Buried in the Red Dirt

T0384583

Bringing together a vivid array of analog and nontraditional sources, including colonial archives, newspaper reports, literature, oral histories, and interviews, *Buried in the Red Dirt* tells a story of life, death, reproduction, and missing bodies and experiences during and since the British colonial period in Palestine. Using transnational feminist reading practices of existing and new archives, the book moves beyond authorized frames of collective pain and heroism.

Looking at their day-to-day lives, where Palestinians suffered most from poverty, illness, and high rates of infant and child mortality, Frances Hasso's book shows how ideologically and practically, racism and eugenics shaped British colonialism and Zionist settler-colonialism in Palestine in different ways, especially informing health policies. She examines Palestinian anti-reproductive desires and practices, before and after 1948, critically engaging with demographic scholarship that has seen Zionist commitments to Jewish reproduction projected onto Palestinians. This title is also available as Open Access on Cambridge Core.

FRANCES S. HASSO is a professor in the Program in Gender, Sexuality & Feminist Studies, Department of History and Department of Sociology at Duke University. She is the author of *Resistance, Repression, and Gender Politics in Occupied Palestine and Jordan* (2005) and *Consuming Desires: Family Crisis and the State in the Middle East* (2011), and a coeditor of *Freedom without Permission: Bodies and Space in the Arab Revolutions* (2016). She has been awarded multiple fellowships, including from the National Humanities Center, ACOR – the American Center of Research (Amman), the Rockefeller Foundation, the Palestinian American Research Center, and the Social Science Research Council/American Council of Learned Societies. She is an Editor Emerita of the *Journal of Middle East Women's Studies*.

Buried in the Red Dirt

Race, Reproduction, and Death in Modern Palestine

FRANCES S. HASSO
Duke University

CAMBRIDGE
UNIVERSITY PRESS

Shaftesbury Road, Cambridge CB2 8EA, United Kingdom

One Liberty Plaza, 20th Floor, New York, NY 10006, USA

477 Williamstown Road, Port Melbourne, VIC 3207, Australia

314–321, 3rd Floor, Plot 3, Splendor Forum, Jasola District Centre, New Delhi – 110025, India

103 Penang Road, #05–06/07, Visioncrest Commercial, Singapore 238467

Cambridge University Press is part of Cambridge University Press & Assessment, a department of the University of Cambridge.

We share the University's mission to contribute to society through the pursuit of education, learning and research at the highest international levels of excellence.

www.cambridge.org
Information on this title: www.cambridge.org/9781009073981

DOI: 10.1017/9781009072854

First published 2022
First paperback edition 2024

A catalogue record for this publication is available from the British Library

Library of Congress Cataloging-in-Publication data
Names: Hasso, Frances Susan, author.
Title: Buried in the red dirt : race, reproduction, and death in modern Palestine / Frances S. Hasso, Duke University, North Carolina.
Description: Cambridge, United Kingdom ; New York, NY : Cambridge University Press, 2022. | Includes bibliographical references and index.
Identifiers: LCCN 2021026753 (print) | LCCN 2021026754 (ebook) | ISBN 9781316513545 (hardback) | ISBN 9781009072854 (ebook)
Subjects: LCSH: Rogers, Vena Winifred Ellen, – Health. | Nurses – Palestine – Biography. | Midwives – Palestine – Biography. | Infants – Mortality – Palestine. | BISAC: HISTORY / Middle East / General
Classification: LCC RT37.R725 H37 2022 (print) | LCC RT37.R725 (ebook) | DDC 610.73092 [B]–dc23
LC record available at https://lccn.loc.gov/2021026753
LC ebook record available at https://lccn.loc.gov/2021026754

ISBN   978-1-316-51354-5   Hardback
ISBN   978-1-009-07398-1   Paperback

إهداء إلى الشعب الفلسطيني
Dedicated to the Palestinian people

Contents

Figures

Tables

Acknowledgments

I began research for *Buried in the Red Dirt* in January 2016. It is difficult to acknowledge in this section every name of the hundreds of people in multiple countries who facilitated the research over five years. I am grateful to every informant, librarian, archivist, translator, reader, interlocutor, secretary, and technical assistant, many of whom I recognize in notes, captions, and the bibliography. Librarians, especially Sean Swanick at Duke University, Brooke Andrade at the National Humanities Center (NHC), and Humi Ayoubi and Samya Kafafi at ACOR – the American Center of Research, warrant special mention for kindly finding sources on short notice. For translation assistance, I turned more than once to Suzan Abdi, Duke librarian Rachel Ariel, and Samya Kafafi. I appreciate the assistance of Duke staff members Julie Wynmor, Jeremy Boomhower, and Jinny Yoon.

Many research projects, and certainly all my books, begin as leaps of faith guided by interest, a hunch, and a commitment to doing the painstaking work without knowing where the path will ultimately lead. Working on this historical project triggered more than the usual humility because it required a methodological shift to archival research, which acquired the status of a terrifying challenge until I started to do it. Many of my meetings and communications were as much about conceptualizing the outlines of the project as determining where I could turn to study non-archival subjects like abortion among Palestinians, Palestinian infant and child death during the British Mandate, or the involvement of the Arab delegation in the race controversy at the 1919 Paris Peace Conference. A number of scholars were consequential and generous in the directing process, including Salim Tamari, Faiha Abdulhadi, Nadera Shalhoub-Kevorkian, Anita Vitullo Khoury, Sonia Nimr, Ylana Miller, Reem al-Botmeh, Ghada Madbouh, Rita Giacaman, Leena Dallasheh, Munir Fakher Eldin, Musa Budeiri, Mahmoud Zeidan, Sharif Kanaana, Rema Hammami, Falastin Naili, Lauren Banko, Roger Heacock, Saleh `Abdel Jawad,

Philippe Bourmaud, Suhad Daher Nashif, Mahmoud Yazbak, Rashid Khalidi, Penelope Mitchell, Beshara Doumani, and Ellen Fleischmann.

I appreciate the former students who engaged relevant texts and ideas with me, with special mention due to Kathryn Medien, Jake Silver, Sinan Goknur, Bill Hunt, Sally Tran, Mumbi Kanyogo, Hadeel Abdelhy, and Jennifer Uzcategu.

I wanted to produce a high-quality, aesthetically pleasing physical text that would also be available to academics and nonacademics throughout the world in the digital Creative Commons without paywall barriers. I am thrilled to have been awarded a 2020 Duke Open Monographs Award, and I am grateful to David Hansen and Haley Walton at the Duke Libraries and to Maria Marsh at Cambridge University Press for working with me to bring this commitment to fruition. I am deeply indebted to Moataz Dajani for giving me permission to use his beautiful art on the cover and inside the book.

Research and writing for *Buried in the Red Dirt* was funded and supported by a 2017 research grant from the Josiah Trent Memorial Endowment Fund (Duke University), a 2018 Senior Residency Fellowship at ACOR, funded by the Council of American Overseas Research Centers, and a 2018–2019 Residency Fellowship at the NHC, funded by Delta Delta Delta. The NHC experience was particularly memorable given the unique intellectual setting and the sociality and friendship that developed among the fellows. I am especially grateful for the support and friendship of Abraham Terian, Lisa Earl Castillo, Weihong Bao, Ling Hon Lam, Lanlan Du, Simonetta Falasca-Zamponi, Julie Velásquez Runk, Meta DuEwa Jones, Yan Xu, Claudia Leal, and Matthew J. Smith.

We too often take for granted and underestimate how much commitment and invisible labor are necessary in academia to help each other, students, and emerging scholars advance knowledge, ideas, and careers. I extend my sincere thanks to Lila Abu-Lughod, Beth Baron, Leo Ching, Sally (Sarah) Deutsch, Leela Fernandes, Ranjana Khanna, Amaney Jamal, Charles Kurzman, Minoo Moallem, Sumathi Ramaswamy, Raka Ray, Judith Tucker, and Kathi Weeks for this labor on my behalf. My friend Nadia Yaqub is a longtime source of ideas, support, and homegrown foods. I am regularly reminded of the gifts of friendship and intellectual community with Patrice Douglass, Jessica Namakkal, and Nayoung Aimee Kwon.

I presented earlier versions of the work in March 2018 at "The Shadow Years: Material Histories of Everyday Life," the fifth annual New Directions in Palestinian Studies Workshop at Brown University, organized by Beshara Doumani and Alex Winder; in March 2018 at ACOR in Amman, for a keynote address organized by Barbara Porter and ACOR staff; in April 2018 at a research seminar at the University of Jordan's Center for Strategic Studies, organized by Sara Ababneh; in September 2019 at the "Death and Afterlives in the Middle East Workshop" at Brown University, organized by Aslı Zengin with Osman Balkan as my reader; and in November 2019 at the Décima Semana Árabe en México, for a keynote address at Tecnológico de Monterrey, Campus Ciudad de México, organized by Camila Pastor and Miguel Fuentes Carreño.

Buried in the Red Dirt benefited from a Franklin Humanities Institute Book Manuscript Workshop, which was scheduled at just the right time to focus my anxious mind in April 2020, early in the pandemic closure. I acknowledge Sylvia Miller's backstage work and support. Karl Ittmann of the University of Houston and Beth Baron of the City University of New York Graduate Center provided invaluable readings and suggestions on the manuscript as the external interlocutors. I am grateful for the time and participation of local colleagues – Leo Ching, Shai Ginsburg, Ranjana Khanna, Anna Krylova, Charlie Kurzman, Kimberly Lamm, Jocelyn Olcott, and Nadia Yaqub. They will notice the impact of their valuable feedback on the final manuscript. Three reviewers solicited by Cambridge University Press asked questions that further strengthened the book. All that said, I take full responsibility for the arguments and apologize *salaf* for any errors in *Buried in the Red Dirt*.

I collected an entire corpus of material – largely interviews – on post-1948 shifts in reproductive healthcare, birthing practices, and birth control in Palestine that is likely to become the basis of another monograph, although I occasionally use sensitive information from these interviews without attribution in *Buried in the Red Dirt*. I thank the traditional healthcare providers, midwives, nurses, health researchers, and physicians who took precious time to answer my questions: `Awdeh Abu Nahleh, Salwa Najjab, Berit Mortensen, Dina Nasser Khoury, Fatima Ahmad, Barbara Ben Ami, Imm `Imad (Bayt Jala), Sahar Hassan, Vartouhi Kukeian, Miriam Shibli-Kometiani, Jantien Dajani, `Aysha Barghouti Saifi, Jamila Qawassmi, and Huda Abu El Halaweh.

There's a special place in my heart for dear friends in Palestine and Jordan with whom I regularly socialized and shared ideas: In`am `Obeidi, Soraida Hussein, Salam Mahadin, Sara Ababneh, Carol Palmer, Rawan Arar, Robert Schick, the late Rula Quawas, Maya Abu-`Ajamiyya, Reem Quawas, Randa Nasser, Maysoon Samour, and Dima Saad. My aunt Bandar Khoury, cousins Evon Rabadi and Majeda Dababneh, and godmother Rahmeh Yatim (Imm Sami) helped fill sometimes lonely weekends in Jordan with company and delicious meals.

Jeff Dillman, my partner and favorite person, keeps my world in balance even when the world is upside down. I love and appreciate him. Our children, Jamal Dillman-Hasso and Naseem Dillman-Hasso, are excellent sources of apropos memes, inside jokes, political analysis, and solicited advice. Possibly more important in this case, they came through repeatedly when I needed difficult-to-access sources in electronic form on short notice in the final stages of writing and revision, helping overcome the research challenges posed by the pandemic closures and slowdowns of the interlibrary loan system.

Introduction

Historiography and History of Missing Palestinian Bodies

"Past and future inhabit the present. History could be a hall of mirrors, a spiral maze ... a door that swings back and forth on its hinges."

Miriam Ghani, 2012

Miriam Ghani makes this point in an interview about her filmic installation "A Brief History of Collapses," a two-screened, floor-to-ceiling visual memoir produced from the perspectives of two iconic buildings, one in Kassel, Germany, and the second in Kabul, Afghanistan, for Documenta 13. Rather than being linear, she argues, time "bends around the tale or the story's will" (Ghani 2012). *Buried in the Red Dirt* shows, to use Ghani's words, how "past and future inhabit the present" in the paradoxical peripheralization and hyperbolization of Palestinian sexual and reproductive life. It makes the case that racism was central to the colonial and settler-colonial order and to the distribution of health, life, and death in British Palestine. Following Ghani's approach to reconstructing the Afghan film archive, in 2016 I entered research on reproduction and quotidian death in Palestine "slantwise," "as if approaching a horse with an uncertain temper" (Ghani 2015, 43, 45).

The 1948 establishment of Israel as a settler-colonial state was radical in its psychic and material impact on Palestinians, most of whom were dispossessed and expelled; more than 150,000 were internally displaced within the borders of the new state (Doumani 2009, 4; Masalha 2008, 127–129). For Palestinian generations living under multiple jurisdictions, 1948 is "not a moment but a process that continues" (Doumani 2009, 4–5). The events of 1948 came to be understood as "the foundational station in an unfolding and continuing saga of dispossession, negations, and erasure" (Jayyusi 2007, 109–110). I sought to avoid such cataclysmic historical points to tell a story about life and death, and about missing bodies and experiences, that exceeds authorized frames of collective pain and heroism. This required pursuing the "non-eventful quality" (Stoler 2009, 107) of archival and other coeval sources and creating new ones, and using transnational feminist reading practices to analyze different kinds of texts.

I imagined a primarily document-based research project on reproductive death during the British colonial period in Palestine (1917–1948). I ultimately conducted substantial archival research, analyzing British vital records, Department of Health and Colonial Office reports, news stories from the Hebrew press, thousands of pages of correspondence in Palestine Department of Health files, and Palestinian oral history interviews conducted by activists and researchers since the 1990s. A brainstorming meeting in Jerusalem with Anita Vitullo in July 2016 made clear to both of us that original interviews with elderly women would be necessary to address Palestinian abortion practices during the British colonial period given the non-archival nature of the subject and deliberate lack of record-keeping.

Palestinian historians I consulted similarly believed that existing government archives held in Israel and England provided limited information on Palestinian abortion practices given abortion's stigmatization and illegality. I ultimately conversed with dozens of informants in person, and hundreds more electronically, and conducted formal interviews in cities, towns, and refugee camps in the Occupied Palestinian Territories, Jordan, Israel, and Lebanon with more than sixty people on matters of healthcare, reproduction, and birth control, including twenty-six Palestinian women born between 1917 and 1933 who met my marital and reproductive criteria.[1]

Since death had thinned the ranks of Palestinian women born in 1933 or earlier, Palestinian communities are dispersed throughout the world, and historic Palestine is difficult to navigate given its apartheid segmentations by Israel, I turned to analog and digital oral history (*al-tarikh al-shafawi*) archives on the Web or held in Beirut, Ramallah,

---

[1] I interviewed other elderly women who ultimately did not fit these criteria, but whose thoughts and experiences I integrate at various points. I gained entrée with little difficulty to refugee camps in Jordan and the West Bank, but in 2017 and 2018 Palestinian refugee camp entrances in Lebanon were extremely militarized, requiring high-level permission to enter, and Gaza was completely inaccessible due to an Israeli blockade.

Birzeit, and Amman to deepen my understanding of Palestinian daily life during the British Mandate period. I learned much of value from the oral history projects, which proliferated from the 1990s as Palestinian activists and scholars interviewed elders before they died in an effort to record Palestinian life before the establishment of Israel in 1948. The oral histories, which recuperate loss and build narrative memory archives, are valuable but limited by the impulse to tell a collective Palestinian story, which by definition is oriented toward historical events considered geopolitically and nationally salient.

The historiography of Palestine similarly continues to be most concerned with the unfolding Palestine Question, and thus with the many dimensions of anti-colonialism, colonialism, settler-colonialism, and national identity. Reproduction and infant and child death are addressed as side notes in some accounts of the 1936–1939 Revolt and the 1948 Nakba (Disaster), usually within authorized registers of traumatic loss, mourning, and resistance. It is unsurprising that the Nakba and its antecedents, which ended a way of life and set in motion multiple situations, sovereignties, and existential crises for Palestinian communities, is overrepresented to a degree that "simultaneously silences" other "lines of inquiry" (Doumani 2009, 6).[2] The historical moment continues to exert its powerful will because it bent time, reshaped space, and ruptured life trajectories on a massive scale. Even feminist scholars who study Mandate Palestine, whose works I reference, do so in a political and discursive context overdetermined by the need to make the case for Palestinian justice. *Buried in the Red Dirt* is not immune from this impulse. Nevertheless, I ask questions on scales less examined, mobilize sources that include literature and film, and rely on my interdisciplinary reading and analytical skills to tell a slantwise story about race, reproduction, and death during and since the British colonial period in Palestine.

Buried in the Red Dirt highlights historical actors such as British Zionist Arthur Felix, who led an antityphoid serum experiment in Palestine; US Zionist nurse matron Bertha Landesman, who led Hadassah's infant and maternal health program in Palestine for decades; and British nurse matron Vena Rogers, who supervised the

---

[2] The term *Nakba* was first used to describe the 1948 war by Constantin Zurayk in his 1948 book, *Ma`na al-nakbah* (*The Meaning of the Disaster*). Honaida Ghanim offers an incisive critique of the word's implications in the Palestine context (Ghanim 2009, 25–28).

nurse-midwifery program in the Jerusalem district. It calls attention
to ordinary colonial subjects such as Palestinian nurse-midwife Alice
Butros, who unsuccessfully battled with British Department of Health
officials as they refused to provide healthcare for a severely ill indigent
child at the Jerusalem Government Hospital; Bahiya Afifi El-Jaby,
a Palestinian midwife who crossed colonial boundaries by internally
examining pregnant women and giving ill women and children injections; Yona Tsadok, the Yemeni Jewish lover of Palestinian driver
ʿAdel Shaʿon, who died in Jerusalem after she received a wanted
abortion conducted by a Jewish German woman physician; and the
many Palestinian women I interviewed whose embodied, affective,
and analytical reflections are woven in throughout to reorient our
understanding of Palestinian reproduction, birth control, illness, and
death in modern Palestine.

  Buried in the Red Dirt "bring[s] out [the Palestinian] dead" (to
appropriate James Baldwin's phrase) (Hong 2015, 126–127) in ways
that scholarship on Palestine has not. A dominant motif foregrounds
the *racialized* distribution of ill health and death in Palestine, attenuated by class and gendered/sexual embodiments and positionalities.
I show how ideologically and practically, racism and eugenics shaped
British colonialism and Zionist settler-colonialism in Palestine in different ways, informing their health policies, investments, and discourses. The book is influenced by Grace Kyungwon Hong's *Death
beyond Disavowal: The Impossible Politics of Difference*, which challenges the disavowal of responsibility for the "exacerbated production
of premature death" (7). Hong calls for a politics of life that acknowledges "the uneven but connected dispersion of death and devaluation
that make self-protective politics threaten to render others precarious,"
especially "occluded and debased subjects" (5–6, 65–66). *Buried in the
Red Dirt* also takes seriously Palestinian anti-reproductive desires and
practices, including abortion, and critically engages with demographic
scholarship that either takes for granted a Palestinian commitment to
reproductive futurity or sloppily projects onto Palestinians existing
Zionist commitments to Jewish reproduction to fulfill a racialized
demographic settler-colonial project in Palestine.

  The British colonization of Palestine began late in British colonial
history and exhibited path dependence in many ways. The imperial
relationship with colonized subjects aimed to assure that on balance
much more was extracted than invested. The colonial enterprise was

expected to pay for itself, which meant the colonized were required to subsidize their colonization. Colonial authorities were typically concerned with health and wellbeing in the colonies as conditions harmed their officials and civilian professionals or their labor and economic priorities. Imperial scientific endeavors also motivated interventions. British investment in healthcare in Palestine was limited and infrastructures (water, sanitation, roads, electricity) were built only when they directly served colonial or imperial priorities. Predatory policies, the raison d'être of colonial and imperial projects, exacerbated Palestinians' poverty and hunger and facilitated their disproportionate and premature death. British austerity with respect to Palestinian maternal, infant, and child health was at least partly influenced by a usually unstated concern to maintain a balance between Muslim birth and death rates. British authorities certainly imposed the most brutal direct violence they could get away with on Palestinian subjects when they rebelled, but in their day-to-day lives Palestinians suffered most as a result of poverty, illness, and high levels of infant and child mortality.

British policies produced consequential patterns that were not mitigated, I insist, by differences of opinion or tensions among specific colonial officials and civil servants in Palestine, the Colonial Office, or other government offices in London. Whatever their ideological, ethical, or strategic disagreements, multiple examples show that British medical practitioners and civilian employees in the Palestine Department of Health and other colonial offices were crucial to the functioning of the colonial project. Moreover, they benefited economically and professionally from their positions. I do not understand them as largely well-intentioned experts caught up in the empire's unfortunate goals.

The Palestinian colonial experience differs from others of the same period because an important third player was in the mix – the Zionist settler-colonial movement, a racialized project whose goals British authorities largely facilitated. Zionist elites understood that investments in science and healthcare in Mandate Palestine strengthened their case to Western powers as a worthy settler-colonial "national" project. Such investments not incidentally improved the "quality" and quantity of the Jewish population in Palestine. Colonized Palestinians were forced to fight two relatively well-resourced Western projects that for thirty years worked simultaneously even if they were not always in harmony. The differential impact of funding, infrastructure, and political agency on health and wellbeing was clear.

The section that follows considers dilemmas in Palestinian archives and archive-based research and discusses my archival sources and practices. The second section explores historiography on the British colonial period in Palestine, which is largely silent on quotidian experiences of reproduction and infant and child death. The third section shows how Palestinian women's lives within their natal and marital families, as well as their reproductive experiences, were crucially shaped by often unremitting physical labor to reproduce households without electricity or running water, class status (that often but not invariably mapped onto urban/rural residency), family gender dynamics, gender inequality in collective beliefs and normative practices, and individual personality. It explores as well Palestinian spiritual and metaphysical explanations and practices related to childbirth, illness, and death. The fourth section discusses the global color line and international discourse on race and racism as relevant to Palestine and Zionism in the twentieth century before the British invasion and colonization of Palestine. The final section briefly summarizes the focus of the remaining chapters.

Value and Vexation: Textual and Oral Archives

I turned to archival research with much trepidation after twenty years as an interpretive and ethnographic feminist scholar primarily working with human subjects and informants and textual and visual sources on contemporary questions. As a late adopter of archival research, I approached the work queerly – that is, by refusing a totalizing methodological or theoretical frame, informed by the Pad.ma collective's "10 Theses on the Archive," which defines "archive" broadly. Recognizing the fragmentary nature of records, members of Pad.ma consider archival work fluid and creative by definition, challenge the bounded and fortress-like model of an archive, and argue for diffusion and distribution rather than "consolidation" and "conservation" (Pad.ma 2010).

Archival researchers in historic Palestine face myriad barriers, much more so for Palestinian researchers with West Bank and Gaza Strip identifications, whose mobility is drastically restricted and who are denied access on the basis of being Palestinian (Banko 2012). As a US citizen from a major university and an experienced researcher in the region, I largely successfully navigated a number of archives and libraries in Beirut, Amman, Jerusalem, Ramallah, and Bethesda, Maryland.[3] In Israeli contexts, my focus on mothers, infants, and abortion seemed benign and even interesting to gatekeepers in comparison to studying Palestinian collaborators or property records during the Mandate, except I was denied access to a Hadassah folder at the Central Zionist Archives from the second decade of the twentieth century for reasons of security. Palestine Department of Health documents held at the Israel State Archives (ISA) were only available in electronic form since all researchers were excluded from accessing the physical material in Jerusalem. From a studio apartment in Ramallah in 2017 and an ACOR: American Center of Research residency in Amman in 2018, I used tens of keyword searches to research ISA material online and made many requests for indexed but unscanned material that was almost always provided electronically after a few weeks. I downloaded and closely analyzed ninety-four such electronic files from the ISA, the large majority of which were hundreds of pages long, with memos and letters bearing the initials of multiple officials as they moved through colonial offices in Palestine. The usually dry formulaic language used in these documents and the many colonial reports I analyzed hid as much as it revealed, although I occasionally ran into documents that produced a shiver of the unusual, what Arlette Farge calls "a sensation" of catching "hold of the real" (2013, 8, 65), always in fragments.

Ethnographic, triangulation, and analytical practices helped me situate and theorize documents that were difficult to understand on their own, as was the case with the antityphoid serum letters discussed in Chapter 3. I walked into this research project recognizing that "the archive plays with truth as with reality" and would include the colonized on the terms of the colonizer (Farge 2013, 27). I puzzled through bits of evidence as researchers always must and built an argument by focusing on their "condition of … appearance," even as I was alert to absences and attempts to obscure (Farge 2013, 30, 71; Stoler 2009, 25). I found most useful what Ann Laura Stoler calls archival "surfeits,"

---

[3] During this project I acquired the Jordanian citizenship and passport I was deemed eligible for based on patrimony because of border and residency difficulties I faced in Lebanon, Jordan, and Israel.

excesses the material itself did not explain (Stoler 2009, 10, 47) because they were central to the ideological and material workings of British colonialism and Zionist settler-colonialism in Palestine.

The 1993 Oslo Accords and the fiftieth anniversary of the 1948 Palestinian Nakba led to a proliferation of oral history projects concerned to document the pre-1948 collective history of Palestine by interviewing particularly Palestinian refugees from villages and communities that Zionist forces ethnically cleansed and appropriated. The oral history projects were partly designed to stave off "forgetfulness" and "growing amnesia" in the present among younger Palestinian generations, as well as to challenge Palestinian "bourgeois nostalgia" (Abu-Lughod and Sa`di 2007, 17, 18, 20). Even earlier, researchers used the oral history method to "recover" and "unsilence" marginalized Palestinian voices given the ideological elisions critical to Zionist and to some degree authorized Palestinian nationalist histories (Masalha 2008, 135–136).

The Palestinian Exodus from Galilee, 1948 by Nafez Nazzal, based on his 1970s interviews with men refugees in Lebanon, is one of the earliest results of Palestinian oral history research (Nazzal 1978). Soon after, Rosemary Sayigh published *Palestinians: From Peasants to Revolutionaries* using oral histories she conducted in 1970s Lebanon with women refugees (Sayigh 1979). Sayigh argues that Palestinian national discourse was at the time biased toward "history," or male memories, activities, and accounts. Women refugees were assumed not to know "the plots," which resulted in researchers excluding their experiences and voices (Sayigh 2007, 138, 139). Sonia El-Nimr is another early adopter of the oral history method in Palestinian scholarship. Her 1990 dissertation is based on a massive study conducted in 1980s historic Palestine with Palestinian men who were rebels in the 1936–1939 Revolt and with British police officers from the period (El-Nimr 1990).

I translated and analyzed interviews in the Jana, Shaml, Al-Musahama al-Siyasiyya (Palestinian Women's Political Participation Oral History Project), Nakba, and PalestineRemembered.com oral history projects with women born in 1933 or earlier, listening for discussion of health, death, illness, and reproduction. I discuss notable characteristics of each of these oral history projects in what follows. As a rule, interviewers did not follow up on expressions of quotidian pain unless they fit within a pre-given collective narrative frame. Lena Jayyusi writes that the collective or "communal voice" is a "feature" in Palestinian accounts of the 1948 expulsions (Jayyusi 2007, 111). Because Palestinians are geopolitically illegible as victims of a collective trauma, the oral narratives make a case for recognition, ending the continuing catastrophe, and undoing "the mythic Israeli narrative" (Abu-Lughod and Sa`di 2007, 11, 12, 23). I learned a great deal about Palestinian life during the Mandate period as well as the commitments guiding scholars and activists involved in these projects. The interviews shaped my analysis of British colonial discourse and its silences, and illustrate the diversity of Palestinian women's experiences based on class, urban or rural residency, region, family of origin, and personality.

In 1989 Moataz Dajani worked with Sayigh and other intellectuals and activists in Beirut to found the Arab Resource Center for Popular Arts (Al-Jana) (http://al-jana.org) as a volunteer project.[4] Al-Jana developed into a continuing multipronged endeavor of "popular arts and heritage" (*al-funun al-turathiyya*) with Palestinian children in Lebanon to raise their consciousness (*shughul taw`awi*) using active learning methods to teach history, creative expression (theater, film), and critical inquiry/journalism. The project was intended to address the alienation and despair of younger Palestinian generations. Al-Jana eventually published a magazine, widely read beyond Lebanon, and oversaw multiple oral history projects designed to remap with first-generation refugees and to re-enliven for the generations born in Lebanon the wedding songs, folklore, superstitions, saint and sanctuary practices, and embroidery in pre-1948 Palestine.[5]

---

[4] Dajani, a Jerusalemite banned from returning to Palestine in 1971 after completing his A-levels at Brumanna High School in Beirut, studied child psychology in Egypt for two years and returned to volunteer in the Lebanon Palestinian refugee camps and to work at the Institute for Palestine Studies. He studied history at the American University of Beirut (AUB) until he was forced to leave in 1983, after which he completed a degree in arts and arts education at George Washington University between 1984 and 1988. Interview with Moataz Dajani on May 17, 2018, in Amman, Jordan.

[5] Al-Jana conducted four kinds of oral histories: first-generation refugee narrations of uprooting and displacement, first-generation narrations of "folktales" and other aspects of "intangible culture," refugee women in South Lebanon narrations of their camp lives and work establishing the refugee camps, and biographical interviews with men and women considered important in their refugee communities (Sleiman and Chebaro 2018, 64–65). I read most issues of *Al-Jana: The Harvest*, a magazine published between 1994 and 2009, which are archived at the AUB Jafet Library.

I transcribed three recommended Al-Jana interviews with four Palestinian women refugees born in my period of interest to get a sense of narrative structure and content.[6] Four prominent themes are worth highlighting from these interviews. First, women reported regular inter-action between Jews and Palestinians before the *hijra* (forced migration) of 1948 if they lived in towns and cities that included Jewish neighborhoods or nearby Jewish colonies, with narrators distinguishing between Yemeni and other indigenous or long-settled Jews, and the mostly European Jewish migrants who "changed everything" from the early 1930s as the Nazis rose to power in Europe. Palestinian respondents reported Jewish women who married Palestinian men, Jewish neighbors and school friends, Palestinian women working in Jewish colonies as nannies and domestics, and everyday commerce between Palestinians and Jews. Second, there is an inexorable weightiness in the narratives to experiences of suffering in 1948 and the years that followed. Third, the interviewers, all men who were younger than the interviewees in these cases, were eager to elicit narratives that remapped places and lifeways they believed they would never be able to see or experience. Fourth, questions and answers were often in the collective mode – how "people" grew food, where they marketed it, how they celebrated feasts, and how they interacted with British colonizers and Jewish settlers. Discussion of intimate and personal matters was often truncated by the narrator or the interviewer.

About two hundred Palestinian refugees were interviewed between the mid-1990s and 2004 in the Shaml (in-gathering) oral history pro-ject, with material stored at the Palestinian Diaspora and Refugee Center in the Birzeit University Digital Palestine Archive.[7] The inter-views reflect great variation in technical quality (digital recordings that were inaudible, too fast, or blank). Most were missing metadata (such as date of interview) and the questions differed by interviewer. Shaml questions about pre-1948 Palestine aimed to remap collective life in destroyed communities. Women were asked to describe healthcare

[6] Interview with Amina Hasan Banat (born 1931 in Shaykh Daud, Palestine), residing in the Burj al-Barajneh refugee camp in Lebanon, on December 6, 1997. Interview with Radiya Muhammad Hammad (born 1918 in Saffuriyya, Palestine) and Ghazalah Ibrahim `Abd al-Ba`ti (born 1927 in Bethlehem, Palestine), in the Nahr al-Barid refugee camp in Lebanon on December 2, 1998. Interview with Watfa `Abd al-Mu`ti (born 1925 in Tantura, Palestine) in the al-Baddawi refugee camp in Lebanon on May 9, 2009.
[7] I am grateful to Suzan Da`na, who helped me access this archive, titled Arshif Mu'assasat Shaml, found here: www.awraq.birzeit.edu/ar/taxonomy/term/943.

practices, weddings (not a particular woman's wedding), and major festivals such as for the (prophets) Nabi Rubin, Nabi Saleh, and Nabi Musa. The collective orientation was signaled by questions that began with *kayf kan* . . . (how were . . . ?) weddings, for example, or medical care, in the village or town. They were asked about their 1948 expulsion and *hijra* experiences and whether they or anyone else from the village or town had tried to return. They were also asked leading questions about identity and political sensibilities relevant after the 1993 Oslo Accords: did she agree with *tawtin* (resettlement in other countries) and compensation proposals, or did she want to keep the right of return to her village or town?

Despite some problems, the Shaml interviews offer much of value for the patient researcher. Women commonly reported poverty – for example, "people barely had bread," and illnesses like measles. Women who were late teenagers or young adults during the Mandate period discussed seeing for themselves or their children Jewish German physicians in *kubayniyyat* (colonies), whose medical offices were typically located at the edge of the Jewish settlement. Others reported traveling to Jaffa or Jerusalem as needed for medical care at private Palestinian clinics. Amina Qasem `Abd al-Haq, born in Silwan, Jerusalem, in 1933, had eleven pregnancies and "11 additional pregnancies that did not live."[8] Few women in their communities gave birth in hospitals, turning instead to home births with a *daya qanuniyya*, a traditional Palestinian midwife registered with the government. In a difficult pregnancy, women were more likely to turn to "*dayat* who worked for the government" (also termed *qabilat qanuniyyat*), referring to licensed nurse-midwives who had completed a government training course, or Palestinian physicians. Larger villages had three or four traditional midwives in residence, and many interviewed women named them and specific physicians, clinics, and hospitals their community used during the Mandate.

In 2017 I listened to fourteen interviews conducted in 1998 and 1999 with Palestinian women who met my criteria completed by the Palestinian Women's Political Participation Oral History Project under the guidance of Dr. Faiha Abdulhadi.[9] The results of this massive

---

[8] Most of the pregnancies and losses occurred after 1948 given her age and her report that she had the third child during the 1948 war.

[9] I thank Iman Ammus, Nisreen `Umar, and Melia at the Palestinian Women Research and Documentation Center in El-Bireh for assisting me in finding and listening to the relevant interviews.

endeavor, which focused on multiple decades and geographic sites of Palestinian political life before and after 1948, were published in a series of books in Arabic and English.[10] The project's aim was to put women into the Palestinian nationalist picture, and as such it did not focus on intimate life. The women interviewed were disproportionately more educated than other Palestinian women living in 1930s and 1940s Palestine, often had worked as teachers, and were more likely to be involved in conferences, women's associations, and social work (`amal ijtima`i) – that is, community activism and philanthropy.[11] The questions and accounts gravitated toward tumultuous moments of political resistance and repression such as the 1936–1939 Revolt (*thawra*) and the 1948 war. While most were not fighters, they had supported battles by giving money, moving weapons, and setting up popular first aid projects. Unmarried women were not asked why they remained unmarried, and women who mentioned loss of children were not asked about the cause.

The Nakba Archive, an oral history video project conducted largely between 2002 and 2005 with first-generation refugees in Lebanon, was led by Mahmoud Zeidan and Diana Allan. Zeidan and Allan trained refugee camp residents to assist with and conduct interviews as part of a collaborative pedagogical orientation to allow people to produce "community histories."[12] The Nakba Archive includes more than 650 participants from more than 150 Palestinian towns and villages. Nakba Archive interviews recall social, cultural, and political life in Palestine, with some emphasis on gathering eyewitness accounts from refugees who experienced violence such as massacres. Narrators were asked about relations with neighboring Jewish communities and British colonial authorities, the 1948 expulsion, and the early years of exile. Relying on a positivistic (rather than interpretive) coding schema developed by archivists at the AUB Jafet Library, I translated interviews

[10] I focused only on women interviewed about their experiences in the 1930s (Abdulhadi 2006a [Arabic]; Abdulhadi 2006b [English]). Faiha Abdulhadi met with me in Amman and Ramallah between 2016 and 2018 and directed me to specific interviews she believed were relevant to my project. Soraida Al-Hussein tracked down the book series, which I purchased.
[11] Some of the women had moved to Palestine with parents or husbands as children or adults from Lebanon or Syria, or they had Hijazi origins.
[12] Zeidan continues to take his camera when he receives a request to interview an elderly refugee. Interview with Mahmoud Zeidan in Beirut, January 12, 2018. Also see www.nakba-archive.org/?page_id=956.

with the only three women who met my age criteria and had discussed health or reproduction.[13]

These refugees, most from northern Palestine, reported that Jewish settlers regularly hired Palestinian women to serve as domestic workers, to care for their children, and to do laundry. The women discussed their weddings, and one even mentioned the suffering she experienced with an abusive husband. They went to Jewish physicians as needed for themselves or their babies when there were no Palestinian physicians. The refugee women interviewed mostly used traditional Arabic remedies (*wasfat `arabiyya*) and healers who directed them to physicians when they could not resolve an illness. The center of gravity in these accounts is again the suffering and shock of the moment of expulsion and the *hijra* that followed. The interviewees frequently expressed nostalgia for land, foods, and hometowns, colored by the diasporic travails of dislocation, poverty, exclusion, and war in Lebanon. One of them described the collective dread that shaped her life in the refugee camp: "we sit in fear and terror here."

The richest set of oral histories for my purposes are available online through the PalestineRemembered.com project, largely in video, although women make up a small proportion of the hundreds of available interviews.[14] In 2018 I translated every interview conducted with women born between 1916 and 1933, a total of thirty that occasionally included a sister or a husband. These interviews were conducted between 2003 and 2011 by `Abdel Majid Dandeis, Sa`id `Ajjawi, Fawwaz Salameh, and Rakan Mahmoud, with Mahmoud as the interviewer or co-interviewer in the largest number. Most of the women lived in cities and refugee camps throughout Jordan, while

---

[13] The interviews did not always include full metadata. I listened to an interview with Amina Husayn Shamali, born circa 1927 in the village of `Ilmaniyya, Palestine, recorded on April 27, 2003, by Amneh Ahmad al-Khatib; an interview with Badi`a Nayfah, born circa 1929 in Qaqun, Palestine, living in the Burj al-Barajneh refugee camp, recorded on May 14, 2003, by a woman (Jihad); and an interview with Tamam Ahmad al-Haj, born circa 1918 in `Amqa, Palestine, recorded on February 15, 2004. I am grateful to Kaoukab Chebaro and Sarah Soueidan, who helped me navigate the Nakba Archive and Al-Jana archival material.

[14] The oral histories are usefully organized by district of origin and further indexed by town, village, or neighborhood. Of fifty-seven interviewed refugees originally from the Jerusalem District, only one was a woman, and no woman was interviewed from the Hebron District. www.palestineremembered.com/OralHistory/Interviews-Listing/Story1151.html.

a few resided in Damascus and one in Lebanon. The women largely originated from peasant families in Palestinian villages and small towns, although some came from the Palestinian urban bourgeoisie in Jaffa, Jerusalem, Tiberias, or Ramleh. A minority worked as teachers before and after 1948.

The PalestineRemembered.com interviewers were uneven in their follow-up questions when women opened threads that veered into intimate matters. Nevertheless, many questions elicited discussion of schooling, as well as religious, holiday, leisure, wedding, conflict resolution, and spiritual healing practices during what some women termed *wakit al-ingliz* (the time of the English). Women described doing paid and unpaid work such as farming, bread-making, laundry, sharecropping, sewing, and transporting water to their homes, sometimes multiple times a day. They explained that their facial tattoos were made by artisans in summer-traveling Romani bands, acquired as teenagers without asking their parents for permission.[15] Interviewers asked about access to running water and sewage systems, electricity, paved roads, and transport. The answers provide a sense of dramatic infrastructural differentials between villages and their urban centers (e.g., Tiberias and its villages), as well as between Jewish and Arab communities. A Haifa District villager described going with her father to a Jewish colony to see "Dr. Sarah" to treat her ill son: "I had no idea what his illness was. He was throwing up. I saw how they were living and I realized we were not living."[16]

Similar to the other Palestinian oral history interviews I analyzed, PalestineRemembered.com interviewers asked about Palestinian-Jewish interaction. Women reported that commerce was common, but not on the terms of equals, and social visiting was rare. Palestinians in some northern towns purchased grapes and apples from Jewish German colonies and occasionally visited them for medical treatment. Palestinians in Tiberias patronized Jewish-owned salons and fabric merchants, as well as private Jewish physicians and dentists. Poorer women reported they worked as domestics and launderers for Jewish residents and better-off Palestinians. Jewish settlers purchased

[15] Practically every woman discussed the tradition of making or having made for her by Palestinian seamstresses seven dresses of seven different solid colors for a trousseau.

[16] Ratibah `Abdel Rahman Mahmoud Abu Fanneh, born 1928 in Chufr/Kufr Qari`. Interviewed in the Husn refugee camp in Irbid, Jordan, on April 4, 2007, by Rakan Mahmoud.

eggs, chickens, cheese, and bread from Palestinians. Women who lived in mixed communities distinguished relations with Jews of Yemeni and other Arab backgrounds, whose language was Arabic and whose life-ways were similar, from those with Jewish migrants from Europe. They expressed abiding affection for Jewish neighbors and friends in towns and cities where communities lived in some proximity to each other and Jewish children attended government schools. In some communities, Muslim and Christian Palestinians helped Jewish residents keep the Sabbath.

Women featured in the PalestineRemembered.com project reported multiple healthcare practices during the British colonial period, includ-ing using traditional providers of Arabic medicine (*al-tibb al-'arabi*) for bone-setting, circumcision, childbirth, and physical and psychological illnesses, as well as Arabic home remedies. For serious medical situ-ations (e.g., appendicitis or difficult pregnancies), they visited mission-ary hospitals, Arab and Jewish private physicians, and British government hospitals. While women were asked about *dayat* (mid-wives, who they often named) and childbirth, these discussions were rarely developed, possibly because all the interviewers were men and may have considered further discussion a source of embarrassment for the women. Women familiarly distinguished between a *daya qanu-niyya* and a *qabila qanuniyya*, indicating internalization of status dis-tinctions instituted by British authorities.

In almost every PalestineRemembered.com interview I analyzed, the woman mentioned she had at least one child who died of illness (typhoid, measles, tuberculosis, influenza, appendicitis) before or dur-ing the 1948 expulsion and *hijra*, or in the early years of waiting in refugee settlements or moving from place to place. Najmeh Yousef Saleh al-Jabir was interviewed by her son Sa'id 'Ajjawi in Irbid, Jordan, on March 16, 2007. Born in 1930 in the village of Kawkab al-Hawa in the Beisan District, she migrated in 1948 with her firstborn, Muhammad, who became ill with fever when they lived in tent encamp-ments in Jericho for five years. She used home remedies and then took him to a physician, but he "got worse and was screaming mother, I want to drink water (*yama badi ashrab mayi*) . . . he was screaming and I was screaming. I fainted. His father finally came. I went crazy over Muhammad when he died. He was a big boy (*chbir*) [about four], playing with the goats and moving around . . . I would wake up at night asking 'where is Muhammad?' He died there, God accept him."

Women often remembered the war and *hijra* as traumatic periods of profound suffering. A refugee from a village near Haifa explained: "We left from fear. My mother was always afraid for her son because he always spoke up fearlessly. So she made us leave."[17] She described her first visit back to Firdis years later as "like *laylat al-`ama* [the night of blindness], it was devastating." Jumping back to the days immediately following the family's *hijra* from the village, she continued. "We died from crying when we knew we could not get back." A Gaza villager randomly commented that "many more people would have died" if the *hijra* had occurred in colder months rather than May through July. She added that there were "no days after the *hijra* where you ate and were full. There was not enough food."[18]

The protocol for the PalestineRemembered.com is preoccupied with mapping pre-1948 communities, villages, and towns, looking for "facts" using "a restricted notion of history" that excludes the so-called domestic sphere (Sayigh 2007, 139). Many questions were about directionality and topography: locations of homes, hills and wadis, saints' shrines, mosques, paved roads, sources of water, and number of kilometers between places. Did the community have a public café (*qahwa*) or public salon (*diwan*), a bathhouse, a church? Was a road, town, water source, Jewish settlement, or other landmark to the east, west, north, or south? While a few women easily answered some of these questions, most did not experience their home of origin in this manner and found the questions confusing. As in other oral history projects, women were asked whether they would accept compensation to give up their claims to property in villages and towns and provided a range of nuanced responses.

Palestinian oral history and interview-based projects are subject, like any other method, to what Abbad Yahya calls "marginalization" and "suppression" organized around the assumption of national unity and "national commitment" (Yahya 2017). His oral history interviews with Palestinian men and women refugees originally from the village of Mughallis, for example, found some peasant women who challenged

---

[17] Ghazaleh `Ali Hamdan Sa`beh (Umm Na'il), born 1922 in Firdis. Interviewed on August 22, 2007, by Sa`id `Ajjawi in Irbid, Jordan.

[18] Interview with Muhammad Salem Rabbah `Abdeljawad (born 1925) and Mariam Musa Rabbah `Abdeljawad (born 1932), married four months before the Nakba in Sawafir al-Shamali, Gaza. Interviewed on November 25, 2007, by Rakan Mahmoud in the Nuzha neighborhood of Amman.

the dominant narrative of 1948 as ruining their lives. For them, the Nakba served just deserts to a previously powerful Palestinian family from a nearby village because it too became disfranchised. The Nakba shifted "power relations and social positions" for these villagers, who experienced "injustice and oppression," including "forceful land acquisition" and being compelled to give up wives and daughters for marriage to powerful Palestinian men from the village of Beit Jibrin. Moreover, most girls and women in Mughallis did not inherit portions of land they had rights to, thus the Nakba did not translate into loss of property for them. Women more than men from the same village violated national unity frames by discussing how their families experienced upward social mobility after 1948 as they moved to towns and cities, studied, and worked hard to become "learned and knowledgeable" (Yahya 2017, 98–102). Yahya argues that oral history is uniquely able to address the phenomenology of individual experience if researchers follow evidence of less normative positions and remain alert to urban, elite, and male biases. Bourgeois "nostalgia," he contends, often represses class conflict in pre-1948 Palestine (Yahya 2017, 104).

Healthcare, Science, and Medicine in British Palestine

Palestinian society during the British colonial period remained ethnically, ideologically, religiously, and culturally diverse, with urban-rural differences and class conflicts. Sherene Seikaly argues against idealizing and "flatten[ing] the topography of Palestinian social" and political life during the British colonial period (Seikaly 2016, 4, 13, 75). Islah Jad, for example, finds that "the Palestinian urban middle class" came to agree with British calls for "advancement" and "modernization," reinforcing a sense of urban superiority in relation to villagers (Jad 2005, 9). Ela Greenberg shows how Palestinian modernists were supportive of a maternal reformation agenda promoted by foreign missionaries, teachers, nurses, and social workers (Greenberg 2010, 135–136). Palestinian physicians, teachers, nurses, and other experts promoted a health and hygiene approach to mothering in lectures and lessons at girls' schools, in articles in Arabic newspapers, and on a program on the British-sponsored Palestine Broadcasting Service (Seikaly 2016, 136–137, 144–146, 161–162).

The genealogy of the commitment to modern maternalism and health and hygiene, certainly among Arab physicians in Southwest

Asia, predates the British colonization of Palestine. After all, they studied in Ottoman, European, and Russian medical schools, as well as missionary medical schools (such as the American University of Beirut and St. Joseph University, the latter established in 1883), which were thoroughly committed to modern science and producers of modern scientific knowledge. Palestinian elites and professionals, almost always men, lived in and helped shape the same intellectual times and spaces as non-Palestinian elites and professionals. The British Empire demoted them to the status of colonial subjects in a tiered system that facilitated Zionist interests by law and policy and treated Zionist organizations as closer to British interests.[19]

Historical scholarship on Ottoman and British colonial Palestine illuminates institutional and political-economic dynamics that shaped Palestinian health and reproduction. German, Austrian, British, French, Italian, and US Christian missions established hospitals during the Ottoman period, and later added maternity wards and children's clinics, primarily in Jerusalem, Bethlehem, Haifa, and Nazareth. Arab and Muslim elites recognized that missionary institutions had conversion and imperialist agendas, as Philippe Bourmaud shows in a rich analysis of local resistance that delayed for ten years the building of a medical mission in late Ottoman Nablus (Bourmaud 2005, 133–135). Missionary institutions were historically protected by their foreign governments in Palestine and their hospitals were "near-sovereign" after they successfully navigated the arduous permission process with Ottoman authorities (Bourmaud 2009, 293, 294, 301). Wealthier Palestinian municipalities such as Nablus created public hospitals to undermine missionary and foreign influences, although even these hospitals were compelled to appoint French sister nurses given the disreputable nature of the occupation for "Syrian women" (Bourmaud 2009, 280–281).[20]

---

[19] Moreover, a handful of powerful British figures in Mandate Palestine, such as the legal advisor to the military administration in Palestine and Attorney-General Norman Bentwich (1918–1931) and the first high commissioner, Herbert Samuel (1920–1925), were in fact committed Zionists who were British Jews.

[20] As was the case during the Ottoman period, British colonial authorities found it difficult to recruit Palestinian women to work in government hospitals as nurses because the educated classes considered it menial and subjecting them to "gossip among [Arab] men in the wards," reducing their chances to marry. Moreover, British nurses typically supervised Arab nurses in segregated wards for Palestinian patients (Fleischmann 2003, 55–56).

Although missionary institutions remained under the authority of foreign powers during the British colonial period, Palestinians ironically came to see them as "national" entities because they employed Palestinian professionals and were not Zionist institutions. Missionary healthcare institutions were under-resourced and overextended in British Palestine because they had "very largely relieve[d] the Government from its responsibility of providing accommodation in its hospitals for the country's general sick."[21]

A less trodden path of investigation is the degree to which Palestine, like other colonized settings, was a laboratory of extraction and advancement for imperial science and medicine. A 1926 article published in *The Lancet* by British colonial physician John MacQueen, who spent the remainder of his career in Palestine and became the government's director of medical services in the 1940s, offers an illuminating early illustration of colonial medicine's impulses. The article describes a native male traditional healer among Palestinians in the village of Duwaymeh (south of Hebron) named al-Hakim (Doctor) Shaheen. Shaheen had taken pus from the smallpox infection of a "negress" in December 1921 in order to inoculate villagers, including more than three hundred children, using tools such as thorns, photographs of which are included in the article. Shaheen reportedly charged villagers "an egg or two" for each inoculation procedure (MacQueen 1926, 213).

British health officials were fascinated with Shaheen's knowledge and incubation and preservation skills. Nevertheless, they imprisoned him for a month, "considerably" enhancing his reputation in the village (213). Although one must read the article carefully to determine this, Shaheen's method was effective for most inoculated villagers in that they acquired a greatly weakened version of smallpox. The inoculation campaign was controversial, however, because the unnamed Black Palestinian woman whose bodily fluid was used seemed to have acquired a strong strain of the virus and a "few [of those inoculated] had almost certainly died," although MacQueen reported no evidence of this and admitted that the British team "were too late on the scene to observe ... ourselves" or "obtain a reliable

---

[21] Government of Palestine Report, Report on Palestine Administration, July 1920–December 1921. London, 1922. In *Palestine and Transjordan Administration Reports 1918–1948, Vol. 1* (1995), 269.

account of the course of symptoms following inoculation" (212, 213).[22]

A line of research inquiry foreclosed by a focus on major geopolitical historical moments, illustrated by the Duwaymeh smallpox case, is the limited usefulness of a modern versus backward understanding of Palestinian cosmologies and practices in relation to healing, illness, science, and medicine. *The Lancet* article reports that Palestinian villagers "readily agreed" to a smallpox vaccine developed by scientists with a different strain of smallpox virus in (colonial) Egypt when they saw it was effective. An initial "lymph" that Palestinian health workers under British supervision had administered to them after scouring the village for hiding children "proved quite unsatisfactory," and "several children developed true small-pox" (213). Not incidentally, the Duwaymeh medical intervention resulted in a sole-authored publication for MacQueen made possible by the work of two Palestinian physicians whom he thanked at the end of the article, Drs. "Ayoub and Mossauba, on whose devoted shoulders fell the heavy load of the routine work" (214).

The Duwaymeh smallpox case serendipitously came up during a February 7, 2018, interview I conducted with Sabha Muhammad Ahmad Hbeid in the Baq`a refugee camp.[23] Hbeid was born in the village of Duwaymeh in 1944, although her ID card gives her birth date as 1940. Her family manipulated Jordanian government officials circa 1957 so as to acquire a birth certificate that legally made her four years older, allowing an imam to marry her as a thirteen-year-old to a twenty-five-year-old man.[24] Hbeid was among the most charming of my interviewees and one of about seven women I interviewed who did not meet my age, marital, and reproductive criteria.[25]

---

[22] For a published scholarly treatment of this case, see Davidovitch and Greenberg (2007).

[23] Baq`a is north of Amman, two kilometers of winding road away from the village in which I lived for part of my childhood.

[24] Many Duwaymeh villagers moved to `Arroub after their 1948 expulsion, which came under Jordanian jurisdiction in 1950. Hbeid said that performance of adulthood included having her chest stuffed with cotton. She ran away in terror when she learned of her impending marriage to "an old man." She said her husband abused her until he died. She reported that her mother had one daughter who died of measles (*hasabat*) in infancy, "before I was born." The mother nursed other babies since "she had so much milk."

[25] I relied on community and family guesses to find women who met my criteria. I did not have the heart to end interviews with eager interviewees when I learned

Answering my question about her memories of childhood diseases and deaths, she shared a story she was told by an older mother-in-law (her father-in-law had married four women because some "did not have babies"). The mother-in-law had two young boys who "got sick. They said they got smallpox. They were quarantined in Duwaymeh in a small room they made like a hospital for all the people sick with smallpox. [Who put them there?] The villagers did it in order not to infect others. It was very infectious. They had brought a Black woman who had smallpox. [Why?] They used a matchstick to take from her smallpox and infect others so that they would heal. They would remove it from her palm. [She gently took my hand and poked my pen into my palm.] They would take from her – [Was she Palestinian?] Yes, she was Palestinian. They didn't know where she was from but she had to leave her own village when she got smallpox. All of this became *labakh*.[26] [Did the boys heal?] No, they died. So this was a mistake. They didn't know."

I draw a number of general points from this case and other evidence. First, scientific knowledge based on empirical observation was part of the repertoire of unlettered Arab healers. Second, local communities widely respected such "traditional" scientific knowledge. Third, Palestinians of all classes used and valued effective biomedical interventions. Finally, respect for both traditional and modern allopathic medicine coexisted with a variety of "nonrational" spiritual and touch healing practices and beliefs, including appeals and protections designed to protect women and children from known and unknown forces. The following section explores some of these indigenous concerns and approaches in relation to pregnancy, childbirth, and health using a phenomenological approach.

Cosmologies of Reproduction, Maternity, and Loss

This section uses scholarship and my ethnographic research to dwell on Palestinian women's health and reproduction accounts and sensibilities. I caution against reading it as a romanticization of pregnancy and childbirth or an account of nationalist mourning for the dead. For one

during the interview they were younger (or in one case never married), given the generosity of my hosts and interlocutors.
[26] I believe this is a colloquial term for the pus-derived inoculation serum, but I cannot be sure.

thing, this is not how women understood life and death or told their stories. The ethnographic work quickly checked any assumptions I held about women's pregnancy and childbirth desires and their affective responses to pregnancy, miscarriage, and child death.

Relying solely on written records marginalizes nonliterate people who primarily use oral expression and certainly women, "who leave fewer written records" behind than men (Fleischmann 1996, 352–353). I interviewed Palestinian women born between 1917 and 1933 in historic Palestine, some of whom had become experienced healers themselves, about folk health knowledge, practices, and beliefs, as well as how, who, where, when, and why individuals in their families and communities used "traditional" or "modern" health providers, especially during the British colonial period.[27] I probed women's memories

---

[27] I interviewed the following twenty-six women who married and had at least one birth before 1948: Victoria Khalil Basir (born 1917, interviewed in Taybeh on March 31, 2018), Amneh `Awadh Khalifeh (born 1917 in Marj [Haifa], interviewed in Suf refugee camp on January 31, 2018), Fatima `Ali Hammad (born circa 1918 in Tamoun [Nablus] and interviewed in Tamoun on June 27, 2017), Khadra `Awadh al-Saleh (born 1920 in Toubas [Nablus], interviewed in Husn refugee camp on January 31, 2018), Wathha Hussein Mathi (born 1921 in Sharrar [Nazareth], interviewed in a town near `Afula on June 14, 2017), Najla Wadi` Khoury (born 1923 in Jifna, interviewed in Amman on July 1, 2017), Zaynab Sa`id Abu-`Ajamiyya (born 1923 in Mughallis [Ramleh], interviewed by Skype in Saudi Arabia on May 14, 2018), Rahmeh `Isa al-Ya`coub al-Yatim (born 1924 in Beit Sahour [Bethlehem], interviewed in Irmemin, Jordan on May 18, 2018), Zahweh Hanna Salah (born 1924 in Ramallah and interviewed in Ramallah on June 18, 2018), Jamileh `Ali Zbeidat (born 1924 in Sakhnin [Galilee] and interviewed in Sakhnin by Skype on May 19, 2018), Kamila Muhammad al-`Othman (born circa 1925 in Deir al-Ghusoun [Tulkarem] and interviewed in Deir al-Ghusoun on March 27, 2018), Fatima `Abdelwafi `Anati (born circa 1925 in Lyd, interviewed in the Jalazon refugee camp north of Ramallah on June 22, 2017), Widad Abu Dayyeh (born 1926 in Beit Jala [Bethlehem], interviewed in Al-Tur [Mount of Olives], Jerusalem, on June 11, 2017), Nadia Shibli Khalil Kayleh (born 1927 in Birzeit [Ramallah] and interviewed in Birzeit on March 24, 2018), Miladeh `Isa Ya`qub Hilweh (born 1927 in Birzeit and interviewed in Birzeit on March 24, 2018), Wasayif Ihmaydeh Ahmad Dallal (born 1927 in Mukhmasiyya [Ramallah] and interviewed in the `Aqabet Jabr refugee camp in Jericho on June 18, 2017), Yumna `Abd al-Rahman (born circa 1928 in Jiflik [Nablus] and interviewed in `Ayn Basha, Jordan [lives in the Baq`a refugee camp] on February 7, 2018), Evelyn Salloum Shalhoub (born 1928 in Haifa and lives in Haifa, interviewed in Jerusalem's Old City on June 6, 2018), `Aysha Mahmoud `Eid al-Kafri (born 1928 in `Annaba [Lyd], interviewed in the Am`ari refugee camp in El-Bireh on June 28, 2017), Jamileh Mahmoud Ahmad (born 1928 in Deir al-Ghusoun and interviewed in Deir al-Ghusoun on March 27, 2018), Hamda Muhammad

of their mothers' reproductive histories and their knowledge of illness, death, and healthcare in their childhoods. I asked women to chart their own reproductive histories, including miscarriages, child illnesses, and child deaths, as well as childbirth, healthcare-seeking and birth control practices. The women expressed their reproductive desires, pain about child loss, happiness or unhappiness with husbands, and frustration with lack of control over frequent pregnancies, stories that circulated among womenfolk and grown children. The interviews ultimately work, I contend, as rejoinders to the dry metrics, self-serving explanations, and racist prose of colonial and settler-colonial documents, as well as to scholarship on British colonial Palestine that does not attend to intimate life.[28]

Women's reproductive experiences and healthcare-seeking practices during the British colonial period were shaped by material circumstances, social networks, and their cosmological orientations to their own bodies, other bodies, and forces in the spirit world. With a few exceptions, the Palestinian girls I interviewed as elderly women were married off by a father, older brother, or uncle at between twelve and sixteen years old, with the average age around fourteen. Husbands were usually older, in good cases as few as four or five years older, but in many cases much older (none of the twenty-six women had

`Odeh (born 1929 in Burqa [Nablus] and interviewed in Beitin [Ramallah] on June 22 2017), Umm Maher `Ubeidi (born 1929 in Jerusalem and interviewed in Jerusalem on July 6, 2016), Fatima Khamis Zaydan (born 1929 in Dayr Yassin [Jerusalem] and interviewed in El-Bireh on June 17, 2017), Wasfiyya `Abdullah Hasan Abu Sa` (born 1931 in Deir al-Ghusoun and interviewed in Deir al-Ghusoun on March 27, 2018), Ruqayya Isma`il (born circa 1932 in Toubas [Nablus] and interviewed in the Husn refugee camp in Jordan, on January 31, 2018), and "Umm al-Khayr" (born 1933 in Qubeibeh [Bethlehem] and interviewed in Qubeibeh on June 9, 2017).

[28] It would not have been possible to find the many people I interviewed without the assistance of people who took me around and introduced me in villages and refugee camps, told me fascinating stories, diligently called, texted, and emailed me back with contact information and even documents, connected me with their relatives, booked rides for me in isolated villages, and kindly hosted me at impromptu meals. Some of these generous folks are: Ayat Nashwan, Najah Muhammad Al-`Azzeh, Khayriyya `Amr, Lina Sa`adeh, Buthina Canaan Khoury, Amneh Sharaqah, Diala Shammas, Ibtisam Zaydan, Maysoon Samour, Ghada Khoury, Habab Khoury, Huda Abu El Halaweh, Hala Hanoon, Khalid Farraj, Nawal Shahin, Sr. Hildegard Enzenhufer, Usama Zahran, Riyadh `Ali `Abed Bani `Odeh, Sami Shunnar, `Aziz Wahdan, Ahlam Bisharat, Sahar Hassan, `Aysheh al-Rifai, Maya Abu- `Ajamiyya, Dina Zbeidy, Miriam Shibli-Kometiani, and Ghaliyya (Umm Muhamad).

a living husband when interviewed). Girls had little recourse if they were unwilling, although some reported running away or behaving obstreperously. Approximately a third of the women discussed being unhappily married because they wanted someone else, did not want or like the man they lived with, were forced into marriage by a family member (one of these reported having a promiscuous husband she ultimately divorced), or were regularly abused by their husband. On the other hand, most women expressed affection for their husbands and a few indicated they were satisfied with their sexual lives.

Most of the women across religions and classes birthed their children at home, usually with the assistance of experienced and admired women healers and midwives – Christian and Muslim – from the 1930s to 1950s. Because even a modest payment to a *daya* was a hardship for the very poor, she was in such cases called only to cut the umbilical cord, if at all. As in the oral history archives, women reported that they and their families saw multiple kinds of healthcare providers, including one respondent born in the late 1920s whose natal and marital family members saw "Dr. Samuel" for nonreproductive healthcare at his clinic in Ramallah, and the frequently mentioned traditional midwife Sultaneh for childbirth.

Most women explained birth, health, illness, and death as in God's hands, even when they tried every method in their knowledge, network, and power to address a problem. Geographic location, access/availability, and reputation of the provider mattered, as did the nature of the illness, its perceived seriousness, and whether there was local ability to heal it. Village women were most likely to travel for healthcare when they or a child were extremely ill, they suffered a reproductive disorder that could not be resolved by local healers, or they had a history of difficult pregnancies. One respondent, born in the mid-1920s in a village near Ramleh, reported her pregnant mother dying in her mid-thirties while on the road to seek medical assistance in a Jewish colony, "which was about thirty minutes from our *balad* by walking." As a young girl she rode to the colony with her father, brother, and pregnant mother in a borrowed cart (*carra*) and horse until they were forced to make their way back to the village when her mother died before they reached their destination.[29]

---

[29] Palestinians associated physicians with death during the Mandate because most only went to see one when nothing else worked, in contrast to the high rates of

Striking in interviews is the tremendous amount of physical labor in and outside homes that was primarily the responsibility of girls and women, in contrast to the idealized image of the cared for and protected pregnant woman and new mother. Women's physical labor socially reproduced households in the broadest terms, extending well beyond cooking and childrearing to farming, caring for animals, bringing water to the household, and hauling wood for fuels since electrified Palestinian villages were the rare exception during the British colonial period. Such unremitting work, combined with lack of money and limited transportation between hilly, distant villages and their town centers, limited girls' and women's access to midwives, doctors, hospitals, and medications.

Spontaneous miscarriages and stillbirths were common and not documented by Government of Palestine Department of Health reports and vital records. Women I interviewed experienced miscarriages as unremarkable unless they were having difficulty sustaining a pregnancy or the miscarriage occurred in a late gestational stage. Women who lived in rural Mandate Palestine reported miscarrying (*al-walad binzil*) while they were working on farmlands (*hasida*) or carrying wood for fuel or water. An interviewee born in the late 1920s in a village near Ramallah reported her mother miscarrying multiple times because "We were farmers and shepherds who followed the animals and carried a lot on our heads, including wood; she miscarried from exhaustion." One of my oldest interviewees reported "losing" one of her pregnancies in the 1940s "because I used to work in the fields. Someone told me to go home because I was bleeding. I rode a donkey home. On the way, I started to have pains. I got off the donkey, may it be far from the hearers, and stood near a rock. I sat and dropped what I dropped [*nazalet il nazalteh*] and buried it in the red dirt [*samakeh*]. I got back on the donkey and went home. My husband's sisters took care of me. I sat two or three days at home and took myself back to the fields." Although this woman knew she was pregnant, many women only learned they were pregnant when they miscarried, and did not typically see a midwife or medical professional afterward. In contrast to their responses to miscarriages, mothers and older children, if the latter were

physician use by European Jewish residents of Palestine. Interview with Sharif Abdelqader Ahmed Kanaana in El-Bireh on June 10, 2017.

in the room during an interview, remembered in vivid terms children who died from illnesses or accidents.

While the peasant Palestinian women in the Bethlehem village of Artas studied by Finnish anthropologist Hilma Granqvist in the 1920s did not necessarily want many children, they believed pregnancy "proved" a husband was sleeping with a wife and avoided him taking another wife. They had many pregnancies given the high infant mortality rate (Granqvist 1950, 80). Fifty years later an ethnography by Sharif Kanaana and his colleagues found that Palestinian village women in the West Bank understood children to provide continuity of the self and family line, social unity, and people who will mourn their death (Kanaana et al. 1984, 21–23, 30). They considered children to bring beauty, amazement, and joy into life (*zinat al-hayat*) and lighten the load of elderly people (42).

Because children were a valued and assumed dimension of marriage, difficulty in becoming pregnant or sustaining a pregnancy was a source of pain, divorce, and plural marriage. A newly married peasant woman who did not become pregnant relatively quickly was subject to unsolicited questions, advice, and treatment suggestions (*wasfat* and `*ilaj*) (34, 36, 62, 63–65). As British nurse matron Vena Rogers wrote in 1934 about Palestinians: "To be sterile is a great disgrace; anything is done to prevent this. When sterile the uterus 'sits in sorrow,' mourning for lost children ... If the wife is unhappy, the uterus grieves and in sympathy refuses to become impregnated" (Rogers 1934, 103). Rogers describes "many strange things" women used to induce pregnancy (103).

In 1920s Palestine preference for boys was prominent because "boys build the house and girls leave to build another family's house," boys provide "working hands" for peasants, and boys become "defenders of the house," although Palestinians also had sayings about the blessings of a woman whose firstborn is a daughter (Granqvist 1947, 55, 79; Canaan 1927, 159n2, 162–163). In Palestinian peasant societies then and now, boys produce `*izweh* for their parents and paternal relatives, a social power that relies on number of men in a clan (Kanaana et al. 1984, 23–25). Women's songs recorded in the ethnographic study extol desire for many boy children who can provide farm labor, social standing, and future support (*sanad*) to aged parents (26, 28). Boys continued to be understood as stabilizing a woman's position in her marital family, tying the husband to her and protecting her from the possibility he would take a second wife (29). Brothers supported each other and their sisters, retained land within a family line after marriage, and were (are?) understood to confirm the masculinity (*rujula*) of a father in peasant communities (30, 31, 32).

My interviews with women born between 1917 and 1933 evidenced multiple examples of decisions around healthcare seeking, reproductive control, and pregnancy determined by a strong bias for boy children, as discussed in Chapter 5. A Palestinian refugee in Jordan born in the late 1920s whose family had been pastoralists in an area near Nablus was one of the most difficult interviews I conducted since she was unhappy and chronically ill. Because she had three daughters (no miscarriages or stillbirths), her much older husband continuously threatened to marry another woman, although he never did because she refused to give permission. A grown daughter in the room expressed her wish that her father had married an additional wife because "she would have had brothers for us."

That said, a number of women shared accounts where the illness or death of a girl infant or child, or losing her to the husband's family upon a mother's widowhood or divorce and remarriage, sat as an emotional weight of grief decades later. A villager from northern Palestine, married off by her brother at twelve to a "very old" (about forty) man in an exchange (*badal*) marriage because the brother wanted to marry the man's sister, had a firstborn daughter who died of an illness at around one year old. The second daughter was an infant when the husband himself died of an illness. The widow's mother-in-law and sister-in-law collaborated with her brother to marry her off and leave the baby behind: "I was widowed and my brother came, God have mercy on him, my mother-in-law told him you must marry her off. My brother-in-law wanted to marry me badly but his mother and sister did not agree. They forced me to leave my daughter behind so young and marry this man. I did not want to get married, I did not want to get married. My mother-in-law insisted, saying you cannot stay for one daughter. If it was for a son, maybe, but not a daughter. What could I do?"

Given my focus on Palestinian infant and child death, it is important to discuss many women's fear of the figure of the Qarina, also called the *tabi`a* (follower) in colloquial Arabic (a woman haunted by her Qarina is *matbu`a* [followed]) and the evil eye, the main negative otherworldly forces understood to explain lack of pregnancy, miscarriages, and mother, infant, and child illness and death (Granqvist 1950, 110–114). Women who had multiple miscarriages or lost babies regularly blamed the Qarina, who "cannot tolerate that women are happy, and as women's happiness consists to a great extent in having children, this is the tender spot where she hurts, by trying to kill their little ones" (112–113). As a result, "great fuss" and "overpreparation" were discouraged for expected children (Granqvist 1947, 99). Palestinian women were assumed to be in danger during and soon after childbirth, as indicated by the expression "For forty days her grave is open." Postpartum women were expected to stay out of sight and take care of themselves and their babies (104–105). Mothers wiped rather than washed infants clean because of their "special fear" of the dangers of "being wet" (Canaan 1927, 174).

This "djinniyeh," writes Palestinian physician and ethnologist Tawfik Canaan about the 1920s, "is dreaded by all the inhabitants of Palestine," who hung, pinned, and hid charms around babies. Even the Muslims among them turned to Christian saint shrines with ill children to protect them from the forces of death (Canaan 1927, 159, 181, 182, 183; Granqvist 1950, 82).[30] Women hung silver or other shiny objects in a child's hair to reflect back "the first glance" of the "admiring" eye rather than absorb it (Granqvist 1950, 110). A raggedy, unclean child was better protected from attracting the notice of the evil eye or a Qarina. Parents dreaded compliments on the looks of their children, fearing they made them vulnerable to death (Canaan 1927, 174–175; Granqvist 1950, 111).

Kanaana and his colleagues continued to find the Qarina "to be among the strongest of unknown forces that affects the woman or the child. She is a female from the other world (the hidden world) who is in conversation with the world of jinns. She is also called *al-ukht* (sister); each woman and man have their own Qarina,[31] who may be good or a problem, as in the earthly world. A woman suffers if her Qarina focuses on her because she is jealous for her gold, nice clothes, or makeup. The Qarina's most effective harms are to prevent a woman from getting pregnant, kill her fetus, or hurt her child" (Kanaana et al.

---

[30] Canaan, who provided free medical care to the needy, accumulated a famous collection of amulets as gifts from grateful Palestinian patients.

[31] *Qarina* comes from the Arabic word for *pair*. I heard examples where the gender of the jinn did not match the gender of the mother or person possessed.

1984, 76).[32] In a 1990s ethnography of spirit possession in the village of Artas, people explained jinns and demons to Celia Rothenberg as "degraded men" – children of Eve whom she denied and hid from Adam in shame. They "enter" a regular person when they have the opportunity. The solution is to call out God's name often, pray, beg pardon, and behave properly in order not to injure them or allow them an opening to hurt one's child (Rothenberg 2004, 30–31).

A number of unlettered Palestinian women insisted "I did not believe in this" or "I didn't know her" when I asked about the Qarina, or they believed in the evil eye but not in the Qarina. Other women explained pregnancies to have been ended by the Qarina, who tried to choke them in their sleep or beat them on their bellies because of jealousy. Muslim and Christian women reported the Qarina to be particularly active when they had an exhausting day. A villager born in the late 1920s in the Ramallah area and her grown daughters described such experiences. "You used to tell us that you dreamt of a Qarina that pressed against your face like this," one daughter prompted her mother, who elaborated. "She always came when I was pregnant. The prayer would protect me. I learned about her from the midwife." The daughter added, "When we were younger, when Mama had just laundered and was tired, she would say that in the night the Qarina came to me, as if it was a nightmare [*kabus*]."

Multiple women I interviewed explained young children to have died from a specific disease or from God, and others to have been afflicted by the evil eye, the Qarina, or the "Kashra" (Granqvist 1950, 81). One interviewee from an area between Jerusalem and Bethlehem explained that her one-year-old son, "born big," had attracted the evil eye and became ill and died: "He was five kilos. While me and my husband's women relatives were bathing him, his father came in with a man who startled the baby and cursed him with the evil eye [*hasaduh*] when he exclaimed to my husband, 'this boy of yours is a man [*hatha ibnak zalameh*].' The boy got sick with *lafhet hawa* [possibly pneumonia, although she described him as crumpled, unable to stretch his arms or legs and refusing to nurse]. We took him to Dr. Salib al-Sa'ideh in Jerusalem and he died while we were there."

An interviewee from the Ramleh area explained that her twins almost died at three days old: "Their father [a teacher] was at the school … I had dreamed when I was pregnant that a man came and

---

[32] My translation and synopsis.

beat my stomach and pulled out a piece of flesh from my chest. As I was watching the infants their faces became yellow and then flush red. Something was choking them. When their father arrived, he wrote a paper and put it under their heads. Thank God, after that, there were no problems."

A respondent born in the mid-1920s in coastal Palestine reported that of two of her children who died, a girl became ill with measles and a boy was "touched by the evil eye." She had left him asleep with his sister after bathing, dressing, and nursing him. She went to visit a friend. The baby awakened and threw up when a woman came by to ask for the mother. After his sister bathed and dressed him, "he began to laugh, got a fever and died the following day at sunset."

A villager born in the late twenties in the Tulkarem area explained that her one-year-old son died without getting ill because she herself was *matbu`a* or had a Qarina who wished her ill: "I would see her as something rotten [*ishi kham*], a snake or a monster, and I would be afraid because they were chasing me. The boy deteriorated [he went *wara, wara*], he changed, he stopped eating and died within a few days." A son she'd named the same as the child who died also died as a one-year-old, this time after an illness, despite her regularly taking him to see an Armenian Palestinian physician in the city named "Dr. Da`das." In addition to visiting the physician, the parents sought a reading (*fatahna*) by a shaykh in Nablus who said the respondent had a Qarina and wrote her a hijab.[33] She reported additionally losing three sets of twins during pregnancies in the 1950s.

Mothers renamed ill children in order to disguise them from these forces and vowed to sacrifice an animal and share the food with the larger community if such a child survived, called a *nidhr* (Granqvist 1950, 114–126; Kanaana et al. 1984, 79–80). The resulting children are called "vow or beggar children" (*shehadeh*), who some Muslims in the village of Artas baptized if they survived (Granqvist 1950, 126–127). Women deemed to have a Qarina may turn to a *tahwita* (or hijab), as did

---

[33] This is a thickly folded triangle of paper on which are written holy words or letters. Muslim midwives, according to Avner Giladi, have a long history of using amulets (*ruqya*) – recitations from the Quran in the form of a spell or in written form (*talasim*), which are "justified by the Quran itself, by the hadith literature and by religious scholars, particularly compilers of Tibb nabawi collections, thus adding a spiritual dimension to their roles" (Giladi 2015, 139, 140–143).

my respondent from Tulkarem, call God's name (*bismillah al-rahman al-rahim*), or read *ayat* from the Quran (Kanaana et al. 1984, 77–78). Christian women have similar practices with different prayers, as indicated by some of my interviewees.

Granqvist's famous scholarship on the Bethlehem village of Artas expressed the dominant Western biblical nostalgia of the period and the modern/backward epistemological frame she shared with Canaan, a Palestinian. Canaan, for example, described how midwives cut the navel cord "after binding both ends with a non-sterilized cloth band, or more often with a cotton cord ... Many still burn the cut surface of the cord with the flame of a candle. In this primitive way they unknowingly sterilize the certainly infected wound" (Canaan 1927, 165). He did not offer the possibility that midwives burned "the cut surface of the cord" because they learned it protected women from infection. Similarly, he wrote, Palestinian children acquired immunity "despite filthy conditions" and the "ignorance of the midwives," whose women patients surprisingly did "not succumb to puerperal infection" (186). In keeping with Western "mothercraft" advice, Canaan encouraged scheduled feeding, although he was not judgmental about swaddling (171, 172, 173, 174, 176).

Palestinians I interviewed greatly respected traditional midwives and healers who had earned community trust by their humility, quality of care, and positive health outcomes. Hacks and quacks quickly earned bad reputations. At the same time, elderly Palestinians who lived during the Mandate gave every indication that they and their elders used every tool at their disposal to address pregnancy, childbirth, and illnesses – traditional healers and midwives, home remedies, amulets, prayers, pharmacies, and the expensive government or private allopathic medical care that was rarely available to most of them. However, they also recognized their limited control. They described hunger and poverty as well as fevers, measles, tuberculosis, malaria, pneumonia, and associated digestive illnesses that produced high infant and child mortality as coming in unpredictable "waves" (*amwaj*). Discourses of native scientific and medical backwardness typically served ideological purposes for colonizers and the modernizers who mobilized them.

Colonial Palestine and the Global Color Line

Race is central to the plot in *Buried in the Red Dirt*. I take as axiomatic that racial projects articulate with sexuality given their concern with biological and social reproduction or, in Michel Foucault's terms, biopolitics: who people have sex with or marry, who has babies and how many, who deserves citizenship, who is worthy of health and life, and who merits illness and premature death (Foucault 1978, 138, 139, 140, 145).[34] White racial and population anxieties and discussions of race more generally were increasingly prominent at global conferences by the turn of the twentieth century. Marilyn Lake and Henry Reynolds write that the "assertion of whiteness was born in apprehension of imminent loss" as colonized peoples continued to revolt (Lake and Reynolds 2008, 2). The racist dimensions of international politics were manifest and explicitly challenged during the many months of intensive meetings at the Versailles Peace Conference of 1919 – at which was established the scaffolding of postwar colonial and imperial arrangements, including the British Mandate over Palestine.

White powers often described the struggle for "world domination" as a "race war" in the late nineteenth and early twentieth centuries (93, 242). British imperialists distinguished between white and nonwhite (or "coloured") peoples and assumed the former should rule and the latter should be ruled, defining "Syrians" and Afghans, for example, as "nonwhites" (9, 6). White supremacy and race consciousness informed national and international discussions about geopolitics, economics, birth and infant mortality rates, the nature of justice, and the social implications of "contact" between populations as Euro-American empires expanded and cross-continental migration became more feasible (e.g., 10–11). These debates among intellectuals, scientists, journalists, professionals, military leaders, and politicians translated into immigration and citizenship policies, international labor regimes, and geopolitical conflicts.[35]

---

[34] Foucault theorizes expansively on reproduction, children, life, medicine, medicalization, and health and their relationships to the fostering of economic and political power. See, for example, "The Politics of Health in the Eighteenth Century" (in Rabinow 1984).

[35] Race-based immigration restrictions did not necessarily align with a sensibility that nonwhite peoples were essentially or fixedly inferior to whites. For example, Charles Pearson's widely read 1892 book *National Life and Character* used his vantage point as a white settler in Melbourne to challenge "Anglo-Saxon" "pride of race" and argue that "black and yellow races" had the capacity to develop their own trade economies, competing with and circumscribing "the industry of Europeans." The book nevertheless "encouraged racist thinking of a kind that his own forecast called into question" by dividing the world into "white and non-white" and was used to justify

Although white racial supremacy was a global concern in the first twenty years of the twentieth century and was absolutely relevant to Zionism and the workings of the Palestine Mandate, scholarship on the British and Zionist colonization of Palestine has rarely addressed these projects as racial and racist, with specificities, to be sure, but in alignment with other Western imperial and settler-colonial projects. Irrespective of anti-Semitism and the historically situated and to some degree malleable nature of whiteness as a social construct, Zionist settler-colonialism was understood by its advocates and their British and US allies to be a *white socioeconomic project*. Racism in Mandate Palestine expressed itself through civilizational discourse, extraction from the native population, the biopolitics of colonial categorizations and counting, and the systematic maldistribution of life, death, and wellbeing by investment priorities. Such maldistribution by priority is underplayed as a *systemically racist dimension* of settler-colonialism and colonialism in Palestine.

Racism and white supremacy have been "trans-statal" and "global" from their genesis (Jung 2015, 193, 194). In 1900, W. E. B. Du Bois famously termed as "the color line" that "belts the world" the ways "differences of race" were used to deny "to over half the world … opportunities and privileges" in presentations at the first Pan-African Congress in London and the third meeting of the American Negro Academy in Washington, DC (Du Bois 1900a, 625; Du Bois 1900b, 47–48). Black, brown, and yellow peoples, Du Bois argued, will be "beneficial" to "human progress" and influence "the world of the future by reason of sheer numbers and physical contact," pointing to the global salience of racial comparative population discourse at the time (Du Bois 1900a, 625). The "color line" was always "plural," argues Moon-Kie Jung, shaped by reigning systems of accumulation and extraction: slavery, colonialism, settler-colonialism, and imperialism (Jung 2015, 195).

Du Bois's 1900 accounts reproduced Orientalist tropes of Asian "moral and physical degeneration" and "dumb submission" with the exception of Japan (Du Bois 1900b, 49). He commended British and Belgian imperialists for ending slavery and introducing "rapid

immigration restrictions and establish or maintain white colonies in the "Temperate Zone" (in Lake and Reynolds 2008, chapter 3). Pointing to early "comparative" global white anxiety regarding population, Pearson emphasized that "the lower races of men ["Africans, Indians and Chinese"] increase faster than the higher" (78–79).

development of trade and industry" in parts of the African continent. Instead of condemning US imperialism ("new ownership") in Puerto Rico, Hawaii, Cuba, and the Philippines, Du Bois aspirationally called for "sympathy and alliance" with the "masses of dark men and women" as they are "united under the stars and stripes for an America that knows no color line in the freedom of its opportunities" (49–53). More critically in the same period, colonial subject and West African and Caribbean intellectual Edward Blyden, speaking before the 1903 meeting of the British African Society, called out the ignorance of Europeans who believed in "absolute racial difference [and] his own absolute racial superiority," physically, intellectually, and psychologically (quoted in Tilley 2011, 222; also see 225–226).

By 1910, Du Bois harshly condemned white supremacy as a "religion" in his essay "The Souls of White Folk," which he updated and published in *Darkwater*, informed by the brutality of World War I (Du Bois 1920, 1921). He analogized the "modern" white man to a thieving "Prometheus" "tethered by a fable of the past" and insisting on his divinity: "Neither Roman nor Arab, Greek nor Egyptian, Persian nor Mongol ever took himself and his own perfectness with such disconcerting seriousness as the modern white man" (Du Bois 1920, 497–501). Du Bois recognized that the extraordinary danger of white supremacy emerged from demographic, economic, and psychological senses of "threat," including from "little Japan," whose government's "eventual overthrow ... became a subject of deep thought and intrigue, from St. Petersburg to San Francisco" (504).

Substantial historical evidence indicates elite white defensiveness in the face of "colored" challenges to global power arrangements in the fin-de-siècle and early twentieth-century world. This was the case despite the fact that "racial thinking could take stronger and weaker forms" – for example, in colonized Africa – and colonial states "employ[ed] multiple and contradictory definitions of race, tribe, and ethnicity" (Tilley 2011, 220; Tilley 2014, 779). The 1911 Universal Races Congress at the University of London, a famous site of inter-national elite exchange on race and racial amity, included multiple plenary sessions with more than fifty English-language papers submit-ted in advance by researchers and political leaders.[36] Although the

---

[36] The papers were read by the more than two thousand attendees, with additional hundreds of intellectuals, politicians, lawyers, and religious leaders who paid to

majority of papers challenged racial supremacy and the coherence of race as a category, the opening address by Sir Phillip Stanhope (Lord Weardale) expressed white global anxiety regarding the "remarkable rise of the power of the Empire of Japan, the precursor, it would seem, of a similar revival of the activities and highly developed qualities of the population of the great Empire of China" (quoted in Lake and Reynolds 2008, 252).

I am mainly concerned with discussion of Jewish settler-colonialism at the 1911 Universal Races Congress. *Drawing the Global Colour Line: White Men's Countries and the International Challenge of Racial Equality* (Lake and Reynolds 2008) offers essential insights that invited my own race-specific questions about the two decades that preceded the British Mandate and intensified Zionist colonization in Palestine. Lake and Reynolds write that Du Bois was impressed with many participants at the 1911 Congress, including (in his words) "two Egyptian Feys"[37] who "were evidently negroid, the Portuguese was without doubt a Mulatto, and the Persian was dark enough to have trouble in the South." Among the presenters who deeply impacted Du Bois and, I contend, informed his ardent Zionism, was the British Jewish novelist Israel Zangwill (Lake and Reynolds 2008, 258, 257).

Zangwill's paper, "The Jewish Race," was rhetorically crafted to first make a case for Jews as a superior race that required "a territory" to "live its own life" (Zangwill 1911, 271). Expressing the eugenicist logic of the era, Zangwill wrote that in comparison to "the yet uncivilized and brutalized masses of Europe, when, for example, the lowest infant mortality or the healthiness of its [Jewish] school children is contrasted with the appalling statistics of its neighbours, there is sound scientific warrant for endorsing even in its narrowest form its [Jewish] claim to be 'a chosen people'" (268–269, 275). In the second half of the

be affiliated with the Congress (Lake and Reynolds 2008, 251). Presenters were predominantly white US, French, and Anglo-Europeans, but included Hungarian, Haitian, South Asian, Chinese, Japanese, US indigenous, Turkish/Ottoman, Persian, Egyptian, Russian, Black South African, and Brazilian people. "First Universal Races Congress, University of London, July 26–29, 1911. Abstracts of Papers." https://credo.library.umass.edu/cgi-bin/pdf.cgi?id=scua:mums312-b007-i068. "Papers on Inter-racial Problems, Communicated to the First Universal Races Congresses held at the University of London, July 26–29, 1911." Edited by G. Spiller. https://babel.hathitrust.org/cgi/pt?id=hvd .32044019018068&view=1up&seq=11.

[37] I wonder if the written or intended word was "Beys," an Ottoman honorific.

essay Zangwill switched rhetorical gears to align with the racial con-
structionist orientation of most Congress papers (including by Franz
Boas) and Jewish European anthropologists such as Maurice Fishberg
(see Falk 2017, 71, 87). Zangwill asserted the "comparative superfici-
ality of all these human differences," that "every race is really akin to
every other" (otherwise how could Jews so easily assimilate?), "every
people is a hotch-potch of races," and Jews were mainly "white" but
included other ethnic groups and colors (Zangwill 1911, 276).

Given Jewish whiteness, Zangwill continued, Jewish religious difference is more important for "surviv[ing] the pressure of so many hostile
milieux – or still more parlous, so many friendly" (277). Zangwill
presented Jews as having limited options: they could assimilate, which
in settings of lower "civilization" (such as Central and Eastern Europe)
was a recipe for their "degeneration" to the level of the majority. In
advanced settings, on the other hand, "emancipation" had brought
"dissolution" of Jewish difference through assimilation.[38] Zangwill
concluded his essay in the white settler-colonial spirit of the times:
A "Jewish State, or at least a land of refuge upon a basis of local
autonomy," was "the only solution left to address this dilemma"
(279). Zangwill had in fact established the Jewish Territorial
Organisation (ITO) in 1903 to acquire land for a Jewish settler-colony
"under British protection," especially for "refugees from Russian persecution," somewhere other than Palestine given Ottoman resistance to
such a project in "Zion."[39] Zangwill's 1911 essay illustrates the importance of a kind of Jewish social-eugenic maintenance project as a driving
impulse for Jewish settler-colonialism, not only anti-Jewish racism.

Du Bois also attended the months-long 1919 Versailles Peace
Conference that helped determine the fate of postwar Palestine as
a reporter for *The Crisis* newspaper and co-organizer of the Pan-
African Congress, which met in parallel in Paris to petition for Black
political self-determination, protection of African natives from state
injustice and violence, and affirmation of Black resource rights (Lake

---

[38] The "nature of Judaism started to change" from the mid-eighteenth century in
Western Europe "when a process of juridical emancipation of the Jews was
initiated." As a result, "old patterns of Jewish life started to crumble" as options
for Jewish lifestyles, religious practices, professions, and trades were liberalized
and Jewish "alienation" decreased. Such loss of difference was less likely in "the
lands of Islam" and Eastern Europe (Falk 2017, 11, 12) for different reasons.

[39] Letters and the ITO, by Israel Zangwill, *Fortnightly Review*, May 1865–
June 1934, London, Vol. 79, Issue 472 (April 1906): 633–647.

and Reynolds 2008, 306, 307). Du Bois's opinion on Zionism can be inferred from the concluding sentence of his February 1919 presentation at the Pan-African Congress, "Africa, Colonialism, and Zionism." Alluding to the Marcus Garvey Movement, the essay argues against the colonization of Africa by African-Americans while expressing sympathy for the diaspora's orientation to the continent: "The African movement means to us what the Zionist movement must mean to the Jews, the centralization of race effort and the recognition of a racial fount" (Du Bois 1919, 637–640).

Du Bois's 1948 essay "The Case for the Jews" expresses a committed Zionist sensibility thirty years later. He passionately insists that the "right" answer vis-à-vis Palestine is "terribly simple." Palestine should be the grounds of a Jewish state because "everyone knows the way in which the history of the Jewish religion is wound about Palestine" (Du Bois 1948, 461–464). The essay reprises the greatest Zionist and Orientalist discursive and ideological hits, including: "Among the million Arabs there is widespread ignorance, poverty and disease and fanatic belief in the Mohammedan religion, which makes these people suspicious of other peoples and other religions. Their rulership is a family and clan despotism which makes effective use of democratic methods difficult." In contrast, "there is no question of the contribution which he ["the wandering Jew"] made to modern civilization." Du Bois seemed to have absorbed the options for Jews from Zangwill's essay at the 1911 Universal Races Congress: "Should he lose himself in the surrounding population and through that give up his peculiar culture and religion; should he keep to himself, an integral unit; or finally, should he try to found a state of his own?" (462). In sum, Du Bois's vigorous criticisms of imperialism and the global color line excluded the British and Zionist colonization of Palestine.

I conclude this section by exploring the 1919 Versailles Peace Conference itself to substantiate my claim that white supremacist thinking deeply informed the approaches of white imperial powers toward Palestine and Zionism. The "Great Powers" at the 1919 Conference, the Allied victors from World War I, were the United States, the British Empire, France, Italy, and Japan, although Japan was not considered an equal. The conference was attended by "signing delegations" from more than thirty political entities, including the four British white settler-colonies (Dominions) of South Africa, Australia, Canada, and New Zealand and the Arab delegation, another eighteen uninvited groups listed as "national representatives," and three "non-national representative" groups, the Pan-African Congress, Western and US suffragists, and the Zionist movement.[40]

The "blueprint" for the Allied postwar geopolitical order, the League of Nations and its Mandate system, was authored by racist war hero Jan Smuts, an Afrikaner from South Africa, at the behest of the British government. Published in December 1918 as *The League of Nations: A Practical Suggestion*, the document became a worldwide bestseller. Its stated purpose was to establish "a means to prevent future wars" (Lake and Reynolds 2008, 298; Smuts 1919). Smuts's use of the terms "self-determination" and "no annexation," drawing on Woodrow Wilson's Fourteen Points released in January 1918, offered thin ideological cover for European and US imperialist aims to control postwar geopolitics and resources. The "peoples left behind" by the dissolution of the Russian, Austrian, Ottoman, and German empires, Smuts rationalized, were "largely incapable or deficient in the power of self-government" (Smuts 1919, 8–9).

The Japanese delegation created an international stir at Versailles when it called for anti-racial discrimination language in the Covenant of the League of Nations, and thus equal status in postwar Allied geopolitical arrangements (Shimazu 1998, 13). More than a top-down Japanese imperial initiative, "the question of racial equality dominated domestic debate in Japan from November 2018 until May 1919," with Japanese citizens demanding that any peace accord "abolish all forms of racial discrimination," including against Japanese nationals who lived in other countries (Lake and Reynolds 2008, 284–285, 286–288). Japan was itself an imperial and colonial power interested in "equal access" to lands that would be redistributed from the losers of World War I. Japan had colonized Korea in 1905, annexed it in 1910 (the Korean Provisional Delegation attended the Versailles Conference as a nonvoting national group), and quickly moved to take over trade and industries in China's Shandong Province after Germany was defeated and hoped to do the same in Pacific territories (Burkman 2007, 5–6, 150, 241n94).

---

[40] The white-ruled Union of South Africa (a British Dominion) was among the signatory delegations, as were Black-ruled Liberia and Haiti. "List of Participants to Paris Peace Conference, 1919–1920." https://tinyurl.com /yxqa7c9o.

Nevertheless, "Japan's cause became a universal one. Supporters and opponents alike came to see the proposal for an end to racial discrimination as a universal crusade" (Lake and Reynolds 2008, 285–288). Naoko Shimazu shows that between late January and the end of April 1919, the Japanese delegation made three formal bids at the Versailles Conference to append to an existing clause on religious freedom (Article 21), and later to the preamble, an equality clause in the final Covenant of the League of Nations. Their efforts were to no avail, despite progressively weakening the language. The delegation originally requested making "no distinction, either in law or in fact, on account of their [all alien nationals of states, members of the League] race or nationality." In response to strong white resistance, especially from the United States, the British Empire, and white British Dominions, the Japanese delegation instead called for language that endorsed "the principle of equality of all nationals of States members of the League." The final failed bid asked that "equality of all nations" be included in the covenant (Shimazu 1998, 13, 16–33).

Delegates from the United States and from the British Empire and its Dominions publicly and privately rejected the proposals. They and their constituents at home expected the envisioned League of Nations to reject challenges to white supremacy domestically and internationally, including existing race-based immigration, labor, and naturalization policies (Shimazu 1998, 14–15, 18–20; Lake and Reynolds 2008, 288–297). Discussing the Japanese proposal with Woodrow Wilson's diplomatic emissary and friend Edward M. House, British foreign secretary Arthur Balfour deemed as "outmoded" the principle of racial equality. Although "all men of a particular nation might be considered to be born free and equal, he was far from convinced that an African 'could be regarded as the equal of a European or an American'" (Lake and Reynolds 2008, 291–292).

Smuts played the most important go-between role in resisting all Japanese entreaties to include antidiscrimination language in the League of Nations Covenant (Lake and Reynolds 2008, 299).[41] Australian prime minister W. M. Hughes was the most belligerent in

---

[41] Smuts remained opposed "throughout his political career" to the principle of racial equality. When white Dominion leaders met at "the Imperial Conference in London in 1921, it was he alone who stood out against the policy of granting equal rights to Indian immigrant communities across the Empire" (Lake and Reynolds 2008, 302).

assuring that no such language would be accepted (Shimazu 1998, 24–25). The US delegation led by Woodrow Wilson was similarly determined not to allow it to come to fruition (Shimazu 1998, 30–31; Lake and Reynolds 2008, 301–302). During the final plenary session of the Commission of the League of Nations on April 11, created to draft and finalize the Covenant, the Japanese delegation insisted on a recorded vote on the "equality of all nations" language. France (two), Japan (two), Italy (two), Brazil (one), China (one), Greece (one), Serbia (one), and Czechoslovakia (one) voted to add the anodyne prose to the preamble (eleven of seventeen present votes).[42] As chair, Wilson did not call for a "negative vote," which served to keep off the record the positions of the British Empire, the United States, Portugal, and Romania. British and US representatives had nevertheless made their opposition clear, and Wilson repeatedly raised the possibility of the language being used to challenge the Monroe Doctrine. After the majority affirmative vote to append the Japanese language, Wilson declared that any such amendment to the Covenant required "unanimous consent" to be "valid" (Shimazu 1998, 30–31; Lake and Reynolds 2008, 300, 301; Miller 1928, 375–392).

Smuts argued in the 1918 blueprint for the League of Nations that the peoples of Palestine and Armenia were too "heterogeneous" to be consulted regarding any future arrangement. Thus "autonomy in any real sense would be out of the question [for them], and [further] the administration would have to be undertaken to a very large extent by some external authority. This would be the case, at any rate for some time to come, in Palestine, where the administrative cooperation of the Jewish minority and Arab majority would not be forthcoming" (Smuts 1919, 13–14). During a meeting in San Remo in April 1920, US and British diplomats, under the auspices of the League (established in January 1920 without US endorsement), finalized Palestine's fate as a Class A Mandate awarded to Britain. The arrangement was approved by the League of Nations Council in July 1922 and came into force on September 29, 1922, although the British had already invaded Jerusalem in 1917 and set up a military administration.

---

[42] The Commission was composed at this point of the five "Great Powers," each with two votes, and nine additional countries, each with one vote (nineteen total). Paul Hymans, who represented Belgium, and Smuts, who held one of the two British Empire votes, were absent.

To my knowledge, no Arab world–focused source on the 1919 Versailles Peace Conference has addressed the prominent racial debates.[43] Alexis Wick finds that scholarship rarely explores with nuance the multifaceted Arab diplomatic negotiations, positions, and constraints before and during the fateful conference (Wick 2004, 3). The Arab delegation, composed of Arab nationalists, included two plenipotentiaries, Prince Faisal of Damascus, a reluctant participant explicitly chosen by the British Empire to represent his father, Sharif Hussein of Mecca (10), and Rustum Haydar, born in Baalbek. The Nablusi `Awni `Abdulhadi was Faisal's general secretary to the conference and the five advisors included Faisal's personal physician, Damascene Ahmad Qadri (11, 20). While Faisal was only fluent in Arabic, Haydar, `Abdulhadi, and Qadri, friends of the same generation, had studied and lived in Paris beginning in 1910, been active together in Arabist movements in multiple settings, and were fluent in the languages and ways of Western Europe, Istanbul, Damascus, Jerusalem, and Beirut (11).

Rather than summarizing dimensions of the fateful conference that Palestine scholars usually focus on, or Wick's valuable study, I looked for evidence of what may be called "race consciousness" among members of the Arab delegation in Versailles in three sources. The "Arab Memorandum to the Paris Peace Conference," submitted in early January 1919 by Prince Faisal and his "translator," British agent T. E. Lawrence, indicates the delegation was not operating on the same logic as Zionist or British imperial participants with respect to "race." The memo recognized the existence of social, economic, and cultural differences among the peoples of "Arab Asia" and insisted on the need for the communities to determine their political leaderships and "frame of government." "Arab unity," it argued, was premised on "closely related Semitic stocks, all [for the most part] speaking one language, Arabic," noting that the "peoples" (in the plural) in different geographic areas had increasingly been able to "communicate common ideas readily." Regarding Palestine, "the enormous majority of the

---

[43] I am indebted to colleagues and friends who helped me with sources to explore this matter, including Beshara Doumani, Rashid Khalidi, Alexis Wick, and Sean Swanick. In a compressed time period, Suzan Abdi carefully read the Versailles sections of two Arabic memoirs for any mention of the Japanese-initiated discussion or of race consciousness generally, and we met virtually to discuss the possibly relevant passages.

people are Arabs. The Jews are very close to the Arabs in blood, and there is no conflict of character between the two races. In principles we are absolutely as one."[44]

Rustum Haydar and ʿAwni ʿAbdulhadi's memoirs yield no mention of the Japanese antidiscrimination debate that was prominent at multiple points from February through April 1919 at the Versailles Conference. This lack is a mystery but may have been partly the result of not being represented on the Commission that wrote the Covenant language. The records at my disposal do not indicate whether they attended relevant plenaries or discussed the matter in informal settings. Given that the Arab delegation was in its own high-stakes negotiations with the British Empire, which had deceitfully promised Arab self-determination in return for participation on the side of the Allies during the war, not discussing the Japanese antidiscrimination proposals may have been a strategic decision. It is difficult to be sure without systematically examining additional primary sources.

Haydar and ʿAbdulhadi were familiar with French racism given their longtime residency in France, aware of French brutality in colonized Northwest Africa, and likely understood the nature of British colonial rule in Ottoman Egypt and the Sudan. Haydar's memoir entries from the Versailles period show his keen recognition of French racism against even the most cosmopolitan Christian Arab. He noted as well that the "American viewed the Frenchman like the Frenchman viewed the Easterner," as an inferior. After writing that he spoke with "Madame Fisher," who boasted of her missionary work in the United States and hoped for entrée to Arab lands, he commented, "The Americans think the Arabs are imbeciles (*hamajan*)" (Safwat 1988, 557, 567, 592). In ʿAbdulhadi's memoir entries from the same time, he wrote that the French assumed Arabs lived like people did "in the middle ages or earlier." He noted that European elites repeated ad nauseam the canard that they occupied other peoples not for imperial benefit but to advance their wellbeing. In another comment in this vein, he observed that the French seemed to think the Arabs naively accepted their claims that their only interest as colonizers was to raise the

---

[44] Notably this is followed with language (likely from Lawrence) accepting imposition of foreign trusteeship in Palestine that is similar to phrasing in British treaties that came into legal force. "Arab Memorandum to the Paris Peace Conference," January 1, 1919: https://en.wikisource.org/wiki/Arab_Memorandum_to_the_Paris_Peace_Conference.

standards of "backward lands," even as France "dreams of adding Greater Syria to its acquisitions" (Qasimiyya 2002, 49).[45]

Importantly, the European war victors hosting the Versailles Conference decided which political entities would have signatory power and which French and British colonial subjects were allowed to cross international borders to attend. The British authorities, for example, banned delegates from the First Congress of the Muslim-Christian Associations (MCA) in Palestine from leaving (Porath 1974, 85). Similarly, elected delegates from "the various parts of Arab Asia" of the "Young Arab Society" were refused permission to attend (Wick 2004, 9n21). The MCA Congress, which was called in Jerusalem in late 1918 to prepare a Palestinian position for Versailles, was infiltrated by Zionist, French, and British agents, although they could not completely control the results (Porath 1974, 79–85). The MCA and the Young Arab Society were dominated by urban elite men, and the MCA included religious leaders as well (Porath 1974, 80; Totah 2018, 435). We do not know if the attendance of these delegates or more radical Arab activists at the Versailles Conference would have influenced the official Arab delegation or the race controversy. Other subaltern and colonized groups had used the Conference as an oppor-tunity to congregate and make political demands, even if they ultim-ately had little influence on the outcomes.

Even white US and European intellectuals, scientists, and politi-cians increasingly criticized "race prejudice" and "race discrimin-ation" beginning early in the twentieth century (Tilley 2011, 221–223). By the 1919 Versailles Peace Conference certainly, British colonial politicians recognized, to borrow Helen Tilley's words, that egregiously racist policies threatened the stability of the colonial order by making "governing far more difficult." At the same time, policies of social equality or parity threatened to "undermine" the (extractive and violent) logic of colonial relationships – the col-onizer must be above the colonized. When such hierarchy was shaken, the "prospects of [the colonized person's] future usefulness

---

[45] `Abdulhadi was at the table or behind the scenes at the most important diplomatic and conflict high points involving Palestinians from 1910 through the early 1960s (e.g., Abdul Hadi and Aouni Bey 1932). He became involved in militant Arab nationalist groups against "Turkification" before the war, first in Istanbul and then in Paris, while studying law and afterward ("Awni Abd al-Hadi," www.paljourneys.org/en/biography/9835/awni-abd-al-hadi).

[to the colonial state] is destroyed" (226, 227). This helps explain why criticism of racial prejudice by some colonial elites "was insufficient to undermine the social hierarchies of colonial states" (225). Despite rebellions against racist systems and challenges to racial thinking, "expansive projects of racial state building around the world" continued in the twentieth century: "colonial and national categories of difference actually proliferated on the ground, increasingly sorting populations by alleged racial taxonomies and granting rights and privileges accordingly" (Tilley 2014, 779). These observations certainly apply to British-colonized Palestine, its indigenous peoples, and all the so-called Mandate relations established by white imperial powers after World War I. Mandate Palestine is too often analyzed and theorized without considering this deep imbrication in the international racial-imperial-colonial order, a global color line that remains alive if not well.

Life, Death, and Futurity

Chapter 1, "We Are Far More Advanced," begins by reconstructing the 1933 story of a Palestinian nurse-midwife in Ramallah, Alice Butros, who destroyed the face of a British training doll after a severely ill infant from Ramallah was repeatedly turned away from the Arab section of the Jerusalem Government Hospital because her indigent mother could not pay the admission fee. The chapter examines the political economy of ill and healthy babies, which included British developmental colonialism and welfare austerity toward Palestinians, and contrasts that with elaborate Zionist healthcare institutions for Jews in the same period guided by competitive demographic and cultural goals. Zionist organizations invested generously in Jewish maternal and infant healthcare in Palestine, facilitated by British policies and funded by Jewish communities in the United States, Europe, and white British Dominions. The chapter ends by examining two cases, one from early and one from late in the Mandate, where Palestinian elites challenged British and Zionist claims that health and healthcare were apolitical, as well as colonial and settler-colonial associations between health status and backwardness or superiority.

Chapter 2, "Making the Country Pay for Itself," opens by summarizing a mid-1940s conflict between British superintendent Vena Rogers and Egyptian nurse Insaf Ali because the latter was using a speculum, refusing to wear the regulation uniform she was required to pay for, administering an antisyphilis medication, and generally behaving as if she were an independent professional making a living rather than a colonial subject in her position as an infant welfare nurse in the town of El-Bireh. The "efficiencies and economies" orientation of British welfare policy in Palestine, the first section shows, contributed to Palestinian starvation, illness, and death. Colonial austerity and extraction coexisted with civilizational and primitivist rhetoric regarding Palestinian nutrition and hygiene practices, the focus of the second section. The final section discusses the gendered-racialized British regulatory approach toward Palestinian traditional and licensed midwives even as the colonial government invested the absolute minimum in infant and maternal healthcare, and fleshes out other occasionally prominent archival examples of unruly midwives.

Chapter 3, "Children Are the Treasure and Property of the Nation," begins by reconstructing two Lister Institute antityphoid serum trials conducted on human subjects in hospitals in 1934 and 1935 with the approval of the highest government officials in London and Jerusalem, and considers their results and implications. The chapter explores the demographic obsessions of British colonial authorities in Palestine, including the special anxiety produced by higher Palestinian birthrates. Comparative snapshots of birth, mortality, and disease rates based on religious category from the late 1920s to the late 1940s point to dramatic patterns. Eugenicist sensibilities, the chapter shows, were prominent among British imperial and Western Jewish elites before the Mandate and shaped the work of Zionist healthcare institutions in Palestine. The final section discusses the close relationship between eugenicist agendas and transnational breastfeeding and mothercraft campaigns, which made appearances in Zionist and British archival records in Palestine.

Chapter 4, "Technically Illegal," shifts the book's focus to anti-reproductive desires and practices. It uses scholarly and legal sources and a historical lens to examine Muslim, Christian, and Jewish religious traditions and state legal regimes over time on sex, contraception, and abortion relevant to historic Palestine. As in every other part of the world, abortion laws and policies were substantially shaped by profane institutional, material, and ideological interests – challenging dominant "culture" and "tradition" explanations.

Chapter 5, "I Did Not Want Children," focuses on birth control in discourse and practice in historic Palestine during the British colonial period and since. One section explores abortion stories, largely relying on accounts in the Hebrew press during the Mandate period, including a prominent case involving a Jewish Yemeni young woman, her Christian Palestinian lover, and the Jewish German physician prosecuted by a British colonial court on the allegation that she conducted an abortion that had gone wrong. The chapter delves into Zionist pronatalism in the face of Jewish refusal to procreate in Mandate Palestine, with attention to early 1930s correspondence regarding the showing in Tel Aviv of the 1929 Swiss film *Frauennot – Frauenglück*, which advocated "medical abortion." The final section uses interviews I conducted with elderly Palestinian women and other sources to foreground Palestinian anti-reproductive desires and birth control practices from the 1940s to the present.

Chapter 6, "The Art of Death in Life," argues that for Palestinians scattered under different sovereignties after 1948, the reproductive family became more important as a source of survival but was not the basis of a reproductive demographic futurity. As was the case before 1948, class, regional, and educational differences and age of marriage led to great variability in Palestinian reproductive desires and fertility outcomes. The chapter critically examines the ideological elisions, obsessions, and empirical problems in demographic and public health scholarship on post-1948 Palestinian fertility, which too often project onto Palestinians a desire to battle with Israel demographically. It contemplates death, reproduction, and liberation in Afro-futurist, Afro-pessimist, and queer scholarship to inform understanding of Palestinian reproduction and death after 1948. The final section examines a selection of Palestinian literature and film produced after 1948 to argue Palestinians were more likely to dwell on life in conditions of death rather than to celebrate biological proliferation.

1 | "We Are Far More Advanced"

The Politics of Ill and Healthy Babies in Colonial Palestine

Vena Winifred Ellen Rogers, a British nurse, is especially prominent in Palestine Department of Health records given the length of her service as a matron and superintendent of midwifery for the Jerusalem District, which included Jerusalem, Hebron, Bethlehem, Ramallah, El-Bireh, and their villages. Government and non-Jewish "government-aided" maternity and infant welfare centers in the Jerusalem District were accountable to Rogers, who in turn answered to the British senior medical officer (SMO).[1]

In rare moments, Palestinian thoughts and feelings forcefully interrupt the supremacist rhetoric of empire in the Department of Health archival record. A startling conflict that unfolded over multiple documents from 1933 captures the tensions between colonizers and colonized around the politics of healthcare and mortality in Mandate Palestine.[2] The interaction involved the sole registered full-time Palestinian infant welfare nurse in the Ramallah Infant Welfare Centre (IWC), Alice Butros, Superintendent Rogers, and G. W. Heron, the director of health, over the treatment of an ill baby named Yasmin.

---

[1] Senior medical officers in Mandate Palestine districts were white British male physicians until 1946, when two Palestinian SMOs were appointed (Sufian 2015, 127), and supervised usually male Palestinian medical officers. The British director of the Department of Health or the director of medical services ranked above the SMO. Rogers's office was in Watson House, a clinic in the Silsileh neighborhood of the Old City that had served as the home of Lady Watson, wife of Brigadier General C. F. Watson, the chief administrator of Palestine during most of the 1920s. The Order of St John seems to have leased out the building to Lady Watson and later to the Department of Health's Maternity and Infant Welfare Centre. Government of Palestine (hereafter GOP), Department of Health, Infant Welfare Centre – Bab-el-Silsileh, Jerusalem, June 1940–November 1946. File location in catalog: 00071706.81.D1.30.56. Israel State Archives.

[2] GOP, Department of Health, Infant Welfare Centre – Ramallah, December 1924–September 1944. File location in catalog: 00071706.81. D0.98.37. Israel State Archives.

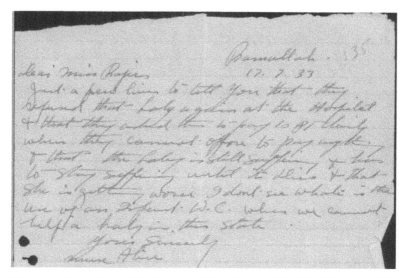

Figure 1.1 Letter from Alice Butros to Vena Rogers, July 17, 1933, Ramallah.
Courtesy of Israel State Archives

My curiosity about Butros was initially captured by Rogers's fruit-less attempts in November 1933 to find a shop in Jerusalem that could repair the destroyed face of a demonstration doll Heron had given to her earlier that autumn "for teaching" purposes. The documentation on the series of events begins with a spirited English-language hand-written letter dated July 17, 1933, from "Nurse Alice" in Ramallah to "Miss Rogers" in Jerusalem (see Figure 1.1):

Dear Miss Rogers
  Just a few lines to tell you that they refused that baby again at the Hospital & that they asked them to pay 10 PT daily when they cannot afford to pay anything & that the baby is still suffering & has to stay suffering until she dies & that she is getting worse. I don't see what is the use of an Infant W.C. [Welfare Centre] when we cannot help a baby in this state. Yours sincerely

Nurse Alice.

A handwritten letter follows dated July 24, 1933, from Rogers to Heron in the Department of Health office in Jerusalem. Rogers tells him she visited the IWC in Ramallah on the "19th" and

saw a baby. T. 40^2 for over two weeks. name Yasmin: complaint right hip very swollen, pain acute, no inflammation. child's condition bad – Dr. Hourani [the medical officer in Ramallah] had sent them to the Government Hospital Clinic in Jerusalem but money was asked. As the mother was too poor to pay the child was not seen.

The notation "T. 40^2" likely refers to Yasmin's body temperature in degrees Celsius, which converts to 104.3 degrees Fahrenheit.[3] Rogers continues,

Dr. Hourani was not there on my visit to the Centre. So I gave the mother a note to the Clinic stating she was poor and the following day I telephoned the M.O. [medical officer] i/t Clinic saying the baby would be there early. I attach the letter I received later from the Ramallah Infant Welfare nurse. Is it possible for something to be done to help in such cases as this?

The archives are silent on the matter for four months, until a November 23, 1933, handwritten letter from Rogers to Heron titled provocatively: "Subject: Ramallah Demonstration Doll." She informs him that the face of a demonstration doll he had issued for pedagogical purposes around September 27, 1933, was "damaged" by "the nurse Alice Butros." Indeed, its face was "smashed," she explains. Rogers adds: "I have taken it to several shops in Jerusalem but am unable to get it repaired. Can you have something done to it?" Heron replies to Rogers a week later that he tried but is unable to fix the demonstration doll, which he returns to her.

We know from Butros and Rogers's correspondence that Yasmin's mother, who lived in the distant town of Ramallah, had repeatedly tried to get the child, suffering pain and a high fever for two weeks, treated at the Jerusalem Hospital Clinic. They likely determined Yasmin needed hospitalization ("pay 10 PT *daily*"), and she was refused admission more than once because her "mother was too poor to pay": "they refused that baby again at the Hospital & . . . they asked them to pay 10 PT daily when they cannot afford to pay anything."

We don't know whether baby Yasmin was ever seen in the Jerusalem Hospital Clinic. It is highly likely she died of her illness, as did tens of thousands of ill Palestinian infants and children during the British Mandate. We can assume Nurse Alice was familiar with the limited British commitment to medical care for Palestinians and unsurprised by the clinic's unwillingness to admit the ill Yasmin without payment of

---

[3] Dr. Herman Staats guessed the likely meaning of this notation in an email exchange (January 12, 2019).

the daily fee. Department of Health records do not reveal when between late September and late November the angry Nurse Alice "smashed" the doll's face.

I conjecture that Alice Butros damaged the doll on her way out of the Ramallah IWC because she quit, transferred, or was fired. The 1930 Department of Health list of licensed healthcare providers in Palestine includes an Alice Butros in the midwives' section (license no. M. 341) whose address is "c/o the Government Hospital" in Haifa. This listing provides evidence that Butros was an experienced nurse who had either transferred or been reassigned to the Ramallah IWC in the early 1930s (GOP 1930). The Department of Health continues to list Butros as a licensed nurse midwife, but affiliated with the Ramallah IWC, in January 1935. Her name does not appear on Department of Health lists published in July 1936 and May 1938, however (GOP 1936, 1938).[4]

The doll symbolizes and materializes, I argue, colonial prioritization of pedagogical training for Palestinian girls and women over the funding needed for preventative healthcare and treatment. Its destroyed face, moreover, viscerally captures Nurse Alice's sense that the situation was untenable. Although the municipality of Ramallah was required to pay the costs of the IWC and her salary through community "fundraising" and "local subscription," Nurse Alice was bound by British colonial rules in Palestine.[5] The archives show frequent turnover of the Palestinian nurses who worked in the Ramallah IWC from the 1920s through the 1940s (no more than one was employed at a given time).

As this chapter explores, lack of British investment in healthcare for Palestinians was systemic and endemic to a colonial ecology segmented by nationality, religion, and "race."[6] Palestinians disproportionately

---

[4] These lists, which were published in Jerusalem as thick pamphlets divided by category of medical profession, were not annually released or necessarily comprehensively up to date when they were published, especially for midwives.
[5] GOP, Department of Health, Infant Welfare – Regulations, December 1921–February 1935. File location in catalog: 00071706.81.D1.32.B2. Israel State Archives.
[6] British "Notification of Birth" forms required "nationality" (citizenship, *al-jinsiyya*), "religion" (*al-mathhab*), and "race" (*al-`unsur*) for the mother and father. Arabs and Armenians typically wrote "Palestinian" for nationality irrespective of religion, even if they were born in Damascus, Beirut, Saida (Sidon), or "Turkia." Some Jews wrote "stateless" under the nationality/citizenship category, sometimes with their former country (e.g., Austria), and others wrote

died very young of poverty, hunger, and disease during the thirty years of British colonial rule, a rate overdetermined by colonial austerity in healthcare and infrastructure provision and systemic extraction from the native population. During the same period, Zionist health and science institutions, funded mainly by investments from Western Jewish communities, improved Jewish infant, child, and maternal health in Palestine guided by a racial demographic impulse and social medicine philosophy. Palestinian elites, in turn, recognized that health-care and health status were political and crucial to the Zionist enterprise.

Developmental Infra/Structures and Health Consequences

The Treaty of Versailles and the League of Nations mandates (based on the ideology of European "trusteeship" over certain populations) imposed some pressure on colonial governments to "invest in public health pro-grammes," as did the League's putative interest in the "health situation in Africa," but did not translate into substantial investments. Differing priorities, population composition, perceived health dangers to European bodies, and indigenous demands in various colonial settings determined British healthcare policies in mandate colonies (Von Tol 2007, 111–112; Lindner 2014, 219, 209). Ulrike Lindner finds that "colonial health policy" in tropical Africa mostly reified "racial demarcation lines" (Lindner 2014, 208, 219). This was also true in Mandate Palestine, intensified by the additional factor of Zionist settler-colonialism.

The League of Nations unambiguously "endorsed a settler project" in Palestine by validating the idea of a "Jewish National Home" (Norris 2013, 11; Norris 2017, 278). Article 11 of the Palestine Mandate gave the British colonial "Administration of Palestine" authority to "safeguard the interests of the community in connection with the development of the country" and "full power to provide for public ownership or control of any of the natural resources of the

"Palestinian," even if they had been born in Poland, or simply "German." Arabs born before 1918 wrote or were required to write "Syrian." The given choices for "religion" were "Moslem," "Jew," "Christian," or "Other" (*ghayr thalik*). For "race," the options given were "Arab, Jewish, or Other Race"; some wrote in "Armenian." GOP, Department of Health, Notification of Birth, 1939–1948. File location in catalog: 00071706.81.D3.A9.DF. GOP, Department of Health, Birth Certificates, 1944–1947. File location in catalog: 00071706.81.D3.AA.51. Israel State Archives.

country or of the public works, services and utilities established or to be
established therein." It allowed colonial authorities to "introduce
a land system appropriate to the needs of the country, having regard,
among other things, to the desirability of promoting the close settlement and intensive cultivation of the land."

Article 11 conjured a "Jewish Agency" with the right "to construct
or operate, upon fair and equitable terms, any public works, services
and utilities, and to develop any of the natural resources of the country,
in so far as these matters are not directly undertaken by the
Administration." The Jewish Agency, which was not formally established until years later, was the only non-British institution the British
colonial government recognized as a competing authority (Seikaly
2016, 5).[7] Article 16 of the Palestine Mandate limited British interfer-
ence "with the enterprise" of religious and charitable bodies "of all
faiths in Palestine" unless "required for the maintenance of public
order and good government."[8]

British colonial authorities in Palestine quickly promulgated ordinances that truncated independent Palestinian initiatives and stripped
all governing autonomy from Palestinian political bodies such as
municipalities, which had had significant local authority under
Ottoman rule (al-Barghuthi 1932).[9] Instead of existing in "dual" or

[7] "The Jewish Agency for Eretz Yisrael was established in 1929 to act on behalf of
the World Zionist Organization in relation to the British Government, the
administration in Palestine, and the League of Nations." Chaim Weizmann was
elected president of both. In 1920, "the Allied Forces Council (preceding
establishment of the League of Nations) approved the British Mandate in
Palestine based on [Article 2 of] the Balfour Declaration to support the building
of a 'Jewish national homeland' and establish[ed] that in order to fulfill the
declaration's promises, a 'Jewish Agency' shall also be formed to 'advise the
Government of Palestine on economic and social issues, as well as other
matters.'" The World Zionist Executive, established in 1920, acted as this
"Jewish agency," working "through the financial institutions of the World
Zionist Organization" (Knesset webpage: www.knesset.gov.il/lexicon/eng/wz
o_eng.htm).

[8] "The Palestine Mandate," Avalon Project: Documents in Law, History and
Diplomacy. Yale Law School Lillian Goldman Law Library: https://avalon
.law.yale.edu/20th_century/palmanda.asp.

[9] The 1864 Ottoman Provincial Law called for application of "Istanbul's
municipal model to the provincial cities and towns of the empire." The details
were fine-tuned in an 1867 law and formally amended and published as the 1877
Municipality Law, which was translated into Arabic "and published in full length
in Beirut's press." Municipalities were required to address "urban planning,
market control, health, public morality, and public welfare." Jens Hanssen

parallel political-economic sectors, Palestinians and Zionists existed in exploitive and extractive *relations*, as did British colonizers and Palestinians (Zu'bi 1984, 91, 107). British colonizers and Zionists were unequal colonial partners, yes, but Palestinians and their lands, labor, natural resources, and very lives were the grounds of colonial and settler-colonial exploitation and extraction for both parties.

Jacob Norris makes the case that British colonial authorities had "earmarked" Palestine for "developmental" colonialism by the end of the first decade of the twentieth century (Norris 2013, 11). Led by the "new imperialists," the "age of colonial development" aimed to develop resources and build infrastructure that strengthened the metropolitan economy (Norris 2013, 2; Norris 2017, 269, 272). For the British government, Palestine was economically valuable in a number of ways. Most importantly, Haifa, already linked by railroad to Baghdad during the Ottoman period, would provide a "Mediterranean coastal outlet" for products from "Mesopotamia," which the British also hoped to colonize (and ultimately did) (Norris 2013, 11; Norris 2017, 272, 274). Significant as well was wealth from Dead Sea mining, which extracted potash, bromine, and potassium salts in joint British-Zionist ventures developed during the Mandate (Norris 2017, 277). Palestine in addition provided a captured market for British products and was a major source of "custom duties" on imports and exports (Asad 1976, 6, table 1). London was most likely to approve "development" projects in colonial Palestine that showed "benefit [to] British industry" and "British imperial interests" (Norris 2013, 14; Norris 2017, 270). Palestinians were explicitly excluded from such projects, and certainly so for rural people, who were understood as "incapable of keeping pace with the changes introduced by Zionism" (Norris 2013, 12).

British "imperialist ambition" aligned with the settler-colonial ambitions of the Zionist movement in Palestine. For one thing, British imperialists understood European Jews as classic mediators for British economic interests (Norris 2013, 10; Norris 2017, 270). A number of prominent new imperialists "viewed Zionist migration to Palestine as the key to realizing" the land's "developmental potential," just as they encouraged British (including Jewish) migration to

argues that advocates of "hygiene and medicine" and Arab and Ottoman "scientific traditions and medical epistemologies" were eager to take up this mandate in Bilad ash-Sham (Hanssen 2005, 115–118).

"white dominions" (Norris 2017, 273). British developmentalists argued that "Jewish colonization" had already helped the "Palestinian Arabs" with "its modern intensive methods of agriculture, its scientific appliances, its western ideas of hygiene and business methods" (Norris 2017, 273).[10]

The British colonizers prioritized keeping British bodies safe and healthy in an environment they considered climatically and politically hostile. In the words of a British surgeon in Jerusalem to the Royal Geographical Society in 1917, "efficient sanitary authority with powers" of enforcement was necessary for the "successful colonization of Palestine" (quoted in Sufian 2015, 115). Colonial authorities emphasized health policies that sustained the economic and military dimensions of rule by serving the basic health needs of British military, police, and civilian forces. Oriented to eradicating contagious diseases, Mandate authorities selectively "constructed the sewage and drainage systems" and "invested in drying up swamps [and] education for hygiene" (Abu-Rabia 2005, 421). They understood and treated the colonized as "vectors" rather than "victims" of disease and illness, to use Mary-Ellen Kelm's analysis of settler-colonial medical approaches to First Nation peoples in early twentieth-century North America (Kelm 2005, 382).

A continuous source of tension with Palestinians and Zionist organizations was that the government of Palestine "consistently prioritized infrastructural projects above the provision of welfare services" (Norris 2013, 13). Infrastructure projects were not designed to serve the needs of the colonized population as the government, for example, neither built nor maintained sewage and water systems in most Palestinian villages. Transport systems facilitated British labor and military priorities rather than indigenous mobility or advancement. A for-profit electric concession monopoly granted by British authorities early in their rule to Russian Zionist engineer Pinhas Rutenberg privileged his private electricity initiative and Zionist towns and settlements,

---

[10] Writing about post–World War I Iraq, Sara Pursley argues that British colonial governance is best understood through the "dual mandate" theory associated with F. D. Lugard, a British member of the Permanent Mandates Commission of the League of Nations, which referred to colonial "exploitation of a territory's resources" ("economic development") while protecting "development 'along native lines'" through indirect rule. This agenda would ideally allow the "native labor force" to reproduce itself while avoiding "unruly demands for popular sovereignty and for a share in economic development" (Pursley 2019, 20).

plotted a map of settler-colonial boundaries for a Jewish Palestine, and bypassed Palestinian villages (Meiton 2019).

Palestinians recognized the relationship between the Rutenberg Jewish Hydroelectric Company grid and the strengthening of the Zionist settler-colonial project. The building of the grid in Jaffa led to a mass mobilization of Palestinians in the early 1920s. In 1923, a nationalist circular titled "Beware of the Rutenberg Scheme" and signed by Hafez Tukan, president of the Jaffa Economic Committee, called on "the people of Jaffa" to boycott the grid since it could not be sustained or maintained without municipal taxes and fees: "Rutenberg wants by means of the force of the occupying authority to help himself out of your own money – he having failed in the matter with his own people's money – and thus get possession of the means of people's livelihood in the country so that he will subjugate you to his rule by lighting your streets and lanes. What will be the use of electrical lights if you lose your wealth and lands?" (quoted in Jarman 2001, 559–560). It is not surprising that Palestinians involved in the 1936–1939 Revolt targeted the Rutenberg electrical grid (Meiton 2019, 4–5, 20).[11]

The majority of Palestinians, most of them peasants, were also constrained by extractive local and absentee Arab large landowners (Khalaf 1997, 93). Beginning in 1858, the Ottoman state required registration of land titles for taxation, destabilizing a system that relied on communal forms of land use and landholding. To avoid taxation and conscription under the new legal regime, villagers often registered property in the name of a clan leader or family member not eligible for military service, which in more fertile areas "institutionalized and re-enforced pre-existing relations of dependence between indebted culti-vators and debt-owning usurers (whether traders or urban notables)" (Asad 1976, 4).

These dynamics intensified and became "more complex" after the devastations of the Great War, which included widespread conscription into the Ottoman army and poverty, hunger, and disease in Palestine. Palestinian revolts during the British Mandate, usually initi-ated by peasants and the poor, typically targeted landlords, merchants, Zionists, and the British authorities (Khalaf 1997, 95, 96). The

---

[11] Research by Tawfik Canaan found that the Rutenberg grid facilitated the spread of malaria in the 1920s and 1930s by bringing down the level of Lake Tiberias (Nashef 2002).

situation for Palestinian peasants and laborers was made worse by the fact that the Jewish sector "did not seek Arab labor but Arab land," which it could acquire only through "market exchange – a slow and politically unsatisfactory process" until the 1948–1949 war, when Palestinians were expelled en masse and their property stolen (Asad 1976, 8).

Talal Asad argues that the economic situation of peasant Palestinians during the British colonial period is best understood as "the articulation of a capitalist with a non-capitalist mode of production mediated by the British colonial state," in a process that began during Ottoman rule. The Mandate's fiscal structure depended on regressive taxation and debt, which "facilitated the extraction of surplus from the non-capitalist sector, and its partial transfer to the expanding capitalist sector," dominated by Jewish enterprises (Asad 1976, 5–7; also see Khalaf 1997, 94–95).

A British-commissioned project undertaken by Palestinian researchers in 104 villages and by Zionist researchers in seven settlements run by the Jewish Agency indeed found in a self-serving 1930 report that the "Arab farmer is paying more than his share of taxation" to the colonial government. Peasants in addition suffered from high levels of poverty because cheaper agricultural products were dumped on the market, a problem the authors considered so "serious" it required immediate government remediation (GOP and Johnson and Crosbie et al. 1930, 49, 52, 54).[12]

Colonial sovereignty, argues Achille Mbembe, "means the capacity to define who matters and who does not, who is *disposable* and who is not" (Mbembe 2003, 27). He draws attention to racialization as the dividing line that "regulates the distribution of death" by sovereign powers (17).[13] He coined the term *necropolitics* to describe sovereign

---

[12] The report concludes that the government should use "compulsory means" to continue to divide and privatize communally owned Palestinian farmland (*musha`*) that surrounded most village settlements, a process begun by nineteenth-century Ottoman land codes that were nevertheless ineffective in transforming peasant practices until British and Zionist colonization and passage of the 1921 Land Transfer Law (Zu`bi 1984, 92, 93, 94, 97; GOP and Johnson and Crosbie et al. 1930, 55–56).

[13] Colonies, Mbembe argues, "are the locations par excellence where the controls and guarantees of judicial order can be suspended – the zone where the violence of the state of exception is deemed to operate in the service of 'civilization'" (Mbembe 2003, 24). For Mbembe, the "most accomplished form of necropower is the contemporary colonial occupation of Palestine. Here, the colonial state [of Israel] derives its fundamental claim of sovereignty and legitimacy from the

and non-sovereign forms of biopower that make "murder of the enemy its primary and absolute objective" using appeals to exception or emergency in the name of preserving the lives of the privileged group (12, 16, 21). British colonial necropolitics, I contend, was operative on a daily basis in Mandate Palestine but on quotidian levels that worked in tandem with periods of intensified military violence. The necropolitics of the Department of Health, which answered to the Colonial Office and the Treasury in London, was built on a logic of austerity and developmental extraction from a Palestinian population considered disposable.

As colonial powers, British authorities regularly reported to League of Nations offices on their "health and hygiene" responsibilities over the population in Palestine, which included venereal disease incidence and infant mortality rates, the latter "generally considered a prime indicator of the state of health of the population" (Bourmaud 2013, 13).[14] As Philippe Bourmaud reminds us, however, while the health-care of the colonized "was one of the core concerns of the mandates, at least on paper," the majority of the members of the Permanent Mandates Commission in Geneva "were former colonial officers themselves and unabashed colonialists" (12). Nevertheless, since the mandates were structured as a "civilizing mission," it was imperative that British and French colonial governments "visibly represent the health improvements" with reports and statistics (15).

Few British-sponsored infant welfare centers were established in Palestine and when they did exist, they were similar to British government hospitals in offering no preventative services such as prenatal care (Kligler 1932, 173), which helps explain the comparatively high rates of Palestinian infant and child mortality. Research commissioned by

authority of its own particular narrative of history and identity" (Mbembe 2019, 80–83).

[14] The infant mortality rate refers to the number of infant deaths per thousand births in a period of time, usually a calendar year. Infancy is the first year of life, composed of the "neonatal phase" of the first twenty-eight days after birth and the "post-neonatal phase that covers the eleven remaining months of the first year." Each of these phases has patterns for causes of death. The "peak of mortality from nutritional deficiencies" is in infancy. A live birth is a fetus outside the mother and breathing, no matter how many gestational weeks old, while a "dead birth" is when a fetus is born after twenty-eight weeks of gestation but not breathing (Khalidi 1996, 10, 11, 12, 13).

US Zionist organizations reported that in 1925, 64 percent of all recorded deaths in Palestine were among children "before the age of five years," which the authors term "staggering" (Rosenau and Wilinsky 1928, 576, 577; also see Canaan 1927, 185; Granqvist 1947, 47, 49, 56–57, 60–66, 116; Granqvist 1950, 74, 80, 81, 83, 90, 110–114).

By 1929, 68.2 percent of recorded "Moslem" deaths (18,131) and 38 percent of recorded "Jewish" deaths (1,820) occurred among children younger than five years (Kligler 1932, 172). In 1930, the death percentages of children younger than five years by religion were 67.9 percent and 34.7 percent for Muslims and Jews, respectively (172). High mortality rates among infants and children continued in the 1930s and 1940s, with substantial gaps between Palestinians and Jews.

A five-year (1930–1934) table compiled from annual Department of Health reports on birth, death, and infant mortality rates, divided by columns for "Jews," "Christians," and "Moslems," offers another snapshot. For 1934, the infant mortality rate for Muslims was comparatively high (175.34), for Jews much lower (77.95), and for Christians closer to the Muslim than the Jewish rate (152.62) (MacLennan 1935, 6). In *Vital Statistics of Palestine Bulletin* No. 1 (1936), Director of Medical Services J. W. P. Harkness notes "the striking fact that nearly 32 per cent. of all deaths in Palestine in 1935 were of infants under one year of age" and half were of children younger than two and a half years old.[15]

Three years later, in 1939, infant mortality rates were once again broken down by religious category in a vital statistics report: "Median age of death for Moslems was between two and three years, while the median for Jewish deaths was a little over fifty years. The median age for deaths for Christians lay in the age group 25–29 years."[16] Late in the Palestine Mandate, the Anglo-American Committee of Inquiry acknowledged that the "provision of infant welfare and maternity

---

[15] GOP, Department of Health, Births, Deaths, Vaccinations and Inoculation – Regulations, 1932–1936. File location in catalog: 00071706.81.D7.1D.D5. Israel State Archives.

[16] GOP, Report for Office of Statistics, Jerusalem: Vital Statistics. Includes quarterly reports for 1940 and totals for 1939 and 1940 and comparisons with earlier years, March 25, 1940–March 1941. File location in catalog: 00071706.81.D3.AA.55. Israel State Archives.

centres [for Palestinians] is admittedly inadequate in a country having a high infant mortality rate" (Anglo-American Committee of Inquiry 1946, 2:618).

Aziza Khalidi's DSc dissertation on infant survival and death in Palestine between 1927 and 1944 finds that while poverty for Palestinian Muslims and Christians existed in both rural and urban areas, government, missionary, and private health services were concentrated in towns, as was infrastructure such as electricity, roads, sanitation, and water systems. Having health institutions and infrastructure was associated with better health outcomes and lower infant mortality rates (Khalidi 1996, v–vi, 197). She found that roads linking predominantly Christian villages to towns were associated with lower infant mortality rates *in those villages* (431). Death during infancy is socially rather than culturally or individually caused, she argues, since it depends on "resources" and their "patterns of allocation" (156).

Without the health infrastructure provided by missionary institutions in major towns, Palestinian infant and child death rates would have likely been higher during the British colonial period. In October 1941 Bertha Spafford Vester, the director of the relatively wealthy Anna Spafford Baby Home sponsored by the American Colony Aid Association (headquartered in New York), approached the British director of medical services to ask the government to take over the home because it was difficult to retain nurses during the war. When he replied, "we [are] not prepared to do so," she asked if the government would take the six hundred babies they cared for if she closed it. If accurate, this was more babies than the number cared for by any other government-sponsored IWC with the possible exception of Watson House in the Old City. He likely refused. The home did close in October 1943 "on account of lack of trained nurses," although it reopened at least by 1947 and continues to exist today.[17]

A 1933 report from the Colonial Office in London to the Permanent Mandates Commission illustrates the disavowal accomplished by rhetorical sleights of hand with respect to Palestinian death, in this case of postpartum women. A 1932 inquiry from the commission asked "whether there was any connection between the high mortality from

---

[17] GOP, Department of Health, Infant Welfare – Anna Spafford Baby Home (American Colony Aid Association), Jerusalem, 1935–1948. File location in catalog: 00071706.81.D1.32.B6. Israel State Archives.

puerperal fever and the number of *dayas* [traditional midwives] permitted to practice midwifery."[18] The official responded that the colonial government in Palestine only counted cause of death certified by
government medical officers in towns. The town rate of puerperal
deaths was not high, he contended, at 1.1 per 1,000. He assured the
Permanent Mandates commissioner that since traditional midwives are
no longer allowed to practice in "the majority of towns" after passage
of the 1929 Midwives Ordinance, they could not be directly linked to
"high mortality from puerperal fever." "If the daya is blameworthy,
her name is removed from the register of persons permitted to practice
midwifery." He explained that the cause of postpartum death was
rather not seeking or delays in seeking professional medical help to
assist with difficult births.[19] The League of Nations query assumed that
ignorant Palestinian midwives were primarily responsible for maternal
death from puerperal fever. For its part, colonial response was contradictory on whether Palestinian postpartum death rates from puerperal
fever were high and used a common (in the archive) passive-voice
construct to evade addressing meta factors that increased the likelihood
of death in difficult labor cases, such as lack of affordable medical care
and transportation.[20]

Using Science and Social Medicine to Make Healthy Jews

Zionist "aspirations to develop a national entity" were understood to
require building "strong scientific foundations" that included research,
education, and treatment institutions, as well as investing in technology

[18] Puerperal fever is produced by a uterine bacterial infection that develops in the
first few days after giving birth or miscarrying. In Palestine, forty-seven cases of
puerperal fever with twenty-two deaths were reported for 1933 (towns only). In
comparison, forty-one cases with eighteen deaths were reported for 1934, and
fifty-four cases with twenty-nine deaths were reported for 1935. GOP,
Department of Health, *Annual Report for the Year 1934*, 28. GOP, Department
of Health, *Department of Health Report for the Year 1935*, 26.

[19] "Report by His Majesty's Government in the United Kingdom of Great Britain
and Northern Ireland to the Council of the League of Nations on the
Administration of Palestine and Trans-Jordan for the Year 1932." London,
1933, Colonial No. 82, 58–82. In *Palestine and Transjordan Administration
Reports 1932–1933, Vol. 4* (1995), 137–138.

[20] In British health reports active-voice prose typically accused the colonized of
cultural and intellectual defects in healthcare practices while distancing and
passive language skirted taking any responsibility.

to "civilize" and transform a "desert wasteland" (Davidovitch and Zalashik 2010, 402, 404). "Re-establishing the health of the country" was seen as a prerequisite for "re-populating" the land with Jews (406). Zionist health activists understood these Jewish bodies and subjectivities as plastic – that is, as highly amenable to social engineering that improves the quality of the population, an environmental eugenic approach that existed in the same welfare and health ecosystem as hereditary eugenic projects.

Health spending by Jewish organizations for Jews far exceeded that of the British government for many more Palestinians, and substantially focused on preventative care (Kligler 1932, 169). The 1920s saw annual reductions in Jewish infant and child mortality rates as a result of such investments (172, 171). Influenced by social medicine, Zionist health projects targeted entire Jewish communities in the multiple locations they lived and worked. The Zionist colonization of Palestine would not have been possible without this massive healthcare and medical infrastructure, facilitated by the British colonial policy of encouraging "private" and "voluntary" investment in "welfare."

Social medicine, which emerged in mid-nineteenth-century Berlin, was concerned with the relationship between the health of individuals and communities and their socioeconomic situations. The field assumed that resolving health issues required treatment and "social work." The public health field, in contrast, was historically more oriented to resolving communicable diseases. Both social medicine and public health have diffracted into multiple ideological and practical directions depending on context and historical moment, however. For example, Salvador Allende, the socialist president of Chile until he was overthrown in a US government-backed coup in 1973, was a public health physician and advocate for the poor who had first served as the minister of health. Che Guevara, who joined the Cuban revolution and became the minister of economy, was first an Argentinean physician (Horton 2013; Anderson et al. 2005). In comparison, British settler social medicine in First Nation communities in North America in the early twentieth century facilitated "the production of racial hierarchies," influenced by the "broader concerns of social medicine – contagion, gender breakdown, racial characteristics," and the "the pathological encounter" between colonists and indigenous people (Kelm 2005, 371, 372).

Examining the League of Nations Health Organisation in the interwar period, Paul Weindling finds that although social medicine was considered "objectively based in social or biomedical science, and benignly reformist," its practitioners had a "range of political interests," including "a prominent concern with eugenics that ranged from providing a rationale for positive welfare measures like maternity benefits to 'negative eugenic' measures such as compulsory sterilisation." In its "biologistic formulations" at least, social medicine facilitated medicalization and support for professionals who created for themselves "new career opportunities in polyclinics and social administration," which functioned as "professional imperialism" in colonial settings (Weindling 1995, 135–136).

In contrast to the rather disinterested health policy of British colonial authorities in Palestine, US Zionist organizations commissioned the 1928 "Sanitary Survey of Palestine" to plan health investments for Jews in the following ten years and to push British authorities to provide increased funding for the Hadassah Medical Organization (the Women's Zionist Organization of America) and Jewish schools.[21] The report challenged British refusal to disburse funds to "private" entities such as Hadassah (Rosenau and Wilinsky 1928, 539, 541, 542, 553–554, 561, 622). According to colonial government budget reports beginning in 1930, the Department of Health came to provide limited "grants-in-aid" to Zionist health organizations using the government's per-patient or per-bed formula for Palestinian patients in response to persistent applications for support by Jewish

---

[21] Hadassah was established by Henrietta Szold (1860–1945) in 1912 in New York City after she joined a chapter of a Zionist women's group. Szold was a Jewish teacher, intellectual, and Zionist activist who grew up and spent much of her adult life in Baltimore as the beloved daughter of a rabbi. Szold and her mother visited Palestine in 1909 for a month, as Henrietta was suffering from heartbreak. Szold became overwhelmed by a need to offer practical help to Jews in Palestine, whom she perceived as backward and disease-ridden. In 1912, "philanthropist Nathan Straus offered [the women's Zionist group in NYC] partial funding to establish district nursing in Palestine" if they could raise the rest of the money and find "a skilled nurse able to depart for Palestine within a few weeks. Ultimately two nurses – Rose Kaplan and Rachel Landy – sailed with the Strauses on January 18 [1913]. In March 1913 they opened an office in a rented Jerusalem house identified by a Hebrew and English sign that read 'American Daughters of Zion, Nurses Settlement, Hadassah.' They saw 5000 patients in their first year ... At the second [Daughters of Zion national] convention in 1914, the group [which included multiple chapters] formally adopted the name associated with the group's medical efforts in Palestine – Hadassah." "Women of Valor: Henrietta Szold," Jewish Women's Archive: https://jwa.org/womenofvalor/szold.

health institutions. British documents frequently complained of Jewish extravagance in healthcare provision, which did look generous in light of the government's absolutely minimal services and financial commitments to Palestinian healthcare.[22]

Zionist health organizations continuously pushed the boundaries set by British colonial authorities in order to extract more money and authority and to improve health services for Jewish communities. The 1940 Public Health Ordinance, which amended rules regarding registration of births and deaths and consolidated circulars from previous years, was first published as a draft in the *Palestine Gazette* so as to solicit comments. The Jewish Medical Association of Palestine's deputy chairman, Dr. A. Wolwelski, wrote to Director of Medical Services John MacQueen seeking, among other things, more leeway for their physicians to make decisions regarding who must be hospitalized for infectious diseases. The organization also sought to make compulsory a second inoculation against smallpox and a first inoculation against diphtheria. Recognizing these were expenses British colonial authorities were unwilling to take responsibility for, Wolwelski assured MacQueen that Jewish localities and institutions would pay for diphtheria inoculations. MacQueen disagreed with both proposals, suggesting these were largely "administrative" rather than ordinance matters and the government had faced few difficulties quarantining infectious Palestinians and vaccinating Palestinian schoolchildren.[23]

Zionist propaganda and fundraising campaigns showcased in documents and visual material the building of an advanced Jewish science and healthcare system of hospitals, research centers, medical schools, and clinics in order to solicit support from Jewish philanthropists and communities. Members of Hadassah continuously raised "Palestine Campaign" funds from the United States, and like British, Australian, and New Zealand Zionist women activists, deployed the ignorant indigenous Muslim or Jewish mother as a foil for its work, although the organization predominantly served Jews.[24] A letter from Bertha

[22] For example, GOP, Department of Health, Public Health: Hospital Accommodation for Jewish Settlements, 1936–1945. File location in catalog: 00071706.81.D3.FB.89. Israel State Archives.

[23] GOP, Department of Health, Laws and Ordinances – Public Health Ordinance 1940, March 1940–1941. File location in catalog: 00071706.81.D08E.66. Israel State Archives.

[24] For example, as early as 1925, "Hadassah: The Women's Zionist Organization in NY" letterhead from the address at 114 Fifth Avenue included a footer:

Landesman (1882–1959), a settler who became the chief nurse of the Health Welfare Department of Hadassah, illustrated the organization's ecological approach to health.[25] Hadassah, she explained, took the Jewish "family as a unit, and not the Expectant mother or Infant." Home visits by nurses allowed them to "supervise the health of the entire family" through the vector of the expectant mother, who was monitored "six to seven months before the birth of her child" and then tracked until "the child finishes its school period."[26] In addition, Hadassah trained nurses in Jewish schools, where they were expected to work with physicians to identify and repair children's "defects." Landesman further explained to Hadassah's acting director, R. Katzenelson, in an October 12, 1925, letter: "The school nurse is to instruct in the home how to care for the school child physically, mentally and hygienically, as well as bring close contact between the school room and the home, the teacher and the mother." The nurse was also required to examine children between their annual physician visits so as to detect and resolve the emergence of "any new defects."[27]

Landesman's correspondence cultivated material, ideological, and symbolic external support for Hadassah's settler-colonial medical and nursing projects in British-ruled Palestine. In a July 14, 1926, letter she wrote from Jerusalem's Hadassah office to Dr. I. M. Rubinow at the *Jewish Social Services Quarterly* in Philadelphia, she boasted that Hadassah had recently "saved every child" among "Yeminite Jews" ("100 families, 300 souls") in the colony of Rehobot despite "epidemics" of measles and whooping cough.[28] Hadassah's modern public

"United Palestine Appeal, $5,000,000. Have you done your share?" Central Zionist Archives 1925, Folder J113/6738.

[25] Landesman was born in Ukraine and immigrated as a teenager with her family to New York City in 1896. She trained in nursing, graduating from Lebanon Hospital in NYC in 1913. From 1913 to 1920 she worked in the NYC public health department in child welfare and hygiene clinics that served public schools. She arrived in Palestine in 1920 and founded Hadassah's Public Health Nursing Services Department, where she worked until 1936. Nira Bartal, "Bertha Landsman [sic], 1882–1962." Jewish Women's Archive: https://jwa.org/encyclopedia/article/landsman-bertha.

[26] September 21, 1926, Landesman letter to Dr. Truby King. Central Zionist Archives 1925, Folder J113/6738.

[27] October 12, 1925, Landesman letter to Dr. R. Katzenelson. Central Zionist Archives 1925, Folder J113/6738.

[28] The letter references "Enclosure No. 5," a report from the Government of Palestine indicating that "1,508 Jewish babies" were born in 1925. Landesman glossed that Hadassah registered in its "Infant Welfare Clinics in Jerusalem"

health work was uniquely difficult and effective, she elaborated, given the backwardness of women in Palestine: "We are far more advanced than in America or European countries. That is, our work is more concentrated. It must be, because the mothers we teach are very primitive and our teaching must be more thorough, each detail demonstrated." To reinforce her point, she explained that "when a baby was really seriously ill, they were rarely taken to the doctor, but all sorts of tortures [were] inflicted upon the poor little babies, such as burning underneath the tongue,[29] or making wounds on the temples hanging all sorts of amulets on their forehead, attached to the front hair, etc.[30] Now, at least they know we do not approve of these methods."

In contrast to her deployment of "Yeminite Jews" as a population, Landesman used individual Palestinian or Muslim women as figures of the ignorant primitive. For example, she illustrated her case for external support by describing a thirty-eight-year-old "woman in the Old City Centre in Jerusalem, who had 24 children, 4 sets of twins, sixteen have died." This prolific unlucky mother eagerly listened to Hadassah nurses' advice to keep her youngest baby alive. Landesman also mentioned a "Moslem mother" who came in with a six-month-old ill baby but violated Hadassah advice on sterilization of rubber nipples and feeding. A visiting nurse had found "the nipple on the floor, with the rest of the family food," maybe referring to trays and dishes from a communal family meal she interrupted. Hadassah nurses "managed to keep this baby alive until 11 months of age, it weighed 12 lbs., then got an attack of diarrhea: was instructed to stop the milk formula for a certain period. The next day mother returned with baby in a much worse condition." The mother pleaded that while following instructions to stop milk feeding, she had given the "thirsty" child "some grapes to eat," which the nurse determined to have "fatal" results.[31]

The ideological and rhetorical weight of these individual stories is indicated by their reuse in a similar letter from Landesman to

"926 new babies," thus "about 60% of the Jewish babies born in Jerusalem" were under its health supervision.

[29] Arab healers frequently burned extra tissue tethering a baby's tongue to the bottom of its mouth, which restricts the ability to nurse and a tongue's range of motion, a condition scientifically termed *ankyloglossia*.

[30] The reference is to amulets or coins braided or tied into a baby or child's bangs to reflect away the evil eye believed to lead to serious illness or death.

[31] Central Zionist Archives 1925, Folder J113/6738.

Dr. F. Truby King about two months later (September 21). King (1858–1938), an iconoclastic and obsessive (described as "zealous" in a hagiographic account by R. M. Burdon) eugenicist physician who held many leadership positions over his long career, became by the early twentieth century a world-renowned infant welfare and "mother-craft" pedagogue. He insisted that white British bourgeoisie women follow "the laws of Nature" by fully devoting themselves to raising healthy children rather than seeking higher education or employment outside their homes (Burdon 1945, 49–53).[32] He was particularly influential in his arguments for breastfeeding rather than artificial feeding, especially timed breastfeeding – or if necessary as a supplement, carefully formulated "humanised milk" – to lower infant mortality rates produced by "careless bottle-feeding ... by the majority of women" (13–25, 25, 34, 35).

Summarizing Hadassah's accomplishments in prenatal and infant care in her September 1926 letter to King, Landesman explained that many mothers in Palestine now understood the superiority of timed rather than at-request breastfeeding and were less likely to use methods informed by "old traditions and superstition" on ill babies. She described in familiar terms the lowered infant mortality rate among "Yeminite Jews" since Hadassah established its health center. She once again told the story of the woman who had twenty-four children (three sets of twins in this version, and eight babies remained alive). Given that the story of this unfortunate woman followed discussion of Yemeni Jewish mothers who previously had "eight, nine, and as many as seventeen births, with rarely more than one to three children living," the "24 children" mother was probably a Muslim or Christian Palestinian rather than Jewish. Landesman now described the mother as thirty-seven years old when she attended the health center with the "24th child."

As Warwick Anderson argues in his study of US medical authorities who colonized the Philippines in 1898, "Hygiene reform ... was intrinsic to a 'civilizing process,' which was also an uneven and shallow process of Americanization" (Anderson 2006, 1). Dafna Hirsch

---

[32] Although Frederick Truby King was born in the New Zealand colony of New Plymouth, his father had been a member of the British Parliament before he came to represent two districts in "the first and second New Zealand Parliaments" (Burdon 1945, 13). The younger King studied medicine at Edinburgh University before returning to New Zealand in 1888.

similarly connects hygiene to instilling manners and civilized behavior, not only health, for Zionist reformers in colonial Palestine. Hygiene science considered "almost everything ... a potential factor of disease or health. The hygienic repertoire contained models for washing, sleeping, eating, dressing, working, organizing time, and much more" (Hirsch 2009, 579). While these hygiene concerns were certainly classed and raced, they were also gendered. Sherene Seikaly writes that British colonizers assumed that "most nutritional, health, and budgetary problems in 20th-century Palestine were a result of bad cooking, inadequate mothering, and ignorant housekeeping, whether Arab or Jewish" (Seikaly 2014, 785).

Consistent with the dominant Western supremacist sensibilities of civilizational superiority, Landesman explained to King in the September 1926 letter that if the mother "understands 1% of what the nurse is trying to convey, we feel satisfied, when one considered the element we have." She retold the story of the "Moslem mother" with a "six months baby weighing 6½ pounds, starved almost to death" because the "mother had practically no milk." Hadassah nurses, Landesman explained, "managed to keep the baby alive until it reached eleven months of age, weighing 12 pounds. The baby had an attack of diarrhea; mother was instructed to stop the [formula] milk for a certain period, the next day mother returned with baby in a much worse condition, but pleading that she followed instructions, not giving milk, etc. but baby seemed thirsty so she gave it some grapes. The result, fatal."[33] In this account, the mother is responsible for the baby's initial low weight because she had no breast milk, the baby's diarrhea at eleven months, and the baby's death.

Zionists understood Jewish science and health institutions to prove the worth of a Jewish homeland to the British colonial overseers of Palestine, but they also made that separatist demographic project a reality on the ground. Israel Kligler, professor of hygiene and bacteriology at the Hebrew University, director of Hadassah's Nathan and Lina Straus Health Centre, and former associate of the Rockefeller Institute in New York City, described the Zionist sense of demographic urgency in the following way: "The Jewish people are in a hurry. They are anxious to improve health conditions with the utmost speed in order to facilitate reconstruction [of a Jewish homeland] and resettlement [Jewish settler-colonialism] with a minimum loss of life and

---

[33] Central Zionist Archives 1925, Folder J113/6738.

health" (Kligler 1932, 167). Demographic transformation of the land was the sine qua non of settler-colonial dominance, even as Zionists struggled with low Jewish fertility rates.

The goal was to bring in and reproduce as many Jewish bodies as possible and cultivate what US Zionists called "Jewish genius" by assuring the health of indigenous Jews and Jewish settlers (Rosenau and Wilinsky 1928, 741). Jewish scientific, hygiene, and health projects aimed to "regenerate" the "health of the nation" (Sufian 2007, esp. 240–287). Sandra M. Sufian shows how Zionist antimalarial campaigns, for example, worked to transform in tandem "the physical topography of Palestine" and "its Jewish inhabitants and their bodies." Zionists considered inculcating "hygienic principles and health habits" necessary for reshaping "an unhealthy, passive people in the Diaspora" into a "renewed and vibrant" Jewish body politic (239–240). Medical and health research, investments, and propaganda were vital to this project (242).

Zionist organizations came at these goals from different ideological perspectives shaped by their leaders, members, and the support and fundraising of Jewish communities in Europe, the United States, and white colonial settlements in places such as New Zealand and Canada.[34] Hadassah nurses in Palestine, who were predominantly settlers from Central and Eastern Europe, followed a hygiene framework that assigned them to be civilizing agents of "social and cultural mediation," a project shaped by early twentieth-century US Progressive ideals (Hirsch 2008, 232, 231, 240) in cities such as New York, Boston, Baltimore, and Philadelphia. Following a gendered model of medicine, Hadassah subordinated Jewish midwives to "public health nurses" and "physicians, who benefited through the outcome of increased hospital birth rates" (Katvan and Bartal 2010, 170). Sick Funds (Kupat Holim) were initially established in 1912 as health care mutual aid systems by socialist Jewish male settlers who were agricultural workers in Palestine. The sick funds were integrated into the General Federation of Labor (Histadrut) health insurance system when the Zionist labor organization was established in 1920. The Histadrut worked closely with Hadassah through the late 1920s to provide healthcare to its members and their dependents until it established its own institutions (Cohen 1987, 144–152).

---

[34] New Zealand became independent of Britain in 1947 and Canada became independent in 1919.

Primary documents illustrate inter-Zionist competition and conflict, as well as coordination, for example between Hadassah and the British-based Women's International Zionist Organization (WIZO), which primarily sponsored Jewish schools run by the "locally" founded (1920) Hebrew Women's Organization in "Eretz Israel/Palestine." The WIZO also established IWCs, and its volunteers and workers conducted tens of thousands of "home visits" to Jewish families.[35] Hadassah additionally competed with socialist and labor Zionist organizations such as Histadrut's Nashim Ibriot women's committees (funded by Jewish women in New Zealand), whose members canvassed Jewish neighborhoods for pregnant women and accompanied them to hospitals to be examined by a gynecologist in the 1920s, leaving them with a ticket that allowed them to be delivered at home or in a Zionist hospital by a nurse-midwife. Another organization, Ezer Leyoldos (Children in Need) served Ultra-Orthodox Jews.[36] Despite their differences Zionist health activists were feverishly oriented toward Judaizing Palestine by populating it with as many Jewish bodies as possible and assuring their survival and health. The final section of this chapter uses examples from an early and late moment in British colonial rule to explore Palestinian elite responses to British and Zionist health projects and priorities.

Palestinian Elites and the Politics of Health

Palestinian elites realized that the heart of Zionist settler-colonialism was transforming the demography of Palestine by populating it with healthy Jewish bodies and that this project was vitalized by investments in science and medicine and a colonial civilizational discourse. A telling early example of conflict involving Palestinian, British, and Zionist leaders centered on Health Week 1924, held in the third week of November. Initiated by Hadassah and led by its director, Dr. Simon Tannenbaum, this massive educational campaign run by "local committees" was aimed

---

[35] July 27, 1926, Landesman letter to Rose Slutzkin in London. Central Zionist Archives 1925, Folder J113/6738. Also see "WIZO: Who We Are": www.wizo.org /who-we-are/our-history.html. In 1931 the WIZO Congress moved the Palestine office from Jerusalem to Tel Aviv because of mass immigration to the municipality from Germany. Central Zionist Archives 1933, Folder A217/29.

[36] *Report of the Central Committee for Maternity and Infant Welfare in Palestine.* This committee was an unfunded British project founded in 1922 by Lady Samuel and largely composed of representatives from Zionist women's health organizations. Central Zionist Archives 1925, Folder J113/6738.

at schoolchildren and their parents. It included posters, "Cinematograph and Magic Lantern exhibitions," essay contests, health propaganda newspaper stories, and a Hebrew curriculum translated into Arabic pamphlets. Health Week was designed to "spread the light of health" by targeting the "person" or "individual" rather than the "environment," according to a Department of Health statement.[37]

British officials made clear to Tannenbaum that their support was conditional on inclusion of Palestinians ("Christians, Moslems"), although the meetings were organized by the secretary of the Health Week Committee, Hadassah's Nellie Mochenson (Straus), and were usually held at the Hadassah office or the Jewish "Lemel" School. The executive committee, whose appointed figurehead chair was British director of health Rupert Briercliffe, expanded over three months but remained composed of Zionist health and education representatives, British colonial officials from the departments of health, education, and public works, wives of high-ranking colonial officials (e.g., Lady Samuel Bentwich, Lady Gilbert Clayton, and Lady Ronald Storrs), and a few representatives from private Christian religious schools serving Palestinian children.[38]

The elephant in the room was the lack of high-level Palestinian participation. "Dr. Canaan" and "Dr. Khalidi," who were mentioned occasionally and expected to write stories for publication "in each of the Arabic newspapers," did not continue to participate in the planning for political reasons despite attempts to frame the Health Week campaign as apolitical. The minutes of a September 10, 1924, meeting of the executive committee, at which only Briercliffe and Hadassah and other Zionist representatives were present, included a section on "Participation of [the] Arab Population": "Dr. Tannenbaum stated that it is very doubtful whether it would be possible to secure the active participation of the Moslem Supreme Council. It was decided that an effort should be made to persuade the Moslem Supreme Council that there is no political significance attached to this plan." A September 10 handwritten note by Briercliffe summarized a meeting with Dr. Tannenbaum:

[37] Environmental campaigns, the focus of the British colonial government, focused on anti-malaria projects, food inspections, and regulations related to sanitation, health, and hygiene.
[38] GOP, Department of Health, Hygiene and Health – Health Week – Hadassah Med. Organization, August–November 1924. File location in catalog: 00071706.81.D0.97.4B. Israel State Archives.

Impressed Dr. Tannenbaum that a meeting which, apart from myself, represented only the Jewish section of the Community, was going to limit Government participation in the Health Week, considerably. Dr. Dajani's resignation at the instigation of the Supreme Moslem Council must be regarded as very serious. One of the conditions of Government cooperation was that the Health Week was on for the whole of the people of Palestine and that it really was backed by Jewish Christian & Moslem public opinion. I had obtained Chief Secretary's approval to take part in the movement because it was presented to him that all communities were willing to help. RB.

A September 12 handwritten note by Briercliffe summarized a meeting with the British civil secretary of the Mandate government: "Asked Col. [George S.] Symes (CS) his opinion of the situation. He considers the movement should proceed purely as a Jewish matter and that at a different time a Health Week should be held for Moslem schools too. I thought this would not be in keeping with the Health Week idea. RB."

A September 16 handwritten note by Briercliffe summarized a meeting with the mufti of Jerusalem:

Asked Mufti reason for Dr. Dajani's non-participation. Mufti most desirous of helping the Government in health work and is not opposed to Health Week. Considers however that as at present organized it is mainly a Jewish affair and that if a Moslem representative takes part in it the Jewish press will make political capital out of the incident and put it forward in light of a rapprochement between Arabs and Jews which would be most undesirable. He will lend his support to the Government but not with Health Week Committee which is predominantly Jewish. RB.[39]

The Health Week events went forward in 1924 without Palestinian participation. I fleshed out this example from the archival records in order to impress that all major players in the political field recognized the implications of health and healthcare in Mandate Palestine: British officials worried about optics and costs; Zionist leaders had demographic, material, and ideological agendas; and Palestinian leaders realized all of these dimensions but had few cards to play, politically or in terms of capital.

Palestinian physicians, exemplified by Tawfik Canaan, invested substantial time and energy appealing to British colonizers for healthcare

---

[39] GOP, Department of Health, Hygiene and Health – Health Week – Hadassah Med. Organization, August–November 1924. File location in catalog: 00071706.81.D0.97.4B. Israel State Archives.

services, often participated in British-sponsored public health projects, and were enamored of the modern as hygienic, "steady development and progress" (Canaan 1946, 1), enlightenment, and rationality. Canaan, born in the Bethlehem-area Ottoman village of Beit Jala to a poor family of Lutheran religious affiliation, trained as an ethnologist in Germany and as a physician at the Syrian Protestant College for Medicine (established 1867, later renamed American University of Beirut), from where he graduated with honors in 1905 (Nashef 2002). He was involved in multiple scientific, health, and medical research projects and institutions, as well as ethnographic scholarship, over sixty years in Palestine, beginning from early in the twentieth century in Ottoman Greater Syria.[40] Salim Tamari, who writes of Canaan's successful work to eradicate leprosy in Palestine, calls him a "nativist ethnographer" who was part of "the attempt to establish sources of legitimation for Palestinian cultural patrimony (and implicitly for a Palestinian national identity that began to distance itself from greater Syrian and Arab frameworks)." Canaan turned to "primordial sources of identity" in response to British superiority frames and "Zionist attempts at establishing their own putative claims to the Israelite and biblical heritage" (Tamari 2009, 95, 99). Canaan's textured folkloric work "contested Zionist claims to biblical patrimonies by stressing present-day continuities between the biblical heritage (and occasionally pre-biblical roots) and Palestinian popular beliefs and practices" (99). Tarif Khalidi similarly argues that Palestinian intellectuals such as Canaan and Omar al-Barghouthi were "striving to show the Semitic roots of the Palestinian peasant as an ancient and continuous occupier of the land" (Khalidi 1981, 65).

---

[40] Canaan wrote for and participated in the editorial board of the British *Journal of the Palestine Oriental Society*, established in Jerusalem in the early 1920s, directed a number of medical and research institutions before and after 1948, including Augusta Victoria Hospital, and cofounded the Palestine Arab Medical Association and its medical journal in the mid-1940s. The society came to be responsible for a number of nongovernment hospitals serving Palestinians until 1948. British colonial authorities arrested Canaan in September 1939 (he was held for nine weeks), the day Britain and France declared war on Germany. His wife, a German national, was arrested the same day and imprisoned for nine months, as was his sister Badra, held for an astounding four years. Accused "of inciting Arab women against Britain," Badra and her mother had indeed been involved in the 1936–1939 Revolt. See "Palestine Information with Provenance Database": http://cosmos.ucc.ie/cs1064/jabowen/IPSC/php/event.php?eid=4237.

While not interested in using Jewish resources to provide for Palestinian health, Zionist political propaganda in the 1940s apparently took credit for lowering Palestinian infant mortality rates. This galled the anti-Zionist Canaan, who acknowledged the lower "general and infantile" death rate in Palestine for multiple reasons over time during the Mandate period but argued it "is a fundamental mistake to attribute it only to one cause, as the Zionists say, i.e. to their influence" (Canaan 1946, 10). He repeatedly pointed to structural conditions that produced high infant mortality, such as lack of roads in Palestinian villages and hamlets and Palestinian physicians settling in towns rather than villages (1).

In a section of a 1946 report titled *The Hygienic and Sanitary Conditions of the Arabs of Palestine*, Canaan dismantled the Zionist argument of hygienic superiority by looking at Jewish and Palestinian infant mortality rates separately. He used British data (provided by Zionist health institutions) to argue that "despite the vast sums of Jewish money poured into the country during the 18 years and which were used for Jewish interest, not least for the sanitation of the [Jewish] colonies and the general standard of health of the Jews, [they] were not always able to decrease the mortality among their [own] infants." He showed that "Jewish total infant mortality was higher in 1938 than in any previous year, except 1935 and 1936, while the total infantile mortality among the Arabs was in 1938 the lowest since 1923."

Canaan realized that counting often tells an ideological story. The report I analyzed at the US National Library of Medicine includes Canaan's taped-in handwritten table showing "Infantile Mortality in Places far from Jewish Influence per 1000 Live Births" (see Figure 1.2). The table lists Palestinian infant mortality rates from 1938 to 1944 for Khan Yunis, Hebron, "Hebron Villages," Bethlehem, "Bet Djala" (Beit Jala), and "Jericho Villages," showing their variability over time and across space despite all of them being "far from Jewish influence" in terms of geographic access to Zionist health institutions (Canaan 1946).[41]

Palestinian elites recognized that the Zionist movement sought to advance the project of a Jewish state in historic Palestine by "proving" its civilizational superiority in economic, health, and scientific development before Western powers. Given that British colonial authorities

---

[41] This report is not paginated sequentially.

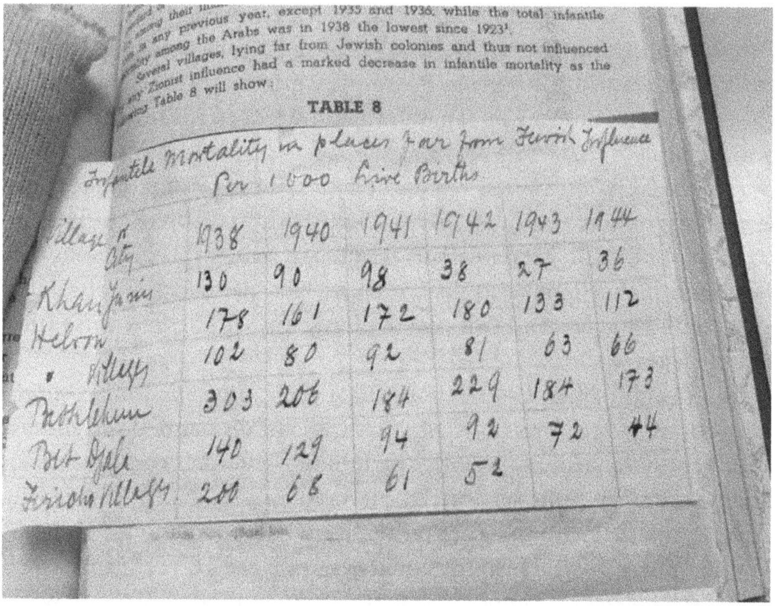

Village or City	1938	1940	1941	1942	1943	1944
Khan Junis	130	90	98	38	27	36
Hebron	178	161	172	180	133	112
" Villages	102	80	92	81	63	66
Bethlehem	303	206	184	229	184	173
Beit Jala	140	129	94	92	72	44
Jericho Villages	200	68	61	52		

Figure 1.2 Handwritten taped-in Table 8 by Tawfik Canaan calculating "Infantile Mortality in Places far from Jewish Influence per 1000 Live Births" (Canaan 1946). Photo by author. Courtesy of Army Medical Library/National Library of Medicine, Bethesda

and the League of Nations connected a population's "civilization" level to its health, "Jews and Arabs would be at odds to link the contrasting levels of infantile mortality among the national population groups in Palestine with their respective contribution to the territory's development" (Bourmaud 2013, 14). Palestinian medical professionals, including the Palestine Arab Medical Association established in 1945, persistently requested an increase in the Public Health Department budget and additional health facilities to address "the real needs of the country for more thorough sanitation and more medical help."[42]

Palestinian physicians also advocated for their professional and economic interests. A July 15, 1945, letter from the Palestine Arab Medical Association signed by Dr. M. T. [Mahmud Taher] Dajani (general secretary) and Dr. Canaan (president) to the director of

[42] The first "Medical Non-Jewish Association" of physicians was established in Jerusalem in 1912, likely initiated by Canaan (Canaan 1946, 4).

medical services in Jerusalem, John MacQueen, included requests for investment in sanitation infrastructure and healthcare as two of five demands from the Arab Medical Congress held in Jerusalem. The third demand was that "one or more young Arab doctors should be sent yearly to British Universities for specialization ... No real scientific work and no real service can ever be done to the country without a backbone of specialists." MacQueen responded they were "endeavouring to send two of our [government-employed Palestinian] doctors this year." The fourth demand was for the Palestine Arab Medical Association to be involved at the decision-making level in any "basic changes ... contemplated" in relation to "sanitation, health or medical services."

The fifth demand, for a "radical change of the present regulations for licensing physicians," took up most of the letter. It noted the high "number of licensed and practicing Jewish physicians," which the Arab Medical Congress expected would increase after the war. It demanded protection of "the vital interests of Palestinian Arab physicians."[43] The association complained that Jewish physicians actively drew away Arab patients from the small number of Arab physicians, with significant impact on their livelihoods, "as (1) the Arab population as a whole is poorer than the Jewish one, as (2) it does not seek the help of the doctors as often as the others, and as (3) practically no Jew will come to an Arab physician for treatment – following the fundamental Jewish National Principle viz., Jewish work only for Jewish workers; non-Jewish work for all." While the phrasing is confusing, the message is clear. Zionists settler-colonial principles considered Palestinians fair and appropriate game for extraction in all realms in order to maintain their livelihoods and cultivate a Jewish National Home. Zionist health institutions had a policy of charging Palestinian patients fees that were "high and at times exorbitant" (Canaan 1946, 14).

MacQueen met with Dajani and Canaan on July 29, 1945, after receipt of the letter. In a September 5 confidential memo to the "Acting Chief Secretary," he summarized the content of the meeting, dismissing the Arab physicians' criticism of the quota system that determined the

---

[43] The letter states there were 2,247 "licensed Jewish physicians" for "600,000 inhabitants [who] are Jews," a ratio of "1 physician for every 267 persons," which it compared to the high ratio of 1 physician per "1067" Norwegians.

number of Jewish physicians allowed to immigrate to and be licensed in
Palestine: there was "no need for a new law," although he agreed that
"numerically we had more than enough doctors at present." He
reported encouraging the physicians "again" to develop a "rural medical service," an idea they "were fostering ... amongst Arab doctors."[44]

In his testimony to the Anglo-American Committee of Inquiry in
1946 about the health of the Palestinian population, Canaan challenged Jewish Agency testimony claiming that lower Arab mortality
rates in Palestine were caused by the treatment of Palestinian out-
patients in Jewish institutions (Sufian 2015, 133–134). The published
Jewish Agency memorandum to the Anglo-American Committee
(Jewish Agency 1946) had made a non-zero-sum case for Zionism
that was crucial at that historical juncture before a Western international audience: Zionists had "common interests" with "Arabs"
and had worked with them in "cooperation" and offered "help" and
"friendship," including healthcare services, during the Mandate. The
Jewish Agency memo recommended that the Anglo-American
Committee support a "Jewish commonwealth" with "a Jewish majority" because of "common economic and social interests" between the
Zionist movement and Palestinians, including "cooperation" between
Arab and Jewish "orange growers," "certain Arab trade unions established with the help of the Histadrut," and coordination between
Jewish and Arab politicians in the municipality of Haifa (33).
Zionists had advanced the knowledge of "Arab farmers," the memo
claimed, and "Valuable pioneer service in the cause of Jewish-Arab
friendship has been rendered by the Hadassah Medical Organisation
whose hospitals have always been open to Arab patients and have also
been frequented by Arabs from the neighboring countries" (34).

[44]   Health and Vital Statistics. "The Palestinian Arab Medical Association Requests
for more medical health by provision of Clinics, Hospitals, Laboratories, Etc."
File location in catalog: 00071706.81.CF.FD.59. Israel State Archives. These
demands may have influenced the 1946 Department of Health investment of
"Approximately £P.5,000 ... for the development of [Arab Palestinian] Village
Clinics," a modest influx that should be understood in comparison to the
£P.81,000 in grants provided for "Jewish health services" in the same year,
excluding additional government investments in bed strength at the Government
Hospital, Tel Aviv, which served Jews, and "staff increases" at the Mental
Hospital, Jaffa, which was more likely to serve Palestinians. GOP, Department
of Health, Health and Vital Statistics, Annual Reports – Annual Report for the
Year 1946. File location in catalog: 00071706.81.CF.FC.FA. Israel State
Archives.

The 1946 "Evidence" document submitted to the Anglo-American Committee by the Arab Office in Jerusalem insisted, to the contrary, that "there are no benefits obtained or to be expected from Zionism commensurate with its evils and its dangers." Responding to claims that Zionist health institutions and knowledge had reduced Palestinian mortality rates, it stated: "The increase in the Arab population is not primarily due to Zionist immigration, and in any case would not necessarily be a sign of prosperity ... The Zionist contention that their social organizations provide health and social services for the Arab population is exaggerated; only a minute proportion of Arabs, for example, are looked after by Jewish health organizations ... Arab voluntary social organizations have grown up independently of Jewish bodies and without help from them" (Arab Office 1946, 4–5). The document emphatically challenged Zionists' claims that they were "mediators of Western civilization to the Middle East ... the Arab world has been in direct touch with the West for a hundred years, and has its own reawakened cultural movement, and thus it has no need of a mediator" (5).

~~~~~~~~~~

Despite the extractive political economies that are the very definition of imperial and colonial relations, health and science nevertheless remain especially amenable to civilizational discourse that posits the colonizer as an advanced purveyor of the good to the benighted colonized. The putative "silver lining" of the stark power differentials of colonialism is an improved lot for the colonized in the arena of health, but that was not the case for Palestinians. Chapter 2 uses archival material to consider the health impact of British "efficiencies and economies" logic in Palestine. It draws links between hunger and poverty on one side and disproportionate morbidity and early death on the other and explores the multiple ways in which Palestinian traditional healers and midwives were situated in relation to the Mandate government. The chapter tracks the material dimensions and embodied outcomes of British healthcare austerity, as well as the persistent rhetorical myth-ology of Western cultural and racial superiority.

2 | "Making the Country Pay for Itself"
Health, Hunger, and Midwives

Limited expenditures and cost-cutting were overriding concerns for British colonial officials with respect to social welfare and health in Palestine. London required British colonies to "pay their own way" by extracting resources from indigenous populations and encouraging private enterprises, especially British ones. London facilitated such enterprises as long as they did not threaten stability in the colonies (Bunton 2007, 25; Constantine 1984, 17–18, 23). Imperial authorities were most willing to assist colonial governments in building "the railways, roads or other facilities needed to attract investment and stimulate exports" and expected local taxes and laborers to meet maintenance costs, including for municipal infrastructures such as sanitation systems (Constantine 1984, 22–23; Palestine Local Councils Ordinance 1921, 1922). The British logic of "efficiencies and economies" also ruled healthcare provision for Palestinians during the Mandate. Zionist institutions provided for Jewish healthcare and Palestinians largely relied on Christian missionary institutions and fee-based medical services.

British colonial welfare ideology was committed to the "march of civilisation" for metropolitan gain, even when some officials recognized the damage done to indigenous health. "Arabs and Yeminite Jews," as well as "Bedouins" ("in many ways a race apart"), had little immunity to tuberculosis, for example, as contact increased "between urban and rural communities," infected poor Jewish settlers immigrated from "Russia and Eastern and Central Europe," and infected Palestinian migrants returned from the Americas, according to a 1935 report by Norman M. MacLennan, the Jerusalem SMO (MacLennan 1935, 22, 102). MacLennan notably did not mention that colonial extraction and austerity contributed to poverty and hunger, which made people more likely to become ill and less likely to recover. Even when British health officials in Palestine recognized these connections and privately argued for more resources for Palestinians, they usually deployed civilizational rhetoric that articulated themselves as culturally superior to backward natives.

Gendered-racialized dynamics and material tensions were prominent in the archives as colonial authorities governed and minutely regulated Palestinian-serving IWC nurses and midwives but provided little money for healthcare. A conflict between Superintendent Rogers and nurse Insaf Ali recorded in a folder spanning 1934 to 1947 illustrates these dynamics and offers insights on the municipality of El-Bireh's ultimately fruitless battle with the Department of Health to acquire first permission and later financial support for a clinic that included an IWC.[1] The colonial government repeatedly insisted that El-Bireh should not establish a clinic, the government could not afford to pay the salary of a nurse, and residents should instead travel to the IWC in Ramallah. The president of the municipal council, `Abdullah Judeh, responded that the distance between El-Bireh and Ramallah was far, transportation was expensive, and long waits ensued for patients in Ramallah, where medical treatment was in any case limited. El-Bireh leaders continually made the case that women, infants, and schoolchildren had enormous medical needs, residents were highly taxed and poor, and the council could not complete many urgent projects because of budgetary limitations. Ultimately the municipal council established an independent clinic and a health insurance system (10 mils per head per month) that it could not sustain.

The El-Bireh folder contains details of a lengthy conflict between June 1944 and May 1945 involving an unruly Egyptian nurse, Insaf Mahmoud Ali, who said she had "graduated from the Egyptian College of Medicine" with "diplomas in Nursing and Midwifery with Distinction," and was finally fired by the El-Bireh Municipal Council after enraging Vena Rogers with her "insolence" and "insubordination." Rogers claimed that the Egyptian nurse did not seem to "know the true purpose of the center," which was baby care and educating mothers. Nurse Insaf was more interested in "showy matters

---

[1] GOP, Department of Health, Infant Welfare Centre, El-Bireh, March 1934–July 1947. File location in catalog: 00071706.81.D1.32.BF. Israel State Archives. I am grateful to Suzan Abdi, Lina Hawari, and Reem Quawas for their generous deciphering assistance with multiple handwritten Arabic letters in this folder.

and in midwifery work in the town." Rogers demanded the nurse only attend to "midwifery cases" in "emergencies" and insisted she was not permitted to "charge fees for such services." Upon visiting the El-Bireh IWC while Nurse Insaf was attending a home delivery, Rogers reported seeing "a vaginal speculum, a scalpel, hypodermic needles, etc.," which she ordered "be immediately removed" since only medical officers, by definition male, were allowed to use them. Rogers accused Nurse Insaf of being more interested in working "in hospitals" and complained of her arrogance in asking the medical officer in Ramallah for "Neo Salvarsan" (a syphilis treatment) because she had a "positive case."

Rogers cited Nurse Insaf for wearing "an Army Sister's Cap," "jewelry" (deemed unclean and not making "a good impression"), a "fancy dress," and "overalls" with "large fancy glass buttons," instead of the regulation uniform. In her own letter in the file, Nurse Insaf responded that the government did not provide a uniform and should pay her to wear one. (It did not pay her salary either.) The president of the El-Bireh Municipal Council described Rogers as coming to "our centre" in "a furious state," "cursing the Nurse before the women and beat[ing] her." The council viewed this as part of (colonial?) "intrigues against the Centre." Rogers denied beating Nurse Insaf but admitted to grabbing her arm and pulling her out of a treatment room when the nurse refused to pay obeisance to Rogers and went so far as to ask her to instead pay "for the necessary things" in the clinic.

The El-Bireh Municipal Council eventually fired Nurse Insaf and the colonial government continued to refuse to pay a salary for a nurse or midwife in El-Bireh through the Mandate period.[2] Like Nurse Butros in the previous chapter, Nurse Insaf was expected to spend a good portion of her time providing "practical training" to teenage "schoolgirls" and mothers about health and hygiene rather than treating patients.[3] Actual treatment of non-acute conditions was the responsibility of the Palestinian medical officer who attended to patients in a clinic he held in the Ramallah IWC once per week.

[2] GOP, Department of Health, Infant Welfare Centre, El-Bireh, March 1934–July 1947. File location in catalog: 00071706.81.D1.32.BF. Israel State Archives.
[3] *Department of Health Report for the Year 1934*, 12, 58. *Department of Health Report for the Year 1935*, 22. These digital reports were kindly provided to me by Dr. Stephen J. Greenberg of the National Institutes of Health/National Library of Medicine (January 2019).

Efficiencies and Economies in Colonial Health

As in other colonies, fiscal austerity policies limited provision of health-care in Palestine. Expanding services for Palestinians always "depended on the generation of adequate [local] revenue" (Miller 1985, 71). The British colonial project in Palestine was expected to pay for itself, with Zionist, missionary, and philanthropic institutions – and especially Palestinians themselves – picking up the tab. In response to a 1929 query from the Permanent Mandates Commission regarding the limited "hospital facilities" in Palestine, the Department of Health reiterated a 1922 colonial policy statement of priorities:

(a) To concentrate on public health and sanitation, and the prevention of disease;
(b) To provide hospital accommodation for infectious and communic-able diseases and for the insane;
(c) To limit as far as possible the hospital accommodation provided by the Government for the treatment of general diseases to the requirements of Government officers and employees, members of the Police Force, prisoners, medico-legal cases and accidents, and *the very poor* [my italics];
(d) To provide hospitals, or, to aid Municipalities to provide hospitals, for the needs of the general population *where no provision or inadequate provision is made by voluntary organizations* [my italics].[4]

A notice on March 2, 1922, marked "strictly confidential," from the civil secretary of the Government House in Jerusalem to "all British high officials in Palestine," highlighted "the urgent necessity of econ-omy in expenditure" and instructed that "any programme of cultural and economic development must be postponed for the present" (Adm. No. 981). An item dated May 1, 1922, from the Colonial Office, labeled "Urgent Confidential," notified the departments of "Public Health and Education" to ask "persons who are in a financial position to do so, [to] repay a larger proportion of the cost of the medical and educational facilities which they receive." A May 10, 1922, confiden-tial memo from the director of health expressed resistance to increased

---

[4] In *Palestine and Transjordan Administration Reports 1918–1948, Vol. 3, 370.* The original memo is in *Palestine and Transjordan Administration Reports 1918–1948, Vol. 1, 257.*

austerity in a complaint he sent to the civil secretary and the treasurer. He explained the department had already cut expenditures in "relief" by "more than half" compared to the previous year. He added that the fee rate for "3rd class treatment" at all government hospitals had already been "doubled" by the Colonial Office, although "it must be understood that a considerable proportion of the latter are infectious diseases, medico-legal cases, and indigents who are certified by Governors as unable to pay" (per item c in the aforementioned statement of priorities). Nevertheless, a May 17, 1922, confidential memo on "Budget Estimates 1922–23" indicates the director of health made "additional economies." Among other things, the Department of Health closed Ramallah Hospital entirely, accruing a savings of almost one thousand pounds, and reduced the number of third-class "diet strength" rations at the Gaza, Haifa, and Jerusalem hospitals.[5]

Halfway through thirty years of British colonial rule in Palestine, the *Department of Health Annual Report for Year 1935* reiterated health-care austerity for Palestinians: "Treatment at Government clinics is restricted to Government employees and the very poor." As illustrated by the case of the infant Yasmin, however, free care for Palestinian indigents in such hospitals was the exception, not the rule. The poor were required to pay the third-class fee, which was not affordable to most. In a critical academic article published in 1932, Israel Jacob Kligler, then the director of the Hadassah Straus Health Centre in Jerusalem and a professor of hygiene and bacteriology at the Hebrew University, found that "the Government provides 10 PT. or less than 50 cents per capita per annum for hospital and public health purposes" in Palestine (Kligler 1932, 169). Despite frequent references to paying "the closest attention to measures for safeguarding the health of the population," the government invested as little as possible to improve health conditions.

British colonial rhetoric, moreover, understated Ottoman investments in public health in Palestine in the same breath it exaggerated British commitments. According to a 1921 report of the Civil Administration of Palestine presented to the British Parliament, for example, "Before the British Occupation there were no government

---

[5] GOP, Department of Health (Reorganization & Finance) Budget Estimates – Health Department – General Correspondence, October 1921–September 1922. File location in catalog: 00071706.81.D1.31.A8. Israel State Archives.

hospitals or dispensaries for the civilian population."[6] However, according to Palestinian physician Tawfik Canaan, there were:

five [Ottoman] government or municipal hospitals (in Jerusalem, Jaffa, Nablus, Tul-Karm and Gaza). They were small and inadequately equipped. The hospital in Nablus was built by voluntary contributions of the Arab inhabitants. Later on it was taken over by the municipality and is now run by the [British] P.H.D. All other hospitals were either missionary (Christian) or philanthropic (Jewish). The first predominated and they treated equally Arabs and Jews. (1946, 1)

Of the twenty-five "non-Jewish" (and nongovernment) hospitals in Palestine before 1914, nine were in Jerusalem and all except a Greek Orthodox (mission) hospital and a Russian hospital were sponsored by (Northern) European Christian missions (Canaan 1946, 2).

From the 1840s to the 1860s, according to Philippe Bourmaud, there were four hospitals in Ottoman Bilad ash-sham (Greater Syria). Similar to Canaan, Bourmaud estimates that by 1914 there were about "thirty such institutions . . . unevenly dispersed in the main population centres and on both sides of the Jordan; most were established after the French-Prussian war in 1870–1871 as part of national competition between the main European powers," largely in the small town of Bethlehem "with its biblical background," which had "no less than three hospitals" by 1909 and was "indisputably over-medicalised" (Bourmaud 2009, 277, 278).

In 1921 the British colonial government in Palestine reported to Parliament that it ran "13 hospitals, 21 dispensaries, 8 clinics and 5 epidemic posts."[7] By 1922 the Department of Health reported sponsoring eleven hospitals (two less than in 1921), one of which was quickly closed for lack of funds (Ramallah), and one of which served Palestinian laborers at the Kantara Railway,[8] as well as a mental hospital in Bethlehem.[9] In "clinics," a 1921 report explained, a medical officer saw patients once "weekly or fortnightly" "during their periodic tours" of some villages, but assured the London Treasury that such

---

[6] In *Palestine and Transjordan Administration Reports 1918–1948, Vol. 1, 1918–1924*, 185.
[7] In *Palestine and Transjordan Administration Reports 1918–1948, Vol. 1, 1918–1924*, 185.
[8] Government hospital locations in 1922 were Jerusalem, Beersheeba, Jaffa, Ramleh, Gaza, Haifa, `Acca, Nablus, and Tulkarem.
[9] *Government of Palestine Department of Health Report for 1922.*

services were not free: "The revenue derived from the village clinics was sufficient to cover the cost of the drugs and dressings expended. This form of medical relief was so much appreciated by the villagers that Governments of Districts made numerous requests for new clinics to be started but limitations of staff usually prevented this."[10] By 1929, "for financial reasons," there were no "adequate hospital facilities" for Palestinians in large areas that included "Tulkarem, Ramleh, Majdal, Ramallah and Hebron."[11] In the early 1930s the medical officers in the large cities of Jerusalem, Haifa, Jaffa, and Nablus were each responsible for visiting as many as "thirty to forty villages about once a month" (Kligler 1932, 168), making the 1921 claim of weekly or fortnightly visits rather impossible.

The Colonial Office in London reported their spending on health services in the 1920s in British pounds to the Council of the League of Nations on the Administration of Palestine and Trans-Jordan. Among other things, the report shows that total spending on healthcare in absolute terms went down from the highest amount in 1921–1922 (146,500), to a much lower plateau in 1928 (73,800), rose in 1929 (101,800) and 1930 (105,400) in relation to spending from 1923 through 1928, but remained lower than spending in 1921–1922.[12]

To give a comparative sense, the 1926–1927 Hadassah annual budget, which served the healthcare needs of a much smaller Jewish population in Palestine, totaled 132,032 British pounds (Rosenau and Wilinsky 1928, 660), 44 percent higher than the 91,676 British pounds the colonial government reported spending on the health of its forces and Palestinians in the same year. Substantially dependent on external funding from the United States, Hadassah did experience funding shortages, for example, in the early 1930s. At that point, it transferred most of its "various health services to the local Jewish Communities," whose health services were "supported for the most part by the Jewish community in Palestine itself" (Simoni 2000, 57). Transferring Hadassah health institutions to local

---

[10] In *Palestine and Transjordan Administration Reports 1918–1948, Vol. 1, 1918–1924*, 30.

[11] In *Palestine and Transjordan Administration Reports 1918–1948, Vol. 3, 1929–1931*, 86.

[12] In *Palestine and Transjordan Administration Reports 1918–1948, Vol. 3, 1929–1931*, 373.

Zionist communities allowed the hospitals to apply for and receive government grants-in-aid (58). With this shift, the Department of Health eagerly took the opportunity to recommend "economies" in the Tel Aviv municipal hospital, according to the Department of Health annual report for 1933 (pub. 1934).

Despite a global economic depression, fiscal years 1932–1936 saw *budget surpluses in Palestine*; indeed the colonial government called it a "boom period" (GOP 1938, Report by the Treasurer, 3). Deficits in fiscal years 1931–1932 (–22,900) and for two years beginning in 1936 (–1,432,600 and –2,434,200) were the result of increased military spending to address Arab "disturbances" (El-Eini 1997, 573, and table 1, 574). Surpluses in 1932–1933 (+499,500), 1933–1934 (+1,280,600), 1934–1935 (+2,222,600), and 1935–1936 (+1,534,200) were the result of parsimonious government spending and the influx of Jewish capital as more Germans emigrated to and invested in Palestine with the rise of Adolf Hitler.

Colonial health officials on the ground were well aware that the Palestine government was held to the British imperial principle of "making the country pay for itself" (quoted in El-Eini 1997, 571). British spending on Palestinian healthcare was miserly as a proportion of the colonial budget and was further reduced over time (Anglo-American Committee of Inquiry 1946, Vol. II, 630, table 2). A five-year snapshot of the spending priorities of the Government of Palestine is presented in an "Ordinary Expenditure" table in the *Report by the Treasurer on the Financial Transactions of the Palestine Government for the Year 1938–1939* (GOP 1939, 19). It illustrates a continued low proportion of spending on healthcare services in the 1930s that ranges from 4.0 to 5.9 percent (rounded) of annual total budgets. I extracted the "Health" and "Law and Order" rows to calculate comparative percentages (see Table 2.1).

These amounts include health services of a higher grade for colonial and military personnel and their families and grants to Jewish healthcare institutions in Palestine. Higher proportions of spending on health occurred in years of lower gross spending. Spending on law and order increased substantially, taking almost half the budget, during the first year of the Palestinian Revolt, and remained high through 1938–1939. Taking a wider historical lens, Department of Health expenditures in Palestine averaged 4.13 percent of the total budget from the years 1923–1924 through 1945–1946, according to my calculation of

Table 2.1 *Health and Law and Order in Palestine Mandate Budget, 1934–1939*

Year	Total Budget (British pounds)	Law and Order (percent)	Health (percent)
1934–1935	2,834,841	32.4	5.9
1935–1936	3,315,531	28.6	5.9
1936–1937	5,159,799	45.4	4.0
1937–1938	4,796,808	43.3	4.5
1938–1939	4,613,611	41.4	5.1

Source: Government of Palestine, from "Ordinary Expenditure" table, in *Report by the Treasurer on the Financial Transactions of the Palestine Government for the Year 1938–1939.* Courtesy of Princeton University Library.

a yearly table of health services spending in colonized Palestine (Anglo-American Committee of Inquiry 1946, Vol. II, 630, table 2).

I analyzed files of Department of Health correspondences involving multiple medical administrators and colonial officials discussing collecting, suing for, or writing off hospital fees in situations where male Palestinian patients absconded without paying, as well as for European indigents such as nuns and nurses working in Palestine. Most patients who used government hospitals were required to pay the first-, second-, or third-class fees. Yasmin's mother was required to pay the daily third-class fee for the Arab section of the Jerusalem government hospital when she tried to get care for her daughter in 1933. Notably, Yasmin was repeatedly *refused* treatment because her mother could not pay rather than being charged after the child was treated. Indeed, I found no billing arrears cases involving Palestinian women and children.

Government employees injured not through their own "negligence," including British members of the Palestine police, were required to pay the hospital diet fee only. Many patients who worked in British government offices or labor projects left hospitals without paying even this fee, the majority of them impoverished Palestinian village men who owed very little, according to an Arabic letter written on behalf of a former (likely illiterate) patient and a list of the names of absconding patients from the Jaffa government hospital. Hospitals quickly learned to "settle accounts" before a patient left, even in "medico-legal cases," and the government only sued for payment when administrators thought a suit would be successful; it did not sue when costs in staff and money would easily exceed the small amounts owed.[13]

A June 7, 1923, circular (No. 153) lists the per diem first-, second-, and third-class fees for "maternity cases admitted to Government Hospitals," which were PT ("piastre tariff"; the Egyptian colonial pound, tied to the sterling, was in common and official use in Palestine until 1927) 75, 50, and 30, respectively. These fees rose substantially by the late 1920s. In the 1930s and 1940s maternity hospitalization was broken down into three parts: the "surgeon's fee," which was paid directly to him (usually a man, although there were a few women obstetricians working in institutions that served Palestinians in the 1940s) and was unnecessary if the birth was only attended by a nurse-midwife; a per diem fee of 230 mils for subsequent "treatment" that did not appear to be differentiated by "class"; and a per diem "maintenance" rate, which covered "diet" (120 mils for second class), for a total of 350 mils per day for second-class maternity care. For comparison, the per diem maternity fees excluding the surgeon cost totaled 450–500 mils in the Princess Mary Maternity Ward of the government hospital in Jerusalem, likely the first-class rate, "where the nursing staff is composed of British Nursing Sisters."[14]

Multiple correspondences in the late 1920s and early 1930s related to the costs of childbirth and postpartum care for the wives of white *British* Palestine police constables in the Jerusalem and Haifa government hospitals, which each had "special accommodations" designed for the "European maternity patient." The second-class rate and the debate about who should carry the costs of "family," reproductivity,

---

[13] Health and Vital Statistics, Remission of Diet Fees, 1933–1944. File location in catalog: 00071706.81.CF.FC.A8. Hospital Fees – Administration and Collection of. File location in catalog: 00071706.81.EE.3A.0C. Health and Vital Statistics, Medical Treatment for Families of British Police, 1929–1946. File location in catalog: 00071706.81.CF.FC.CD. Israel State Archives.

[14] The Jerusalem government hospital had a highly developed British section that served colonial military and civilian officials and their families from throughout Palestine, including the private Princess Mary Maternity Ward established in the late 1920s for pregnant and birthing women and (white) "foreigner visitors." Department of Health annual reports summarized in some detail the nature of medical services provided in the hospital's British section each year. GOP, Department of Health, Infant Welfare – Regulations, December 1921–February 1935. File location in catalog: 00071706.81.D1.32.B2. GOP, Department of Health, Equipment – Hospital – Princess Mary's Ward, Maternity Hospital, Jerusalem. File location in catalog: 00071706.81. D0.95.0E. Israel State Archives.

and healthcare illustrate the continuing relevance of class among white subjects in the empire. In January 1929, in response to long-standing entreaties from the police inspector-general in Palestine, the Colonial Office in London agreed to pay for "medical and dental treatment," *but not for hospital stays or maternity care*, for wives and children of British constables if family members were "resident in Palestine." Although no wives and children of other British colonial "officers" in Palestine were reportedly provided medical and dental treatment, the stated principle for agreeing to do so for constables was to be consistent with the policy for the wives and children of "British Army and Air Force" members serving abroad. Correspondence from 1933 indicates there were ninety-seven married British constables in Palestine remunerated with an average monthly pay of eleven Palestinian pounds and government provision of housing.[15]

Maternity coverage for the wives of British police constables remained a source of tension. In 1929 "Mrs. Dove" stayed in the second-class ward of the British section of the government hospital in Jerusalem. Her husband owed twenty-seven Palestinian pounds for this stay, "approximately, two months' pay to the Constable." Based on a ruling by the secretary of state, colonial officials repeatedly refused to provide free maternity treatment for Mrs. Dove and other constables' wives and "prohibit[ed] the grant of a free diet." In a late 1933 letter to the police inspector-general (likely) from the treasurer, he stated he was "reluctant" to ask the secretary of state to reconsider government coverage of maternity hospital per diems for British police wives, emphatically reminding him of class-based reproductive ideology in England: "I would point out that very few of us can hope to finance an increase of family strictly from income: it is usually a question either of drawing on capital or borrowing. There seems no particular reason why the British Constable should be relieved of a similar necessity at public cost."

---

[15] Health and Vital Statistics, Medical Treatment for Families of British Police, 1929–1946. File location in catalog: 00071706.81.CF.FC.CD. Israel State Archives. According to Matthew Hughes, the Palestine police force "attracted former soldiers, initially from the British paramilitary 'Black and Tans' force used against Irish rebels in the early 1920s, a force that established the basis for police forces across British colonies." Such demobilized British soldiers, who tended to come from the social "margins," worked in Palestine through 1948. They served as a violent "crack force" "alongside the Army" and were known for drinking heavily and being brutal (Hughes 2013, 697–698).

In the same letter, the author noted that Director of Health Colonel George W. Heron (whom he seemingly had reapproached, contrary to his reluctance) had offered a "reasonable compromise" and "alternative": a constable would be responsible for fees accumulated in the "first ten days of his wife's stay in hospital but that if complications arise requiring her to remain in hospital after that period then no [additional] charge should be made for medical treatment." Each constable would continue to be responsible for the second-class per diem maintenance (diet) fee after the ten days as well. This directive, which ultimately came from High Commissioner A. G. Wauchope and the secretary of state, was implemented beginning January 1934 and remained in place through the 1940s. If British constables found it difficult to pay the cost of maternity treatment and hospital stays for their wives, which the police inspector-general described as imposing a "severe strain on the resources of the average constable," most Palestinians could certainly not afford such care.[16]

Government-sponsored IWCs that served Palestinians were always limited in number and remained underfunded during the Mandate. Palestinian municipal leaders repeatedly requested that British health officials open or support IWCs. Infant Welfare Centres serving Palestinians closed or opened year to year depending on financial support and staffing by a nurse-midwife, who was required to be licensed by and under British supervision whether or not the government funded an IWC, as was the case with Nurses Butros and Insaf. According to annual Department of Health reports, by the end of 1927 the government ran five IWCs, the Palestinian municipalities of Ramallah, Bethlehem, and Nablus sponsored one each, Hadassah sponsored seventeen, the Women's International Zionist Organization sponsored three, and one each was sponsored by the Committee of Jaffa Ladies, the Haifa Social Services and Infant Welfare Committee, and the American Colony Aid Association. By the end of 1934 the government sponsored eight IWCs (in Jerusalem, Ramleh, Nablus, `Acca, Gaza, Jenin, Jericho, and Kfar Kama) and provided minor support to Palestinian communities that ran an additional eleven. By the end of 1935 the government sponsored only five

[16] Health and Vital Statistics, Medical Treatment for Families of British Police, 1929–1946. File location in catalog: 00071706.81.CF.FC.CD. Israel State Archives.

IWCs, dropping responsibility for Jenin, Jericho, and Kfar Kama, and provided some assistance to Palestinian municipalities that sponsored an additional seventeen IWCs. In 1934 and 1935 the municipalities of Bethlehem and Ramallah continued to sponsor their own IWCs, as they had since 1925 and 1926, respectively, but were persistently asking the government to take them over financially because of lack of funds. Jewish mothers and babies continued to be primarily served by Hadassah and WIZO health centers, which in the mid-1930s had increased to twenty and four, respectively. Two other IWCs were "maintained by voluntary committees," likely including the American Colony Aid Association.[17]

By mid-1946, according to my careful tally of registered government midwives who listed their address as a "Government Infant Welfare Centre" in a particular locality (by definition serving Palestinians), only 23 IWCs sponsored to any degree by the British government operated in Palestine (GOP, List of Medical Practitioners, 1946). The *Department of Health Report for the Year 1946*, in contrast, states that the government "maintains 39 Infant Welfare Centres in towns and villages and participates in the administrative support of 8 others." Palestinian "local voluntary committees" ran an additional "7 Arab centres." The government also provided £P. 6,000 "towards the maintenance of the infant welfare centres and school medical services administered by various Jewish medical organisations." Of 61 total IWCs "maintained for Jewish children," 7 were "conducted by the Tel-Aviv Municipal Council, 37 by the Hadassah Medical Organisation, and 17 by the Sick Fund of the Jewish Federation of Labour."[18]

Hundreds of memos from the 1930s and 1940s focused on building permissions, inspections, and costs related to IWCs, clinics, and staffing. The documents included Palestinian voices from all over Palestine – nurses, physicians, municipal officials, midwives – begging for resources, advocating for their communities, themselves, or local nurses and midwives, and complaining of broken government promises. For example, a folder on the IWC in the village of Beit Sahur indicated that the SMO promised in March 1934 to provide a nurse for the IWC provided locals found a "suitable" location and furnished it,

[17] In *Palestine and Transjordan Administration Reports 1934–1935, Vol. 5*, 161.
[18] GOP, Department of Health, Health and Vital Statistics, Annual Reports – Annual Report for the Year 1946. File location in catalog: 00071706.81.CF.FC. FA. Israel State Archives.

which they apparently did with "heavy furniture." In September nurse `Afifeh Najjar wrote to say the government had not, as promised, paid a cleaner who had worked for two months, so the "municipal road sweeper" was now cleaning the IWC, which looked "very dirty." The authorities responded they made no such promise, but by 1935 paid a cleaner six LP per year because the Beit Sahur "Local Council" had "no funds." In addition to the loved Nurse Najjar, whom the villagers fought to keep when the government tried to transfer her, registered nurse-midwife Katrina Shomali treated and helped "poor women" in Beit Sahur without charge. The government denied Shomali's repeated requests for a government grant or to be issued drugs without cost.[19] In a typical response from the Department of Health to Palestinian entreaties for resources, a February 13, 1935, memo from Colonel G. W. Heron expressed his belief that Palestinian municipal contributions in Bethlehem, Hebron, and Ramallah for IWCs were "insufficient." He expected them to contribute more since the Department of Health was not provisioned to pay for anything, not even the salaries of nurses.[20]

In the 1940s the government's closure of Italian, Austrian, and German-affiliated missionary hospitals and the prisoner of war status of their foreign staff because their governments were part of the Axis Powers led to an "acute" crisis, particularly in "hospital accommodation

[19] According to an April 1936 correspondence from the director of medical services, it cost the colonial government forty LP per year, excluding the salary for Nurse Najjar, to run the Beit Sahur IWC in 1936–1937. GOP, Department of Health, Infant Welfare Centre – Beit Sahur, February 1934–November 1947. File Location in catalog: 00071706.81.D1.32.BE. Israel State Archives. Other records indicated that Shomali was among the most prolific registered nurse-midwife deliverers of Palestinian babies in the Jerusalem District between 1936 and 1938, about 85 per year. She joined registered nurse-midwives "J. Fayoumy," "Zahieh Bastieh," and "Maria [Jadallah] `Awwad." The latter by far delivered the highest number of Palestinian babies in the district, 179 in 1936 and 169 in 1937. Two elderly women I interviewed from the Bethlehem area, one of them my godmother, mentioned Rifqa Abu `Aytah had birthed women in Beit Sahur in the 1920s, sequentially followed by "Hanneh" (possibly Dawud `Afaneh), and Maria `Awwad in the 1930s. The latter two had by 1932 taken a six-month training at the "Government Maternity Centre" in Jerusalem. GOP, Department of Health, Regulations – Training of Midwives, July 1925–May 1945. File location in catalog: 00071706.81.D1.33.72. Israel State Archives.
[20] GOP, Department of Health, Infant Welfare – Ramallah. File location in catalog: 00071706.81.D0.98.37. Israel State Archives.

for the Arab population of the country," to use the words of MacQueen in a January 1942 letter to the chief secretary in Jerusalem. He noted, at the same time, "the steadily growing appreciation of the value of hospital treatment by the Arabs," including villagers.[21] Lack of hospital beds for Palestinians remained a crisis, with health authorities noting that Arab tuberculosis and mental patients circulated in their communities: "many patients in the earlier stages of progressive disease are unable to obtain appropriate treatment until irreparable damage has taken place."[22]

Mid-1940s correspondence in a secret file labeled "Rural Health Centres" illustrates British recognition of the resource basis for dramatic disparities in mortality and morbidity rates between Palestinians and Jewish settlers despite pro forma disavowal that blamed Arab cultural backwardness. Sir John Valentine Wistar Shaw, "Officer Administering the Government," forcefully outlined the disparities in a fourteen-page letter ("secret") dated November 12, 1945, to G. H. Hall, a member of the British Parliament and His Majesty's Principal Secretary for the Colonies from August 1935 until October 1936. The letter requested permission to submit a grant application under the Colonial Development and Welfare Act "amounting to LP 1,090,000" to build a "National Health Service" in Palestine. Shaw argued that hospital facilities were completely inadequate in Palestine, "especially for Arabs." Limited government investments in health, he appealed, would encourage "self-government." He presented an ambitious ten-year proposal to build eighty-six "rural health centres," establish a nurses' training school to accommodate sixty students, increase hospital bed strength for infectious diseases, and increase hospital beds "for general and maternity cases from 3,148 to 8,500." More radically, Shaw advocated for an excellent health system accessible to all in Palestine and delinked from ability to pay. Laying out the separate and unequal health system set up by British colonial policy, he pointed to the dilemmas produced by generous Zionist capital investment and institution-building in healthcare:

---

[21] GOP, Department of Health, Health and Vital Statistics, "Hospital Accommodation for the Arab Population, 1942." File location in catalog: 00071706.81.CF.FC.F6. Israel State Archives.

[22] GOP, Department of Health, Health and Vital Statistics, Annual Reports – Annual Report for the Year 1946. File location in catalog: 00071706.81.CF.FC. FA. Israel State Archives.

The Jews are insistent on health services to the standard appropriate to their way of living. They are equally insistent that the services provided by Government fall short of the minimum. Accordingly, while Government tries to provide for both communities without discrimination, for as long as the Jewish services are so extensive and of such high standard, Jews will continue to use them exclusively. In seeking to improve its own health services, therefore, Government must have the appearance of contriving to benefit the Arabs at the expense of the Jews, while depriving Jewish services of their due allocation of public funds.

This tension, Shaw argued, would not exist if the government: "had secured within the last quarter of a century the raising of Arab standards of existence to the level of Jewish standards," although Zionist health investments and standards in Palestine "need not and, I think, should not be regarded as the appropriate norm. The objective of Government should be, I would urge, the achievement of a standard equally appropriate to both communities ... The only standard of general application should be of efficiency and modernity."

Correspondence through November 1947 shows how the grant proposal Shaw ultimately submitted was cut by two-thirds to build only twenty-four rural health centers and one training center between 1948 and 1952. London officials insisted that loans and "local contributions" instead of grants finance the project. Member of Parliament Arthur Creech Jones, who was His Majesty's Principal Secretary for the Colonies (October 1946 through February 1950), supposedly supported the application. But in his May 23, 1947, dispatch to High Commissioner for Palestine Sir Alan Cunningham, he partly framed the health disparities between Jews and Palestinians, reflected most dramatically in infant mortality rates, in terms of a "primitive outlook" and "cultural deficiencies": "The marked difference in the health standards of the Arab and Jewish population in Palestine at the present time is very largely due to a lack of understanding on the part of the former community of the simple principles of hygiene, and this, in turn, is due in no small extent, to a lack of education."

By November 24, 1947, British authorities cancelled all such plans given financing disputes and conditions of war in Palestine. A letter from Maurice H. Dorman, the principal assistant secretary to High Commissioner Cunningham, to Sir John Gutch, the joint head of the Middle East Department in the London Colonial Office, explained: "We have reluctantly decided to abandon the whole project. Not only is there the difficulty of financing the scheme, but it is now unlikely that there will be time in which to complete even buildings. We could not expect a scheme of this nature to function in the future unless we could leave it as a well established going concern. This is now quite impracticable."[23] The following section investigates the coexistence of austerity and racializing logic with welfarist discourse on nutrition, hunger, and illness in Palestine.

Nutrition, Hunger, and Illness

British health officials recognized that "under-nourished children" who contract a disease such as whooping cough or measles have lower resistance to tuberculosis and that hunger decreases a child's resistance to pneumonia and enterica (MacLennan 1935, 10, 17, 18). Norman MacLennan "confidently" assumed in a mid-1930s report on tuberculosis in Palestine that hunger extended beyond children: "many of the villagers are suffering from malnutrition, have a low resistance to disease generally and are incapable of sustained effort" because they are "living in conditions of poverty, aggravated in recent years by a series of partial crop failures and poor harvests" (17, 18, 9). Indeed, "During the winter of 1933–34 conditions bordering on starvation were observed in some districts and organised relief by Government was considered essential" (10, 6).[24]

MacLennan's report used a racialized imperial frame to call for government investment in the colonial health system, whose lacks included no tuberculosis service for Palestinians (100–101). Despite

[23] GOP, Department of Health, Rural Health Centers – Application for Grant under Colonial Development & Welfare Fund, October 1, 1946–March 31, 1948. File location in catalog: 00071706.81.CF.C2.19. Israel State Archives.

[24] According to the Department of Health's *Annual Report for the Year 1934*, because of drought, "from April onwards, water supplies of the majority of the villages in the hill country failed, and both villagers and Bedouins were almost starving on account of failure of crops and death of their milk producing animals." The year 1932–1933 was "a very bad year for the rural population of Palestine. The year 1933–34 was infinitely worse." So much so that the Department of Health issued "tinned milk ... in large quantities to ailing mothers and children in Arab villages throughout the country" and sometimes provided either "cooked or uncooked" "subsistence rations" to "whole villages and tribes" undergoing "special suffering." The government was even compelled to sponsor waged "relief work on roads etc." that circulated "money" into the communities.

acknowledging the structural production of hunger, poverty, and disease, MacLennan justified his call for health investments by culturally
condemning Palestinians, saying that the "masses of the population are
living in appalling ignorance of the first principles of maternal care, and
where parental inefficiency is so manifest" (101, 110). On the nutritional front, he criticized widespread consumption of olive oil, which
"contains practically no vitamins," and noted the low consumption of
meat and milk, especially among children (15). Palestinians, he wrote,
depended on "wells, cisterns or springs, usually grossly contaminated
by manure and refuse," and "Arab village sanitation is deplorable."[25]
He inveighed against the "confined life" of "the Moslem woman" in
towns (who rarely left "her frequently ill-ventilated house"), as well as
"promiscuous spitting," "communal feeding," shared coffee cups,
"unhygienic" food preparation, and lack of bathing and clothes washing (11, 12). MacLennan reminded readers that Palestine was part of
the British imperial "march of civilization" when he quoted from
a 1935 article by Lyle Cummins, "Studies in Tuberculosis among
Africans": "It may be urged that an imperial race such as our own,
owes at least this debt to our subject populations, that even if we do
introduce our infections along with our culture, we offer at the same
time the full fruits of our more advanced civilisation in the provision of
facilities for prevention and treatment" (109).

　While providing some support to the Jewish Agency for Jewish
healthcare in Palestine, it was verboten for "private" organizations
such as missionary hospitals, which primarily served Palestinians, to
receive British grants-in-aid or other government support. Palestine
Department of Health archived correspondence includes desperate
requests from missionary health institutions for water, tinned milk,
and other supplies for infants and children. In October 1932 the
mother superior (Mary Mayaud) of the Sante Famille Hôpital in
Bethlehem (a French hospital) wrote to the district commissioner in
Bethlehem and the SMO in Jerusalem asking not to be charged for
water since the institution was a "hospital, an orphanage and a home
for abandoned children." She continued, using the typical language of
European racist contempt. "It is next to impossible to contend with the

---

[25] He also wrote, however, that many Arab towns and villages had introduced
"piped water supplies in recent years," were installing borehole latrines, and
collected refuse (MacLennan 1935, 9, 8).

prevalent diseases and the absence of the most elementary cleanliness among the natives if we have to stint the water." The records do not indicate how the water matter was resolved, but given other evidence in a file focused on the French hospital in Bethlehem, it is unlikely the authorities approved the request.[26]

In late May 1935 Vena Rogers wrote a letter marked "confidential" to the Department of Health SMO in Jerusalem that she "occasionally" went to the French hospital in Bethlehem "to help them in the feeding of children, at their own request." Rogers added that she had visited "Sister Mary" because she had "left a telephone message" saying she believed two cases of British powdered milk from Cow and Gate, likely purchased by the hospital, were "impure, which was not the case, but while there I saw the [foundling] babies 41 in all, nearly all suffering from Marasmus [severe undernourishment] and Rickets, the ward was a mass of flies and the air foul, the fact that one child was dying was unpleasantly evident. Certainly there were mosquito nets but none fitted the cots, the children were in a sad and pitiable state. These children are sent from all over Palestine and belong to each faith, some are sent by Government."

These communications from the mother superior to Rogers appear to have been savvy attempts to encourage Rogers to come and see the situation in the Bethlehem hospital and advocate for resources, which worked. Given the institution's poverty and that most patients and residents were indigent, wrote Rogers, Mayaud had asked her to "enquire as to whether Government could help them with milk, no matter if only to a small extent. On an average £10 is spent monthly for milk, this sum they find it hard to find. Is it possible for some help to be given here, and one feels that a regular inspection should be made regarding the conditions of these children." In early June 1935 the SMO in Jerusalem firmly responded to Rogers: "I disagree to the supply of milk to private institutions for distribution. I suggest that deserving cases should be referred to the Infant Welfare Centre, Bethlehem, for the supply of milk." In his direct response to the mother superior at the French hospital a day later, he tersely wrote: "I have to inform you that milk cannot be supplied to Private or Voluntary institutions." Even in IWCs partially or wholly funded by the colonial government, British

---

[26] GOP, Department of Health, Public Establishments – Insp. of (HP & Institutions) – French Hospital, Bethlehem. File location in catalog: 00071706.81.D1.30.96. Israel State Archives.

Department of Health documents from the 1920s and 1930s expressed concern that free portions of milk not be given out promiscuously to Palestinians in order to avoid making them dependent – only the "destitute" who turned to these centers were eligible.

In a February 1936 memo titled "Foundlings Cared for by the French Hospital. Bethlehem," Rogers once again asked whether it was possible "for milk to the value of £1 pound to be given to them monthly or a case of tinned milk such as Cow and Gate." The foundlings, she repeated, came from "all over Palestine and are of all creeds and usually tiny babies. At present the number is 30 but it is usually 40. The hospital authorities have great difficulty in providing for these babies, they have no special grants or funds." "Help is badly needed," she insisted. "Dr. Maloof," the Bethlehem medical officer, had informed Rogers that the "majority of deaths among these foundlings are due to Marasmus." Rather than denying the request directly, the short memo from the SMO referred her to his response from June 1935 that denied the request based on a "ruling of the Director of Medical Services." Six years later, in March 1942, a new mother superior (Soeur Gravier) from the same hospital asked for "20 large tins of Cow and Gate milk having 18 babies under one year" in its "baby-home" for orphans and foundlings. The SMO responded using different reasoning. "I regret very much that I am unable to supply Cow and Gate milk as we have insufficient supply."

Consistent with long-standing Western state, imperial, and colonial practices, British medical researchers and health and welfare practitioners in Palestine frequently folded together racialized and classed value judgments about food with concerns for efficiency and economy – or how to determine the minimum nutrition necessary for the least expenditure. From the late nineteenth century, scientists in the United States focused on making "precise comparisons between the diets of different social classes and nations" (Cullather 2007, 341). The guiding logic of what I would term *nutritional governmentality* constituted food as "uniform and comparable between nations and time periods" in order to determine the least amount needed by a person to live (342, 361). Nutritional science sited in multiple countries quickly became central to the mechanics of efficient colonization and imperialism. By the late 1920s, Nick Cullather argues, health practitioners and scientists increasingly believed that "physical differences identified as eugenic might in fact be nutritional" (355). Such science nevertheless always seemed to have in mind what Chikako Takeshita's (2011) research on reproductive technologies terms "implicated bodies" – a hierarchical, usually socio-biological, under-standing of groups based on "culture," "race," gender, and class.

Kligler illustrated the "national diet" concerns of Zionist public health researchers in a 1931 study focused on the nutrition of Jews in Palestine. Kligler studied from "six months to a year" the dietary practices of 74 Jewish families of "Ashkenazic," "Sephardic," and "Yemenite" or other "Oriental" backgrounds, or 389 people (Kligler 1931, 391, 390). For comparison, his "faithful Arab assistant Ahmed abd el Ganni was responsible for gathering diet data [on 24 families] in the Arab villages," or 157 people (389, 394). Assuming that "nutrition plays an important part in the national economy" (389), Kligler's goal was to "gather and evaluate the data relating to nutrition with the ultimate purpose of developing a rational Palestinian diet" for Jews (391). Although "milk and butter are known to be ideal foods," he found that most Jewish settlers did not consume enough because they were unaffordable (391).

I encountered similar corporate and medical promotion of "pure milk" for building "energy" (Cullather 2007, 346, 359) in Palestine Department of Health folders, which included film advertisements, some marketing a product and the film and others touting educational health films only.[27] The distributor Educational Motion Picture Films in Mooresville, Indiana, for example, sent a 1933 solicitation letter and brochure for the film *Milk: The Master Builder*, which promoted drinking cow's milk and demonstrated the methods of pasteurization and cleanliness used in its production. Usually US-made, health propaganda films were mostly shown to Jewish settlers and English-speaking communities in Palestine.[28]

---

[27] Films on the dangers of flies and avoiding eye diseases proliferated. Goldwyn Mayer had an office in Alexandria, Egypt, from which a representative communicated with the Palestine Department of Health on promotions. In addition, the American University in Cairo had an extension office that circulated and promoted science and health propaganda films to the Department of Health in Palestine. GOP, Department of Health, Health & Hygiene – Health Educational Films, January 1, 1933–June 30, 1935. File location in catalog: 00071706.81.D0.97.3F. Israel State Archives.

[28] *Milk: The Master Builder* was paired with another pedagogical film on preventing the spread of disease, with each film costing eighty-five US dollars purchased alone but seventy-five US dollars each if purchased together. *Milk: The Master Builder* was produced in 1920 by the Child Health Organization in New York City. *Mother and Child: A Magazine Concerned with Their Health*, published by the American Child Hygiene Association, Baltimore, MD, June 1920, Vol. 1, No. 1 (in "recent literature on mother and child" section, 333).

W. J. Vickers, an SMO in the Palestine Department of Health, published the results of a major nutritional "economic survey" of fourteen hundred Arab and Jewish (divided between "Oriental" and "European") "family units" in urban and rural Palestine that began in April 1942 and extended over eighteen months (Vickers 1944).[29] The study was motivated by bad press ("public attention") about Palestinian starvation ("undernourishment") (4, 6). While colonial officials framed such criticisms as unwarranted, preliminary survey results led to immediate interventions for Palestinian communities in 1943, before the study was completed.

The study's detailed "nutritional and somametric analysis" of children found "Arab children were clearly far below the Jewish in general condition from every angle. This was due to the school meals in the case of the Jews in 1942, and was corrected to some extent in 1943 after local Arab subscription and subsequent Government grants had provided meals for the undernourished in urban Arab schools" (Heron quoted in Vickers 1944, 2). To emphasize, the emergency school feeding program was implemented because "interim reports" from the Vickers study showed widespread hunger among Palestinians exacerbated by a controlled low wage, wartime food-rationing schemes, and inflation. The preliminary survey results also forced the colonial government to implement "supplementary feeding" in towns and food rations for villages.[30]

In comparison to the mere 9.3 percent of Palestinian schoolchildren fed by colonial interventions in 1943, in 1942, "44% of Oriental and 29% of the European Jewish school children received school meals, but practically none of the Arab children" (28). The report noted the "considerably" higher "nutritional state of the people in general" *since 1939* in sleights of language that did not address improvement resulting from the implementation of substantial feeding interventions for Palestinians *in 1943*, before the study was completed (4).

---

[29] However, my calculation of family units surveyed (from a provided table) totals to 1,041, slightly more than half "Oriental" or "European" Jews. In comparison, 221 "Arab families" were studied in 1942 and 279 (different) "Arab families" were studied in 1943, for a total of 500 Palestinian families (Vickers 1944, 28).

[30] Officials complained in the 1946 Department of Health annual report that the village food ration system had given "advantage" to "suppressing death registrations." GOP, Department of Health, Health and Vital Statistics, Annual Reports – Annual Report for the Year 1946. File location in catalog: 00071706.81.CF.FC.FA. Israel State Archives.

In keeping with the venerable colonial tradition of disavowing structural responsibility and blaming mothers, Vickers claimed to have found "bad cooking" in "both Arab and Jewish houses in all expenditure groups," or lack of economy. He found "a saving of over 25% in a food budget in the case of a good housekeeper in families of the same social level" (28, 53). Such "ignorance" in "house-keeping and cookery" required "organised guidance to mothers ... just as we try to provide for it in regard to the feeding of infants at Infant Welfare Centres" (52, 53). The report also expressed the colonial obsession with "long-continued breast feeding indulged in by the Oriental mother." It claimed that this practice "continues to adversely affect infantile mortality and general physique" (47, 15). In one place the report defined extended nursing by Palestinian women as continuing for "up to two years" (71). Paradoxically, elsewhere the report criticized "the European Jewish mother" because she did "not indulge in sufficient breast feeding. This should not completely cease until the end of the first year of life" (63). In the same vein, Vickers wrote that in villages, "Racial custom and habit deprive the infant of sufficient sunlight, fruit juices are never given except at Infant Welfare Clinics, and prolonged breast feeding deprives the baby of many essentials" (71). The next section delineates the British regulatory approach to Palestinian traditional and licensed midwives, and analyzes occasional moments in the archives when they speak back to their colonizers.

Governing Palestinian Midwives

An early report from the Palestine Women's Council, led by the Zionist British high commissioner's wife, Lady Samuel, stated plainly that after two years of effort the council had failed to fulfill a government request to reign in indigenous women healers and midwives because "the present mentality of the women of the country was such that they do not seek professional skill" (Palestine Women's Council 1922, 5). The Women's Council recommended that the government instead establish "Infant Welfare Centres" and disseminate "simple pamphlets on the subject of health and hygiene to the people of Palestine in Arabic and Hebrew."[31]

---

[31] Ellen Fleischmann kindly provided a scan of this document from her own archival research.

A 1922 government report complained in a similar vein about the "most unsatisfactory" quality of midwifery in Palestine, noting "no less than 884 untrained, and, in most cases, grossly ignorant, practising midwives registered in the District Health Offices." This type of early framing of Palestinian midwives emerged repeatedly but with nastier valences in private correspondence. The report discussed the "urgent" problem of establishing "centres for the teaching of midwifery and infant management," but noted that "Government funds are not yet forthcoming" and colonial health officials were trying to "obtain voluntary subscriptions to effect this end."[32]

The underlying logic of the few British-sponsored IWCs eventually established was to teach Palestinian girls and mothers British health, hygiene, and mothering principles rather than serve their healthcare needs. Similarly, curriculum for girls in the limited number of government schools in Palestine stressed "the value of a good home where cleanliness, sanitation and above all care of the children are to be regarded as the main aim of every woman" (Miller 1985, 103). English colonial women working, living (usually spouses), or visiting in Palestine frequently represented Palestinian women as dirty, wretched, neglectful, and ignorant in childrearing, housekeeping, and mothering (Fleischmann 2003, 32, 33, 37; Stockdale 2007, 123, 128, 129). Similarly, British colonial authorities seeking to reduce indigenous infant mortality in African colonies from the 1920s onward focused on "educational measures" rather than "costly investments in a large expansion of health services" (Lindner 2014, 220). Nigerian and other African mothers not surprisingly demanded treatment rather than "education" and advice on their mothering skills (Von Tol 2007, 118, 120–122, 124; Lindner 2014, 220, 229).

Healthcare austerity and a racialized pedagogical orientation to health went hand in hand with energetic regulation in Palestine. The Department of Health was full of "technical supervisors." I read hundreds of communications between superintendents of midwifery matrons, SMOs, and directors of the Department of Health with Palestinian midwives, nurses, physicians, and municipal officials about drains, doors, disinfectants, vacations, pay, milk and food rations, and hours of work at clinics and IWCs. Many of these scribbled or typed notes related to policing the boundaries of registered Palestinian

---

[32] In *Palestine and Transjordan Administration Reports 1918–1948, Vol. 1*, 271.

midwives who dared to use specula to examine pregnant women, give injections to the ill, or independently set up shop. Licensing and regulation in health domains in Palestine were the responsibilities of a matrix of offices that employed hundreds of military and civilian British men (most) and women health professionals, bookkeepers, and statisticians. They moved from London, Dublin, or Edinburgh, or more typically from colony to colony, as opportunities arose. It is naive to accept at face value claims that health-related regulations and requirements were primarily or even secondarily attached to improving the health of the colonized population or the quality of care.

The 1918 Public Health Ordinance No. 1 set up a regulatory framework for midwifery in Palestine: "No person shall exercise the profession or calling of a physician, surgeon, dentist, midwife, pharmacist, or druggist, unless he has previously obtained a license to be granted by the Public Health Department." The ordinance required a midwife to pay PT 25 for issuance of said license but made no mention of training and did not use the terms "unqualified" or "dayah." Article 26 stated that exercising the profession or calling of midwife "in contravention of this Part" would lead to a fine of up to a half English pound or "imprisonment . . . not exceeding one month."

By the end of 1921 most licensed doctors (274), pharmacists (99), dentists (43), and midwives (51) in Palestine were Jewish and working for "voluntary" health organizations that served Jews.[33] In 1927, according to the annual British government report to the League of Nations, 221 "trained and licensed midwives" were working in Palestine, but colonial health officials complained they were "reluctant to settle in villages to practise among the peasantry, where their attendance is a crying need."[34] Although unremarked upon, the vast majority of these were Jewish women of European or US origin, with a few additional European women affiliated with the colonial government or missionary institutions. A limited number of them were Palestinian women of Christian background, disproportionately Arab Armenian.

In 1928 this group of "trained and licensed" midwives coexisted with "over 1,300 women" registered as "dayahs," "with very few of them being able to read or write," according to the Zionist Boston health professionals sent primarily to assess the health situation for

---

[33] In *Palestine and Transjordan Administration Reports 1918–1948, Vol. 1,* 266.
[34] In *Palestine and Transjordan Administration Reports, 1925–1928, Vol. 2,* 404.

Jews in Palestine (Rosenau and Wilinsky 1928, 637). Traditional Palestinian midwives "learned their trade predominantly through oral transmission and hands-on experience" (Young 2011, 106), with a daughter occasionally following in a mother's footsteps. Rather than reducing their number, licensing requirements restricted the domains of work for "unqualified" and "qualified" Palestinian women healers and midwives over time.

To further this end, the high commissioner of Palestine imposed the April 1929 "Ordinance to Regulate the Practice of Midwifery," also called "Midwives Ordinance, 1929."[35] The ordinance authorized who could and could not practice *midwifery*, defined as "being prepared to examine, diagnose, prescribe for, treat or deliver any woman in connexion with child-birth." It made clear that "the practise of midwifery by a licensed medical practitioner" was unrestricted. However, even licensed midwives were excluded from "gynnecology [*sic*] or any other branch of medicine" and from granting any "certificate of death or stillbirth." The ordinance even distinguished a licensed midwife from a "licensed medical practitioner," the latter physicians. To become licensed, the 1929 ordinance required candidates of "good character" to be "Palestinian citizens" or have permission to remain permanently and to have studied midwifery for at least six months at an "approved institution." In 1932 Harkness banned from midwifery training women not "of Palestinian nationality" (or "citizenship"), at least partly because lectures were given by Arabic-speaking medical officers. Nevertheless, some Jewish women tried to sign up for training in Jerusalem, Jaffa, "Quarantine & Haifa," and "Samaria & Galilee."[36] With limited exceptions, the licensing fee for midwifery was 230 mils.[37]

To assure that the government had information on birthing practitioners – and cognizant of its inability to pay for or to train women to provide such healthcare – the 1929 ordinance did allow the "practise of midwifery" by "unqualified persons practising Midwifery" whose names "have been entered in the Register," on condition they did *not*

---

[35] Its final article repealed "Part VI" of Public Health Ordinance No. 1 of 1918 as it applied "to the licensing of midwives."

[36] GOP, Department of Health, Regulations – Training of Midwives, July 1925–May 1945. File location in catalog: 00071706.81.D1.33.72. Israel State Archives.

[37] "An Ordinance to Regulate the Practice of Midwifery." *Official Gazette of the Government of Palestine*, April 1, 1929, 260–264. http://sesame .library.yale.edu/fedoragsearch/ameelreader?pid=agaz:87247&size=1.0

practice in "prescribed" towns without the director of the Department
of Health's explicit permission. A 1929 Colonial Office report to the
League of Nations explained that based on the ordinance, "27
Municipal and Local Council areas" are "prescribed, and henceforth
only fully trained or qualified midwives may apply for licences to
practise therein."[38] Registered "unqualified" persons practicing midwifery paid 250 mils for a permit with free annual renewals, but were
not allowed to use the term "midwife" to describe themselves and were
not permitted to be registered if a medical officer deemed "sufficient
numbers of persons registered" in an area. They were only allowed to
call themselves "Registered dayah," pinpointing the discursive legal
point when one of the Arabic terms for midwife, *daya*, signifies
unqualified, Arab, and backward. The 1929 Colonial Office report
made clear that the ordinance was enacted to give "powers of inspection and control to officers of the Department of Health."[39] Indeed,
item 17 of the ordinance gave an "officer of the Department of Health
authorized for the purpose" the right to "enter at any reasonable hour
upon the premises" of a licensed midwife *or* registered "unqualified
dayah" "for the purpose of inspection and supervision." This system
presumably required keeping track of all midwives, Jewish and
Palestinian, which was impossible.[40]

Implementation and enforcement of the 1929 ordinance, largely the
bailiwick of women "Superintendents of Midwifery and British Nursing
Sisters," remained difficult and frustrating for British authorities
(Brownson 2000, 73n150, 76, 78n164; Fleischmann 2003, 54–55).
Through 1935, there were four district-level superintendents of midwif-
ery (also called infant welfare supervisors), based in Jerusalem, Haifa,
Jaffa, and Nablus, each a British civilian nurse-midwife such as Vena

[38] In *Palestine and Transjordan Administration Reports 1918–1948, Vol. 3*, 365.
[39] In *Palestine and Transjordan Administration Reports 1918–1948, Vol. 3*, 85.
[40] In 1937 licensed midwives were required to notify the Department of Health of
any change in address at risk of losing their license by a "rule 2," which modified
the 1929 Midwives Ordinance. Multiple orders from Director of Medical
Services J. MacQueen in the 1940s listed the names of midwives whose address
was "unknown for over two years" to be advertised in the *Palestine Gazette*.
While officials recognized that most had likely "died or left the country or ceased
to practice," those practicing were required to provide a written statement of
a new address within ninety days. The overwhelming majority of names on the
lists were Jewish. Midwives Ordinance – Cancellation of Midwives Licences
under Section 7 of Midwives Ordinance, 1940–1945. File location in catalog:
00071706.81.CF.FD.04. Israel State Archives.

Rogers, who worked for the Department of Health. Superintendents were responsible to "supervise and organize Government Infant Welfare and ante-natal work" as well as "assist and supervise the work of practicing midwives and dayas in the towns and villages of their respective districts." In 1936 a superintendent of midwifery was appointed for the Gaza District.[41] In 1946 a sixth superintendent of midwifery was appointed for the "newly-formed Galilee District."[42]

Scholarship by Ellen Fleischmann and Elizabeth Brownson, as well as my analysis of primary sources, indicates that "unqualified" *dayat*, whether in "prescribed" areas or not, worked around restrictions, including by having a "father [of a newborn] or village leader" inform the Department of Health of a birth and "collect the birth certificate" (Fleischmann 2003, 55; Brownson 2000, 77–80, 80n169). These "unqualified" women, after all, served the large majority of Palestinian women, infants, and children. While British regulation was certainly a mechanism of control over traditional healers and midwives (Brownson 2017, 27–28), Palestinian healthcare workers had substantial leeway because providing healthcare to Palestinians was never a colonial priority.

A 1934 article published in a nursing journal by Rogers illustrates both the high social status of Palestinian women expert at delivering babies and negative colonial judgment toward them. Rogers writes that the *daya* was powerful in Palestine, "her word was law," and her "equipment was of the simplest, often consisting merely of the famous chair, on which the patient sat for her delivery. Some midwives carried a pair of shears, a ball of string for ligatures, and a basin of filthy oil for lubricating" (see Figure 2.1). Rogers describes birthing rooms full of women and children honored to be invited, noting: "only two years ago a woman complained of our cleanliness and quietness, saying she was not used to it" (Rogers 1934, 103).

Hilma Granqvist, a Finnish anthropologist who lived in Palestine twice between 1925 and 1931 for a total of about three years, studied birth, childhood, and death in the Bethlehem village of Artas.[43] She

---

[41] In *Palestine and Transjordan Administration Reports 1936, Vol. 6*, 199.
[42] GOP, Department of Health, Health and Vital Statistics, Annual Reports – Annual Report for the Year 1946. File location in catalog: 00071706.81.CF.FC. FA. Israel State Archives.
[43] Granqvist returned to Jerusalem for four months in 1959, reconnecting with Bertha Spafford Vester of the American Colony and her Arabic teacher at "the

Figure 2.1 Image of a Palestinian traditional midwife in a courtyard preparing for a home birth with her equipment, circa 1934. Extracted by author from "Midwifery Work in Palestine" (Rogers 1934)

describes with less judgment the great honor accorded Palestinian midwives, who had to be paid for their work, otherwise a person was "indebted to them for all eternity" (Granqvist 1947, 103). Invited women surrounded a woman in labor in her home, replacing each other as needed, although they could not be menstruating and must have bathed if they had had sex in order to protect the woman and baby from the many dangers perceived to abound from the spirit world. In cities, midwives brought with them a "birth chair" that had been forbidden "since the English came into the country." British nurse-midwives instead expected women in labor to lie down (58, 62). Rogers's account and my interviews with elderly women who gave birth in the 1940s indicate that many Palestinian *dayat* continued to use such a chair. Women also described perching over large rocks in courtyards and fields during labor.

British-licensed nurse-midwives represented the minority of women delivering Palestinian babies throughout the Mandate period and were not evenly distributed throughout the country. According to annual Department of Health and British government reports to the League of Nations, the number of licensed midwives increased from 221 in 1927 to

Newman School of Mission in Jerusalem." Zionists had expelled her teacher and his wife from their house in Jerusalem. She reports she had last been in Palestine in 1931 (Granqvist 1965, 1).

332 by the end of 1929. By the middle of 1930, when the ordinance was fully in effect, they numbered 211.[44] My analysis of the names of these licensed midwives, which were published in a July 1930 register, indicates that more than 80 percent were Jewish and a few were English; the remainder were predominantly Christian-origin Armenian and Arab Palestinian women.[45] By the end of 1931 the number of licensed midwives was 355, of whom 205 were denoted as "Jews" and the remainder as "Others." Among the 1,185 "Unqualified Midwives" enumerated through 1931, 10 were categorized as "Jews" and the remainder as "Others," that is, Arab or Armenian Palestinians.[46] By the end of 1935, according to the annual Department of Health report, 445 midwives were licensed to work in Palestine. By the end of 1938, according to the annual Department of Health report, the total was 532 licensed midwives. In 1946 there were 504 licensed midwives in Palestine, of whom 236 were categorized as Christian, 79 as Muslim, and 189 as Jewish.[47] More Muslim women's names appeared on published British lists of licensed midwives in the late 1930s and 1940s in comparison to earlier, although Jewish women's names comprised well over half of the total until the mid-1940s. When I tabulated and organized by location and institutional affiliation the approximately 257 *total* Palestinian (including Armenian) licensed midwife names on the 1940 and 1946 Palestine Department of Health lists of medical professionals, the largest number worked in Jerusalem or its villages (68 women) and the second largest worked in Haifa or its villages (47 women).

Participants in a six-month government-sponsored midwifery training course were required to pay for it and speak, read, and write Arabic or English. According to a 1932 handout, they were also required to "supply themselves with six white calico overalls with short sleeves and 4 kerchief caps. Shoes – black in winter and white in summer – with rubber heels must be worn." In 1935, an Armenian Palestinian (who

---

[44] In *Palestine and Transjordan Administration Reports 1918–1948, Vol. 3*, 369.
[45] GOP, *List of Doctors, Pharmacists, Dentists and Midwives Who Have Been Licensed in Accordance with the Various Ordinances Regulating Their Professions* (1930).
[46] In *Palestine and Transjordan Administration Reports 1918–1948, Vol. 3*, 668.
[47] The government had reported 216 licensed Jewish midwives working at the end of 1945 – the number had dropped by 27 people a year later. GOP, Department of Health, Health and Vital Statistics, Annual Reports – Annual Report for the Year 1946. File location in catalog: 00071706.81.CF.FC.FA. Israel State Archives.

signed in English) and three Arab Palestinian (who signed in Arabic) midwifery students sent an English-language letter asking for a partial refund of the ration (boarding and laundry) fees they had paid to the government hospital in Jerusalem after the price had been reduced by the director of health.[48]

Government midwifery training largely consisted of Arabic lectures by Palestinian male physicians and English lectures by British matrons.[49] The lectures in Jerusalem relied on a biomedical English-language curriculum, including the book *A Short Practice of Midwifery for Nurses*, originally published in 1901 and written by Irish-born gynecologist Henry Jellett (1872–1948), who moved to New Zealand in the 1920s.[50] The text was issued in thirteen editions over the course of the first half of the twentieth century.[51] Chapter VI, titled "Ante-Natal Care," begins by delimiting the "General Duties of the Midwife" to being "entirely responsible" for a pregnant woman only as long as her "condition" "remains normal" (Jellett and Dawson 1948, 87). Any "abnormal" condition made it incumbent on the midwife to "insist on her patient obtaining medical advice [from an obstetrician]." The text stresses that "the midwife must remember that she is not allowed to make vaginal examinations during pregnancy" (88). While antenatal care was central to "lessening the dangers of childbirth," it "must be supervised by a medical practitioner whenever possible" (89). Notably, the curriculum lectures and midwifery text did not address contraception or abortion methods or care.

Licensed midwives in Palestine remained on a tight leash by colonial policy, irrespective of their talents, experiences, and who paid them. British nurse matrons long complained of Palestinian midwives who "appear to have the idea that they are entitled to do gynaecological

---

[48] GOP, Department of Health. Regulations – Training of Midwives, July 1925–May 1945. This file spans twenty years of documents and lists the names of many Palestinian midwives, licensed and unlicensed. File location in catalog: 00071706.81.D1.33.72. Israel State Archives.

[49] GOP, Department of Health, Regulations – Training of Midwives, July 1925–May 1945. File location in catalog: 00071706.81.D1.33.72.

[50] GOP, Department of Health, Regulations – Training of Midwives, April 1946–January 1948, 6579. File location in catalog: 00071706.81.D1.33.71. Israel State Archives. "Obituary: Henry Jellett, M.D., F.R.C.P.I." in *British Medical Journal*, June 26, 1948, 1262–1263.

[51] The fourteenth edition, revised with New Zealand gynecologist J. Bernard Dawson, was published in 1948, the year Jellett died.

work. For instance they install themselves in a sort of clinic, use specula, make vaginal examinations, give douches and insert medicated tampons." The "worst offenders are those who are not trained nurses," according to a 1935 letter to Department of Health Director Heron from Jerusalem SMO J. MacQueen.[52] A November 1934 letter from an outraged Vena Rogers raised similar concerns about Jewish nurse-midwives who, with permission from Jewish male physicians, sutured women's torn perinea, inserted tampons, and advertised their services in Jewish newspapers, "contrary to all rules and regulations." Rogers also accused such women of having "unspeakably filthy" homes where they delivered babies, judgments that cannot be taken at face value, as is the case when colonial authorities lodged them against Palestinians. British treatment of Jewish midwives, whether they worked independently or were affiliated with Zionist health institutions, nevertheless did not parallel the treatment of Palestinian women health providers.

In a 1939–1941 case discussed in the archives, British authorities suspended for one year the midwifery license of twenty-four-year-old "Bahiya Affify," a single Palestinian woman from the Jerusalem village of Wadi al-Joz whose wages supported a household that included her mother and brother, according to an August 22, 1941, self-defense letter she originally wrote in Arabic. She acquired the license on November 25, 1938, and worked independently rather than in a government hospital or clinic, a Palestinian IWC, or a Palestinian physician's private office.[53] The lists of registered licensed midwives for 1940 and 1946 render her full name as "Bahia Afifi El-Jaby." An August 19, 1941, letter from "Dr. D. Boulos" on behalf of the SMO in Jerusalem informed Midwife Bahiya of the government's plan to suspend her license "on account of your unprofessional conduct as a midwife and grossly negligent performance of your duties." The letter began with a chronological list of grievances and warnings that dated back to April 26, 1939, when Rogers informed the SMO that Bahiya was "practising Gynaecology, you use a speculum, tampons, and you call yourself a trained nurse. I was also told you give injections." The

---

[52] GOP, Department of Health, Regulations – Training of Midwives, July 1925–May 1945. File location in catalog: 00711706.81.D1.33.72. Israel State Archives.

[53] Health and Vital Statistics, Midwives Ordinance – Cancellation of Midwives Licences under Section 7 of Midwives Ordinance, 1940–1945. File location in catalog: 00071706.81.CF.FD.04. Israel State Archives.

assistant SMO warned Bahiya against these practices in May of the same year.

In November 1940 Rogers repeated to the SMO in Jerusalem the charges she had levied against Bahiya. You "openly state[d] you give injections and that you were seen by Dayah Khadijeh Asfourah at a delivery case giving an injection. You also refused to call a Doctor for a case of Eclampsia, stating it was all due to the 'evil eye.'" Midwife Bahiya received a second warning as a result of this complaint from the assistant SMO. In May 1941 Bahiya was for the third time reported to Rogers for giving "an injection to Im Daud Fedi of Wad el Joz, a woman four months pregnant and bleeding." Bahiya was also accused of "attending" a woman admitted to the Jerusalem government hospital with "Puerperal Sepsis" without notifying her own "liability to be a source of infection" or following "the rules regarding disinfection." She was warned that any additional "such offence" would lead to her "license being withdrawn." On July 17, 1941, Rogers reported Bahiya for the fourth time to the SMO for giving "an injection to Muhadieh Mussa el Imshaasha of Akabat Suwani, the woman later aborted and bled profusely," leading to the August letter transmitted by Dr. Boulos threatening her with suspension.

Bahiya was advised to submit a defense of herself before September 15, 1941. In a short letter dated August 21, 1941 (translated from Arabic) to the high commissioner, Bahiya conceded, presumably with very little choice in the matter: "I contravened the Midwives Regulations of the Government of Palestine." She asked for "pardon" and "kindly request your Excellency to permit me to take a refresher course at the Maternity and Infant Welfare Centre in the Old City Jerusalem and to return to me the licence at the end of the year." On the following day, August 22, she submitted a less concessionary detailed letter to the SMO in Jerusalem (translated into English) asking him to reconsider her situation. Since the time she acquired her certification as a midwife, she explained,

there is an old midwife over 50 years old, named Zahya El Bastiya, always urging the other midwifes to submit reports against me, this is due to the fact, that I am now a well known [*sic*] to all the inhabitants of Jerusalem, that I am well practiced better than the old midwives who are over 50 years old, such as Zahiyeh Khalil, Zafiyeh Sandowa and [Khadija] Assfoura, they are hating me too much, and always stir up the supervisor in charge of all the midwives in Jerusalem District, that I am breaking the midwife's law (Ordinance). Such as miscarrying the women or using the injections or enema to them, etc., I never did such things to any lady, but by the order of the doctors Barnaba and Dajani who trained me how to give an injection to a lady [who] was sick [and] unable to leave her house to take the injections by a nurse. Anyhow, sir, if you forbid to give injections by the order of a doctor, I will not do it again. I like to draw your kind notice that I am so poor that the Arab ladies society in Jerusalem paid the sum of £P.9. – to the Health Department when I took Midwife's course as a fee.

In a September 4, 1941, letter to the chief secretary of the government in Jerusalem, the director of medical services deemed Bahiya's claim of being the "victim of jealousy and persecution on the part of other midwives" as "hardly worthy of any consideration." I have run into this exact dismissive British phrase in other correspondence involving Rogers and the SMO of Jerusalem in relation to obstreperous Palestinian midwives. Nevertheless, Bahiya's appeal may have influenced the fact that her license was not permanently revoked as the SMO had threatened, although it was suspended for a year: "Bahia Afifi El-Jaby" remained listed as a licensed and working midwife in Jerusalem in the 1946 Government of Palestine Department of Health list.

Delimiting the treatment practices of licensed and unlicensed midwives was based on the logic that the British authorities controlled "technical" aspects of healthcare and locals were responsible for "administrative" dimensions, irrespective of how much or how little the colonial government materially contributed. Colonial authorities assured that unlicensed Palestinian midwives would remain numerous given the limited and expensive nature of government-sponsored healthcare. Despite colonial restrictions, Palestinian nurses, midwives, and healers worked and collected fees independently of government-sponsored clinics, since officials complained to each other about these practices. Indexing how often Palestinian women healthcare providers violated the rules, they were frequently warned of the limits, as in a June 10, 1933 circular (No. 884) from SMO J. W. Harness titled the "Functions of Infant Welfare Centres." The notice reminded Palestinian midwives to "confine themselves to incidental treatment of simple ailments." Only the (Palestinian) medical officer may "see" and "treat" "_any_ sick children brought to him" (underlining in document). He insisted that IWC nurses were only allowed to educate mothers and maintain the health of children until they got to school, when they would "normally come under the supervision of a school medical service." Adding insult to injury, the circular instructed licensed midwives that their "supervision" of children was designed "to prevent ailments and defects in early years which are likely to retard development and which are in a large degree attributable to an insufficient knowledge of simple rules of health on the part of the mothers."[54]

Harkness must have recognized the speciousness of the claim that "children" eventually came under the care of "a school medical service" since most Palestinian children lived in villages and did not have access to government schools. In 1934, 63 such schools were operating in Palestinian towns, with about 15,000 girls and boys (almost even) attending, and 257 were operating in villages, serving 15,281 boys and 852 girls, according to the annual Department of Health report. A year later, 10,044 boys and 7,123 girls were enrolled in 67 government town schools, and 17,693 boys and 1,145 girls were enrolled in 283 government village schools, according to the 1935 Department of Health annual report. The estimated population of all residents of Mandate Palestine at the time was a little over 1 million people. Without breaking out Jewish children (who largely attended Jewish schools) from the total of about 36,000 children in government schools, if 50 percent of the total population was composed of Palestinian children 5–17 years of age, only 7.2 percent of them would have had access to annual school medical exams.[55]

---

[54] GOP, Department of Health, Infant Welfare – Regulations. File location in the catalog: 00071706.81.D1.32.B2. Israel State Archives.

[55] Moreover, "Arab local educational societies" paid for the education of Palestinian schoolchildren in "government schools," and "village local authorities" paid most of the costs for construction of school buildings (Canaan 1946, 4). The *Department of Health Report for the Year 1946* lists 518 "government schools" serving 75,371 predominantly Arab Palestinian children, although the government reported it could not "maintain a thorough inspection of all pupils on pre-war lines, on account of the low ratio of medical officers to student population." In comparison with 1935, an additional 168 schools were established for Palestinian children, a 48 percent increase, serving 39,238 more Palestinian children, a 108.5 percent increase. According to the same report, the "Jewish school medical service, which receives an annual grant from the Government, provided for the needs of 548 schools with a student population of 44,248." GOP, Department of Health, Health and Vital Statistics, Annual Reports – Annual Report for the Year 1946. File location in catalog: 00071706.81.CF.FC.FA. Israel State Archives.

The conflicts with and about nurse-midwives presented in the available Department of Health documents invite a few observations. First, we see multilayered but porous surveillance of Palestinian midwives and healers as well as a gendered and racialized colonial decision-making structure. Rogers, a never-married British nurse matron, was subordinate to higher-level colonial officials in Palestine, all male, who left to her and the limited number of Palestinian male physicians employed by the government the dirty business of "fieldwork" with women and children. But she was high in relation to Palestinian midwives, whether licensed or unlicensed, because the colonial system required they recognize her as their teacher, surveyor, and gatekeeper.

Second, while we cannot know the full situations or experiences of each patient referenced, any British rendering of the story will be self-serving and ultimately distorted by a colonial lens structured by their racial and gendered assumptions and priorities.

Third and related, the triggering event in the Bahiya case illustrates one of the issues that made Rogers and other British health officials apoplectic: she violated colonial racial and gendered boundaries of scientific knowing and health practice. Under no circumstances was she to represent herself as a "nurse." Bahiya admitted to giving injections with the permission of two Palestinian physicians and was accused of using a speculum and tampons on women, likely by competing midwives who recognized well the colonial red lines that would force a response. The inside of women's bodies, however, was the "territory," to use Takeshita's (2011) evocative phrasing with respect to the global development of the IUD, of male gynecologists who wanted to know better and control access to this inner terrain. Injections, specula, enemas, and examining hands were prized expert tools of bodily penetration allowed only to European and non-European men physicians and to a lesser degree British nurses in Palestine. David Arnold argues it is difficult to understate the centrality of "the body as a site of colonizing power" despite colonial medicine's inability to erase multiple "readings" of the somatic in indigenous epistemologies and cosmologies (Arnold 1993, 7, 10). The corollary is that Western medicine "cannot be regarded as merely a matter of scientific interest" or "abstracted from the broader character of the colonial order." Rather, it was "intimately bound up with the nature and aspirations of the colonial state itself" (8–9). "Modern medicine" seeks "monopolistic rights over the body" through professionalization and "exclusion of 'folk' practitioners" (9). In light of the these observations, the differences between licensed Alice or Bahiya and unlicensed traditional midwives were likely not dramatic in the eyes of colonial officials, who considered all of them inferior subjects, although Bahiya was literate in Arabic and Alice in Arabic and English.

This brings me to the fourth observation: We should not be surprised that licensed or unlicensed Palestinian women healthcare providers competed with each other, motivated first and foremost by a desire to sustain an independent livelihood.

~~~~~~~~~~~

For all their finger wagging and stated concerns with the health of women and children, British colonial authorities determined early on that healthcare for Palestinians was not a worthy investment. They occasionally took note of poverty and even "starvation" of the "Arab fallah," to use language from the annual health report for 1933, but funding or policy changes rarely followed. More often than not, evaluations of hunger and disease were filtered through a racialized and gendered logic of cultural and civilizational backwardness. The burden of remaining alive and healthy was almost entirely on the colonized. Colonial priorities, rationalized by the repetitively brutal language of "economies" and "efficiencies," were devastating in their health outcomes when combined with lack of capital and substantive restrictions on Palestinian political agency. The fact that austerity decisions were channeled through multiple layers of colonial bureaucracy that distanced decision makers from implementers does not lessen the significance of the underlying calculus or its consequences. The next chapter examines racial and demographic anxieties in colonial Palestine, placing them within a longer eugenicist genealogy and comparative colonial frame.

3 | "Children Are the Treasure and Property of the Nation"
Demography, Eugenics, and Mothercraft

This chapter examines British and Zionist demographic anxieties and their eugenicist inflections in Mandate Palestine, which came from different places and had global precursors and diffractions. British authorities frequently expressed concern with higher Palestinian birth-rates, which they racialized from early in the occupation. These concerns were balanced by a rarely expressed calculus that recognized that limited investment in Palestinian welfare and in infant, child, and maternal healthcare produced higher mortality rates. The second section explores Jewish and British eugenicist discourse that predates and overlaps with the Mandate period and its iterations among Zionist health workers as they built a Jewish settler colony in Palestine. The final section discusses transnational maternalist and breastfeeding campaigns, which were motivated by classed and racialized eugenicist concerns to reduce infant mortality and increase fertility among "white" better-off married women, and the conditions of the appearance of these discourses in Zionist archival records in Mandate Palestine.[1]

By way of introducing the argument that racialized and classed evaluations of human value were central to the decision-making of British colonial authorities, I examine two antityphoid serum trials conducted in Palestine in the mid-1930s under the auspices of the Lister Institute in England. According to the first journal article published about the Palestine study (Felix 1935) and many publications that followed, the 1934 human trial of antityphoid sera confirmed the

---

[1] "White" is a historically constructed sign and category the content/meaning of which has never been stable. This chapter benefited from being workshopped at the Death and Afterlives in the Middle East conference at the Watson Institute of Brown University in late September 2019. I am grateful to organizer Aslı Zengin for inviting me, Osman Balkan for his close engagement with the chapter, and other workshop participants for their suggestions and comments.

existence of a Vi (virulence) antigen that produced protective anti-bodies against *B. typhosus* in humans.[2] I analyze published medical scholarship and an electronic file of British correspondence about the trials in the Israel State Archives in Jerusalem.[3]

The first therapeutic trial in Palestine was conducted on patients in hospitals in Jerusalem, Jaffa, and Tel Aviv over six weeks in October and November 1934. Dr. Rudolph Reitler, a research pathologist and German settler, was the medical officer in charge of the government hospital in Jaffa and the serum trial. Palestinian Dr. N. Hamzeh was the medical officer responsible for the trial in the Jerusalem government hospital. Jewish settlers Drs. M. Levontin and W. N. Wolff were responsible for the trial in Hadassah's Tel Aviv Municipal Hospital. Palestinian Dr. N. T. (Tawfik) Canaan was responsible for the trial at the German Deaconness Hospital in Jerusalem. Also involved in analysis was Dr. K. S. Krikorian, an Armenian Palestinian bacteriologist who worked in the central laboratories of the Government of Palestine Department of Health.

Typhoid fever, acquired by consuming food or liquid contaminated with the feces of carriers of salmonella bacteria, was a significant septicemic disease in Mandate Palestine, although the most prevalent diseases and sources of death for Palestinians were pneumonia, tuberculosis, measles, diarrhea, and malaria. In addition to high fever, typhoid symptoms include abdominal pain, skin lesions, and mental disturbances. Typhoid infection rates are higher in settings lacking safe "drinking water, food handling, and sewage disposable and isolation," and without healthcare systems that identify and treat infected patients with antibiotics (Robbins and Robbins 1984, 436). While many anti-typhoid vaccines were developed over the twentieth century, even

---

[2] Lister scientists tested an initial serum produced from the blood of immunized rabbits by inoculating mice in laboratory conditions (Felix 1935; Felix and Pitt 1934). They concluded that a serum containing both Vi and O antibodies "will prove to be of value in the treatment of typhoid patients" (Felix and Pitt 1934, 190). They then produced two versions of antityphoid serum from two immunized horses and one control serum from a normal horse for use in the Palestine trial (Felix 1935; Felix and Pitt 1934).

[3] I did not track additional information that is likely available in non-British archives or in London. GOP, Department of Health, Communicable and Other Diseases – Treatment of Typhoid by Anti-Typhoid Serum – Dr. Felix of the Lister Institute, August 1934–May 1938. File location in catalog: 00071706.81. D1.33.57. Israel State Archives.

today they are only 50–80 percent effective, and any protection they offer is temporally limited (436).[4]

In 1934, 2,002 cases of typhoid fever and 185 deaths from the disease were reported to the British colonial government in Palestine, almost double the number of cases in 1933 (1,055/107), with a 4 percent fatality rate for the 998 cases among Jews and an 11 percent fatality rate for the 1,004 cases among Palestinians.[5] Thus typhoid fever was almost three times as likely to kill Palestinian Arabs as Jews in 1934, with those living in the Haifa District suffering the highest number of cases and those in the Nablus District experiencing the highest proportional death rate.[6] In Palestine typhoid fever patients ranged from children to adults.[7]

Archival correspondence among high-level officials in London and Jerusalem between August 1934 and January 1935 about the antityphoid trial largely focused on permissions, expenses, access to lab facilities, and who was responsible to pay for what aspects of a research trip to Palestine by renowned bacteriologist Dr. Arthur Felix of the Lister Institute in England.[8] Discussions involved the high

[4] I learned about typhoid from meeting with Herman Staats, a professor of pathology at Duke University, who patiently answered my questions about the disease, contexts of prevalence, and other medical matters. I read the research of Marc Jeuland at Duke on the economics of investing in infrastructure versus typhoid vaccines in poor countries. I thank Provost Sally Kornbluth for connecting me with scholarship by Staats and Jeuland.

[5] GOP, Department of Health, *Annual Report for the Year 1934*, 27, 28. These numbers exclude village cases because the Department of Health required cause of death to be determined by a town- or city-based medical officer.

[6] "Case and Death Incidence of Infectious Diseases by Location for the Year 1934." GOP, Department of Health, *Annual Report for the Year 1934*.

[7] In contrast to other "encapsulated" bacterial infections, typhoid sufferers are infrequently children younger than two years of age. In most countries "the peak incidence" occurs "between the ages of four and 12 years" for reasons "that remain obscure" (Robbins and Robbins 1984, 442).

[8] The Lister Institute funded serum development (trial and control), shipping and air costs of lab material, and Felix's regular salary, whereas the Colonial Office in London funded his trip to and from Palestine (he came with five "family members"). The Government of Palestine provided facilities and funded his transportation between Jaffa and Jerusalem and his accommodations in Jerusalem (thirty-seven pounds haggled over in many memos). Felix stayed with extended family when in Tel Aviv. GOP, Department of Health, Communicable and Other Diseases – Treatment of Typhoid by Anti-Typhoid Serum – Dr. Felix of the Lister Institute, August 1934–May 1938. File location in catalog: 00071706.81.D1.33.57. Israel State Archives.

commissioner for Palestine and Trans-Jordan, the acting chief secretary of the Government of Palestine, the secretary of state in London, the chief medical officer in the Colonial Office in London, the director of the Department of Health in Palestine, the acting deputy director of medical services in Palestine, the director of the Lister Institute, and Felix.[9] A confidential memo dated September 26, 1934, from Acting Director of Medical Services J. W. Harkness in Jerusalem asked the chief secretary of the government offices (also in Jerusalem), Sir John Stuart Macpherson, to cover Felix's local expenses. Harkness stressed the value of testing an antityphoid serum on humans and the possibility of "considerable saving in hospital accommodation and cost of treatment of typhoid fever by reducing the duration of incapacity caused by the disease. This is of very great importance in Palestine where Government hospital accommodation is taxed to its utmost during the [summer and fall] months when the disease is most prevalent."

The clinical trial, led by Felix, was run on sixty typhoid patients in four hospitals: the Jaffa Municipal Hospital (thirty-four patients),[10] the Jerusalem government hospital (seven patients), the German Deaconness Hospital in Jerusalem (three patients), and the Hadassah Municipal Hospital in Tel Aviv (sixteen patients). While I found no information on

---

[9] Arthur Felix (1887–1956) was born in Silesia, Galicia (later Poland), of Orthodox Jewish parents and died in London. He studied chemistry at the University of Vienna, where he became interested in Zionism, and later trained in mycology. The Austrian Army commissioned him during World War I to serve in laboratories on multiple fronts, working to develop a typhus fever serum (not typhoid) under Austrian bacteriologist Edmund Weil. When the war ended in 1918 they continued to work on serums for paratyphoid and typhus fevers in Prague. In 1920 Felix moved to Palestine, where he became the chief bacteriologist, supervising Hadassah's four laboratories. He married Leah Gluckman of Tel Aviv in 1923. He left Palestine with his family in 1927 to work at the Lister Institute in England, although he frequently returned to Palestine for visits. Felix shifted to typhoid research in earnest in the early 1930s (Wilson 1957).

[10] The Jaffa Municipal Hospital was established by city officials in this busy Arab port town under Ottoman rule in approximately 1908, and was "financed (at least partly) through an increase on the fees paid by travelers alighting at Jaffa port" (personal email correspondence with Philippe Bourmaud, July 11, 2019). In 1934 three-quarters of the population of Jaffa – which attracted hundreds of (male) Palestinian laborers from villages who were compelled to live in "insanitary conditions" – did not have a "public water supply and utilize[d] easily contaminated wells, and there is no sewerage except in some of the Commercial Quarters." GOP, Department of Health, *Annual Report for the Year 1934.*

the ethnic or religious backgrounds of the typhoid trial patients at the Jaffa and Jerusalem government hospitals, Jews comprised only 6.67 percent of the 2,280 non-British patients who used the Jerusalem government hospital and 17.2 percent of the 1,928 non-British patients who used the Jaffa Municipal Hospital in 1934. The overwhelming majority of patients were Palestinians.[11] Given the racial geography of healthcare in Mandate Palestine, we can assume with some confidence that all three trial patients at the German Deaconess Hospital were Palestinian and all sixteen trial patients at the Hadassah Hospital were Jewish.

At the government hospitals twenty-eight of the forty-one patients (68 percent) were in the trial group (receiving serum), whereas twelve of the sixteen patients (75 percent) at the Hadassah Hospital and all three patients (100 percent) at the German Deaconness Hospital were in the trial group.[12] Six of the forty-three patients in all four hospitals who received the antityphoid serum and three who received the control serum were children younger than fourteen years of age, with doses attenuated by age (Felix 1935, 800).

The two antityphoid sera seemed to work for some patients, although Felix concentrated them as results were observed during the trial. Five people in the treated group died, all in the "extremely severe" category of twelve patients (801). The published article did not share the hospital distribution of the patients who died or how many (if any) deaths occurred among patients in the control group. The scientific community deemed the results of the Palestine antityphoid trial "promising but inconclusive"; Felix admitted the serum was less likely to work on "extremely severe" cases (Wilson 1957, 288; Felix 1935, 801).

---

[11] "Table of Patients in Government, Municipal and Voluntary Hospitals – 1934," 57. GOP, Department of Health, *Annual Report for the Year 1934*.

[12] While the control placebo serum was discontinued when patient health clearly worsened, control patients did not receive the experimental sera (Felix 1935, 800). A trial of the Lister sera in a Dublin hospital during the same period offers a comparison of trial and control group assignment and treatment. In September 1934 Dr. C. J. McSweeney, the medical superintendent of the Cork Street Hospital in Dublin, began independently testing the Lister sera on typhoid patients, systematically assigning every other case of eight patients to the trial or control group. After increasing the dosage, medical staff gave the trial serum to all subsequent severe cases when they saw "the beneficial effects" (McSweeney 1935). McSweeney continued using fifteen different batches of sera on sixty-one total "bacteriologically confirmed" typhoid cases in the Dublin hospital with "good" or "excellent" results on forty-four patients and "no effect" on ten patients who died (McSweeney 1937).

A published study based on analysis of typhoid patient blood sera from the 1934 trial in colonial laboratories in Palestine concluded that any future antityphoid serum or vaccine must have the Vi antigen to be effective and the treatment would not work with patients suffering from paratyphoid fevers A or B (Felix, Krikorian, and Reitler 1935, 424). The significance and results of the 1934 Palestine trial were discussed in optimistic terms in medical journal publications and a few positive news stories were published in Britain in 1935. Nevertheless, the Department of Health *Annual Report for the Year 1934* makes no mention of the experimental trial, despite including a section on typhoid fever and typhoid in disease tables and touting "measures" taken to ameliorate, for example, malaria and starvation.

I found no academic publication discussing an additional trial of two revised Lister antityphoid sera conducted at the Jaffa Municipal Hospital in 1935, a year later. In London Felix wrote to colonial officials repeatedly and unsuccessfully from January through May 1935 seeking support and permission to return to Palestine to oversee such a trial. A handwritten 1935 memo (whose month is indecipherable) to the director of medical services initialed by multiple colonial health officials in Palestine points to one possible reason they refused to pay for a second trip: they believed the 1934 trial results were exaggerated. Referring to an attached newspaper column from London titled "New Serum to Fight Typhoid: Striking Results," the memo's author stated: "Seems an optimistic view is taken regarding the efficacy of sero-therapy in the treatment of the Enterica. I wonder!"

The records at my disposal do not directly say that Felix did not come to Palestine to supervise the second trial because the colonial government refused permission or to pay for the trip. They do show that Felix wrote to "Sir Thomas" (Ambrose Thomas Stanton) in the London Colonial Office on July 3, 1935, this time seeking permission to send two versions of antityphoid sera "free of charge" from the Lister Institute for a second trial at the Jaffa Municipal Hospital, which he said would be supervised by Reitler. When Heron agreed, Felix sent a detailed handwritten letter to Reitler on August 9 instructing him on methodology: he wanted the two versions of sera tested on twenty each of "preferably adult patients only" and "only on selected severe cases." Heron strongly suggested to Reitler that a control group be included, but Reitler wrote he did not think they would have enough severe typhoid cases at the hospital to conduct the experiment on two let alone three groups.

Reitler agreed to conduct the trial for Felix, but stated in advance that "he will not be in a position to see if the serum treatment is of advantage or not." Reitler's second trial at the Jaffa hospital, built slowly with typhoid patients over September and October, ultimately included twenty-four cases "over 15 years old," twelve for each anti-typhoid serum. Reitler deemed the results "good" for both sera but did not believe a general conclusion of efficacy could be made given the small number of cases. Three of the twenty-four patients in the trial died. Heron was less generous in his assessment. He considered the trial methodologically weak ("inadequate and indeed inacceptable"), with "inadmissible" conclusions made by Reitler, which is probably why no results were published.

A few issues stand out from analysis of this case. First, as shown with the smallpox story in a Hebron village in the early 1920s, Mandate Palestine was an important research laboratory used to advance colonial and settler-colonial science and the professional and economic statuses of individual scientists. Helen Tilley finds that interwar British colonial Africa was similarly used as a "medical laboratory." The Colonial Office encouraged "fieldwork" in colonial settings for biomedical experiments and interventions, as was done in "virtually every [colonial] territory" (Tilley 2011, 171, 173). Such research was viewed as necessary for "development" and assuring that colonial subjects were healthy enough to be "industrious" (172, 169). Illustrating how the colonized served as guinea pigs for advancing the health of "Man," an August 29, 1935, letter from a Palestine Department of Health official to Felix matter-of-factly shared the disappointing results of a separate government typhoid study on Palestinians:

We have now finished our vaccination of the Arab College with vaccines prepared from typhoid bacilli containing much Vi antigen. Our analysis of the resultant sera [blood whey] has been rather inconclusive so we are sending on 40 to you for disposal. If you are interested you can analyse them, if not you can return them to us or have them destroyed.

Notably the 1934 Palestine findings and the studies that followed allowed the Lister Institute, governments, and international entities to develop multiple T.A.B.C. vaccines against typhoid and paratyphoid fevers beginning in 1938 and to use them in wartime settings.[13]

Second, although the material I analyzed did not indicate that the 1934 and 1935 antityphoid serum trials were diabolical in intent, we can ask why they were conducted in government hospitals at all given that Palestine was full of Zionist medical institutions (hospitals and laboratories) sponsored by Hadassah, Kopat Holim, and other organizations. Indeed, Felix was supervisor of all four Hadassah laboratories in Palestine before he left for England in 1927, and he had the professional relationships to acquire such access. Moreover, Jewish residents of Palestine were more likely to be infected with typhoid fever, more likely to seek hospital care, and more likely to have bed space available to them. The Lister Institute would have required colonial government approval whether the institutions chosen for the trial were Zionist, missionary, or British run.

Third, a coda to the typhoid story illuminates the persistent capitalist and austerity angles with respect to science and medicine in colonized Palestine. The Lister typhoid treatment serum was apparently greatly improved by 1938 and the institute advertised it widely for sale, including to colonial markets. Referring to a May 1938 letter from Felix to the chief secretary in Jerusalem on the "3rd instance" (third time) that expressed surprise at the Department of Health's "apparent neglect to take advantage of what is now proved to be of positive value in the treatment of typhoid fever," Macpherson wrote to another government official that the "Department's attitude ... is one necessarily governed by financial considerations," given the serum's "almost prohibitive cost – nearly £3 per patient treated – and there seems no possibility of this cost being appreciably lowered in view of the difficulty of production and the estimation of its Vi and O antibodies." In a letter to Felix, Macpherson similarly explained the colonial calculus: it must be "borne in mind that the numbers of enteric cases in Palestine are so considerable. Thus in 1934 there were 2002 cases with 185 deaths, in 1935 there were 2060 with 204 deaths, in 1936 [there were] 1148 cases with 143 deaths and in 1937 there were 2049 cases with 194 deaths." Treating these cases at three pounds per head would be "wholly out of

---

[13] Effective inoculation continued to face the problem of preserving both the O and Vi antigen components and thus was not necessarily protective against typhoid (Climie 1942; Felix 1951; Williams 1941).

the question," he continued. The government in Palestine conceded to purchase serum for ten typhoid fever cases in 1939, at a cost of thirty pounds in total, for use in what officials described as "special" or "selected" cases.

Demographics of Life and Death

As examined in some depth in the introduction, racial-demographic anxieties were prevalent and intensified by the turn of the century among white Western imperial powers and white British dominions. Moreover, white supremacist geopolitics was a contentious topic at the 1919 Versailles Peace Conference that determined the postwar fate of Palestine and other territories. In *A Problem of Great Importance* (2013), Karl Ittmann argues that demography, also known as population science, became even more important to British colonial policy in the interwar years "as concerns mounted about the stability of imperial rule." While colonized populations grew in some parts of the world, there was a "steep fall in British and white settler birth rates, which appeared to threaten the racial and ethnic balance of power in the empire" (1–2).

Particularly problematic were the "efforts of the colonial state to map race and ethnicity" in this process (6), which was partly done through counting and categorization. Such "recording and analyses of populations both created and measured social phenomena – whether disparities in health, differential fertility, or the status of ethnic and religious minorities " (5). This section provides evidence of British racialized demographic anxiety regarding the higher birthrate among Palestinians, especially Muslims, in comparison to Jews, and invites us to consider healthcare austerity in Mandate Palestine in light of such concerns. It ends by examining the 1945 published report of leading demographer Frank W. Notestein on the "population problems of Palestine," which he presented before the Anglo-American Committee in 1946 (Hourani 2005, 86).

Poor recording of vital data must be kept in mind, especially for villages and pastoral communities whose members moved seasonally for water and agricultural work. Between 1923 and 1931, for example, recorded Palestinian infant mortality, which the British estimated at "one third of total reported deaths," "was much too low," according to Justin McCarthy (1990, 31–32). Department of Health officials complained until the bitter end in multiple documents of inconsistent records for births and deaths of the Palestinian population. Moreover, the colonial government recorded cause of illness or death only if it was determined by a physician and communicated to the British-appointed town medical officer. We can comfortably assume that vital numbers were most likely to be accurate for Jews given the proliferation of Zionist health and other institutions and the high use of them by Jewish people in Palestine. Zionist organizations were required to report population, health, and healthcare data to colonial offices and did so. Palestinian vital data, in contrast, were poor quality because of limited government investment.

The May 16, 1918, Public Health Ordinance No. 1, titled "Ordinance to Provide for the Registration of Births and Deaths, Vaccination, Burials, Licenses to Medical Practitioners, and Other Matters Concerning Public Health," amplified by amendments in Public Health Ordinance No. 3 of 1920 (Bentwich 1926, 45, unnumbered footnote), was among the first acts of the British military administration in Palestine. It required "every birth" in Palestine to be notified to the "Public Health Office within fifteen days" by the "father, the mother, the midwife attending the birth, the Imam," or "the Mukhtar of the village or quarter" (45). Deaths were required to be reported to the "Mukhtar or Imam" and the "Public Health Office" within forty-eight hours by "the head of the family" or "medical practitioner" who last attended the patient (45). The Ordinance made such registration "free of charge," attaching a fee of P.T.1 to the issuing of a license only, and "rewarded" each notification by a *mukhtar* with P.T.1 (46). Nevertheless, the colonial government remained vexed by "under-notification" of Palestinian deaths and births throughout the Mandate to the point of seeking in 1934 to "prosecute the parents" for notifying infant deaths whose births were not recorded in the coastal town of `Acca and likely other places.[14] The colonial government increased by a small amount the payment to *mukhtar*s for each report of a birth or death, especially infant death, but this did not resolve the problem. It never employed staff to systematically gather and maintain such records. Registration and notification of Palestinian birth and death had political valence not only for the demography-transforming nature of the Zionist

---

[14] GOP, Department of Health, Births, Deaths, Vaccinations and Inoculation – Regulations, 1932–1936. File location in catalog: 00071706.81.D7.1D.D5. Israel State Archives.

project but also because the data were used for budget and advancement metrics in reports produced for the London Treasury, London Colonial Office, the British Parliament, and the League of Nations Mandates Commission.

Only two censuses of Palestine were conducted during the entire Mandate. The 1922 British census was designed to enumerate "Palestine residents by religious group as the basis for proportional [notably sect-based] voting for a projected Legislative Council" that was never established (McCarthy 1990, 28). This hyperbolization of religious difference was a common European method of divisive governmentality in the colonies. In most Palestinian regions the British relied on local leaders to provide the census counts for Arabs. The weaknesses of the 1922 census included undercounting younger Palestinian women and children. The 1931 census of Palestine used similar methods, estimating "Bedouins" (pastoralists) and undercounting younger women and Muslims, who largely lived in rural areas (29–30). Selig Brodetsky, a British member of the World Zionist Executive and professor of mathematics at Leeds University, was an important member of the colonial committee that designed the 1931 census. He and other Zionist experts asserted themselves as equal to British government statisticians to assure census results did not disadvantage settler-colonial "political interests" by, for example, measuring Palestinian landlessness produced by Zionist land purchases in the previous decade (Sasson and Shamir 2020, 239, 240, 241, 242–243). No other census of Palestine was undertaken during the Mandate and all additional annual population counts *for Palestinians* were estimates.[15]

The British government in Palestine nevertheless produced dozens of statistical reports on population, health, mortality, disease, fertility, and morbidity based on "religion." While the Ottomans had established religious affiliation in population registers of the *sanjak* of Jerusalem beginning in 1860, they only included citizens and differentiated between different categories of Jews, Christians, and Muslims in the city, including by regional origin if they were not Jerusalemites (Sufian 2015, 118). British authorities, in contrast, created a registration system that reduced, racialized, and essentialized religious and cultural differences, which included counting Jews in annual vital records without

---

[15] A reviewer of the manuscript noted that this was "the situation throughout the empire in the interwar years. Several colonies canceled their 1931 censuses due to lack of funds or only took surveys."

differentiation. British religious categorization in Department of Health tables typically relied on an "Other" category as well. Based on religious categories enumerated in the 1922 and 1931 censuses, "Other" consolidated Druze, "Metawilehs" (Shi`a), Bahais, Samaritans, Hindus, Sikhs, and "no religion" residents.[16]

The category of religion as a technology of colonial rule confounded Zionist with non-Zionist Jews, as well as Jewish white settlers with indigenous Jews and Jews who had migrated from Yemen and elsewhere over the decades. Such categorizations articulated "Jew" as a separate national project in legal, material, and practical terms and reinforced the divide-and-conquer logic on which the colonial and settler-colonial projects were built. Combined with the apartheid structures built by Zionist institutions in Palestine during the Mandate, these technologies consolidated the Jewish/non-Jewish divide on which Zionism is premised.

When differentials in infant mortality based on religion appeared in British health and vital reports, they were sometimes explained by cultural arguments and other times understood to be caused by poverty and lack of healthcare. A rare example of explicit prose discussing the demographic "balance" produced by high birth *and* high infant mortality rates among Palestinian Muslims, and connecting mortality levels to healthcare access, appeared in the Department of Health's *Annual Report for the Year 1931*. The author, likely George Heron or J. W. P. Harkness, commented on the high incidence of Muslim infant mortality in comparison to Jewish infant mortality, attributing the difference to "the adequate chain of [Jewish] Infant Welfare Centres" and hospital "confinements" for Jewish women giving birth in comparison to the limited number of such institutions and hospital care for Palestinian infants and mothers. The author then mentioned the differential in "natural increase of population"[17] between Jews and Muslims

---

16 The highest numbers categorized as neither Muslim, Christian, or Jewish in the two censuses were Druze and Hindu. The number of people in these religious categories substantially differed depending on the Palestinian district because they were regionally concentrated. Hindus and Sikhs were notably all men (with exception of one woman listed in 1931), indicating they were British colonial subjects brought in as laborers. "Other" birth, illness, and infant mortality rates, then, largely referred to Palestinians of Druze religious affiliation (extracted from McCarthy 1990, appendix three).

17 In demography "natural increase" is the difference between annual births and deaths per thousand (Notestein and Jurkat 1945, 333). Immigration is a "non-natural" source of increase.

that year, describing the figure for Palestinians as "alarming in light of the apparent impossibility of providing outlet for the population which is already in a state of financial depression, and will soon be unable to feed itself. The high Moslem figure suggests that the fellaheen [peasants] are not yet feeling the pinch of hunger, but when this occurs the death rate is likely to go up and the birth-rate down."

In a chapter focused on infant and child mortality in British colonial Egypt, Beth Baron found similar "ambivalence among colonial officials about lowering the high infant mortality rate" twenty years earlier because they were "fearful of fueling population growth." The author of the 1910 Department of Public Health annual report explained that government efforts to address infant mortality "should be directed to avoiding any serious disturbance of the balance between the birth-rate and the death-rate." Colonial public health investments in Egypt were mainly concerned to mitigate diseases that damaged the health of military forces and their families (Baron 2020, 199–200). British colonial governments in early twentieth-century Uganda and interwar (1925–1945) Nigeria expressed concern, in contrast, about low birth and high infant mortality rates – resulting from conquest and new labor management systems – because they threatened colonial labor needs (Summers 1991; Von Tol 2007, 114, 124, 126, 127; Lindner 2014, 210, 217). Infant mortality rates remained high in British African colonies through the 1940s (Lindner 2014, 230).

In colonial Palestine British reports often commented with trepidation on the family size of the "Arab peasant household," especially the number of "children born per woman." The *General Monthly Bulletin of Current Statistics* from July 1945, which relied on a study of five villages in the Ramleh area, noted the average number of persons in such households without a married child was 5.6 because of "the high fertility of the Arab family" (Waddams 1945, table 9, 434, 438). My calculations of data in table 13 of the report show that 61.9 percent of families in the five Palestinian villages studied were composed of four to eight total members. My calculations of data in table 23 indicate that Palestinian women from four age categories ranging between thirty-three and fifty-two years old averaged 7.04 pregnancies and 4.13 surviving children (445). The report's prose amplified colonial concern with Palestinian village women's "fertility career" of more than seven children without noting the high proportion of infant and child death. A separate item noted an infant mortality rate in villages of 35 percent for women thirty-five years old or younger and 40 percent for women between thirty-five and fifty years old.

A few known elements of fertility the world over may be helpful for processing information on Palestine. Barring infertility or systemic use of prophylactics, number of pregnancies is negatively associated with age of marriage – the earlier a girl or woman marries, the more childbearing years and pregnancies she is likely to have. Palestinian girls and women married almost universally and did so at young ages in comparison to Jewish women in Palestine. Second, literacy and years of education are negatively associated with number of pregnancies for girls and woman because marriage is more likely to occur later and birth control methods are more likely to be used. Third, the preponderance of Christian Palestinians lived in towns and the preponderance of Muslim Palestinians lived in villages during the Mandate. Where one lived differently shaped cultural sensibilities, educational opportunities, and age of marriage – government and private elementary and secondary schools were much more available to town than to village Palestinian girls. In addition, cities and towns offered wider networks and easier access to information, pharmacies, and medical institutions.

A 1931 study of Jewish nutrition and diet in Palestine (Kligler 1931, 394) that for comparison purposes included six Arab Palestinian families *each* from a "Poor Village" (Vuzije), a "Well to do Village" (Kaabah), a "Well to do Bedouin camp" (Heb), and a "Poor Bedouin camp" (Krad) in northern Palestine offered me a serendipitous opportunity to examine fertility and family size. Table VI ("Composition of Families of the Bedouin Camps and Arab Villages") illustrated that *even in non-town settings*, Palestinian girls' and boys' age of marriage and Palestinian family size were shaped by level of wealth and type of residency and work. The poorest Arab villagers were the most likely to marry off their daughters (but not sons) before they reached fourteen years of age, and well-to-do Arab villagers were the least likely to do so. Well-to-do Palestinian village families were the largest, with an average 8.67 members per family unit ranging from 5 to 14. Poor villagers and well-to-do Bedouins averaged 6.17 members per family unit; family size ranged from 5 to 7 among poor villagers and from 4 to 10 among the well-to-do Bedouin families. Poor Bedouin families were the smallest, averaging 5.16 members in family units ranging from 3 to 7.

Colonial vital records and health reports provide comparative snapshots of fertility, illness, and death rates for the years 1927, 1931,

1939, and 1946, which I selected to span most of the Mandate period, recognizing that crude birthrates are a "blunt instrument," to use the words of a reviewer, without other data on age distribution and marriage rates in the different groups.

A comparative table of **birthrate** by religious category for *1927* showed the highest rate, 56.09 per thousand births, among Muslim Palestinians, 50.35 among Other Palestinians, 38.92 among Christian Palestinians, and 35.08 among Jews.[18] A comparative table for *1931* showed a birthrate of 60.29 per thousand among Muslim Palestinians, 51.70 among Other Palestinians, 38.96 among Christian Palestinians, and 32.66 among Jews.[19] Jumping ahead to *1939* and *1946* using an eight-year (1939–1946) table broken down by religion, birthrate increased for each group when comparing 1946 with 1939, proportionally the most for Jews and the least for Christians. Among Muslim Palestinians, the birthrate went from 46.4 per thousand in 1939 to 54.2 in 1946, a 16.8 increase; among Other Palestinians from 40.9 to 47, a 14.9 percent increase; among Christian Palestinians from 31.3 to 33.3, a 6.4 percent increase; and among Jews from 23 to 29.1, a 26.5 percent increase (Table 3.1).[20]

Muslim Palestinians had the highest **death rate** in *1927*, at 33.07 per thousand, Other Palestinians at 28.19, Christian Palestinians at 20.10, and Jews at 13.45 per thousand.[21] In *1931* Muslim Palestinians again had the highest death rate at 29.63 per thousand, Other Palestinians at 16.53, Christian Palestinians at 15.66, and Jews at 9.72 per thousand.[22] The death rate among Muslim Palestinians went from 17.4 per thousand in *1939* to 15.9 per thousand in *1946*, an 8.6 percent decrease; among Other Palestinians, the death rate went from 17.6 to 17, a 3.4 percent decrease; among Christian Palestinians it went from 11.5 to 9.1, a 20.87 percent decrease; and among Jews, it went from 7.6 to 6.4, a 15.78 percent decrease (Table 3.2).[23]

[18] *Palestine and Transjordan Administration Reports, Vol. 2*, 404.
[19] *Palestine and Transjordan Administration Reports, Vol. 3*, 664.
[20] GOP, Department of Health, Health and Vital Statistics, Annual Reports – Annual Report for the Year 1946. File location in catalog: 00071706.81.CF.FC. FA. Israel State Archives.
[21] *Palestine and Transjordan Administration Reports, Vol. 2*, 404.
[22] *Palestine and Transjordan Administration Reports, Vol. 3*, 664.
[23] GOP, Department of Health, Health and Vital Statistics, Annual Reports – Annual Report for the Year 1946. File location in catalog: 00071706.81.CF.FC. FA. Israel State Archives.

Table 3.1 *Palestine birthrate by religious category, 1927, 1931, 1939, 1946*

(per thousand)				
Year	Muslim	Others	Christian	Jewish
1927	56.09	50.35	38.92	35.08
1931	60.29	51.7	38.96	32.66
1939	46.4	40.9	31.3	23
1946	54.2	47	33.3	29.1

Sources: Palestine and Transjordan Administration Reports 1918–1948, Vols. 2 and 3. Courtesy of Bilad ash-Sham Library, University of Jordan. Department of Health Annual Report for the Year 1946. Courtesy of Israel State Archives.

Table 3.2 *Palestine death rate by religious category, 1927, 1931, 1939, 1946*

(per thousand)				
Year	Muslim	Others	Christian	Jewish
1927	33.07	28.19	20.10	13.45
1931	29.63	16.53	15.66	9.72
1939	17.4	17.6	11.5	7.6
1946	15.9	17	9.1	6.4

Sources: Palestine and Transjordan Administration Reports 1918–1948, Vols. 2 and 3. Courtesy of Bilad ash-Sham Library, University of Jordan. Department of Health Annual Report for the Year 1946. Courtesy of Israel State Archives.

The Muslim Palestinian **infant mortality rate** in *1927* was 216.79 (6,631 deaths), the Christian Palestinian rate was 187.22 (560 deaths), the Other Palestinian rate was 153.68 (68 deaths), and the Jewish rate was 115.79 (598 deaths) per thousand births.[24] In *1931* the infant mortality rate was 187.55 (6,877 deaths) among Muslim Palestinians,

[24] *Palestine and Transjordan Administration Reports, Vol. 2*, 404.

Table 3.3 *Palestine infant mortality rate by religious category, 1927, 1931, 1939, 1946*

		(per thousand)		
Year	Muslim	Others	Christian	Jewish
1927	216.79	153.68	187.22	115.79
1931	187.55	113.36	133.27	81.60
1939	121	108	101	54
1946	91	98	56	32

Sources: Palestine and Transjordan Administration Reports 1918-1948, Vols. 2 and 3. Courtesy of Bilad ash-Sham Library, University of Jordan. Department of Health Annual Report for the Year 1946. Courtesy of Israel State Archives.

133.27 (441 deaths) among Christian Palestinians, 113.36 (56 deaths) among Other Palestinians, and 81.60 (452 deaths) among Jews.[25] In *1939* the infant mortality rate was highest among Muslims at 121 per thousand live births, followed by Others at 108, Christians at 101, and Jews at 54. In 1946 the infant mortality rate was 98 for Others, 91 for Muslims, 56 for Christians, and 32 for Jews.[26] In *1946* all four groups had lower infant mortality rates in comparison to 1939, keeping in mind the problems of birth and infant death reporting for Palestinian villagers, and the lowest rate was among Jews, which fell an impressive 40.74 percent. The Christian Palestinian infant mortality rate fell by 44.55 percent in comparison to the rate in 1939, although such infants were 75 percent more likely to die than Jewish infants in 1946.

In 1922, 1924, and 1925, measles and its attached illnesses were the primary **causes of death** in Palestine (Rosenau and Wilinsky 1928, 604, 605). With a few exceptions, most deaths each year between 1927 and 1937 were caused by measles or pneumonia, according to my analysis of annual health department reports.[27] In 1931 influenza was the main

---

[25] *Palestine and Transjordan Administration Reports, Vol. 3,* 664.

[26] GOP, Department of Health, Health and Vital Statistics, Annual Reports – Annual Report for the Year 1946. File location in catalog: 00071706.81.CF.FC. FA. Israel State Archives.

[27] In the 1946 annual health report the colonial government continued to deem measles "the most important cause of child morbidity and mortality in Palestine, although its notification is far from regular."

cause of illness and death by far, while typhoid was the second most prevalent disease and pneumonia was the second most likely to kill.[28] In 1939 the main **causes of death** were "diarrhea and enteritis" (1,336 deaths), followed by pneumonia (1,258 deaths), and the main **infectious diseases** were typhoid (1,235 cases), followed by tuberculosis (461) and dysentery (409).[29]

In 1946 the **diseases most likely to kill** fell into the categories of "pneumonia and broncho-pneumonia" (1,362 people) and "diarrhea and enteritis" (1,165 people). Of the 1,362 pneumonia and broncho-pneumonia deaths, 989 (72.6 percent) were infants or children under five years and 999 (73.3 percent) were Muslim or Other Palestinians. Of diarrhea and enteritis deaths, 1,122 (96.3 percent) were infants or children under five years.[30] Those who died of diarrhea and enteritis were disproportionately Muslim Palestinians: 1,005 of total reported death cases from diarrhea and enteritis were Muslim or Other Palestinians (86.27 percent). Overall in 1946, of all 8,838 deaths recorded, 2,318 were infants (26.23 percent) and 3,957 were infants or children under five years (44.77 percent).

The idea of "demographic transition" became prominent in geopolitical discourse on Palestine in the 1940s and is most associated with Frank W. Notestein, a Michigan-born demographer who oversaw the founding of the Office of Population Research at Princeton University in 1936 (Coale 1983, 3, 5). In Notestein's work on "differential fertility" at the Milbank Memorial Fund between 1928 and 1936, he "foresaw, before almost anyone else," that the "large reduction in birth and death rates that had occurred in the nineteenth and early twentieth centuries in the economically and technologically more advanced countries" would also occur "if and when the less advanced areas experienced economic and technological progress" (4). He argued that attitudes and motivations were more important than

---

[28] *Palestine and Transjordan Administration Reports, Vol. 3*, 132. This report includes a table comparing 1931 and 1932 rates.

[29] "Vital Statistics of Palestine 1939," 3. GOP, *Vital Statistics Bulletin (Annual)*, No. 2. Office of Statistics, Jerusalem (April 1940). GOP, Office of Statistics, Report for Office of Statistics, Jerusalem: Vital Statistics. File location in catalog: 00071706.81.D3.AA.55. Israel State Archives.

[30] Table 10, "Deaths of Residents in Towns, Classified According to Cause, Sex and Religion, during the Year 1946." GOP, Department of Health, Health and Vital Statistics, Annual Reports – Annual Report for the Year 1946. File location in catalog: 00071706.81.CF.FC.FA. Israel State Archives.

biology or contraceptive method to procreative and birth control practices. He concluded, however, that development lags in less advanced
countries combined with improved life expectancy would produce
population growth that impeded "progress" (5).

Notestein was invited to testify before the Anglo-American Committee
of Inquiry on Palestine, which met in the early months of 1946, and
learned years later from "the attorney for the Zionists" that "his testimony had helped the Jewish leaders decide in favor of the partition of
Palestine" (5).[31] In "Population Problems of Palestine," Notestein analyzes the demographic past and forecasts the demographic future in
Palestine, using what he recognizes as poor British data, filtered through
his commitment to the Malthusian theory of "carrying capacity,"
whereby population density should match economic resources and development. He defines the appeal of "small family patterns" as modern and
associates such cultural desires with urbanization (Notestein and Jurkat
1945, 311, 331). He argues that in Palestine, "Modern influences
introduced by Western government [i.e., British colonial] and Western
immigration [i.e., Zionist settler-colonialism] in the interwar period
brought a substantial decline in the death rate." At the same time, he
finds a lower birthrate among largely rural Muslim Palestinians than
among Jews, although it was declining in the 1940s (307, 315, 343).

Rates of "natural increase" were highest for "Moslems" and lowest
for Jews in Palestine between 1922 and 1940, "a disparity increasingly
favorable to Moslem growth" (335–336, 343–343). Jewish fertility
could not match Palestinian fertility, Notestein found, unless immigration of Jewish women of childbearing age was continuous and indefin-
ite (342, 344). Forecasting through 1970 (!), Notestein writes that
given Palestinian Muslim age distribution, "it would be unwise to
count on fewer [than 1.6 million] Moslems by 1970" (347–348). He
opines in the essay that "all parties in the region have a stake in the
maintenance of Jewish interest, as a means of attracting both the
needed capital and skills." Based on his Malthusian "carrying capacity"/density perspective, he writes it would be "a catastrophe of
major proportions ... if enthusiasm for a Jewish state should result in

---

[31] The British Peel Commission of 1937 (Palestine Royal Commission Report),
responding to the Arab Revolt, had recommended the partition of historic
Palestine into an "Arab" and a "Jewish" state, with "exchanges of land and
population," divided by an internationally accessible area under British rule:
https://unispal.un.org/pdfs/Cmd5479.pdf.

the really heavy immigration sometimes talked of" (349). Moreover, he notes "that the rigid segregation of Jews and Muslims presents difficulties if the object is to spread a Western way of life and Western fertility patterns"; among its "difficulties," segregation reduced "imitative" potential (350).

For Notestein, it was "difficult to imagine the conditions under which Jews could become and remain a majority group in Palestine" (351). He glosses further in conclusion:

Should the Jews achieve a national state, it is unlikely that in the long run it could be maintained, either as part of the region ... or as a minority ruling group supported by outside power. Under these circumstances, the chances are great that the Jews, having made possible the development of a modern Palestine and a healthy and relatively prosperous country, would have no share in the fruits of their labors ... The demographic and economic prospects of the region point to the need for the cooperative Jewish and Moslem development of Palestine as an integrated region – the trading and light manufacturing center of a Near East in which the process of modernization may be expected to go rapidly forward. (352)

While Notestein's demographic analysis was reportedly influential with Zionist leaders, his recommendations were not since ethnically cleansing as much of the Palestinian population as possible from the land was definitive to the establishment of Israel as a Jewish state (Pappé 2006). Racial biopolitics was clearly at the core of British colonialism and Zionist settler-colonialism in Palestine. The next section considers this matter further and explores its eugenic components using a wider historical and geographic lens.

National, Colonial, and Imperial Eugenics

In 1859 British naturalist Charles Darwin argued in *The Origin of Species by Means of Natural Selection* that all life traced to a singular biological origin and variation over generations occurred naturally by reproduction through principles of selection that facilitate adaptation and survival in different environments. "Social Darwinism," a concept whose meanings are plural, developed alongside and after Darwin's theory of evolutionary biology. It is (fairly or unfairly) most associated with nineteenth-century British inventor and philosopher Herbert Spencer, who argued against welfare interventions by the state because they disrupted the "survival of [only] the fittest" humans (Becquemont 2011).

The term *eugenics* was coined (combining the Greek prefix *eu*, "good," with *genesis*) in 1883 by Charles Darwin's cousin Francis Galton "to express the science of improving stock ... to give the more suitable races or strains of blood a better chance of prevailing speedily over the less suitable" (Mukherjee 2016, 64–65). Galton's goal was to "mimic the mechanism of natural selection," imagining a system of "accelerating the process of refining humans via human intervention" (64, 72). On this logic, married men and women with the "best traits" from the "best families" (higher social class) would produce the "best offspring, in a manner akin to basset hounds and horses" (73). In 1909 Galton founded the *Eugenics Review*,[32] "which endorsed not just selective breeding [by the strong][33] but selective sterilization [of the weak]"[34] to improve "race hygiene" (76–77).

Eugenicist and social Darwinist sensibilities often came together with British economist T. R. Malthus's late eighteenth-century theory of population. In addition to his understanding of land having a limited "carrying capacity" in its ability to grow food for promiscuous population growth, Malthus blamed the English poor for having "large families" that increased the number of laborers competing for "a limited number of jobs," driving down wages (Ledbetter 1976, 4). One hundred years after Malthus published his work, fin de siècle worries about the racial fitness of the British poor and working classes led to the 1904 *Report of the Inter-departmental Committee on Physical* Deterioration, which, writes Richard Soloway, determined that most British children were born healthy but deteriorated from "ignorance, neglect, malnutrition, poor housing, fetid air ['pollution of the atmosphere'], polluted water, minimal hygiene, excessive drinking, and inadequate medical care." The report responded to long-standing anxieties that British soldiers, drawn from boys and men of the laboring classes, were of poor "quality" in terms of their physical health and anthropometric measures, which served to weaken the empire.[35] The 1904 report concluded that state and voluntary institutions should work on a massive

---

[32] The journal published sixty volumes through 1968: www.ncbi.nlm.nih.gov/pmc/journals/1186/.
[33] Termed "positive eugenics."   [34] Termed "negative eugenics."
[35] The almost nine-hundred-page report from 1904 may be found here (accessed December 24, 2020): https://archive.org/details/b21358916.

scale to "preserve and improve the health of the young." Indeed, legislation from 1906 and 1907 established feeding and medical inspection programs for schoolchildren, by 1911 Parliament passed the National Insurance Act, and the British government eventually established a welfare state (Soloway 1990, 45).

"Race degeneration" fears "chilled" members of the British elite before World War I; they were concerned about the relative strength and vitality of the white middle and upper classes. The poor and working classes, British eugenicists feared, would "produce bushels of children, dominate the gene pool, and drag the nation toward profound mediocrity" (Mukherjee 2016, 75; Soloway 1988, 370–371). By 1911 better-educated British couples were giving birth to an average of 3.4 children while "the more numerous coal miners, boiler-makers, general laborers, shipyard workers, dockers, riveters, pig iron workers, coal heavers, and scavengers" were siring an average of 6.1 children (Soloway 1990, 11). A halving of the birthrate by 1917 combined with fear of being "swamped by the socially . . . and genetic-ally unfit" exacerbated "race suicide" discourse (xv). Birthrates actu-ally dropped "rapidly and relentlessly virtually everywhere in Europe between 1880 and 1930," with a later decline (by World War II) in Ireland and several countries in eastern and southern Europe (xii).

British pronatalists who campaigned for "non-selective social reform" that *overall* reduced infant mortality rates and improved health existed in "uneasy alliance" with eugenicists in the second decade of the twenti-eth century (Soloway 1988, 369). British eugenicist and social reformer Norah March, for example, whose name I came across in Palestine Department of Health correspondence, uses environmental rather than hereditary logic in her 1917 article "The Eugenic Aspects of National Baby Week." She argues that factors such as "poverty, parental intem-perance, poor housing, inefficient mothercraft, defective sanitation" and so on "form a vicious cycle, very complex in its balance, of detrimental influence" (March 1917, 102). The "State" should have an interest in the preservation of life, a matter made more urgent by the massive loss of British soldiers in World War I, she insists. Infant and child mortality rates were too high, as was the rate of miscarriage and the number of "seriously defective children" born that way because of malnutrition, disease, and infection produced by congested housing in British indus-trial cities (97, 98, 102, 103). These problems were preventable with proper "ante-natal supervision" (96) and the establishment of social policies such as pensions to support single mothers (104). The hereditary school of eugenicists continued to argue, in contrast, that the high infant mortality rate in England was not a problem because the weak were dying.[36] March was appealing to them when she explains that while National Baby Week embraces the needs of all British babies and mothers, "the ultimate benefit will tend to gravitate eugenically": "The most intelligent parents will be those most likely to avail themselves of facilities offered for their help, and the most intelligent – particularly of the mothers – be most likely to put into effective practice the teaching given them. Thus, their children will tend to survive" (107).

As the birth control movement became more successful and birth control technologies became more effective in interwar Britain, gender was brought to "the center of the debate about population and empire," drawing on a tradition of "imperial feminism" that proclaimed "shared bonds" among women worldwide (Ittmann 2013, 38–39, 64). This feminism "coexisted with ideas about race and culture that portrayed non-European women as backward and in need of aid from their more advanced British sisters," especially as "victims of colonial men." Some imperial feminists saw colonized women as also punished by "poverty and poor health," and partly blamed the situation on colonial rule, distinguishing themselves from "the patriarchal and paternalistic attitudes of the population movement, especially eugenicists" (40, 41, 46).

The ideological scaffolding of eugenics developed in the metropoles of Western colonialism, imperialism, and racism. Galton wrote that his sense of human hierarchy was strengthened by his visits to the Sudan and Egypt in the summer of 1844: "I saw enough of savage races to give me material to think about all the rest of my life" (quoted in Mukherjee 2016, 65). "Race" and "racial difference" were even more explicit in "the new imperial eugenics and the broader population movements" that emerged after World War I (Ittmann 2013, 32). Harkening to long-standing racialized demographic anxieties, British elites were especially concerned with the implications of differential world fertility rates for maintaining imperial power (32–33, 16, 37).[37]

---

[36] "National Baby Week Council" London meeting notes in *The Lancet*, November 5, 1921, 979.

[37] One of the most extreme forms of interwar British scientific racism, studied by Chloe Campbell, was developed by settler-colonial psychiatrists and

As "class differentials in fertility" lessened in Britain and were "coupled with fears of depopulation," Ittman writes, concerns shifted to "the overall health and size of the [white] population," as well as its "quality" at home and in white dominions, although this school of thought "competed with environmental arguments and proposals for improved conditions" (32, 36). Given "expanding populations in Asia and elsewhere," British eugenicist activists in the interwar period promoted birth control for non-Europeans in the colonies (18). The goal was to find "a simple and cheap contraceptive that would be suitable for both colonial peoples and poor whites, who were thought to present similar problems of ignorance and improvidence" (37, 36).

Among *geneticists*, a substantive shift away from eugenics was facilitated by their increased recognition based on scientific research that:

inheritance . . . is polygenic, involving a multiplicity of genes combining in an infinite variety of unpredictable ways and interacting with environmental factors so as to muddle further the controversial relationship between nature and nurture. Not only were thoughtful eugenicists increasingly uncertain about what to breed for, or even able to agree on the relative racial value of the characteristics they wanted reproduced, but the more the most advanced students of human heredity learned about the complexity of their subject, the more doubtful they became about predicting with any accuracy the outcome of selective reproduction. (Soloway 1990, 659–660)

Nevertheless, in the decades after World War II, US and British eugenics movement leaders shifted to a "crypto-eugenics" program – that is, a focus on birth control and immigration restrictions targeting *racialized* populations, showing the degree to which racial supremacy inflects even modern forms of imperialism and capitalism; British eugenicists generally remained committed to Galtonian principles, however (Ramsden 2009, 861, 875n19; Schenk and Parkes 1968, 154–155). Eugenics in Britain was a "social ideology with eclectic appeal that cut more widely across the social and political spectrum than has been appreciated" (Soloway 1988, 370, 371).

Before exploring eugenics in Zionist settler-colonial health projects in Palestine I discuss nineteenth- and early twentieth-century European

dermatologists in 1930s Kenya who were determined to "prove" the hereditary failings of Africans. They studied Kenyan patients in mental health institutions and prisons in collaboration with eugenicist colleagues in London to "fortify the ideology of imperialism" (Campbell 2007, 3, 6, 7, 26).

and US eugenic discourses in relation to Jews by engaging with Mitchell Hart's *The Healthy Jew: The Symbiosis of Judaism and Modern Medicine* (2007). Hart attests to "the power that science, including racial, evolutionary, and eugenics-based science, possessed for Jews and non-Jews alike" (118). The Jewish and non-Jewish theologians, physicians, and scientists whose writings Hart examines deployed Social Darwinism and eugenics in multiple, partial, and inconsistent ways in relation to Jews. They combined hereditary, environmental, and personal agency to explain "aspects of Jewish history and Jewish collective behavior and traits" (106). Studying their popular and academic writings from the nineteenth century, Hart makes the case for two underestimated and understudied eugenic strands regarding Jewishness. The first position, held by "Gentiles" and "a significant proportion of Jewish elites" in the nineteenth century, promoted Jewish emancipation and integration into European societies in order to "free the Jews of the negative influences of both rabbinism and Christian oppression," a "transcendence" they believed "would produce a healthy Jew" (3–4). The second position, "rendered through the prism of Darwinism," held that "the historical experience of isolation and oppression, suffering, violence and death could be seen to act as a natural selection process, removing the weak and leaving a stronger, more vital Jewish people" (6, 11).

Both strands responded to nineteenth-century medical, racial, and nationalist anti-Semitic ideologies that constructed Jews "as essentially different from and dangerous to civilization and culture," using images and language that pathologized them as diseased "in body and soul." Jewish elites were especially likely to internalize and reproduce such understandings, and sought to "reform and regenerate Jewry" (7, 3). An "effort to represent Judaism and Jewry as healthy, and linked in multiple ways to the history of western medicine and science," was an alternative "response to a medicalized and racialized anti-Semitism" (7). This Jewish literature, which Hart terms "apologetic," celebrated Jewish "racial hygiene" and hygienic principles and traced such projects back to "the ancient Jewish authorities – the patriarchs, Moses, and the rabbis" (10, 106). These biblical figures, the authors Hart studied maintained, were "racial hygienists" and "sex hygienists" concerned with "judicious selective mating" and "intelligent antenatal and postnatal care." Jews, they argued, were a "virile race" because they survived "persecution and physical as well as mental stress."

William Feldman, a lecturer in hygiene and pediatric physiology in London, went further, stating that Judaism permits the sterilization of a woman "if she is likely to bear children who are going to be tainted with physical or mental disease" (107, 108, 109, 112–123).

This apologetic school of thought claimed that European Jews were more committed than their "Aryan" compatriots to marriage, mother-hood, and breastfeeding, and had lower infant mortality rates as a result (135, 141). On this logic, "Jews had been healthy and civilized since long ago," well before European and US societies, and Western civilization owes its existence to such Jewish ethics and practices (10). These findings support Hart's contention that "narratives of medicine, of health, and of hygiene were always also about civilization. Where did it originate? Who contributed to it? Who is capable of shaping and being shaped by it? Who, today, upholds its standards, embodies its ideals?" (34).

Eugenicist impulses of the biological and environmental varieties were important to the Zionist settler-colonial movement from the late nineteenth century, as Nadia Abu El-Haj explores in *The Genealogical Science: The Search for Jewish Origins and the Politics of Epistemology* (2012) and Israeli geneticist Raphael Falk examines in some depth in *Zionism and the Biology of the Jews* (2017), a book whose initial Hebrew version was published in 2006. Abu El-Haj examines the writings of late nineteenth-century and twentieth-century Jewish phys-icians and social scientists in the United States and Europe who studied "disease and pathology ... within the parameters of the scientific study of race." These scientists were invested in the idea of Jewish "biological difference" in light of their commitments "to improving the status and health of Jewish communities in the diaspora and/or realizing the nationalist cause" (Abu El-Haj 2012, 15–16). Falk contends that "Jewish identity became 'biological' only in the last decades of the nineteenth century," as essentialist arguments were used to rationalize discrimination against Jews (Falk 2017, xi, 4–5). By the "end of the [nineteenth] century ... Zionists-to-be stressed that Jews were not merely members of a cultural or a religious entity, but an integral biological entity," thereby adopting a "Blood and Soil" notion com-mon in central Europe (4–5, 49–50). Within this frame, "national variation is founded on racial differences" (Nathan Birnbaum quoted in Falk 2017, 50; also 52, 57–58). Community "self-studies" by Jewish intellectuals served as "biological projects of Jewish self-fashioning" preoccupied with establishing and bolstering origin stories of Jewish coherence and relatedness in relation to Palestine (Abu El-Haj 2012, 5, 14).

Postulating Jewish biological coherence and difference came to be connected by the turn of the century with the strains of Zionist ideology that advocated for and established Jewish settler-colonialism in Palestine, even as other Jewish scholars "made enormous efforts to deny any racial or national distinctness of Jews" (Falk 2017, 29–30; Abu El-Haj 2012, 18). The definition of Jewishness as a racial category was integral to affirming a biological distinction "between Jew and Arab in the Israeli imagination" (Abu El-Haj 2012, 19). After 1948, argues Falk, "genetics, it was hoped, would uphold not only the historical evidence [of Jewish diasporic connection to Zion], but would also provide biological evidence" that dispersed Jewish groups "are indeed one people whose roots trace back to Eretz-Israel" (Falk 2017, 3).

As scholars of Palestine know all too well, Zionist intellectuals in the late nineteenth and early twentieth centuries widely pitched Jewish settler-colonialism as an opportunity to undertake Jewish regeneration while building a Jewish state. Abu El-Haj contends that the Jewish intellectuals she studied embraced a "Lamarckian perspective on the inheritance of racial traits" with the aim of resolving the perceived problem of Jewish "degeneration," which they explained to be the "consequence of historical and environmental circumstances."[38] European Zionist and physician Max Nordau (1849–1923), Falk writes, was an "avid supporter" of Social Darwinism and convinced by biological rather than anthropological explanations for culture. He believed in "neo-Lamarckian evolution," or that characteristics could be inherited or reshaped relatively quickly (Falk 2017, 57–59). Informed by German nationalism, Nordau was deeply concerned about "degeneration" based on poverty, nonnormative sexuality, and the social transformations produced by capitalism,

---

[38] French naturalist Jean-Baptiste Lamarck (1744–1829), who began his career as a botanist and became an expert on invertebrates, developed an evolutionary theory that organisms that change their behaviors to adapt to shifts in their environment during their lifetimes end up using a "given structure or organ" more or less, changing its size and significance and passing such changes onto offspring. "Jean-Baptiste Lamarck (1744–1829)," University of California Berkeley, Museum of Paleontology: https://ucmp.berkeley.edu/history/lamarck .html. "Early Concepts of Evolution: Jean Baptiste Lamarck," University of California Berkeley, Understanding Evolution: https://evolution.berkeley.edu/e volibrary/article/history_09; Mukherjee 2016 (399, 400–401).

especially Jewish biological degeneration resulting from living as a "persecuted community" in European contexts (58–59). For Zionists such as Nordau, only "reconnecting with the soil" in Palestine "would rejuvenate the Jewish race" (Abu El-Haj 2012, 49, 68; Falk 2017, 59 and 62–63 on Zeev Jabotinsky). These activists:

> aimed to cultivate a "new Hebrew" who would be radically different – biologically and not just culturally – from the "diaspora Jews." And they took the biological piece of that regeneration seriously: the Jewish *body* had to be rejuvenated; Jewish degeneration had to be countered, even as who it was who qualified as the most degenerate Jew would shift over time. (Abu El-Haj 2012, 67)

While the Zionist movement primarily lobbied for and facilitated Jewish immigration to a land populated by people they aimed to remove, displace, and contain using every means at their disposal, its activists and workers were also concerned to reshape especially European Jewish bodies and psyches to fortify a Jewish settler-colonial body politic in Palestine. For the Zionist "pioneers who settled Palestine," an essential goal was "revival" of "the physical health of the younger generation and that of future generations." From the 1920s Zionist leaders, "primarily the physicians and the educators among them, emphasized the eugenic aspects of their responsibility to improve the hygiene of the race," which included "the need to control the immigration of persons with hereditary and other diseases" through the 1930s and 1940s (Falk 2017, 12).[39]

The Hadassah Medical Organization was established in Palestine by Jewish public health nurses from cities that included Baltimore and New York. These Zionist medical professionals were socialized in the eugenicist orientations of their times and places. Hadassah's Nathan and Lina Straus Health Centre in Jerusalem was the engine of the annual Palestine-wide Health Week festivals discussed in Chapter 1. Health Week curriculums illustrated the centrality of Zionist environmental eugenics, even as investments in healthcare and health education were also motivated by the salutary goals of improving Jewish health and wellbeing. The May 1933 "Programme for Health Week" was typical

---

[39] I am not concerned with determining genetic or biological bases of belonging, or the "Who is a Jew?" debate (Kahn 2013). Research by geneticists undermines biological bases for "natural" belonging and exclusion, I am not a geneticist, and the debate is ideologically saturated given its political stakes.

of this complex and labor-intensive occasion and demonstrates a Lamarckian approach oriented to fulfilling Zionist settler-colonial aims.

Harkening to similar public hygiene events in Western and colonial settings in the twentieth century, Health Week exhibits included "welfare stations" where experts examined infants between 10 and 15 months and awarded "prizes to mothers rearing their babies best." Hygiene was the focus of lectures and visual presentations as well, which among other things instructed mothers to schedule the feeding of infants and "the necessity of giving water between feedings." The curriculum encouraged reproductive "maxims," many of biblical provenance revised to serve Zionist purposes, although the translations from Hebrew were occasionally awkward: "1. Children are the treasure and property of the nation." "8. Blessed is the man who filled his yard of them," presumably referring to Psalm 127:5, which blesses men whose "quivers" are full of children when enemies are at the gate. "9. Your sons are as the seedlings of olive around your table," referring to Psalm 128:3. "10. Healthy children are the elements of a healthy nation" (Figure 3.1).

There is no doubt that health activists viewed their work as an important element in a Jewish demographic competition with Palestinians over racial-national fitness as reflected in comparative birthrates and maternal and infant mortality rates. The 1933 "Child Hygiene Exhibit" in the Straus Centre included "charts" that compared Jewish and non-Jewish infant mortality "curves," Jewish and non-Jewish births, and Jewish and non-Jewish "maternal mortality" over the previous ten years.[40] The next section examines mothercraft and breastfeeding pedagogical discourse to further substantiate my point that transnational racialized demographic concerns were relevant to Zionist health projects in Mandate Palestine.

Mothers and Their Milk As Transnational Eugenic Concerns

Concerns about infant mortality in the nineteenth and twentieth centuries were linked to class and racial anxieties in metropolitan and colonial settings, and were invariably worked out on women's bodies

---

[40] GOP, Department of Health, Hygiene – Health Propaganda – Nathan and Lina Straus Health Centre, Jerusalem. January 1933–December 1937. File location in catalog: 00071706.81.D0.97.44. Israel State Archives.

```
Maxims for the "Health Week" - year - 693.

1.Children are the treasure and property of the nation.

2. Health is dearer than silver and gold.

3. Health is easily acquired.

4. Hygienic feet bring health to their owner.

5. Cleanliness is the royal road to divinity.

6. Accustom the child in hygienic manners, as manners form habits

7. The right instruction given during childhood reflects during
   adolescence.

8."Blessed is the man who filled his yard of them".

9."Your sons are as the seedlings of olive around your table.
   It is in this way that a man is called blessed".

10. Healthy children are the elements of a healthy nation.

11. Good carriage facilitates the duties of the muscles of
    the body.

                                                    ./.
```

Figure 3.1 First eleven "maxims" from "Programme for Health Week, 693," Nathan and Lina Straus Health Centre, Hadassah Medical Organization (translated into English for British authorities). Hygiene – Health Propaganda – Nathan and Lina Straus Health Centre, Jerusalem. January 1933 to December 1937. Courtesy of Israel State Archives. I am grateful to Eeyi Oon for technical assistance that significantly improved the legibility of the clip.

and sexual and mothering practices, as indicated by Hadassah Health Week curricula in Palestine. Mothering, as well as human, cow, powdered, and "tinned" milk, made repeated appearances in British colonial and Zionist archival discussions of health and hygiene during the Mandate. These transnational projects were eugenicist insofar as they were concerned to reduce infant mortality rates and improve the health of only some children.

The National Baby Week Council in London, whose secretary for many years was eugenicist Norah H. March, discussed earlier, repeatedly wrote to the director of the Department of Health in Palestine from 1926 through 1938 begging for their participation in the "Imperial Baby Week Challenge Shield."[41] While the reigning British director of

[41] March authored the book *Towards Racial Health: A Handbook on the Training of Boys and Girls, Parents, Teachers & Social Workers* (1919), which argued

health dutifully distributed the brochure and application to medical officers each year throughout Palestine, including to the Hadassah Medical Organization and the American Colony Aid Association, no infant welfare centre or clinic ever agreed to participate, as far as I could tell. Many health officials who received the request wrote back to the Department of Health in Jerusalem that they lacked staff resources and doubted "people here would really appreciate such a competition." In a 1933 handwritten note, Vena Rogers obliquely communicated the problem at least for the Palestinian subject population: "I do not think Jerusalem with its mixed population – particularly its Moslem section – ready for a public demonstration in the above," predictably suggesting that a midwifery demonstration would be more useful.[42] Muslim or not, most Palestinians would have considered showing off children in public displays to make them vulnerable to illness and death.

Baby week competitions, "largely a propaganda effort" focused on "the needs of child life and maternal well-being" (March 1917, 101), began in English towns before World War I. The first *national* Baby Week in 1917 was cosponsored by ninety British pronatalist and eugenicist organizations, although individuals in the latter groups were against "indiscriminate" welfare activity that encouraged the health and reproduction of the lower classes (Soloway 1988, 373). Colonial officials encouraged the competitions as inexpensive health propaganda in Lagos, Nigeria, in the early 1920s. The Lagos Baby Week festival included displays of housing deemed fit and unfit, posters illustrating appropriate antenatal and birthing conditions and practices, talks against "native superstitions and practices," and a "Baby Show" for the healthiest infants and children in three age categories up to five years old.[43] The 1920s (and even earlier) saw the development of

for eugenic sex and parenthood instruction for children and advocated barrier contraception by women as a "social hygiene" tool against venereal disease given the promiscuity of men (4, 6). The text aimed to instill in children self-control and "a keen sense of racial responsibility" to avoid "race decay" (7).

42 GOP, Department of Health, Infant Welfare – Imperial Baby Week. File location in catalog: 00071706.81.D1.32.BA. Israel State Archive.

43 In Lagos, Baby Week included no "regular follow-up treatment" if infants were treated for an illness and was not attached to the development of substantial services. The "best babies," evaluated by white Europeans, were "well-fed toddlers in European baby clothes" (Lindner 2014, 222–223; Von Tol 2007, 113).

similar competitions at US agricultural fairs, where "the public encountered Better Babies Contests, in which children, often as young as one
or two years old, were proudly displayed on tables and pedestals, like
dogs or cattle, as physicians, psychiatrists, dentists, and nurses in white
coats examined their eyes and teeth, prodded their skin, and measured
heights, skull sizes, and temperaments to select the healthiest and fittest
variants" as winners (Mukherjee 2016, 84–85).

Tracing the genealogy of promotional materials for films advocating
breastfeeding in Palestine Department of Health folders took me to
a leading public health advocate and eugenicist, physician John
N. Hurty, who was the secretary of the Indiana State Board of Health
from 1896 to 1922 and "an outspoken supporter of the sterilization
and marriage laws" (Stern 2002, 746; Reilly 2015). In 1931 the
National Motion Pictures Company, an Indianapolis corporation
that produced and distributed "Educational Motion Picture Films,"
as well as "slides and machines," promoted to the director of the
Department of Health two films on the benefits of breastfeeding over
artificial feeding. One of them, *The Long vs. The Short Haul or
Mother's Milk Best for Baby*, was produced in collaboration with
Hurty.[44] These materials cultivated mothering that reduced white
infant mortality rates and increased "racial" fitness.

Debates regarding "natural" versus "artificial" feeding, timed feeding, and the weaning of babies in Palestine were most relevant to
Zionist health practitioners in their work with Jewish women, infants,
and children, which was guided by the logic of improving the racial
fitness of the Jewish "nation." I ventured into colonial and settler-
colonial discourse on mothering by startling references to massage of
women's breasts in letters dated May 31, 1925, and September 21,
1926, from Hadassah's Bertha Landesman (then the chief nurse) in
Jerusalem to, respectively, Mabel Liddiard, a nurse midwife who was
the matron of the Mothercraft Training Society in London (which
applied Truby King's methods), and Truby King, the director of child

---

[44] The film brochure warned that "Over 1,500 Babies Die Annually of Summer
Diarrhea in Indiana | When Baby Has Diarrhea Take No Chances But Send for
Doctor." The synopsis for the second film, *The Best-Fed Baby*, included
a mother telling another that "the breast-fed baby has four times the chance to
live than the artificially-fed baby has and that the problem of nursing her baby
lies largely in her hands." GOP, Department of Health, Health and Hygiene –
Health Educational Films, January 1931–January 1933. File location:
00071706.81.D0.97.42. Israel State Archives.

welfare in Wellington and the founder of the Plunket Society of New Zealand.[45]

A series of letters between Landesman and Liddiard from May to June 1925 followed a visit by Landesman to the Mothercraft Training Society in December of the previous year. Landesman asked Liddiard whether "massage of the breast" was King's "special method" and sought information about nurse midwife training expectations in London. Landesman explained that only "the Plunket Centre" fol-lowed "Sir Truby King's method of feeding" in Palestine. A branch of the Plunket Society was indeed established in Tel Aviv (Burdon 1945, 49) and apparently more than one existed. The branches were affiliated with the British Zionist women's organization, WIZO, and funded by Jewish women in Dunedin, New Zealand, "with the aim of introducing and supporting Plunket societies in Palestine" (Baumberg 1998, 53). The white settler men and women who organized Plunket committees in New Zealand hoped to improve "racial fitness" and increase "demo-graphic advantage" against the "Asian hordes," who they feared would rise up against the British Empire (Olssen 1981, 10).

Liddiard responded to Landesman that "massage of the breasts" "has been used since the beginning of the Plunket system," and insisted that Palestine was not dramatically different from other parts of the world in terms of successful applicability of King's methods.[46] In a letter from Landesman to King the following year, a subsection titled BREAST MASSAGE began:

May I ask, whether this is your special method and whether you believe this is the old method of producing milk. There is of course great differences of opinions among the doctors with regard to the methods. In New York City, where I conducted the Infant Welfare work for the Health Department, breast massage was not recommended. Proper diet, proper hygiene, and living conditions for the mother, expression of the milks, (emptying of the breasts) recommended etc. Our doctors here in Palestine do not recommend breast massage, except in perhaps very specific cases of a primipara, with undeveloped milk glands.

---

[45] The Society for Promoting the Health of Women and Children was renamed for the British governor-general of New Zealand and his wife, Lord and Lady Plunket, when they became its patrons (Olssen 1981, 7–8).

[46] May 31, 1925, letter from Landesman to Liddiard in London and June 11, 1925, letter from Liddiard to Landesman in Jerusalem. Central Zionist Archives 1925, Folder J113/6738.

Landesman continued that Hadassah nurses in Palestine followed the "system" of the German settler "Dr. [Benno] Gruenfelder," including in how to prepare nonhuman milk to feed infants. She elaborated: "In Palestine there is not a single doctor who is specially trained in the Plunket method of feedings" and the climate was less temperate and housing more overcrowded than in New Zealand. She proudly listed the decreasing annual Jewish infant mortality rate in Jerusalem: 151 per thousand births in 1922, 141 per thousand in 1923, and 137 per thousand in 1924.[47]

Research and writing on breastfeeding versus bottle-feeding in relation to infant mortality was incubated in the late nineteenth and early twentieth centuries. King wrote the widely read and multiply reprinted pedagogical texts *Feeding and Care of Baby* (1913)[48] and *Natural Feeding of Infants* (1918). With the increasing "acceptance of germ theory," King was part of a turn-of-the-century reorienting of physicians' focus from the "environment" to "humans as agents of disease" (Beattie 2011, 297; Burdon 1945). King believed motherhood is learned and mothers should be responsible for regulating and managing children's feeding, sleeping, clothing, discharge of bodily waste, and stimulation for the "sake of permanent health and happiness" (King 1913, 122, 123; Liddiard 1925, 146–147). In addition to the Plunket Society in New Zealand, King established the Mothercraft Training Society and was the medical director of the Babies of the Empire Society, both in London.[49] He interacted with health researchers and practitioners working to reduce white infant mortality and increase fertility among white middle and upper-class women in late nineteenth- and early twentieth-century Germany, France, Austria, Hungary, and the United States, as well as British sites of white colonial settlement (King 1918, 10–25).

---

[47] September 21, 1926, letter to Dr. Truby King. Central Zionist Archives 1925, Folder J113/6738.

[48] The manual I read was reprinted seventeen times through 1928 by MacMillan and Company, and listed publishing offices in London, Bombay, Calcutta, Madras, Melbourne, New York, Boston, Chicago, Dallas, San Francisco, and Toronto.

[49] James Beattie argues that Scottish-educated physicians (at Edinburgh and Glasgow universities) played important roles in developing "imperial science" for the "rational and systematic exploitation of colonial resources" in New Zealand and elsewhere (Beattie 2011, 281–282).

Pedagogical material in the mothercraft genre insisted that "Mother's milk" is a "birthright" for the infant and a "maternal duty" for the first nine to twelve months, but must be timed to avoid overfeeding and digestive problems (King 1913, 10, 11, 30; King 1918, 9, 10, 18–20; Liddiard 1925, 50–51). King minutely instructed girls and women on how to prepare and tend to their bodies during pregnancy and afterward through healthy diet, exercise, sufficient sleep, cleanliness, "regular solicitation of bowels," and avoiding alcohol and overeating. Women were told how to undertake "hygiene" of their breasts using cold and hot sponging baths and massage during pregnancy and nursing (King 1913, 6–7, 8, 9, 11; King 1918, 12; Liddiard 1925, 10). King was against unnecessary education for girls, as well as women's employment, to assure their physical and mental orientation toward maternity and domesticity (Olssen 1981, 15–19). His concern was to stem white racial and national "deterioration" and gendered forms of "social disorder" (4, 6).

In the wake of World War I, a substantial circle of eugenicist pediatricians, obstetricians, and nurse matrons linked breastfeeding to "the need for a strong and sturdy population for a nation that is to survive in the struggle for existence, and especially for a nation like ours with all its daughter-nations [white British colonies] calling for children of the parent-stock" (Fairbairn quoted in King 1918, 5). The copyright page of *Feeding and Care* (1913) emphasizes that King's concerns were for more and "fitter" white babies, with illustrative images of light-skinned mothers, nurses, and babies. The final section is unambiguously titled "Parenthood and Race Culture," and drew on quotes from "Dr. C. W. Saleeby" (1878–1940), a widely followed British eugenicist whose last name indicates the Christian Arab origins of his father (Elias Saleeby).[50] King discussed the importance of "MOTHERHOOD," not only "inheritance," for determining "the character of the individual," since babies only have "potentialities" even in the "most perfect system

---

[50] Saleeby, a "charter member of the Eugenics Education Society," became annoyed with colleagues in the "better-dead" school of "class eugenics" who "condemned the infant and maternal welfare movement for interfering in natural selection" (Soloway 1988, 372). He was "aware of the importance of prenatal care in reducing the high rates of miscarriage, stillbirth and infant mortality," which "cost the nation millions of potential [male] recruits who were now desperately needed" for the war, but made little headway influencing his colleagues (379, 380). After 1918, he "withdrew from the [Eugenics Education] Society's affairs" (382).

of selection of the finest and highest individuals for parenthood" (King 1913, 152). To secure "nations" required not only guns, "but also the man behind the gun, and he is mainly the resultant of the grit and self-sacrifice of his mother. If we lack noble mothers we lack the first element of racial success and national greatness," which depended on white women breastfeeding (King 1913, 153). Indeed, King opposed "Chinese wet-nursing, or bottle-feeding" of white infants in colonial Hong Kong unless absolutely necessary because breast milk was understood to shape character (156).[51]

In *Natural Feeding of Infants* (1918), a shorter manual published five years later, King drew on research on breastfeeding in Germany "by the leading authorities" whose goal was "to fight the death rate of infants in the German Empire" (14–15, 17), which from 1871 to 1918 spanned much of central and eastern Europe. He again linked breastfeeding with baby health: "The death rate among artificially fed babies is seven times as great as among those who are breast-fed" (17). The eugenicist impulses were clear in his conclusion, which warned about "race suicide" by drawing on recently published US "Birth Statistics Reports" that found "native born Americans contributed at the rate of only about 16 births per 1,000, whereas the immigrant population shows over 40 per 1,000" (32). King stressed: "In all civilized countries a smaller and smaller percentage of new population is being derived from the best sources, and from quarters where there would be ample to provide for larger families if they were desired" (32).

Manuals repeatedly discussed the necessity of nursing a baby and food, housing, and regular healthcare for pregnant women, new mothers, infants, and children. Research and pedagogical manuals on mothercraft were attached to policies when it came to the mothers and children eugenicists considered worthy. In comparison, while Palestinian women widely breastfed their children and neighbors'

---

[51] Ranjana Saha's work (2017) on breastfeeding, milk, and race in late nineteenth-century and early twentieth-century British colonial Bengal finds similar white racial anxieties as *memsahib*s (white colonial women in India) turned to native wet nurses, since their breast milk was deemed to impinge on the shape of "British character" (149–150). She shows, in turn, how the most popular early twentieth-century childcare manual in Bengal, written by nationalist Bengali physician Sundarimohan Das and published in nine editions, was influenced by King's lectures and writings combined with "Ayurvedic sources" (155–156). The Bengali middle-class nationalist project "championed motherhood" and lactation as a defense against "disease and colonialism" (155, 151).

children as necessary, British and Zionist experts often judged them as dirty and ignorant for nursing on demand or beyond a child's infancy. As in other colonial contexts, Palestinian girls and women received lectures and judgments but little to no resources and care for themselves and their children.

~~~~~~~~~~~

It is widely accepted that Zionist settler-colonialism was and is a demographic project oriented to displacing the native Palestinian population. British colonial interests in Palestine, by comparison, are largely understood to have been demographic only to the degree they facilitated Jewish immigration to Palestine. This chapter shows corollaries between British and Zionist demographic priorities in Mandate Palestine as well as the importance of eugenics to both projects. It further builds the argument that British healthcare austerity *toward Palestinians* was underlined by racialized calculations that balanced birth against death rates. Despite their variety, eugenics projects evaluated some human life as more valuable "to the state, the nation, the race, future generations – than other human life" (Levine and Bashford 2010, 3–4). The next chapter shifts the focus of the book to *the desire not to reproduce*. It examines religious (Islamic, Jewish, and Christian) legal traditions, as well as Ottoman, British colonial, Israeli, Jordanian, and Palestinian National Authority laws on birth control. If law is diagnostic of social practices, the chapter shows that anti-reproductive desire was always a prominent yet vexed matter for elites and regular people, including Palestinians.

4 | *"Technically Illegal"*
Birth Control in Religious, Colonial, and State Legal Traditions

An account by Mary G. Blacklock, who worked in the Liverpool School of Tropical Medicine and was "a member of the Women's Medical Service for India, and later of the Colonial Medical Service in Africa," is distinct among documents by colonial figures in mentioning both "Palestine" and "birth-control." Blacklock had used a grant to take a "study tour" in the summer and autumn of 1935 "of the colonies of Hong Kong, Malaya, Ceylon and Palestine, and also to pay a short visit to China, Burma and India, to see something of the work which is being done there" (Blacklock 1936, 222). Blacklock wanted "to assess the welfare of women and children" (Manderson 1998, 42), rhetoric evoking familiar colonial feminist themes and concerns. In the resulting published article, "Certain Aspects of the Welfare of Women and Children in the Colonies," Blacklock associates poverty, hunger, and lack of healthcare education for women and children in the colonies with high rates of maternal and infant death and even infanticide and calls for colonial investment, employment of British "medical women," and training indigenous women as health workers and midwives. Illustrating the immanence of the racial-colonial calculus in relation to birth and death that I argue has not been addressed in scholarship on Mandate Palestine, she anticipates the resistance of those "in a few colonies" with a "tendency to decry welfare work for women and children" and who "in all seriousness" say such investment is a waste "until the economic and general health conditions of the country have improved; that the high infant mortality-rate strikes a balance between the population and the means of subsistence, and that it is better to let the children die if the world is not a fit place for them to live in" (Blacklock 1936, 224).

In her response to such British critics, Blacklock insists that "population and means of subsistence do not necessarily balance each other" and strategically (and not surprisingly) deploys a miserly pedagogical approach to native health: "welfare clinics are meant primarily for the education of mothers and not for the treatment of sick children." Her persuasion takes an explicitly eugenicist turn as she continues, while it was true that "many infants will die off" with no welfare work, "many of those who survive will grow up in a weak and sickly state" (224). She argues for "courageous thinking and planning for a policy of economic improvement and for the better equalization of wealth." If such redistribution is "impossible," an alternative is to "face the advocacy of birthcontrol; yet in a colonial empire of two million square miles with a population of only fifty millions, this seems not only a feeble but a dangerous policy to adopt" (261). Blacklock's lack of enthusiasm for birth control was consistent with an imperial demographic agenda in many colonial sites that sought the reproduction and survival of enough laborers to serve extractive aims. Lenore Manderson argues that ultimately Blacklock's welfare-of-women-and-children goals "reflected the thinking of other colonists concerned to dilute the exploitative costs of empire and justify continued control" (Manderson 1998, 42).

This chapter shifts the focus of the book to *nonreproductive desire* in Palestine by comparatively examining relevant legal genealogies and coexisting layers of law on birth control, especially abortion. The purpose is to undermine simplistic reliance on "religion" or "culture" to explain birth control ideologies, practices, and restrictions in historic Palestine. This and the following chapter show that contraceptive use was licit and available, and abortion, while often "technically illegal," was always an important method of birth control for women in all communities. Most people made complex or simple anti-reproductive decisions best understood by accounting for personal situations and options, as well as material and structural conditions.

The first section offers an abridged comparative overview of Muslim, Jewish, and Christian religious legal traditions on contraception, abortion, and sex. The second examines late Ottoman laws, policies, and priorities as they interacted with birth control practices. The third summarizes British colonial law on birth control including in Mandate Palestine. The final section discusses Israeli, Jordanian, and Palestinian National Authority abortion laws and policies applicable since 1948. Modernity, which in this chapter I operationalize as the rise of state legal codification and policies in the nineteenth and twentieth centuries, reinforced male-dominated governmental and medical expertise over women's reproductive and nonreproductive lives to serve various demographic, professional, and geopolitical ends, even as improvements in scientific and medical knowledge increasingly provided additional birth control options.

Jewish, Muslim, and Christian Birth Control Traditions

This section uses scholarly sources to summarize Jewish, Islamic, and Christian legal traditions on contraception and abortion in that order given the similarities between Jewish and Muslim traditions. Jewish, Muslim, and Christian legal traditions are all pronatalist within licit marital relations. Judaism and Islam are more similar than different in the importance assigned to sexual pleasure within marriage, as well as the noncontroversial nature of contraception. They are also more similar than different in their acceptance of abortion and understanding of the fetus as part of a woman's body rather than a separate being. All three traditions have dogmas as well as internal debates and disagreements about marriage, sex, reproduction, contraception, and abortion shaped by sacred texts, legal methods and codes, influential intellectual personalities, and the profane knowledges and priorities dominant in particular places and historical moments.

The Jewish Torah does not address contraception, and neither do the major Talmudic codes for the most part. Rulings on contraception come largely from Responsa, which like the Islamic fatwa tradition are "formal replies to legal queries addressed to scholars of all generations." A response is often from one rabbi to another about a specific case. Responsa emerged from the multiple geographic locations of these experts and although addressing specific cases, they "become part of 'case law' and enter the legal mainstream as precedent" (Feldman 1968, 17–18).

Approaches to contraception are informed by the status of marriage within Jewish cosmology. Judaism considers marriage a religious duty for men linked to licit sexual pleasure, companionship, and love (21–22, 27, 36, 41). Jewish women may remain unmarried, although they are encouraged to allow men to fulfill their obligation to God (55). A Jewish man has a duty to initiate regular sex with his wife when she is not in her menstrual cycle and to give her pleasure, irrespective of the possibility of procreation (36, 41, 60–61, 64–65, 69, 71–72, 76–77, 79–80, 81–105, 152–153). While sex outside marriage is considered sinful, Judaism does not traffic in the Christian belief in "original sin" linked to the story of Adam and Eve illicitly fulfilling their sexual desires; indeed, it discourages abstinence as a "hard blow to body and soul" (32, 78, 81–105).

The religious duty to follow God's command to the sons of Noah to "be fruitful and multiply" is separate from his command to men to marry and their obligation to provide a wife with sexual pleasure. Jewish women are not required to procreate (28, 46, 50–51, 54, 124–125). Couples may use certain forms of contraception, especially in cases of "physical hazard" to themselves or the health of existing children, but "never" for reasons of "self-indulgence or convenience" (53). Using contraception is acceptable as long as the form does not block passage of the sperm to its destination and sexual gratification of men and women is not obstructed. Men may not improperly emit their semen or destroy it through onanism or coitus interruptus, although some exegetes argue they may do the latter to save the health of a pregnant wife (109–131, 155–156). At least by the late 1960s, condoms were rejected unless other forms of contraception were unsafe to the woman, while spermicide use was acceptable. Jewish religious scholars considered chemical oral contraceptive use by women the "least objectionable" (190, 229–233, 244–247). Even doubtful forms of contraception were acceptable to fulfill the command to marry and maintain the marital relationship (42).

Islamic approaches to birth control were shaped by the religion's understanding of marriage: polygamy was accepted, concubinage coexisted with contractual marriage, and divorce was easy. Sex within marriage "needed no justification for procreative purpose." Within this cosmology, "Contraception was permitted and abortion tolerated" (Musallam 1983, 11). The Quran makes no explicit mention (prohibitive or accepting) of contraception, so Muslim jurist rulings from the eleventh century CE onward relied on analysis of valid transmissions of the practices (sunna) and reported statements (hadith) of the Prophet Muhammad during his lifetime (Musallam 1981, 182). Given the dearth of material explicitly addressing birth control, Muslim jurists' rulings on these matters were more likely to draw on "profane biology and economics than … strictly religious sources of law" (183).

The Muslim jurists were almost unanimous that coitus interruptus by men (`azl`) was permitted provided "a free woman … gives her permission" since she has the right to have children and "complete sexual fulfillment" (181). They used analogical reasoning and consensus to extend the permissibility of coitus interruptus to all forms of contraception. Women's use of contraception was particularly noncontroversial (Musallam 1981, 182; Musallam 1983, 120). Jurist rulings also articulated the right of fathers to control family size to enable them to materially support all their progeny (an obligation); recognized that women's frequent death in childbirth was a good reason for women to avoid pregnancy; understood that nursing infants whose mothers became pregnant frequently died of starvation; accepted that avoiding pregnancy "preserve[d] [a wife or concubine's] beauty"; and argued that settings of war and insecurity *required* Muslims to use birth control (including abortion) to avoid children being enslaved or converted (Musallam 1981, 189–190, 193–194; Giladi 2015, 35, 149–150).

In *Sex and Society in Islam: Birth Control before the Nineteenth Century*, Basim F. Musallam finds that "intra-vaginal suppositories and tampons [to impede sperm] were the mainstay of medieval Arabic contraceptive medicine" as reflected in the detailed medical text published in the mid-ninth century CE in Persia, which "became the standard reference work of Arabic medicine" for centuries and was even used in fourteenth-century CE Spain (1983, 61, 62, 63). The "physical clogging capacity" of "honey and oil" were widely recognized and used as were many other contraceptive and abortifacient methods (63, 77–82 [table 1], 83 [table 2], 84 [table 4], 85 [table 5], 86–87 [table 6], 87 [table 7]).

Islamic acceptance of birth control was shaped by a Hippocratic biological understanding that both men and women emit "seed" during sexual intercourse and each equally contributes to the creation of a child (Musallam 1981, 190–192). This contrasts with the Aristotelian privileging of semen as the sole source of human life and soul and by extension `azl as killing a person since it destroys semen (185–186, 188–189). While drawing on secular concerns and anatomical knowledge, Islamic rulings on birth control existed "in the context of [medieval Islamic jurists'] fundamental belief in God's infinite power" (188). Nevertheless, Muslim jurists recognized that abstaining from sex guaranteed non-conception and birth control limited the possibility of a woman becoming pregnant (188–189).

Christianity, in contrast to Judaism and Islam, has a strong ascetic tradition that associates sex with the original sin of Adam and Eve, inherited by man and not even "effaced by baptism," an idea consolidated by the fifth century in the Catholic Church with the writings of St. Augustine (Noonan 1986, 37, 133–135). Christian sexual ethics came to consider celibacy and virginity as ideals and coitus as defiling, drawing from Greek Stoicism, which argued for the "rational use of sexual faculties" and challenged "bodily immoderation" (37, 46–47, 48, 49). The idealization of virginity in the Gospels meant that marriage had to "justify its existence" in Christianity and ultimately did so on the argument that "passion" could not be its sole basis (37–39, 41, 42, 46–49, 76). The Catholic Church eventually consecrated "sexuality in marriage" as "holy" when reproduction was possible. It rhetorically framed marital sex with reproductive potentiality against condemned sexual behavior such as oral sex, anal sex, and coitus interruptus (Breslow 1991, 55; Noonan 1986, 40, 53, 54, 76–77, 123, 126–127, 144; Feldman 1968, 145–148).

In establishing any form of birth control and non-procreative sex as a "sin against nature" that condemned one to "eternal damnation," the Church drew on the theories of Jewish Alexandrian philosopher Philo and the Stoics, who denounced profane dependence, including on sexual urges (Breslow 1991, 55–56, 59; Noonan 1986, 49, 53–54, 74–75, 76–78). Church fathers considered birth control to interfere with the "natural and legitimate foundation for marriage," which for St. Augustine was "the preservation of the race." Only "delight of the mortal flesh" with the possibility of procreation within marriage was acceptable (Breslow 1991, 58; Noonan 1986, 46–49).[1]

Judaism considers independent life to begin at parturition. Before that, the embryo or fetus is not a person and is inseparable from the mother's body (Feldman 1968, 253, 275). Judaism offers *no legal basis* for

---

[1] Lori Breslow argues that Christian norms on sexuality and reproduction were articulated in a period when the Catholic Church was consolidating itself as the center of true orthodoxy as it competed against challenges from two anti-natalist movements: the Gnostics included several trends ranging from advocates of complete celibacy to "complete sexual freedom," but were "hostile to all procreation," and the Manichees were pro-sex and anti-reproduction (Breslow 1991, 57, 58; Noonan 1986, 56–63). Protestantism was more accepting of marriage than the Catholic Church but not necessarily sex for pleasure, although by 1958 the Anglicans advocated for marriage on "relational" and "procreative" grounds (Feldman 1968, 25).

making abortion at any stage impermissible; only moral inhibitions have relevance (262–264, 267). Although the rabbinic tradition includes many debates and disagreements, "abortion is a noncapital crime at worst" (259). While Judaism condemns infanticide, a newborn is not considered "viable" until thirty days after birth (254–257). Within Jewish cosmology then, therapeutic abortion is generally noncontroversial and not even considered abortion in early gestational stages (275). A pregnant woman cannot be forced to give birth against her will since her desires are paramount (287, 292, 294). Judaism understands the "eternal soul" of a fetus to ascend to heaven if it is terminated given the religion has no theory of original sin (274). As a Jewish state very much committed to Jewish demographic expansion, the openness to abortion in Judaism has challenged Israel's ability to restrict abortion in legal and practical terms, although the practice was illegal for a period.

Intentionally inducing abortion is not addressed in the Quran or "the Sunna (exemplary practice) of the prophet" (Katz 2003, 25). The Quran sternly and explicitly condemns infanticide (killing after parturition) for any reason and especially because of poverty or female gender. Muslim jurists were most likely to address loss of a fetus through accident. In comparison, their "Remarks relating to deliberate termination of pregnancy ... tended to be incidental and unsystematic," possibly because induced abortion "generally remained within the purview of individual women and the midwives or other folk practitioners who assisted them" (25). Islamic jurisprudence and fatwa rulings on abortion were guided by the Quranic "theme" that fetal life developed gradually (Katz 2003, 26; Rogers 1999, 125–126). Thus, abortion's level of wrongness and tort value depends on gestational stage (Katz 2003, 26; Musallam 1981, 183–185; Rogers 1999, esp. 123–125).

The unintentional death of a fetus in its early stages by the act of someone else was expected to be compensated in an amount analogous to damage done to a woman's body part "such as fingers or teeth"; in later stages, penalties and compensation levels became progressively closer to requirements for the death or killing of a human being (Katz 2003, 28–29; Rogers 1999, 127–128). In the eleventh century Zahiri jurist Ibn Hazm used Quranic language that recognized the biologically developmental nature of fetal life to rule that "ensoulment" occurs from 120 days after conception, when "the fetus is indubitably alive," whereas before that point "it is not a separate life at all" but part of its mother and if recompense was demanded it went "exclusively" to her. Other jurists "retained [ambiguity] as a fruitful tension in their general understanding of fetal life" (Katz 2003, 29). None of these "tort debates" addressed "intentional abortion," however. If intentional abortion cases came up, some rulings required a woman to compensate "the fetus's remaining heirs or . . . the father of the child" and others ruled that if "a woman aborts with her husband's permission" she owed no payment (29–30).

Using the point of ensoulment as a demarcation, "passing remarks" and "marginal commentaries" on other matters (e.g., burial rituals for a fetus, vengeance for the killing of a fetus, or inheritance rules in case of fetal death) in the four dominant Sunni schools of jurisprudence *generally* consider induced abortion to be "forbidden after ensoulment (literally 'the inbreathing of the spirit')" unless the wellbeing of the mother is endangered because her life supersedes the value of the potential life of a fetus at any stage. The jurists offered conflicting opinions within and across schools about the "permissibility" of abortion before 120 days (Katz 2003, 30–31, 34; Rogers 1999, 123). Most considered "a fetus before the gestational age of 120 days" as "not a Muslim or even a person, although the fetus is treated as a 'potential' person in some sense" (Rogers 1999, 122–123).

Marion Holmes Katz concludes, as do other scholars of Islamic jurisprudence, that "medieval Islamic discussions of abortion" were similar in recognizing the validity of different juridical opinions and having a "high level of tolerance for ambiguity and complexity, which avoids absolutist simplifications of the intricate moral issues raised by fetal life" (Katz 2003, 45). Moreover, no matter now "influential" the jurist criteria for establishing the humanity of the fetus on its own or in relation to the fully human mother, Katz argues that Islamic jurisprudence has never "represented the sole system of moral guidance for Muslims. Rather, legal texts are best understood within a larger religious world, one that includes mystical and philosophical discourses" (25).[2]

---

[2] Shi`a jurisprudence is distinguished from Sunni legal traditions by its reliance on the Quran *and* the legal reasoning of the twelve consecutive successors (Imams) of the Prophet, who are considered infallible, as well as the guidance of living Grand Ayatollahs (*maraji` al-taqlid*) (Sekaleshfar 2008). Given lack of reference to abortion in the Quran and traditions of the Prophet, Shi`a "legal reasoning (*usul*) dictates the principle of 'prevalence of liberty'" based on "rational and textual reasoning" (2). In response to questions from the faithful, the Imams

Abortion and its methods were familiar in the "Greco-Roman" times that overlapped with the development of Christianity (Noonan 1967, 86), but Christine Gudorf argues there was limited early church language on contraception and abortion because infanticide and abandonment were the "most common birth limitation practices" (Gudorf 2003, 59–60). Infanticide "was more effective than contraception, less dangerous to the mother than abortion, and it allowed for sex selection, which was the prime concern for premodern groups who generally wanted to maximize their males to increase production without either increasing community size beyond available resources or draining family resources to pay daughters' dowries" (57). The Romans encouraged abandonment of newborns as more "civilized" than infanticide.[3] Between 600 and 1600 CE in Western Europe "abandonment seems to have outnumbered infanticide by a factor of several hundred to nearly a thousand" (58).

The fourth century CE Canons of St. Basil of Cappadocia, which remain influential in the Coptic and Eastern Orthodox rites, condemned "all women who commit abortion" at any stage of fetal development as well as the providers of abortifacient drugs (Noonan 1986, 88; Noonan 1967, 97). Roman Catholic traditions prohibit abortion at any stage of gestation for some of the same reasons that contraception is largely condemned, an approach that developed gradually in a context considered by early church leaders to be "indifferen[t] to fetal and early life" (Noonan 1967, 86–88). By the fifth century CE St. Augustine condemned contraception and destruction of a fetus without distinguishing between the two practices (Noonan 1967). Between 500 and 1100 CE, the period of Monk dominance in the Catholic Church, John T. Noonan argues, an even "more pessimistic and severe" approach to sexuality developed. Both contraception and abortion were condemned as associated with "magic" and paganism (Noonan 1986, 143–144).

Crucial to the abortion ban in Christianity is belief in original sin, which requires an embryo or fetus to be baptized for its soul to achieve salvation in the afterlife. Within this cosmology, inducing abortion is damning and even worse than murder because the aborting person

offered different positions on the permissibility of abortion and punishment for fetal death based on whether they considered the fetus ensouled (3–12).
[3] The Catholic Church condemned infanticide in the fourth century CE (Gudorf 2003, 57; Noonan 1967, 93–94).

condemns a soul to hell (Feldman 1968, 269–270). Following Greek
Pythagorean teaching, early Christianity tentatively understood the
soul to enter the body at conception, but this was distinct from considering the embryo a person. The Catholic Church came to accept
St. Augustine's contention that a male embryo was a person forty
days after conception and Leviticus's argument that a female embryo
was a person after eighty days of gestation (Noonan 1986, 90, 122;
Noonan 1967, 95; Feldman 1968, 268–269). The focus of the following section is Ottoman law, which was next in chronological relevance
to contraception and abortion in Palestine, although it always overlapped with regional and community customs and religious legal
traditions.

Abortion in Law and Practice in the Late Ottoman Empire

Ottoman abortion-related policies and laws, the focus of this section, came to be embedded in one way or another in the criminal
codes relevant to Palestine after the end of Ottoman rule. I found
no scholarship and did not conduct archival research on contraception and abortion in Ottoman Palestine, when its five districts
were part of the province of Greater Syria. We know from scholarship on other settings that Muslim Ottoman women widely used
contraception, considered abortion a relatively noncontroversial
method of birth control, and substantially relied on the method.
Abortion was "seemingly free and unlimited," according to the
observations of European Christian foreigners in the eighteenth
and early nineteenth centuries who accused residents of the empire
of "lack of moral restraint" (Somel 2002, 340–341; Demirci and
Somel 2008, 385).

  During the nineteenth century, antiabortion policies and public discourse increased as pronatalism intensified among Ottoman elites for
geopolitical reasons. Pronatalism manifested in law as early as
January 1786, when "a non-Muslim pharmacist" was punished "for
selling prohibited plants." In May 1789 a different sultan issued
a decree forbidding "physicians and pharmacists from selling drugs
that induced abortion," with an additional order to enforce it "in the
provinces." In March 1827 the government issued an order against two
Jewish midwives in Constantinople "accused of providing abortifacients to pregnant women," exiling them "to Thessalonica" (Somel

2002, 341; Demirci and Somel 2008, 386).[4] According to an antiabortion account published in 1872 by Ottoman journalist Basiretçi Ali (1845–1910), women seeking to abort "deliberately miscarry their infants immediately after they realize their pregnancy" (quoted in Demirci and Somel 2008, 411), indicating that abortion practices were guided by developmental gestational thinking.

In her doctoral dissertation on abortion in the empire from the 1840s until about the end of the century, Gülhan Balsoy finds elites were mainly worried about "depopulation," since population numbers were understood as crucial to economic, military, and international vitality; they worried about not having enough laborers for agriculture and industry and soldiers to conscript (Balsoy 2009, 9, 10, 13, 19–20, 125). In addition to aiming to reduce the widespread practice of abortion, especially among Muslim women, nineteenth-century Ottoman pronatalist policies focused on lowering infant mortality rates and ameliorating epidemics and diseases by developing public health projects and by building medical institutions (2, 7, 25–29, 126–127).

Midwives were often blamed for infant mortality, especially by physicians, leading to a variety of policies, including disallowing midwives from using forceps or their hands to turn a fetus in a woman's uterus early in the nineteenth century, establishing a midwifery curriculum within the medical school in 1842, and vigorous licensing and regulation policies (72–73, 86–87, 89–90, 220). In 1842 the Constantinople government required midwives, "whether Christian, Jewish, or Muslim," to register for a midwifery course at the medical school. They were prohibited from using "a midwife chair" without a diploma from this course, which was taught by two midwives, one French and one Austrian, who were hired by the government (Demirci and Somel 2008, 394–395).

Midwives resisted these attempts to control them because "midwifery was one of the very few profitable career paths for Ottoman women, and entry into the profession was not controlled as in other trades, which were under the rigid control of either guilds or state

---

[4] Jewish midwives were popular with Ottoman women of all backgrounds because they were considered "modest and calm" in the dramatic setting of childbirth (Demirci 2008, 396 N60).

regulations" (395–396). By 1845 a mere thirty-six women had received the midwifery diploma, twenty-six of them Christian and the remaining Muslim; most of the certified midwives were "later employed at civil and military hospitals." The overwhelming majority of working midwives "shunned this professional training" and continued to practice, even in Anatolia (396, 399).

The early nineteenth-century Ottoman Egyptian state under its independent-minded viceroy Mehmet Ali was similarly concerned with the abortion practices of independent midwives, so it invited French physician Antoine Clot (Clot Bey) to establish a medical school in 1832 to train women to become *hakimat* (health workers) and midwives. As occurred later with certified midwives in Constantinople, these women ultimately came to work directly for the state, for example conducting autopsies on women's bodies (Hatem 1997, 70–71). State-employed Egyptian *hakima*s worked to control Egyptian women's reproductive practices through "sanitary policing" that included registering births, verifying "causes of death among women," and requiring a "death certificate by an agent of the state before burial" (67, 74). By the 1890s the Ottomans in Constantinople were appointing licensed and salaried (by "local budgets") midwives in many major cities in the empire. Appointed midwives received pensions upon retiring and their children received death benefits (Balsoy 2009, 104–106). Balsoy mentions a Midwife Emetullah appointed to Jerusalem in 1898 (104n80).

The "major obstacle" to the Ottoman state agenda to "prevent abortion and promote maternity" was "Islamic law, which considered conjugal issues an inviolable realm, sheltered women from disciplinary interventions," and considered women part of family units (Demirci and Somel 2008, 378). Long-standing societal and Islamic jurisprudential and medical respect for midwives – as well as gender segregation and bodily privacy norms that facilitated female spaces and socialities – posed considerable additional barriers to state interventions in reproduction. As Avner Giladi explains, Islamic scholars and jurists "in the central and western areas of the Islamic world" for centuries considered midwives trustworthy professionals "skilled in medicine" and especially knowledgeable about girls' and women's bodies and health. Islamic elites in law and medicine similarly recognized midwives as experts in gynecology and obstetrics and differentiated them from nonexpert but experienced birthing assistants. Usually referred to in the Arabic singular as *qabila* ("receiver of the newborn"), "Midwives represent the epitome of the physical essence of femininity, with its periods of impurity – during menstruation and childbirth and after delivery; they are associated with its creative power and threatening mystery alike" (Giladi 2015, 56–58, 60–63, 66, 118).

Legal steps against the provision of abortion "remained piecemeal and ad hoc" in the empire until November 1838, when an imperial edict (*firman*) consolidated three proposals and reports issued in Constantinople by the "Council of Public Works, the Council of the Sublime Porte, and the Sublime Council for Judicial Ordinances" (Demirci and Somel 2008, 385, 386, 387; Reşit Paşa 1872, 750–757; also Balsoy 2009, 139–144).[5] The Council of Public Works report accused women in Constantinople especially of "habitually committing the shameful act of abortion which is against the will of God" (Somel 2002, 341–342; Reşit Paşa 1872, 750–752). Its authors argued that the two main causes of abortion were "hedonism and comfort" and "material difficulty to raise a child," recommending "coercion" against the former and state support to address the latter if "a poor family has more than five children" (Somel 2002, 342). The document affirmed the sultan's commitment to "realize the religious commands as well as prohibitions" in the "measures [that] will be taken to prevent abortion," indicating recognition that Islamic jurisprudence was flexible on this matter. It called for the government's chief physician to warn non-Muslim "midwives, physicians and druggists … not to provide the population with abortifacient drugs" and to require them to "give oath to their religious leaders not to sell abortifacients," and for Muslim midwives to do the same before an Islamic judge in Constantinople (342).

The Council of the Sublime Port then published its own memo warning that "many women already knew how to prepare" abortifacients and did not need the assistance of "physicians, druggists and midwives"; it also drew attention to "Jewish midwives in Istanbul," recommending they be prohibited from abortion activities (342–343). The memo suggested punishment for residents who did not notify the government of abortion activities, and "the necessity" of

---

[5] Special thanks to Brooke Andrade at the National Humanities Center, who found a number of important Ottoman texts for me, and Günay Kayarlar, who was kind enough to skim ten pages in Ottoman Turkish to confirm their contents.

extending "the policy to all of the Ottoman provinces" (343). The two documents' "considerations and ... measures ... were accepted by the Sublime Council for Judicial Ordinances," which additionally *recommended* punishing pregnant women "willing to abort their foetus" and the consenting husband, and imposing this policy "throughout the Empire" (Somel 2002, 343; Demirci and Somel 2008, 393). The "propositions and measures" were "approved by [Sultan] Mahmud II" as a consolidated decree in 1838 (Somel 2002, 343).

The results were distributed as an announcement (in Turkish) that was word-for-word distributed "throughout Ottoman lands," using the following language: "since the prosperity of a country was dependent upon the magnitude of its population, avoiding unwanted acts that would decrease the population was not only meritorious, but also a religious duty that was to be rewarded by God." The announcement called abortion "against the will of God," "homicide," and a "grave sin" (Balsoy 2009, 143–144). However, not a single article from the 1838 decree was included in the 1840 Ottoman Penal Code or its comprehensive revision in 1851 (Demirci and Somel 2008, 391), both of which applied to the Palestinian districts of Greater Syria.

A legal turning point occurred in August 1858 when the Ottoman Penal Code punished providers of abortion services. Article 193 sentenced any person helping a woman commit abortion or providing her with methods to do so with "six months to two years of imprisonment." If such assistance came from "a physician, surgeon, or pharmacist," they would additionally "be sentenced to forced labor" (392). Coming as it did after a shift to a more Westernizing Ottoman leadership following the Crimean War (1853–1856), during which the Ottoman government sided with the British and French against the Russians, the 1858 Penal Code adapted aspects of the 1810 French Penal Code. Nevertheless, the articles related to abortion remained "in full harmony" with Islamic jurisprudence by not penalizing women who freely underwent an abortion (392–393).

Ottoman elite concerns with imperial population strength became more Muslim after the Russo-Ottoman War (1877–1878), when the empire's borders shrank with the loss of the majority-Christian Balkans (402). Nevertheless, cases where Ottoman midwives and pharmacists were punished for facilitating or botching an abortion remained relatively rare in nineteenth-century records (Balsoy 2009, 144–146). After the Ministry of the Interior appointed a commission to determine causes of abortion in 1892, the latter published an antiabortion pamphlet in Turkish that was translated into Arabic for distribution to the provinces. The pamphlet relied on public health rather than moralist rhetoric to discourage abortion. It condemned abortionists on "religious and humanitarian" grounds and advertised state policies that established mobile health units where needed and provided financial support to needy larger families (156–158, 161). Pronatalist efforts continued with a 1904 declaration "proposing additional material support" to parents of twins, triplets, and adoptees to encourage Muslims to have more children, and lawsuits against pharmacists who supplied drugs to pregnant women, for example in Ottoman Belgrade (Ertem 2011, 51). After five years trying to overcome "a long lasting resistance of [the] German embassy," in 1905 the Ottoman government expelled "a very famous German physician who practised abortion in Istanbul," Madame Zeibold (51).

Despite these efforts, no legal penalty existed for women who chose to abort a fetus until the Ottoman Parliament passed a revised Imperial Ottoman Penal Code on June 4, 1911 (Schull 2007, 85). Inspired by the Committee of Union and Progress (CUP),[6] the Young Turks/Unionist party that came to power in 1908 shifted the government from absolutist to constitutional rule. The 1911 code represented "the most extensive and sweeping reforms to the Imperial Ottoman Penal Code of 1858 (IOPC) that had ever been enacted" (85). It followed the French Penal Code (1810) in "its classifications and divisions," but expressed many differences in content (Bucknill and Utidjian 1913, xv).[7] The code served the government's goal of rationalizing, "centralizing and expanding the

---

[6] The CUP was a nationalist modernizing group that emerged in late nineteenth-century Constantinople and aligned with the Young Turks in the early twentieth century.

[7] I rely on the 1913 English version of the Ottoman Penal Code, translated and notated by John A. Strachey Bucknill, the attorney general of colonized Hong Kong and "King's Advocate of Cyprus (1907–1912)," and Haig Apisoghom S. Utidjian. Utidjian was an Armenian member of the colonial Cypriot Civil Service and official translator of Turkish documents for British authorities. Ottoman law remained applicable in Cyprus at this time although it was "applied by English judges, trained in the common law and following the English procedure that had already been introduced in 1882," after the Ottoman government ceded the island to Great Britain in 1878. Cyprus was annexed and came under direct British military occupation from 1914 to 1925 and was a British crown colony from 1925 to 1960 (Symeonides 2003, 447–448).

Ottoman bureaucracy's authority and power over the adjudication of criminal matters at the expense of Islamic law and courts" (Schull 2007, 85, 135). Consistent with this agenda, argues Kent Fielding Schull, the code increased "the state's ability to intervene in familial and personal matters," including substantially restricting abortion (85, 132–133, 135).

The 1911 code increased the penalties against providers and imposed penalties against women who aborted a pregnancy and their husbands. Article 192 of Part II ("The Punishment for Persons Causing Abortion, Selling Adulterated Drinks, or Poisons without Surety") stated: "The woman miscarrying her foetus by making use, or by giving her consent for the making use by another, of special means, is imprisoned for from six months to three years. The individual causing a woman to miscarry her foetus by preparing special means with her consent, is condemned to imprisonment for from one year to three years. If as the result of such miscarriage of foetus, or in consequence of the means made use of for miscarriage, destruction of person [pregnant woman] comes about, he is put in kyurek [hard labor] for from four years to seven years." According to the two clauses that followed: "If a person, without the consent of a woman whose pregnancy he is aware brings about miscarriage by making use of special means, or by beating, wounding, or committing other acts, he is condemned to kyurek for from three years to ten years." "If as a result of such miscarriage, or in consequence of the means made use of for miscarriage the woman dies, the punishment is kyurek for not less than fifteen years." If "these acts" were committed by "physicians, or health officers or persons practising under Government supervision such as midwives, the specified punishment is increased by one-sixth" (Bucknill and Utidjian 1913, 146, 147n5, 11). Article 193 penalized any person who with or without the consent of the pregnant woman provided "drugs" or instructions to undertake an abortion with six months to two years of imprisonment, with additional temporary *kyurek* if the person is "a physician, surgeon or druggist" (147n1). The less Islamic and more "modern" the Ottoman government became, the more it was able to impose restrictive laws against abortion to serve state biopolitical goals. The next section turns to legal developments related to abortion applicable in British-ruled Mandate Palestine (1918–1948) and considers them in light of Ottoman and other legal regimes.

Abortion in British Colonial Law

Colonial authorities in Palestine largely relied on the 1913 Cyprus translation of the 1911 Ottoman Penal Code until the Palestine 1936 Criminal Code Ordinance was implemented in 1937.[8] This section compares British penal legislation on abortion during the Palestine Mandate to Ottoman, English, and other British colonial codes to situate abortion practices and colonial responses to them during the Mandate. Contraception was not mentioned and abortion was illegal in the applicable laws. However, the British government rarely criminally prosecuted cases of induced abortion, despite – or maybe because – it was a frequently used birth control method by Jewish settlers and Palestinians.

From the early nineteenth century, British state and colonial antiabortion legislation drew on UK common law (court judgments) that deemed it "an offence to procure a miscarriage after the stage of 'quickening,' that is the stage at which movement of the foetus could be felt by the pregnant woman, marking the entry of the soul into the foetal body" (Milns and Thompson 1994). John Keown shows that the "quickening" gestational boundary was largely linked to a court's ability to prosecute an abortion (Keown 1988, 3, 5). The general trend from 1803 to 1861 in English law was increasingly severe statutory punishment for attempted abortion and abortion (27). Antiabortion legislation in nineteenth-century England was propelled by three factors: protecting fetal life, protecting women from injury or death, and, most importantly, campaigns by physicians determined to limit competition from "irregulars" such as midwives and herbalists in the arena of childbirth (24, 27–33, 35–47).

The British Offences Against the Person Act 1861 (still in effect), revised by statutes in 1891, 1892, and 1893, reiterated the severe punishments in nineteenth-century English law for procuring and administering abortion. Section 58 provided that a woman "with

---

[8] I serendipitously borrowed a marked "personal copy" of the 1913 translation of the 1911 Ottoman code from a university library in New York previously owned by the British "Chief Justice" of Palestine, either Sir Thomas Wagstaffe Haycraft, chief justice from 1921 to 1927, or Sir Michael F. J. McDonnell, chief justice from 1927 to 1936. According to a commercial embossment on the front matter, the text was originally purchased at the Jerusalem branch of "Tarbuth Booksellers & Stationery's," which also had shops in Jaffa and Haifa (Bucknill and Utidjian 1913).

intent to procure her own miscarriage" using any method, and a person "with intent to procure the miscarriage of any woman, whether she be or be not with child," who "unlawfully administer[s] to her or cause[s] to be taken by her any poison or other noxious thing ... with the like intent, shall be guilty of felony and being convicted thereof shall be liable ... to be kept in penal servitude" for at least three and at most five years. Section 59 created an additional offense by providing that any person who "unlawfully" supplies or procures methods "knowing that the same is intended to be unlawfully used or employed with intent to procure the miscarriage of any woman, whether she be or be not with child, shall be guilty of a misdemeanor and being convicted thereof shall be liable ... to be kept in penal servitude" for "a minimum of three and a maximum of five years" (Sections 58 and 59, quoted in Keown 1988, Appendices, 167 with amendments in notes 1, 2, and 3).[9]

Section 312 of the 1860 (British colonial) Indian Penal Code (IPC), which was applicable beginning in 1862 and remains in effect with revisions, provides that whoever causes a pregnant woman to "miscarry," including the woman herself, "if such a miscarriage be not caused in good faith for the purpose of saving the life of the woman," would receive a prison penalty "for a term which may extend to three years, or with fine, or with both; and, if the woman be quick with child, shall be punished with imprisonment ... for a term which may extend to seven years and shall also be liable to fine (Raghavan and Bakshi 2000, 222). Notably, the commentary defines "miscarriage" to occur only between "the fourth to seventh month of gestation" and states that "prevention of conception is not an offence" (223). The fourth month seems to be the definition of the "quickening" point, so induced abortion before that gestational stage was legal in British-colonized India but not in England as far as I can determine from the sources I examined. Section 314 of the IPC provides that a person intending to cause a miscarriage who also causes a woman's death "shall be punished with imprisonment ... for a term which may extend to ten years,

---

[9] The 1861 act was perceived not to cover "the period during which the child was being born, a time at which some women allegedly killed their babies." As a result, the British Parliament passed the Infant Life (Preservation) Act of 1929, "which criminalised 'child destruction'" of a life "capable of being born alive" but extended the period of viability from twenty-eight weeks to birth (Milns and Thompson 1994). Article 1.1 of the 1929 act, which may be found in *Blackstone's Statutes: Medical Law*, provides an exception for saving the life of the pregnant woman (Morris and Jones 2007, 2).

and shall also be liable to fine" (224–225). Section 315 provides that a person acting to prevent a "child from being born alive or causing it to die after its birth, and does by such act prevent that child from being born alive, or causes it to die after its birth, shall, if such act be not caused in good faith for the purpose of saving the life of the mother, be punished with imprisonment ... for a term which may extend to ten years, or with fine, or with both" (226).

Mitra Sharafi finds that colonial authorities rarely enforced the antiabortion provisions in the IPC, despite abortion being "very frequent" in India. The only cases that made it to court involved situations where a woman had died and even these rarely resulted in conviction, at least partly because Indian physicians were reluctant "to cooperate with the criminal justice system" (Sharafi 2020, 2–3, 19). British colonial officials "regarded abortion as an unfortunate corrective to an oppressive [Indian] norm" that expected widows to remain "chaste" in order to continue receiving financial support from the families of deceased husbands. They believed that in-laws falsely accused widows (understood as "victims") of having had an abortion motivated by economic interest. Moreover, enforcing antiabortion provisions would have affected separated "imperial couples" engaged in "extramarital relationships" whose pregnancies required termination (3, 19, 25).

The Cyprus Criminal Code Order in Council 1928, which applied to the British colony of Cyprus, drew from Sections 58 and 59 of the Offences Against the Person Act 1861 (Dickens and Cook 1979, 427–429) rather than the IPC of 1860, although the abortion-related penalties were more severe in the Cyprus Criminal Code. In Chapter XVI, "Offences Against Morality," Article 153 states that any person who intentionally procured a "miscarriage of a woman, whether she is or is not with child, unlawfully administers to her or causes her to take any poison or other noxious thing, or uses any force of any kind, or uses any other means whatever, is guilty of a felony, and is liable to imprisonment for fourteen years" (Government of Cyprus 1928, 29). Article 154 provides that a woman who "with intent to procure her own miscarriage," whether or not she is pregnant, "unlawfully administers to herself any poison or other noxious thing, or uses any force of any kind, or uses any other means whatever, or permits any such thing or means to be administered or used to her, is guilty of a felony, and is liable to imprisonment for seven years" (29). Article 155 states that any person who "unlawfully supplies to or procures for any person anything whatever, knowing that it is intended to be unlawfully used to procure the miscarriage of a woman," whether or not she is pregnant, "is guilty of a felony, and is liable to imprisonment for three years" (29).

The Criminal Law of Palestine 1928, "compiled by Norman Bentwich," was described by him as "being the parts of the Ottoman Penal Code which are still in force and the principle [*sic*] ordinances of the Government of Palestine replacing parts of that code" (Bentwich 1928).[10] On abortion, the 1928 British Criminal Law followed the 1911 Ottoman penal law. Part II, titled "Procuring Abortion, Selling Adulterated Liquors or Poisons," largely repeats the language and penalties in article 193 of the 1911 Ottoman Criminal Code without the legal nuances and notes (64–65).

Criminal Code Ordinance No. 74 of 1936 (Leon 1947), which came into force on January 1, 1937 (and remains in effect), in contrast represented a radical legal rupture whose *Palestinian social and political history* is yet to be written as far as I am aware. It replaced the Ottoman Penal Code of 1911, as Part I, Chapter I, Article No. 2 declares: "the Ottoman Penal Code shall cease to be in force in Palestine" (5). With respect to abortion, the code makes procuring, assisting, or using methods to induce abortion illegal, but in comparison to the 1911 Ottoman penal code the penalties for women who acquire an abortion and those who assist them are substantially higher (nos. 175–177 of chapter XVII). As with the Cyprus Criminal Code, abortion is addressed in a lengthy chapter (XVII) familiarly titled "Offences against Morality," loaded Western colonial prose that contrasts with the descriptive title used in the 1911 Ottoman penal law.

---

[10] The British barrister and lifelong Zionist was the first attorney general in Mandate Palestine, serving between 1922 and 1931. British authorities in Palestine urgently sought to replace the 1911 Ottoman Penal Code to control Arab anti-colonial and anti-Zionist resistance, but faced fifteen years of obstacles, especially from Palestinians (Bentwich 1938, 71–72). Bentwich viewed "the serious rioting in Palestine of 1929" to require stronger punishment for homicide than allowed by Ottoman penal law. The Shaw Commission explicitly recommended such punishment after the 1929 riots (72). While he dismissed Palestinian criticisms of the draft penal law, the "disfavor of the Colonial Office" in London, which "desired a Code based primarily on English and not on French models," was taken more seriously (72). It seems that the Indian Penal Code of 1860 was version 1 of British colonial penal law, followed by the "Australian Queensland Code" of 1899 (version 2), the "Codes of East Africa" (version 3), and the Cyprus Code of 1928, which became "the basis of the Colonial Office Code" (version 4) (Dickens and Cook 1979, 425–426).

Chapter XVII also discusses sodomy, underage sex, carnal knowledge of animals, indecent acts, marriage with underage persons, procuring prostitutes, and unlawful sexual intercourse (40–45).

Three articles address induced abortion in the 1936 law, Nos. 175, 176, and 177. The definition of crimes and the penalties are identical to those in the Cyprus Criminal Code of 1928. Article No. 175 (like Art. 153) states: "Any person who, with intent to procure miscarriage of a woman, whether she is or is not with child, unlawfully administers to her or causes her to take any poison or other noxious thing, or uses any force of any kind, or uses any other means whatever, is guilty of a felony, and is liable to imprisonment for fourteen years" (45).[11] This penalty is substantially harsher than the relevant article in the 1911 Ottoman code and the language does not distinguish whether a woman was in fact pregnant or had sought assistance. Article No. 176 (like Art. 154) states: "Any person who, with intent to procure her own miscarriage, whether she is or is not with child, unlawfully administers to herself any poison or other noxious thing, or uses any force of any kind, or uses any other means whatever, or permits any such thing or means to be administered or used to her, is guilty of a felony, and is liable to imprisonment for seven years" (45). In comparison, the 1911 Ottoman code does not categorize a woman who successfully acquires an abortion as a "felon" and the penalty for such a woman is less, imprisonment "for from six months to three years." According to Article No. 177 (like Art. 155): "Any person who unlawfully supplies to or procures for any person anything whatever, knowing that it is intended to be unlawfully used to procure the miscarriage of a woman, whether she is or is not with child, is guilty of a misdemeanour" (45).[12] Article 193 of the 1911 Ottoman code is similar, providing for "six months to two years of imprisonment" for such accomplices and additional hard labor if they are medical practitioners (Bucknill and Utidjian 1913, 147n1).[13] The final section of this chapter brings the legal story of abortion in historic Palestine to the present.

[11] A "felony" is defined in the 1936 criminal code as "an offence which is punishable, without proof of previous conviction, with death, or with imprisonment for more than three years" (Leon 1947, 6).
[12] The 1936 criminal code defines a "misdemeanour" as "any offence which is not a felony or a contravention" (Leon 1947, 7).
[13] The 1936 criminal code includes no penalties for providers of abortion or its means where a woman dies as a result (Leon 1947, 45, 55–56).

Post-1948 Legal Developments on Birth Control

This section provides a digest of Israeli, Jordanian, Egyptian, and Palestinian National Authority legal developments on abortion after 1948 since all of them were or remain sovereign in different parts of historic Palestine. While changes occurred over time in both restrictive and expansive directions, one continuity is the politically and socially situated nature of abortion laws and policies. Another is they are most relevant in how, whether, and when states enforce them, as well as how and when people violate or skirt them as they live their sexual and reproductive lives.

Pronatalism dominated in the Israeli state established in 1948, which was built on a Zionist logic of Jewish demographic dominance, with further preference for reproduction by and in-migration of Jews from better off "advanced" communities (Rousso-Schindler 2009; Kanaaneh 2002, 43–47). Contraceptives remained illegal in Israel until the late 1950s and even through the 1980s "were available primarily through private physicians and were not covered by insurance" (Kanaaneh 2002, 35, 37). Abortion was illegal by dint of incorporating the British 1936 Palestine Criminal Code (Basker 1980, 19).

However, the law against abortion was "virtually unenforced," at least partly the result of a 1952 ruling in the District Court of Haifa regarding "a physician accused of performing an induced abortion." The judgment argued that the term "unlawfully" in the 1936 code implied that "certain situations must exist in which abortion would indeed be 'lawful.'" The judge further ruled that induced abortion was permissible on "medical grounds" (such as preserving the life and health of the mother) determined by a physician, if the procedure was conducted "in good faith and skillfully" in a recognized medical facility (Basker 1980, 20, 29; Steinfeld 2015, 5).

An account of the 1952 Haifa abortion trial published in a Hebrew-language newspaper associated with the Irgun movement shows, among other things, the influence of licensed physicians on abortion matters. Dr. Mosheh Horvitz, a German speaker, "was accused of murder by performing an abortion" on Tsiporah Noyman. Horvitz testified that Noyman was referred to him in her "fifth month of pregnancy" by "Dr. Kraus" from the kibbutz of Hanitah. Horvitz learned from examining Noyman that she "suffered from chronic asthma," had already delivered three babies, and had had "three surgeries," likely referring to medical abortions, which Horvitz argued justified the abortion he conducted. After the abortion, Noyman was transferred to a facility in the kibbutz to recover and "her condition was satisfactory." When Horvitz visited to examine her at the request of Dr. Kraus, he reported he "found her playing with her son" with a normal temperature and pulse. After this, Noyman "suddenly and spontaneously began hemorrhaging and complained of lack of appetite." The two physicians determined that Noyman was suffering from "an intestinal infection" and there was some discussion in court of the culpability of another physician at the kibbutz hospital, "Dr. Hefets," who should have "performed a surgery immediately."[14]

The attorney general of Israel followed the Haifa judgment with "directives to the police not to prosecute in cases of induced abortion unless" a woman died as a result, the woman had not consented to an abortion, the abortionist was not a licensed medical practitioner, or the abortion procedure was "conducted in a negligent manner" (Basker 1980, 20–21). While this directive was "officially abolished due to doubts about … legality" in 1963, no cases of induced abortion "per se" were discussed in Israeli courts after 1960 despite 20,000–30,000 pregnancy terminations annually, with "at least two-thirds" of them being "technically illegal" (Basker 1980, 21; also, Steinfeld 2015, 7). In 1966 Israel lifted any penalties against a woman undergoing an abortion procedure and reduced from fourteen to five years any sentence "against a procurer" (Steinfeld 2015, 7).

Coexisting with state law was the decision-making structure of Kupat Holim, the Sick Fund of the General Federation of Labor (Histadrut), estimated to include as members approximately 80 percent of Jewish Israelis in the 1970s. The organization established a "Committee on Matters of Pregnancy" or "Committee on Interruption of Pregnancy" at ten hospitals. Each committee included a gynecologist, "a specialist physician, and a psychiatrist," as well as a nonvoting woman social worker (Basker 1980, 61). The committees used four criteria for abortion

---

[14] "Defense Testimony of Dr. Horvitz," *Herut*, Wednesday, May 14, 1952 (page 4): https://web.nli.org.il/sites/JPress/English/Pages/herut.aspx. Also, "The Trial of Dr. Mosheh Horvitz from Haifa, who is charged with causing the death by abortion of a woman from Hanitah, will take place in the Haifa District Court on May 5, [1952]." *HaBoker*, Monday April 21, 1952 (page 2), a newspaper associated with an older right-wing Zionist organization. I appreciate Duke librarian Rachel Ariel, who was kind and generous enough to find these accounts and translate them.

requests: "danger to the mother's life," "a defective fetus," pregnancy resulting from "rape and/or incest," or "psycho-social reasons" such as "social problems with severe mental ramifications" for the pregnant woman (29–30). To legally protect themselves, the committees "classified all approved applications under the first category of their operating instructions: danger to mother's life or health."[15] To avoid lawsuits they "required the husband's written permission before granting abortion to a married woman." In 1976 Kupat Holim committees approved an average of 89 percent of applications for 7,724 cases. Although the committees operated "extra-legal[ly]," the Histadrut was powerful and antiabortion penalties were not enforced (30–31).

In 1977 a "sparsely attended" Knesset meeting passed Penal Law 5737 (which came into effect on February 9, 1978), making abortion legal in Israel if the procedure was carried out in a medical institution registered with the Ministry of Health and if a committee of three people at that institution ruled it permissible (21, 23). The familiarly named Committee for Interruption of Pregnancies (CIP) at such medical institutions had to be composed of an obstetrician-gynecologist, a second medical practitioner (in ob-gyn, internal medicine, psychiatry, family medicine, or public health), and "a registered social worker" (Israel: Reproduction and Abortion: Law and Policy 2012, 13). With a woman's informed consent, the law allowed five conditions for such a committee to permit pregnancy termination: if she was under seventeen years old or over forty years old; if the pregnancy occurred "from a relationship that is prohibited under the penal law, is incestuous, or is out of wedlock," if the fetus is deemed to have "a physical or mental disability," if the pregnancy endangers the woman's physical life or causes her mental or physical harm, or if pregnancy continuation "might cause serious harm to the woman or her children," the latter labeled "the economic clause" or "the social clause" (Basker 1980, 22; Israel: Reproduction and Abortion: Law and Policy 2012, 13).

The last condition was repealed in December 1979 as a result of strong opposition from rabbis and right-wing Zionist religious political parties given its demographic impact – most abortions were approved

---

[15] Eileen Basker found the Kupat Holim committees actively considered "psycho-social reasons" in their discussion of actual cases, however. Her dissertation offers fascinating discussion of the flexible bases of such reasoning (Basker 1980, 52–60).

on this basis (Steinfeld 2015, 10–12). Nevertheless, in 2008, CIPs approved 98 percent of all applications for an abortion in Israel (Israel: Reproduction and Abortion: Law and Policy 2012, 17). Since 2014 the Israeli government "pays for the legal abortions of many women, regardless of circumstance." Lack of a gestational limit means that late-term abortion is relatively easy, if one is willing to subject themselves to the intrusive examinations of CIPs. Late-term abortion is especially easy in cases of fetal "defects," given an "Israeli obsession with pre-natal testing, combined with a program of free services for the prevention of inborn abnormalities (started in 1978)" (Steinfeld 2015, 15–16).

The second set of relevant abortion laws in historic Palestine is Jordanian.[16] Technically, if not substantively, Jordan gained independence from the British in 1947. Its forces entered "the West Bank" including East Jerusalem in May 1948 and the Hashemite rulers expanded Jordan's borders in 1949 by annexing the territory. Until promulgation of the Penal Code of Jordan 1951, a Jordanian military proclamation declared that "all laws and regulations in force in Palestine up to the termination of the Mandate should remain in force unless they were in contradiction to the Transjordan Defence Regulations" (Mogannam 1952, 195–196).

Jordan's Penal Code (qanun al-'uqubat) No. 85 of (February 1) 1951 largely followed the Ottoman Penal Code of 1911 on abortion.[17] Chapter three (*al-fasil al-thalith*) dealt with abortion (termed *ijhadth*) in five articles. Article 315 punished a woman who aborted her own pregnancy or sought methods to do so with six months to three years of prison, exactly the same penalty as in Article 192 of the 1911 Penal Code. Article 316 punished any person who provided a *consenting* woman with an abortion or its means with one to three years of prison

---

[16] When Egypt had jurisdiction over the so-called Gaza Strip between 1949 and 1967, the British Palestine Criminal Code of 1936 remained in force, including its articles on abortion. We have no social or political history of whether or how the abortion articles of the 1936 penal code were relevant in Gaza during that period. Nor do we have studies of women's reproductive and anti-reproductive situations or experiences.

[17] I am grateful to Lynn Welchman at SOAS and Sean Swanick and other staff at the Duke Library for assistance acquiring primary legal sources. Ultimately, ACOR librarians found the 1951 code by contacting librarian Nawal Raga Alageel at the National Library in Jordan, who kindly scanned the necessary pages of the Arabic law.

and no less than five years of hard labor if the result was the woman's death.[18] Article 317 punished the deliberate perpetrator of an *unconsented* abortion with no more and no less than ten years of hard labor if such an abortion led to the woman's death, whereas Article 192 of the 1911 Ottoman penal code punished such a perpetrator with three to ten years of hard labor and a minimum of fifteen years of hard labor if the woman died. Article 319 increased the punishment by one-third if the facilitator or provider of an abortion was a physician, surgeon, pharmacist, or midwife (*qabila*). Article 193 of the 1911 Ottoman Penal Code, by comparison, penalized with six months to two years of prison a person who provided a woman with means or instructions to self-abort, irrespective of her consent, and included "additional temporary" hard labor if such a facilitator was a physician, surgeon, or pharmacist.

Article 318 was the most innovative dimension of the 1951 Jordanian Penal Code, if we can use this negative term from Islamic jurisprudence to describe state law. The article provided mitigation for the woman who aborted her own pregnancy to protect her honor (*muhafatha `ala sharafha*) and similar mitigation for family members who facilitated a woman's abortion for honor reasons under Articles 316 and 317 if they were related to her up to the third degree (*hata al-daraja al-thalitha*). The article constituted and reified *honor* in legal discourse at the same time that it offered mitigation, which allowed for legal abortion in pregnancy resulting from, for example, nonmarital consensual sex, rape and incest. Notably, Article 318 also offered honor mitigation to perpetrators of an unconsented abortion or when a woman died from an unconsented abortion (Art. 317). Article 318 illustrates how postcolonial legal developments affecting gender and sexual relations are often more restrictive and stigmatizing in comparison to customary and religious jurisprudence and even to the relatively harsh "modernizing" Ottoman penal code of 1911, which did not use moralizing language or mention honor in discussion of abortion.

Chapter three (Articles 321–325) of Jordan Penal Code No. 16 of 1960 declares abortion illegal following the language of the 1951 code it replaced. Article 321 ("Self-Induced Abortion"), Article 322 ("Abortion with a Woman's Consent"), Article 323 ("Abortion

---

[18] Article 192 of the 1911 Ottoman code differs in punishing for a woman's resulting death with four to seven years of hard labor.

without a Woman's Consent"), and Article 325 ("Aggravating Condition"), the latter addressing physicians, surgeons, pharmacists, and midwives, closely follow the language and punishments in Articles 315–319 in the 1951 Jordan Penal Code (DCAF 2012, 36). As in the 1951 code, the 1960 law includes Article 324 ("Honour-Related Abortion"), which states: "A woman who performs an abortion on herself to protect her honour, and a person who commits the crimes provided for in Articles 322 and 323 to protect the honour of a descendent, or a relative up to the third degree, shall benefit from a mitigating excuse" (DCAF 2012, 36).

Articles 59 to 62 of the 1960 Jordan Penal Code, in the chapter titled "Justifications" (*asbab al-tabrir*), are legally relevant to abortion because they allow general "exceptions from penalty and criminalization" in situations where a bad result was not intended, occurred by necessity (*durura*), or occurred while obeying the law. Article 62.2.c. is a justification specific to medical professionals: "a surgery or medical treatment is used according to the rules of the profession on condition it was carried out with the consent of the patient, their parents, or their legal representative in situations of urgency" (*halat al-durura al-masa*).[19]

I asked Dr. Niveen Jamil Faek Tutunji about contraception and abortion practices in Jordan in the 1950s and 1960s during an April 8, 2018, interview in Amman.[20] Tutunji and her older sister Nermeen were the first women from Transjordan to travel to the American University of Beirut for college and then medical school; they had studied at the CMS high school in Amman. In 1954 Niveen Tutunji returned to Amman from Beirut to run the maternity and surgery sections of the Red Crescent Hospital as a twenty-four-year-old. In 1955 she took over the Motherhood and Health Project of the Ministry of Health, which established a clinic focused on infant and maternal health and home birth training of young women who had graduated high school, in coordination with UNICEF and the World

---

[19] Jordanian Penal Code No. 16 of 1960 with Amendments. Arabic, my translation. Accessed January 15, 2020: https://jordan-lawyer.com/2017/04/05/jordan-criminal-law/.

[20] Tutunji's father (a Syrian from Aleppo born in Ottoman Izmir) was the first minister of health in Jordan; he had been appointed in 1939 by King Abdullah to lead the Transjordan branch of the Palestine Department of Health and before that had been his personal physician.

Health Organization. As cohorts of these women graduated beginning in 1958, the Ministry of Health established additional clinics.

Tutunji explained that contraception was not controversial, although it "was not desired a lot" in the 1950s and 1960s. Women nursed babies to space children, couples used withdrawal, men wore condoms, and women who had just given birth had "caps" placed over their uterus or were implanted with a "loop" when they had a reason to avoid another pregnancy. The problem with the pill, she noted, was that it "stopped milk" for breastfeeding, so physicians usually waited at least a year after the birth of a child before prescribing it. When I prodded about abortion practices, Tutunji explained "they used to do curettage but it was illegal ... It remained illegal but they did it in hospitals secretly. Or if the mother had a heart condition or kidney disease or something like that, they would do it." Physicians also gave pregnant women an ergot drip, "which tightens the uterus," when there was a reason to induce premature birth. Generally, however, the goal of state-sponsored medical professionals in the 1950s and 1960s was to improve rather than limit birth (*tahsin al-nasl mish tahdiduh*) given the high rate of infant and child death.

After the Israeli invasion of the West Bank, Gaza, and the remainder of Jerusalem in June 1967, Israel annexed East Jerusalem and appended it to a "unified" city under Israeli jurisdiction (in violation of international law). In the West Bank and Gaza, existing systems of law, the 1936 British criminal code in Gaza and Jordanian laws in the West Bank, remained in effect. Israel amended or replaced them by military orders "mainly in the field of security" (Qafisheh 2012, 359).

Two additional sources of law became relevant in Jordan and the West Bank in relation to abortion, according to a legal PhD dissertation by Abdennaim M. A. Wandieen, but they developed after the expansion of the Israeli settler-colonial project over the remainder of historic Palestine. First, the Jordanian Medical Constitution of 1970, a document governing the practice of licensed physicians, made abortion legal "to save the life of a pregnant woman." Such a decision requires the recommendation of two physicians and agreement by the woman or her husband. This was followed by state-level legislation giving a similar imprimatur with Article 62 of the Jordanian Law of Public Health of 1971, which allows an abortion to be performed "in a hospital or a licensed clinic" if it is necessary to save the life of a pregnant woman with her written approval or her husband's written approval if she is incapable of deciding. Again, "two registered medical practitioners must certify that the operation is necessary for the preservation of the life or the health of the pregnant woman" (Wandieen 1987, 74–75). Wandieen, a practicing lawyer in Jordan when he completed his dissertation in the late 1980s, disapprovingly indicates that the law was stretched to allow an abortion in Jordan "when it is certain that continuance of the pregnancy would cause serious damage to the *mental* or physical health of the woman" (my italics) (76).

The noncontiguous Israeli-Occupied West Bank and Gaza Strip came under the partial jurisdiction of the Palestinian National Authority (PNA) in 1994. The PNA is not the government of an independent or sovereign state with, for example, the right to control internationally recognized borders or issue currency. The PNA "retained the previously applicable law" and "started a process of unifying and harmonising the legislation of the West Bank with that of the Gaza Strip" (Qafisheh 2012, 359). Contraception is legal in the Occupied Palestinian Territories under the PNA and available without cost to married people at United Nations Relief and Works Agency (UNRWA), Palestine Red Crescent, and Makassed hospitals or clinics, as well as at Palestinian Association for Family Planning offices.

With respect to abortion, the combinations of Jordanian and PNA laws applicable in the West Bank "apply to all Palestinian institutions, including in Occupied East Jerusalem, as well as the Qalqilya Hospital," the only UNRWA hospital in the territory (Alrifai 2018, 385). The West Bank laws applicable to abortion include Articles 321 to 325 and Articles 59 to 62 of the 1960 Jordan Penal Code, and Clause 8 of Public Health Law (*Qanun al-Siha al-`Amma*) No. 20, which was passed by the Palestinian Legislative Council in 2004 and applies to all healthcare workers (Alrifai 2018, 385; Shahawy and Diamond 2018, 301). PNA Law No. 20 largely follows the 1971 Jordanian Public Health Law, although it seems to be stricter in its language. Article 8 of chapter two ("Mother and Child Health") "forbids" the aborting of a pregnant woman by any method except to save her life as documented by "two specialized physicians," one of them a gynecologist. Article 8 requires the advanced written consent of the pregnant woman or if this is not possible because of disability, of "her husband or her legal guardian," to perform an abortion; abortions must be "performed in a health institution," and the institution must keep a specific register with the woman's "name, date when the operation took place, the abortion type, and its justification," as well as all documentation, for "ten years at least."[21] In practice in the West Bank, married women are reportedly required to bring to a physician "a medical report," *as well as* a fatwa (ruling) from a religious leader, to justify an abortion.[22]

~~~~~~~~~~

This chapter's historical and comparative approach to law and jurisprudence in relation to contraception and abortion elucidates a number of points. First, Muslim and Jewish religious traditions are far more flexible and plural than Christian traditions on these matters. Second, it would be a mistake to understand the birth control positions and rationales of modern religious authorities, governments, and movements in Palestine and more widely, which are sometimes restrictive and conservative, as based in deeply rooted philosophies anchored in incontrovertible sacred truths. Third, all three religious traditions are guided as much by profane (social, philosophical, and political) as by sacred concerns in given historical contexts, even on the most seemingly fundamental or dogmatic questions. Fourth, Ottoman, British, Israeli, and Jordanian legal restrictions on birth control illustrate state interests to shape or direct to their ideological or material ends the reproductive and anti-reproductive practices of populations. Fifth, these efforts usually failed so they were often altered to some degree in text or application to meet actual sexual and reproductive needs and practices. The next chapter, which spans from the British Mandate to present-day historic Palestine, uses archival sources, interviews, and scholarship to explore the actual birth control practices of women who did not want to be pregnant as well as Palestinian experiences of child death.

---

[21] I translated the original Arabic from the *Palestine Official Gazette*, Issue 54, April 23, 2005, found on the Birzeit University electronic archive Muqtafi on January 15, 2020: http://muqtafi.birzeit.edu/en/pg/getleg.asp?id=14778.
[22] Email correspondence with Reem Al-Botmeh. January 14, 2020.

5 | *"I Did Not Want Children"*
Birth Control in Discourse and Practice

"Whether it was common or uncommon will not be told in books or records."[1]

The seed of this book's focus was planted during a nine-day exploratory research trip to Palestine in January 2016. A *Foreign Policy* essay titled "Palestine's Abortion Problem" (Schwartz 2015), recently published online, had incensed a number of Palestinian feminist friends. I recognized its familiar framing of uncivilized, patriarchal Palestinians set against the foil of advanced and liberated Israelis in the realms of sex, gender, and reproductive rights. As I quickly did the math, I realized an egregious error in the scene-setting lede about a forty-year-old Palestinian woman from Halhul (near Hebron) who was married off to her thirty-two-year-old second cousin when she was fourteen. The woman reported aborting a five-month fetus during her first year of marriage by jumping "belly first" from a "9-foot stone wall," which the reporter claimed was because abortion "is illegal under Palestinian law." However, the West Bank was under full Israeli military rule at the time. I was nevertheless intrigued by the essay's mention of common use of the drug Cytotec (available over the counter in West Bank pharmacies) to induce abortion, which opened the conceptual aperture of exploring Palestinian nonreproductive desires in a nationalist context as part of a project on death.

I came to appreciate that researching contraception and abortion in historic Palestine could not primarily depend on archival methodologies because colonial records were not kept as far as I could determine, medical records were not available, and Palestinian memoirs and oral histories typically do not address intimate and embodied life to some

---

[1] From a July 2, 2016, interview I conducted with renowned attorney Fuad Shehadeh in his law office in Ramallah, Palestine, in response to my comment that abortion was not uncommon among married Palestinian women during the Mandate.

degree because sex and birth control are trivialized by colonial and nationalist frameworks. Additionally, researchers may mistakenly translate the illegality or stigma of abortion, especially in socially conservative societies, to lack of reliance on the method, as admitted by Berit Mortensen, who trained midwives in contemporary Palestine and Norway (Mortensen 2011, 50). Challenging the assumption that reproductive desire reigns supreme reorients how we understand Palestinian history and social life.

This chapter explores Palestinian Muslim and Christian as well as Jewish contraception and abortion practices during the British colonial period and since, despite legal restrictions. It takes seriously the material and personal situations and dynamic cultural milieus that produce nonreproductive aspirations and desires and limit sexual and reproductive agency. In this chapter and elsewhere, *Buried in the Red Dirt* insists on remembering that communities lived in the same times and places in historic Palestine – usually but not always in extractive, exploitive, and apartheid relations. In Mandate Palestine Palestinians were required to negotiate different regimes: the racial settler-colonial capitalism of Zionism, the racial capitalism of British colonization and imperialism, and the class and gender inequalities that structured Arab societies.

The first section analyzes abortion prosecutions reported in Hebrew-language newspapers during the Mandate period, using them as a lens to illuminate public tensions and actual practices, including sex, that crossed religious and ethnic boundaries, as well as regular interactions between Jews and non-Jews in medical and legal realms. The second section focuses on a failed application by a German Zionist sexology institute to the British censorship board to show a Swiss film advocating medical abortion. It also examines Zionist pronatalist discourse for Jews during the Mandate and the status of birth control for Jews in the colonial Yishuv and early Israel. I show the ongoing coexistence of Zionist pronatalism with Jewish refusal in reproductive realms, with some ethnic differences. The final section focuses on Palestinian infant and child death, contraception, and abortion practices during the Mandate period and since, using archival sources, scholarship, reports, conversations, and interviews I conducted with elder Palestinian women as well as scholars, lawyers, midwives, obstetrician-gynecologists, public health professionals, and nurses.

Abortion Stories from Mandate Palestine

Abortion was not a documented phenomenon in the colonial health records I found as a consequence of its illegal status, not to mention approbation. Abortion does appear in the Hebrew press because midwives, physicians, and "accomplices" were sometimes prosecuted if sued in court, which occasionally occurred and was reported, especially when a woman died after an abortion or an attempted abortion. We can comfortably assume that some deaths resulting from botched abortions or lack of care after an abortion never reached the point of being known to colonial authorities given how little healthcare they provisioned to the native population and Jewish settlers.

Press stories indicate that Christian Palestinian cases of abortion death were more likely to reach an awareness threshold that led to state intervention, although Muslim Palestinian women, especially in and near urban areas, also turned to such services. Palestinian women were unlikely to seek abortion assistance from registered ("qualified") Palestinian nurse-midwives, who were closely supervised by the British Department of Health. Moreover, registered ("qualified") Jewish nurse-midwives working in Zionist health service organizations served few Arab Palestinians and, by policy at least, provided neither contraception nor abortion services to Jewish women. British Department of Health clinics and hospitals apparently did not provide abortion services because the procedure was illegal. Finally, Christian missionary medical institutions did not provide such services for ideological and legal reasons.

That left the provision of abortion services to unlicensed Palestinian and Jewish midwives and healers, and Jewish and Arab medical practitioners, especially obstetricians, in private practice. We can extrapolate that Palestinian physicians were familiar with abortion and postabortion care from the story of young Yemeni Jew Yona Tsadok and (likely Russian) Jewish physician Martha Tchernihovsky, which attracted intense press attention in Hebrew-language newspapers in mid-1930s Palestine.

I worked with Duke University librarian Rachel Ariel, who searched for Hebrew press stories about abortion prosecutions in Palestine after I read a footnote mention of three such cases in an article by Lilach Rosenberg-Friedman (2015, 341n48). On June 12, 1931, the Jewish newspaper *Ha-Am* published in its police blotter for Haifa that a Christian Palestinian woman from a village near ˋAcca had traveled to Haifa to abort her fetus, requesting help from a female paramedic, likely Jewish (*hoveshet,* as distinct from a qualified nurse). The unnamed woman died as a result, and the paramedic was arrested.[2] A June 13, 1935, newspaper column in *Doar Hayom* reported that Dr. Alfred Levine was charged in the Jaffa District Court on the recommendation of the Department of Health for doing an abortion that caused the death of a Palestinian Arab nurse, Nasima ˋAwadh; her husband, Saliba Tarazi, was charged as an accomplice. Defense lawyers argued that the woman had tried to perform the abortion herself before seeing Levine for treatment. After only two of five medical experts ready for the defense were called to testify, the colonial court decided it could not accept the medical testimony of the prosecution and released the physician and dead nurse's husband on June 6.[3] A frustratingly short piece in *Ha-Mashkif* newspaper on November 13, 1941, mentioned a trial in closed session in which a Jewish woman and her husband were suing "Dr. Sh." for a failed (unsuccessful) abortion.[4] A Hebrew-language account in *Haaretz* from July 6, 1944, reported that a twenty-eight-year-old woman was brought the previous evening to Hadassah Hospital in Tel Aviv "in serious condition" and died afterward. The reporter learned the cause was an abortion procedure, which led the police to open an investigation.[5]

The most detailed attention to an abortion story unfolded in the Hebrew press between March 1936 and April 1938. It focused on "Frau" or "Mrs." Dr. Martha Tchernihovsky, who was charged, tried, and ultimately imprisoned in relation to the abortion and later death of a Yemeni Jewish woman, seamstress and nanny Yona Tsadok. Yona was in a long-standing relationship with a Christian Palestinian man from

---

[2] "Abortion and Its Fruits," *Ha-Am*, June 12, 1931. Translated by Rachel Ariel. Jewish Historical Press (www.jpress.org.il). National Library of Israel and Tel Aviv University.

[3] "Physicians Were Cleared of a Severe Charge," *Doar Hayom*, June 13, 1935. Translated by Rachel Ariel. Jewish Historical Press (www.jpress.org.il). National Library of Israel and Tel Aviv University.

[4] "An Abortion Trial in Closed Session," *Ha-Mashkif*, November 13, 1941. Translated by Rachel Ariel. Jewish Historical Press (www.jpress.org.il). National Library of Israel and Tel Aviv University.

[5] "A Tragic Incident," *Haaretz*, July 6, 1944. Translated by Rachel Ariel. Jewish Historical Press (www.jpress.org.il). National Library of Israel and Tel Aviv University.

Ramallah, driver `Adel Sha`on. I reconstruct the drama from seven accounts in the *Doar Hayom* and *Davar* newspapers. The story began in the "news from Jerusalem" section of the March 26, 1936, issue of *Doar Hayom*, which reported that earlier that month in Jerusalem "Frau Dr. Tchernihovsky" conducted surgery on a pregnant woman who became ill after the abortion procedure and was transferred in critical condition to the French hospital. The patient would not disclose who conducted the procedure for some time, but after she did, the police arrested Tchernihovsky, who was brought before a British judge. He issued an arrest order and ordered an investigation.[6]

On March 29, 1936, *Doar Hayom* reported that on the previous Friday the Palestinian "Judge Hanania" in the Jerusalem District Court heard from two witnesses in the ongoing investigation of "Mrs. Dr. Tchernihovsky": the investigating "Officer Sofer" and "Mrs. Dr. Margaret Nussbaum." Readers learned that after Tchernihovsky arranged an abortion for "Yona Ts.," the young woman hemorrhaged and was "brought to the French Hospital in dangerous condition." Nussbaum testified that Tchernihovsky "invited her to assist with the young girl's surgery." Much of the investigation and hearing centered on whether Yona had been "sick with a severe disease that made the surgery necessary, or whether she came for an abortion."[7]

A lengthy account published a week later in the April 5, 1936, issue of *Doar Hayom* reported the testimony of Yona Tsadok's lover, "Arab driver" `Adel Sha`on, that seventeen-year-old Yona arranged the abortion surgery herself. `Adel had known Yona for twenty months and "visited her often." He told the court he took Yona to a rented room to recover from the procedure and brought the physician Tchernihovsky to see Yona a number of times to treat her continuing pain. Yona continued to feel badly on Wednesday morning, so `Adel decided to bring "a better doctor," a Palestinian, "Dr. Said." Since this physician was unavailable, `Adel found "Dr. Dajani," who examined Yona, immediately ordered her admittance to the French hospital in Jerusalem, and sent a note to Dr. Tchernihovsky.

[6] "Accused of Abortion," *Doar Hayom*, March 26, 1936. Translated by Rachel Ariel. Jewish Historical Press (www.jpress.org.il). National Library of Israel and Tel Aviv University.
[7] "An Abortion Trial in Jerusalem," *Doar Hayom*, March 29, 1936. Translated by Rachel Ariel. Jewish Historical Press (www.jpress.org.il). National Library of Israel and Tel Aviv University.

During the hearing, Tchernihovsky accused `Adel of telling her that he and Yona were "Christians from Ramallah." He responded that he told her he was a Christian from Ramallah, but not that Yona was his wife. Dr. Dajani testified that the patient had a forty-one-degree (Celsius) fever when he saw her and lobbed a charge against Tchernihovsky: "You're not a good doctor." Notably, Dajani did not accuse the Jewish physician of being a terrible person or a criminal for doing a requested abortion.

Yona's testimony was acquired at the hospital. Court officials allowed the reporter to follow them and attend the interview, which required the removal of two additional patients sharing Yona's room. Readers learned that Yona, who spoke in Arabic to a Palestinian magistrate who translated into English, was a nineteen-year-old who lived on Shari` Pina.[8] She rented a room so that her mother and sisters would not learn of her pregnancy (and no doubt her affair). She testified she was ashamed and afraid, so she explained her illness to her family as appendicitis. She had not told `Adel she was pregnant.

Yona had found Tchernihovsky eight months earlier, and had paid her six Palestinian "lira" for an abortion. Three weeks previous to her court testimony, Yona said she visited Tchernihovsky to abort a second pregnancy. The physician gave Yona one injection each day for seven days, during which she experienced no bleeding and did not abort. Surgery became necessary because Yona was in her third month of pregnancy. When Yona arrived to the medical office for the procedure, she also found Dr. Margaret Nussbaum. Yona reported paying five Palestinian lira for the second surgery and one and a half lira for the medications. She said that Tchernihovsky refused to allow her to stay in the clinic more than three days after the surgery despite her offer to pay more. Everyone in the hospital room felt badly during Yona's testimony, including Officer Robinson, who opened the window, according to the reporter. The reporter added vivid details to the story, describing two bouquets of flowers in the hospital room from her lover and sister, an attending nurse ("sister") who was "sad" and worried that Yona would die, and Yona as looking "terrible" and "pale," but "beautiful," with "big eyes."[9]

---

[8] There are discrepancies in the reporting of Yona Tsadok's age, having to do either with poor sourcing or legal concerns.

[9] "The Dramatic Testimony of Yona Tsadok," subtitled "in the investigation of Dr. Martha Tchernihovsky," *Doar Hayom*, April 5, 1936. Translated by Rachel Ariel. Jewish Historical Press (www.jpress.org.il). National Library of Israel and Tel Aviv University.

On April 16, 1936, the same newspaper published a short report that after hearing from Officer Robinson of the Criminal Investigation Department, the Palestinian investigating magistrate, "H. Hanania," charged Tchernihovsky with violation of Article 192 of the 1928 Criminal Code (the same article in the 1911 Ottoman Criminal Code)[10] because she arranged "an operation of artificial abortion" for Yona Tsadok on March 18; he referred the case to the Jerusalem District Court.[11] Well over a year later, on October 5, 1937, a notice in *Davar* reported that the trial against Tchernihovsky, "who is accused of causing an abortion to a Jewish girl," ended yesterday and the verdict will be issued on Friday.[12] On October 10, 1937, *Davar* briefly reported that Yona Tsadok had died. During a "closed session hearing" attended by "Officers Riggs and Sofer," among others, Tchernihovsky was sentenced to one year of prison, which she was appealing.[13]

A lengthy op-ed by Bina Wallfish titled, "About a Topic That We Don't Like to Talk About," was published six months later in *Davar*, when Tchernihovsky's appeal of her prison sentence was rejected.

[10] Article 192 of the 1911 Ottoman Penal Code condemns "to imprisonment for from one year to three years" the person who prepares "special means with her consent" for a woman to abort, and if the pregnant woman dies, the person is condemned to hard labor for from "four years to seven years."

[11] "The Court Case of Dr. Martha Tchernihovsky," *Doar Hayom*, April 16, 1936. (A typo in the article lists the year of the Criminal Law as 1927.) Translated by Rachel Ariel of the Duke Library and my colleague Shai Ginsburg, whose grandfather was editor and publisher of *Doar Hayom*. Jewish Historical Press (www.jpress.org.il). National Library of Israel and Tel Aviv University. In conducting an internet search to confirm Hanania's Palestinian ethnicity, I found he signed a June 30, 1936, memorandum submitted by more than 150 "Arab Senior Government Officials" from throughout the country to "his excellency the High Commissioner for Palestine" regarding "the Present Situation in the Country." The memo called for an end to violent repression of the Arab revolt and demanded the government address the main cause, continued Jewish immigration to Palestine, which they called for halting: www.paljourneys.org/en/timeline/historictext/6718/memorandum-submitted-arab-senior-government-officials-high-commissioner.

[12] "Tomorrow – the Verdict in the Trial of Physician Tchernihovsky," in the "Jerusalem" blotter, *Davar*, October 5, 1937. Translated by Rachel Ariel. Jewish Historical Press (www.jpress.org.il). National Library of Israel and Tel Aviv University.

[13] "Verdict in Court Case of Physician Tchernihovsky," *Davar*, October 10, 1937. Translated by Rachel Ariel. Jewish Historical Press (www.jpress.org.il). National Library of Israel and Tel Aviv University.

Wallfish rhetorically asked whether the physician was the main culprit, or the "men who brought women to such despair?" She posed an additional question. "Aren't social conditions to blame?" She explained that abortion is a "natural" method that women turned to regularly. Most women and their husbands sought abortion for economic reasons. "They worry about giving the child what they need." Deploying her Zionist demographic perspective despite every indication that Jewish women were not heeding this priority, she argued that couples who abort may regret their decision since this is how "we lose a lot of power." Moreover, "children are sources of joy and blessing." She advocated for changing Jewish mindsets so that "our sons" are satisfied with less and for establishing a children's home for unmarried pregnant women. Addressing social conditions, she continued, was the solution, "not jailing one woman who wanted to help her woman friend."[14]

Zionist Pronatalism Meets Jewish Refusal

This section delves further into the coexistence of Zionist pronatalism with rank-and-file Jewish commitment to birth control, especially abortion, in British colonial Palestine. While Zionist political and public health institutions actively discouraged abortion among Jews, married and unmarried, residents of Palestine made reproductive decisions informed by different priorities. The complex sexual and reproductive positions at play in the British colonial and Zionist settler-colonial setting are illuminated by a set of correspondence from June 1932 between physician Avraham Matmon of the Institute for Hygiene and Sexual Research in Tel Aviv and the Central Censorship Board of the Government of Palestine in Jerusalem regarding the screening of a controversial film that advocated "medical" rather than "artificial" abortion, as well as Cesarean birthing.[15]

The institute, according to research by Liat Kozma, was one of "three sex consultation centers" opened to serve Jews in Tel Aviv in

---

[14] Bina Wallfish, "About a Topic That We Don't Talk About," *Davar*, April 27, 1938. Translated by Rachel Ariel. Jewish Historical Press (www.jpress.org.il). National Library of Israel and Tel Aviv University.

[15] GOP, Department of Health, Health and Hygiene – Health Educational Films, January 1931–January 1933. Location in file: 00071706.81.DO.97.42. Israel State Archives.

fall and winter 1931–1932 (Kozma 2010, 231, 232). Illustrating the pertinence of eugenics in Jewish Palestine, one of the "main purposes of the [sexual consultation] stations was to prevent eugenically unsound [marriage] unions" that would lead to procreation between "the invalid, the insane, ... alcoholics, prostitutes, and homosexuals" (238). Born in Odessa (Russia) in 1900, Matmon immigrated with his family to Palestine in Ottoman Greater Syria in 1904 or 1905. He established the institute in 1931 after completing his medical degree in Switzerland and additional training and work in Germany, Vienna, and Egypt, including a brief internship at a German sexology institute (237–238).

In addition to running the institute in Tel Aviv, Matmon served as the "in-house doctor at Nordiya School, a vocational school targeting lower-class, lower-income [Jewish] families" (238). In 1932 Matmon's sexology institute sponsored "public lectures as well as two courses on sexual anatomy, development, and hygiene attended by 145 individuals, more than half of whom were women" (238). Lest sexology be confused with sex positivity, informed by an ideology of "self-discipline," Matmon used his widely read advice column to counsel men against "obsessive" masturbation (240–241). In the correspondence I examined, Matmon described his Tel Aviv institute to the colonial authorities as "giving lectures on various subjects on sexual research (sexual life of men, marriage, pregnancy etc.)."

In a June 2, 1932, letter to the Central Censorship Board, Matmon sought permission to show institute members in a private setting the "scientific-educational" 1929 Swiss film *Frauennot – Frauenglück*, or *Misery and Fortune of Woman*, which in his description "combatted artificial abortions." "Artificial" refers to *induced* abortion (deliberate rather than spontaneous miscarriage) in Hebrew, but the semiotic slippage is apparent, since the film and Matmon argued for the superiority of "medical" abortions (which are also induced and thus "artificial") – that is, abortions conducted in a physician's office. He appealed to the censorship board in a manner that illustrated the regularity of abortion in Palestine while insisting that only medical "specialists" should be allowed to conduct them. "Now is the right time to project a film of that sort as the number of abortions is increasing daily, and propaganda is made in certain circles in favour thereof, abortions are made by persons who are not specialised to do it (like the case of the midwife Micola [*sic*] in Jerusalem); these show that there is a vital necessity to clear this question by showing this picture whose aim is to combat artificial abortions."[16]

Just two months earlier, according to an April 2, 1932, police blotter for Jerusalem published in *Haaretz*, the court of appeals had approved a verdict of "seven years of hard labor" for "the deadly midwife" Klara Mikola. Mikola, who was clearly on the minds of Zionist elites and British authorities, was a resident of Palestine convicted of "causing the death of a woman during an artificial abortion." A short report in *Doar Hayom* included information that Mikola was German, the investigation of her was complete, and the case was transferred to the Jerusalem District Court.[17] Mikola's name did not appear in any variation on British lists of registered nurse-midwives in 1930s Palestine.

Matmon assured the censorship board that the audience for the film showing would be composed of invited men and women over eighteen years old "who have already completed their studies" and "who have already their opinion on the matter." He suggested that the institute could host gender-segregated showings if the colonial government required. He explained that as a "specialist on Sexology and Hygiene," he would give a lecture in advance of the screening "on the subject of abortion, the dangers thereof, and their result." The Central Censorship Board refused permission to show the film, but its letter stated it would "reconsider the application for its projection as a special performance by invitation under medical auspices." When Matmon reapplied, the censorship board sought the advice of the director of the Department of Health (Col. G. W. Heron), who in a letter dated June 24, 1932, refused permission to project the film "under the circumstances proposed" since "it is superfluous if shown to doctors, and very undesirable if shown to other persons."

The 1929 film in question, *Frauennot – Frauenglück*, is a character-driven series of vignettes about abortion and childbirth captioned in Swiss, French, and English and rendered in silent picture form at first and later with speaking characters. By the second half of the film, an authoritative male narrator represents the position of modern

---

[16] GOP, Department of Health, Health and Hygiene – Health Educational Films, January 1931–January 1933. Location in file: 00071706.81.DO.97.42. Israel State Archives.

[17] *Doar Hayom*, April 6, 1932. Research and translation by Rachel Ariel. Jewish Historical Press (www.jpress.org.il). National Library of Israel and Tel Aviv University.

science.[18] The initial paragraph of the lengthy "précis" included in the scanned Palestine Department of Health archival folder summarized the first vignette: "A woman whose husband earns no money – four children at home with insufficient food. A fifth child about to be born, which will add to the distress, hunger and suffering of the household. The woman out of despair goes searching for a 'certain address' in a quiet street. She wishes to get rid of her burden by artificial means. Would not proper advice help her in her misfortune?" Proper resolution, the film itself makes clear, is induced abortion in a doctor's office to avoid the "tragedy" of "illegal abortion." Additional vignettes focus on differently situated women who find themselves with unwanted pregnancies.

The second half of *Frauennot – Frauenglück* promotes "modern" surgical Cesarean childbirth. Like the film, the précis offered a rhetorical bridge between medical abortion and medical childbirth, in both cases deploying a gendered ideological frame: "Science shows that 'abortion' by primitive and unhygienic means, does not take place without leaving an effect on the woman; the reason being nature has decreed that the aim and happiness of a woman are reproduction. A woman is born to be a mother, and in case she is not physically fitted to normal bearing of children, artificial means are used for accomplishing this, i.e. by the 'Kaizershnit,'" or Caesarean surgery.

Hygiene films such as this one, which combined character-driven story lines with science and health information, were understood to be pedagogically effective because they appealed to emotion (Laukötter 2016, 183). Anja Laukötter argues that *Frauennot – Frauenglück* provoked "the wrong emotions," however, because it stirred "controversy, demonstrations, and denunciations in Germany, France, and Switzerland." Indeed, when in "July 1931, the production company Präsens-Film-AG filed a lawsuit against the Munich police department for prohibiting the film from being shown," the police claimed it "would jeopardize the health of those who watched it" and even create "fear of childbirth" (189).

Denial of permission to screen the film in Tel Aviv was likely motivated by its controversy in Europe and the fact that abortion was illegal

---

18 Shot in Switzerland, *Frauennot – Frauenglück* was directed by Russian filmmakers Eduard Tiss and Sergej Eisenstein, written by Grigori Aleksandrov, and produced by Lazar Wechsler. The film and its production details are available here: https://abortionfilms.org/en/show/3436/frauennot-frauengluck/.

in British Palestine. A point Stephen Constantine makes for bureaucratic decision-making by the Colonial Office in London regarding development policy is likely equally applicable to this case: officials in London had a "preference for a quiet life," thus their primary impulse was to avoid controversy to maintain "local law and order" and "stability" in the colonies (Constantine 1984, 18).

Abortion remained widespread among Jews in colonial Palestine. In an op-ed titled, "The Escape from the Child," published in the "Guarding Health" section of the social democratic Mapai Party's Hebrew-language newspaper *Davar* on March 2, 1934, "Y. R-N" wrote that "the fear of the child has become a sickness that has spread in a frightening way" through the "extreme expansion of birth control." The author continued, surely with some exaggeration, that the "system of two children" (among Jews) was now gone, as some could not afford to have any children. The author expressed sympathy with poor and unemployed Jews in Palestine and asked why the law prohibited abortion, especially because there was no financial support for having children. The author implied that many women aborted because couples could not afford to marry and railed against an unfair situation whereby the wealthy could get proper abortions with good doctors, whereas the poor and the working class were forced to depend on charlatans to provide contraception that did not work.[19]

Zionist pronatalism, on the other hand, was motivated by the racial demographic competition that defined the settler-colonial project in Palestine. As Lilach Rosenberg-Friedman finds in her research, "Striving to establish a Jewish majority in the country was perceived as critical for the establishment of the Jewish state" (Rosenberg-Friedman 2015, 337–338). While sexologist (and eugenicist) Matmon advocated condom use to prevent pregnancy, Zionist public health organizations resisted provision of contraceptive education let alone contraception in order not to "risk the Jewish future as a whole" (Kozma 2010, 244, 245).

Clearly, abortion was used and available in the 1930s, certainly by members of the Yishuv (Rosenberg-Friedman 2015, 339–340). Married Jewish women, worried about losing their jobs with a pregnancy as well

---

[19] Y. R-N, "The Escape from the Child," op-ed in "Guarding Health" section of *Davar*, March 2, 1934. Translation by Rachel Ariel. Jewish Historical Press (www.jpress.org.il). National Library of Israel and Tel Aviv University.

194   *"I Did Not Want Children"*

as political instability in Palestine and Europe, were eager "to control
births" (332). Coitus interruptus, the most widely used contraceptive,
often failed, forcing women to turn to abortion; other contraceptive
methods were "expensive and not readily available" (340). By the
1940s Jewish women in Palestine underwent "thousands" of abortions
per year and "many doctors," especially in Tel Aviv, performed them
"for just a few pounds," as did "amateurs who used primitive tech-
niques" (341). "Voluntary sterility," as the commitment to control
family size was called by the Jewish community in 1940s Palestine,
was widely accepted (340). Indeed, 1941 was a "low point" of Jewish
total fertility (2.12) in Mandate Palestine (Bachi and Matras 1962, 207).
Women usually turned to private providers for abortions, "leaving no
medical records at all," according to the 1943 minutes from the
Committee for Birthrate Problems established in Tel Aviv the
same year (Rosenberg-Friedman 2015, 333–334, 338, 340; Kozma
2010, 242).

Other sources give a sense of contraception and abortion practices
among Jewish women after Israel was established. A systematic study
in twenty-three hospitals of almost all married Jewish women giving
birth during particular windows of time in 1958 found that 40.5 percent of them practiced some form of contraception, the vast majority
after the birth of the first child, and 9.7 percent reported having an
induced abortion (Bachi and Matras 1962, 209, table 2, 211, 212).[20]
Jewish women born in "Europe-America" were the most likely to
report using contraception (64.6 percent), followed closely by Jewish
women born in "Israel" (60.6), an impossibility for those giving birth
in 1958. These two groups were dramatically trailed in contraceptive
use by Jewish women born in "Asia-Africa" (24.8), who composed
a little over half of the 3,006 women in the study. Jewish women born
in "Asia-Africa" were the least likely to report inducing abortion
(4.8 percent), followed by Jewish women born in "Israel" (11.1 percent), and Jewish women born in "Europe-America" (20.8 percent)
(table 2, 211).[21]

---

[20] Of women who used contraception, 62 percent "reported withdrawal as the
only method used" (Bachi and Matras 1962, 224).
[21] Jewish total fertility in Palestine peaked in 1947 (3.54), and peaked again in
1951 (4.01), and averaged between 3.40 and 3.70 between 1952 and 1960, with
higher fertility rates among Jewish women of "Eastern origin" that decreased
with length of residency in Palestine (Bachi and Matras 1962, 207–208, 209).

Palestinian Child Death and Birth Control since the 1940s

In 2016, 2017, and 2018 I interviewed twenty-six Palestinian women born between 1917 and 1933 who had married and had at least one child before 1948 about their health and reproductive practices, experiences, and memories. Because of their reproductive ages, most experienced pregnancy after 1948 as well.[22] When I noticed two or more years between childbirths in a reproductive history, I asked further regarding miscarriages, stillbirths, early child deaths, and birth control practices. This section draws on the women's stories about contraception and abortion, as well as scholarship and my interviews with Palestinian midwives, nurses, physicians, public health professionals, and other informants on the same topic to bring the discussion close to the present time.

Early during the interviews with elders, I realized my focus on the past disconnected me from women focused on more vivid and present grief, pain, and loss related to adult children who preceded them in death, siblings who died, and their own physical deterioration. That is, their accounts and embodied sensibilities exceeded my initial historical endpoint of Mandate Palestine. I learned to better attend to stories that told quotidian, embodied, and collective accounts over time, including other wars, dislocations, and sufferings in Lebanon, Jordan, Palestine, and Syria. Similarly, casual conversations and formal interviews with midwives, nurses, obstetricians, researchers, and friends, especially about abortion, produced unexpected intimate revelations about selves, mothers, and acquaintances of multiple generations that mapped beyond the colonial era and even beyond Palestine for professionals familiar with international midwifery, nursing, and obstetric protocols and trained in the United States, England, the Soviet Union, Jordan, Palestine, and Israel.

Given the passage of time, women's ages, their current aches and pains, and memory lapses, I did not belabor date inaccuracies, inconsistencies, and gaps during interviews, although I often followed up with them or younger relatives electronically and in person. I occasionally corrected numbers and dates from the fuller story and additional research. I took for

---

[22] I interviewed thirty-three elderly Palestinian women in Jordan, Palestine, and Lebanon. In this section I only analyze the interviews with the twenty-six who met my demographic criteria.

granted that respondents had their own agendas regarding what to tell me
and what to hold back. I was rarely alone with an elder woman, which
I generally found to be the ideal situation because children, grandchildren,
in-laws, and neighbors filled out hesitations and memories and asked the
women for particular stories. When I sensed tension in an interview
setting, I asked for privacy or for younger children to leave, but this was
not a matter I had any illusion I controlled. Most elder women
I interviewed lived in extended households, whether in refugee camps,
cities, or villages, and many community members were very interested in
the foreign researcher and her agenda. I relied on this interest to find
willing and able women whose marital and reproductive experiences
occurred in the period I wanted to study. While not pretending to be
systematic, these interviews illuminate a domain of Palestinian life during
the Mandate not previously considered important enough to study.

Contraception was noncontroversial and available to Palestinian
married folks, and women relied on abortion as needed. Married and
unmarried Palestinian women terminated pregnancies with home remedies, pharmaceutical products, and physicians. Informal pregnancy
termination methods included falling, jumping, taking quinine pills,
sitting on hot tiles in Turkish baths while massaging a woman's belly
button until she bled, inserting a *surra*, sage stick, or *mulukhiyya* stick
into the uterus, putting sugar cubes into the belly button, and drinking
castor oil (which contracts the uterus) or boiled cinnamon. In physicians' offices and hospitals, women in the first trimester of pregnancy
received a dilation and "curettage" procedure (D&C), in Arabic called
tanthif (cleaning), or a dilation and evacuation procedure (D&E) in
later gestational stages. Additional termination methods used in physicians' offices included taking pills, getting injected, and getting an IUD
inserted and removed in one session. Palestinian women today also
take Misoprostol/Cytotec,[23] Mifepristone (a synthetic prostaglandin),
or Methotrexate to chemically induce an abortion.[24] Misoprostol is
widely available in pharmacies in the West Bank, according to research

[23] Misoprostol "was introduced in Brazil for the prevention of gastric ulcers" in
1986. Its "abortifacient properties" became "well known" in the country by the
1990s, and "physicians, pharmacists, and women themselves spread
information about the medication." Women use it to "initiate the abortion
process and subsequently gain admittance to a public health facility and access
to legal postabortion care" (Daoud and Foster 2016, 63).
[24] "Medication Abortion," Feminist Women's Health Center: www
.feministcenter.org/medication-abortion/ and "Methotrexate (MTX) for Early

with pharmacists conducted by Francoise Daoud and Angel M. Foster (2016). More than three-fourths of the eighty-seven pharmacists they interviewed reported that women obtained Cytotec without a prescription, although the pharmacists' knowledge of the regimen "for early pregnancy termination" was "uneven and inconsistent" (66).

Nine of the twenty-six (34.6 percent) elder women I interviewed did not answer direct questions about birth control. Three women (11.5 percent) said they did not try to control their reproduction.[25] In three cases (11.5 percent) women struggled with infertility or inexplicably long periods without being pregnant.[26] Fourteen of the twenty-six women (53.9 percent) experienced at least one miscarriage or stillbirth, and typically more than one.

Fifteen (57.7 percent) of the elderly women had at least one infant or young child who died. The number of infant and child deaths ranged from one to five per woman, with an average of two infant or child deaths per woman. The following account is my translation and edited excerpts from an interview I conducted in spring 2018 in an Israeli town near `Afula with a Palestinian woman born in the area in 1921. It illustrates the everydayness of children's death:

[When did you marry?] I was 14 years old. [How many *butun* (pregnancies) did you have?] I gave birth to 12. [Did they all live?] Two died, Fatima and Abdullah. There was an illness that used to come for the children. My mother would make an oil and *qizha* treatment. She would also cut him on his back and chest [*tushatibuh*] and rub him with the oil and put the situation in God's hands. It would be five to six cuts. This is what my mother did. [How old were the children when they died?] Fatima was about three months old, she had a fever. We didn't give them milk from goats and I didn't have enough milk. They drank breast milk from neighbor women who had given birth. That's what women did, if they had the milk and others did not; the others would feed the baby. [What were you doing at that time? Did you work a lot?] I was working in the house, making bread, cooking, bringing wood from the hills. I was breastfeeding her and she died [*matat*] while we were sitting there, in the daytime. `Abdullah, `Abdullah was walking, he was

Abortion," All about Abortion, Feminist Women's Health Center: www
.fwhc.org/abortion/mtxinfo.htm.

[25] One of these women had infertility issues and the oldest responded, "I would find myself pregnant."

[26] Only one of these women was among the nine who did not answer direct questions about birth control.

walking. It was when I moved into this house. He got malaria. I took him to the Lebanese doctor in Nazareth on a female donkey, *hayshach*, do you know the female donkey? [Yes, I know it.] I put him in my lap and took him to Nazareth. The same thing – my mother had cut him and the malaria was all through his body. The doctor was very upset at me and said human beings are made of blood, how could you do this to him? I said these are our habits; this is what older women do. I never did that to a child again. I brought `Abdullah back home and he died on the way home … [Did you always take the children to the clinic?] There were also doctors in `Afula and I took them. There were no buses. If a woman's husband had a horse, he would ride it with the sick child and I would walk.

A Nabulsi I interviewed in her village, which was many winding kilometers from the town of Nablus, was a renowned traditional healer before age weakened her hands. She had many miscarriages and lost five children (four girls and one son) before a son born in 1948 lived after she used a traditional spiritual healer. She reported they all died of measles before that, including her talkative firstborn three-year-old daughter: "She died of measles, measles is what killed the children … Sometimes we put the ill children on our backs and walked to Nablus to get them to experienced doctors. They would treat them, but some healed and some died."

Importantly, women reported infant and child losses through the 1950s and 1960s. Ethnologist Sharif Kanaaneh noted that many children (and elderly people) died in the *hijra* (forced migration) between 1948 and the 1950s, when Palestinian refugee families typically moved six to eight times.[27] I heard similar stories of illness, starvation, poverty, and child death during the *hijra* in the recorded oral history projects with women refugees. Some of the twenty-six elderly women I interviewed also discussed child deaths during these years.

On June 28, 2017, I interviewed Imm `Eid in the Am`ari refugee camp. Born in 1928, she was forced to leave the village of `Annaba in 1948, where she had married two years previously.[28] Two daughters and one son died in the 1950s when they were living in a holding pattern in an area called Mizra`a in Birzeit village. Her firstborn (a boy) was five years old and a daughter was four when they died from

---

[27] Interview with Sharif Abdelqader Ahmed Kanaaneh in El-Bireh, Palestine, June 10, 2017.
[28] All of respondents in this section are assigned pseudonyms.

the same bout of measles. Imm Wafi, who I interviewed in the Jalazon refugee camp on June 22, 2017, was born in Lyd in 1924 or 1925, married around 1941, and left the town with three young children after her husband was assassinated by Zionist forces with six other men. She married another refugee who had lost his wife and had seven more children with him "in a hospital" in Jalazon. A set of twin girls and three boys died during her early refugee years. The first boy from her second husband "became yellow" and died at about four months old, although she'd taken him to the doctor, and the twins lived for about four days. Imm Wafi believes these children were touched by the evil eye. The other two boys "died from God" at six and three months old. She explained they would "become feverish," she would "take them to the doctors, they would give me medicine, they all died in Jalazon."

Nine of the twenty-six elderly women I interviewed (34.6 percent) explicitly said at some point during the interview that they did not want to have children or many children, did not want to become pregnant or have additional pregnancies, or dreaded becoming pregnant for a variety of reasons. Women and husbands who tried to control repro- duction were most often motivated by a woman's health situation, a woman's exhaustion, and financial worries related to supporting children. Some mentioned adopting a culture of smaller family size from better-off men and women in their families or from others in their work and living milieus, especially in towns. Women often heard of birth control methods from other Palestinian women and reported that their husbands purchased prophylactics from Arab pharmacies.

Imm George, who was born in 1926 and ultimately had two boys and two girls, reported she did not want children, insisting, "I never liked children." Imm Hasan illustrated the health and exhaustion motivations for limiting births. After having a few children, "I got treatment because I had infections when I became pregnant. I did not want children. I have an infection that continues until today. I was injured when I had the *bikr* [firstborn] outside and inside [her body]. Before they did not used to suture, *ya habibti*. I got ill in the *'iyal* [uterus]. We kneaded and baked bread."

I followed up. "When you said you were hurt inside and outside, what does that mean?"

She explained that her vaginal canal and uterus were injured by the first pregnancy and labor, "from the boy. I was young and I was injured because my flesh was tender. I was maybe sixteen or seventeen when I had my first baby ... I used to hemorrhage from the injuries. Every labor produced a hemorrhage." When asked if she used birth control, she explained that having or not having babies was from God, although she "nursed the babies" to reduce the likelihood of pregnancy and stopped getting her period from her tendency to hemorrhage. Prodding further about how she reduced her pregnancies, I directly asked if she continued sleeping with her husband. She replied, "We didn't sleep together. He got older (*chibr*)" – the women relatives in the room laughed – "I got sick of the older men (*ba`ouf hali min al-chbar*)."

In a number of cases women had additional children because of their or their husbands' desire to have a boy or more boys, even if they reported wanting fewer children. These examples were numerous and disproportionately mentioned as a source of anxiety by women of Christian background. For example, Imm Khader had two boys and a daughter with her first husband; they stayed with his mother when Imm Khader divorced him for beating her and philandering. During her second marriage, she "got pregnant immediately; my husband wanted a boy." She had five additional children in a row, the middle one a boy, and they used birth control for five years between the fourth and fifth children, both girls. Imm Nabil refused to nurse or name the fifth girl born in a row "to punish her. [Why were you upset?] Because she was the fifth girl. I went forty days without giving her a name. I also did not want to nurse her. [Why?] I was really upset (*inqaharit*). We didn't want more children, that's it." When I asked what she fed the infant, the grown daughter in the living room replied, "My aunt took and fed me." I asked Imm Nabil if it was her husband or her who was upset when girls were born. She insisted: "It's not because she was a girl. We didn't want a lot of children. My husband just wanted two children, at most four children, two boys and two girls. We didn't get what we wanted [*ma ajash mithl ma badna*]." The daughter added: "After me, she had a boy, Nabil." I asked Imm Nabil why she got pregnant with that sixth child: "Because I wanted to have a boy, we were hoping, we said this is the last time. I was begging, only this time, only this time, to my husband and God heard us this time."

Boy desire and family size came up explicitly as well with (Muslim) Imm al-Khayr, who was born in 1933 in a village between Jerusalem and Bethlehem and miscarried (*saqatit*) after carrying a tank of water. She already had her firstborn daughter. Following the miscarriage, which she attributed to God, she did not get pregnant for three years, leading women in the village to question her about this matter. Although her husband traveled to Kuwait for twelve years to work after the Nakba, visiting every one and a half or two years, husbands leaving Palestine for long periods to work did not pose a barrier to pregnancy for most women. To address her inability to get pregnant again, Imm al-Khayr visited an elderly woman (*hajjeh*) who "closed her back" with a plaster (*lazga*) mixture of two eggs, wheat flour, and the shavings of a new bar of olive oil soap from Nablus. The *hajjeh* placed a rag soaked in the mixture on Imm al-Khayr's back for about an hour, until it hardened, and then removed it. She explained to Imm al-Khayr that "my back was open (*zahri maftouh*) from the fear I experienced when I miscarried. I immediately got pregnant and had a boy."[29] From then on, Imm al-Khayr would get pregnant during every months-long visit by her husband until they had three girls and three boys. He decided they should stop having children and took her to "the women's doctor, Dr. Rashid Nashashibi" in Jerusalem, who prescribed her the pill (*habb mani*). After a while, they tried for "maybe one more boy but I had three more girls. Each of them about three years apart using the pill [for spacing]. But girls would come and thanks be to God . . . I have six girls and three boys."

Nursing or weaning was the most common reproductive control method used by the twenty-six elder women I interviewed (six women or 23.1 percent), although they realized the method became less effective as a prophylactic after children began to eat table food. Extending lactation is a long-standing low-technology method for postponing the next pregnancy and is mentioned in a 1927 article on

---

[29] Sharif Kanaana, `Abd al-`Aziz Abu Hadba, `Umar Hamdan, Nabil `Alqam, and Walid Rabi` published a singular text in 1984 based on extensive oral histories with Palestinian women in the Ramallah and El-Bireh areas about birth and childhood. Being "blocked" with a *kabseh* (usually of someone else's doing, a sister-in-law or a visitor) is one of three popular "hidden reasons" that a woman's pregnancy is delayed. The envious spirit Qarina and experiencing a *khawfeh* (fear or shock, such a woman may be called *mar`oubeh*) are two additional reasons for not getting pregnant or losing a pregnancy. When a woman's back is open she feels excruciating back pain to the point where she cannot stand or sit up, usually from carrying heavy items on her head or doing arduous work such as digging or rolling a large stone. In such situations she will be unable to get pregnant or will lose a fetus (*janine*). This malady requires closure of her back (*qafl al-thahr*). One of the many methods to close the back is a *lazga* (Kanaana et al. 1984, 67, 68, 69, 70, 73, 76, 77). I translated most of this book with the assistance of Samya Kafafi, who read and notated the text with me in lively sessions in Amman in 2018, supported by ACOR funds.

the "child in Palestinian Arab superstitions" (Canaan 1927, 171) and *Birth and Childhood among the Arabs* (Granqvist 1947) for the same period. Granqvist found that boys were "suckled" as long as two and a half years to postpone a pregnancy, while girls were nursed closer to one and a half years (108, 109).

Imm Isma`el, a refugee camp resident in Jordan born in 1932 who was forced to leave her Nablus village in 1967, responded the following when I asked about a five-year gap between two children: "As long as I was nursing, I did not get pregnant." I followed up: "So you nursed for a long time. You did not want to get pregnant." "I did not want to (*badeesh*)." Later in the interview, she explained she was exhausted by the work required to reproduce the household. "We did not sleep at night because of the work inside and outside. There was no time to sleep. I had 150 heads of cows to milk, not including shepherding the *ghanam*. All of it was work on work." An ethnographic study completed in the El-Bireh–Ramallah area in the early 1980s also found women who nursed children past thirty months of age for contraceptive reasons (Kanaana et al. 1984, 313).

Six (23.1 percent) of the twenty-six women used devices such as a "ring," pills, or "medicine" to avoid pregnancy. For example, Imm `Abdullah would get pregnant within three or four months of giving birth. "They came one after the other," she explained. When I asked if she tried to use birth control, she replied in the negative, but added, "There was a British woman in Nazareth who worked with Arab women. If the woman did not want to get pregnant, they would put something in for her so she would not get pregnant, five months, six months, or a year."

"So she gave you something?" I asked.

"Yes, like a ring. I kept it for a year, or over a year, and then I went to take it out ... She would put the ring inside the *malada* [uterus] ... The woman who didn't want babies for a while would go to her and she was free how long she wanted to use it, a year or two. She would return to her to remove it if she wanted to get pregnant." Imm `Abdallah was likely referring to the "Graefenberg ring ... comprised of silk threads and bound by silver wire, which was invented by Ernst Graefenberg, a Berlin doctor, in 1928" (Feldman 1968, 234).[30]

---

[30] W. Oppenheimer of the Department of Gynecology and Obstetrics, Sbaare Zedek Hospital, Jerusalem, published a 1958 article that begins: "At a time when so many countries are overpopulated, the prevention of pregnancy has become a consideration of increasing importance," whether for "medical" or

Four (15.4 percent) women regularly used coitus interruptus, described as "we took care" (*nadir balna*), two (7.7 percent) refused to have sex with their husbands, and the husbands of two women (7.7 percent) used a *balon* or *jildeh* (condom) as a *wasta*, or barrier method. Half of the twenty-six women interviewed reported using at least one contraceptive method, and five (19.2 percent) used more than one method over their reproductive history. My research with Palestinian midwives indicates that some women living in coastal cities such as Jaffa soaked a sponge from the sea in vinegar, olive oil, or castor oil and inserted it into their uterus before intercourse, removing and disposing of it afterward.

Four of the women interviewed reported attempts to abort a pregnancy themselves (15.4 percent), and two (7.7 percent) admitted to successfully aborting at least one pregnancy. Imm Khalil, born in the late 1920s, tried to abort her last child soon after the Israeli occupation of the West Bank by jumping off a village rock fence (*silsileh*) – the boy was nevertheless born in 1968. Imm Nabil, who ultimately had six children, "tried but couldn't" abort at least one pregnancy. She explained, "I drank many things, I ran, I jumped ... I was having children one after the other. Then later I did a hysterectomy, that's why it finally stopped."

I found interesting a woman who admitted inducing miscarriages but did not consider such terminations "abortion." Imm Khader, born in the late 1920s, said she used a Jewish doctor in the 1950s to end pregnancies that occurred between the last five children she birthed, calling it "removing children" (*qimet awlad*). "At no time did anything bad happen to me, thank God." She explained, "All the time I would become pregnant. At night I could not sleep with all the little ones. I would get yellow (*asafrin*) from the exhaustion. I was working as a seamstress." When I asked how she heard of the physician, she replied, "My friends told me there are ways to avoid pregnancy. I couldn't bear it. I had no strength." She tried to induce a miscarriage with "Dr. Fox," a German physician, about seventeen times by "swallowing five pills at home," although "it did not [always]

"eugenic" purposes. He indicates the ring was widely used in Palestine and he inserted it "866 times" in "329 women" from 1930 to 1957, and an additional 150 rings were inserted since he started writing the article. He writes that other gynecologists also found the device "reliable," effective, and safe for preventing pregnancy and allowing pregnancy to resume with removal (Oppenheimer 1958, 446–447, 449–450).

work." When I used the word *ijhadh* for abortion, she insisted, "I never aborted while pregnant, never aborted while pregnant. As soon as I got pregnant, that's it, one or two months, before the two months, I must remove the egg. He would do a surgery. They gave me injections to sleep so I didn't feel it and they would take it."

Imm Bader, born in the mid-1920s, used more than one method to control fertility over her reproductive history. When I asked her about birth control, she reported using withdrawal, assuring me that "it worked." When I asked if her husband agreed, she said yes, "because I, see, began to teach ... I did not want to begin teaching with a large belly." She shared a formative experience that occurred before beginning the withdrawal system two years into her marriage. Her period "was one week late and I didn't understand anything. My women friends who graduated [from high school] with me said, *yeeeh, min halla badik tihmali?* [You want to get pregnant from now? It's too early!] So, I took a few *keena* [quinine] pills, which people took for malaria. I took a number of the pills at once and I felt like I was going to die. My family brought me to Dr. Suleiman, and he gave me something to throw up. He said, 'Why did you do this, my daughter?' I told him that I do not want to get pregnant now. I was afraid I was pregnant ... After that, it was four years of withdrawal."

Imm Khalil, also from the Ramallah area, but born a few years later than Imm Bader, similarly used more than one method because she would get her period forty days after giving birth: "So we began to do *wasta*, he would not complete – he completed outside ... He was loving and he agreed. He did it for my health." After having a few children, she and her husband "did seven years of *wasta* in order not to get pregnant." Her husband, she admitted with embarrassment, also "used to wear a *balon* [condom]."

The women who reported actively trying to control their reproduction were distributed in age range (born between 1917 and 1933) and rural, town, refugee camp, and urban residency; they included two women whose own mothers died in childbirth. I assume that my findings on contraception and abortion use among this generation of Palestinian women are underestimations rather than overestimations given some avoidance or embarrassment about directly addressing my questions and the number of women who initially replied no to a direct question and later described a birth control practice. I found no evidence that Palestinian women were having babies motivated by a nationalist or demographic agenda. Nor do the interviews indicate that legal fears or religious sensibilities informed women's decision-making around childbirth and birth control.

A 1964 "Arab Family Planning Survey" in Israel found that only 1.2 percent of married Muslim Palestinian women and 2.7 percent of married Christian Palestinian women reported having had an abortion (Bachi 1970, table 1, 277). A 1965 "Haifa-Nazareth Maternity Survey" seems closer to accurate for abortion among Palestinian women at the time, showing 27.9 percent of all Jewish women (the fewest were reported by women of Yemeni origin at 4.6 percent), 7.3 percent of "Arab women," and 1.3 percent of "Druze women" reporting at least one induced abortion. In the same study, 35.9 percent of "Ashkenazic" Jewish women and 2.4 percent of "Arab women" reported having had between seven and nine induced abortions (table 2, 277).

The "problem" of abortion in Palestine drew the attention of the Medical Committee of the Jordan Family Planning and Protection Association (in Jerusalem) in the mid-1970s. This resulted in a 1975 stratified random sample study of 1,364 married Palestinian "mothers" who in 1974 "at least once" visited one of fourteen family-planning centers in three cities, four towns, and seven smaller towns and villages in the West Bank (Husseini 1981, 1, 2–3). The study offers a valuable snapshot of induced abortion among married Palestinian women in the mid-1970s West Bank. It found that 8.36 percent of the women (114) had undergone an induced abortion and these women induced an average of 1.41 abortions. The women who induced abortion were disproportionately from the town of El-Bireh. Seventy of the 161 total induced abortions reported occurred in El-Bireh.[31] Residents of Jerusalem, Nablus, and Hebron undertook 33 (20.5 percent) of the 161 total abortions. Those who lived in seven villages including Jericho undertook 30 (18.6 percent) of the 161 total abortions (5, 9). Women in the study reported having a "large family" to explain 39.1 percent of the 161 induced abortions,

[31] Almost fifty percent of mothers from El-Bireh in this sample had an abortion (Husseini 1981, 24).

followed by "financial reasons" (21.2 percent), illness of the pregnant woman (14.9 percent), and oldness of the father (8.1 percent) (25, table 23).

In the 1975 study the highest proportion (26.7 percent) of the 161 abortions was done in a physician's office using the D&C method. The next highest percentage (23 percent) resulted from injection of hormones, camphor, or an unspecified matter, although a majority of these required a D&C for completion. Other methods used, in descending order of proportion, were deliberate physical trauma such as hard physical labor, carrying water, pulling or pushing furniture, kicks and blows to the abdomen, jumping over stairs, and carrying heavy objects on the back, often requiring a D&C to complete the abortion (20.5 percent). "Oral" methods were mostly unspecified, with the specified including ingestion of aspirin, quinine, and castor oil, in that order, and drinking hot concoctions of herbs and spices (such as cinnamon, ginger, parsley, and onion skin), which often required a D&C in a hospital or clinic (26–32).

Palestinian society is not particularly unusual in abortion being stigmatized and widely used at the same time (e.g., Shahawy and Diamond 2018, 299–300). A Palestinian nurse-midwife interviewed in January 2016 explained, "women do abortions silently." A gynecologist who had referred abortion cases explained in a July 2016 interview that "it's okay to do it in hiding and not to discuss it." Her own mother told her she had a painful abortion in a clinic in the 1960s without anesthetics. A scholar and political activist who had abortions as an unmarried and married person in the Occupied Territories explained in a January 2016 interview, "women do not usually talk about abortions, even married women who have them avoid it because of society and religious sensibilities." When she was unmarried in the 1980s, she and her boyfriend convinced a physician in a private clinic to induce an abortion, although it was not a "proper procedure" and she woke up in the middle of the operation with "horrendous pain." A younger Palestinian woman interviewed in January 2016 described abortion as "a form of resistance" among a generation of unmarried women who came of age after the Oslo Accords between 1994 and 2000.

By the late 1990s the Palestinian Authority (PA) began implementing strong "education" campaigns with physicians, threatening them and a consenting woman with three years of prison for doing an abortion, and any other assistant with one year of prison, which "reminded a lot of doctors not to do abortions." As another physician explained, "now the situation is much worse than in the 1970s and 1980s in the Occupied Territories in terms of access to physician abortions." Beyond the law, seasoned gynecologists and nurse-midwives explained that younger generations of Palestinian nurses and physicians hold more restrictive attitudes about abortion because of their conservative sexual and religious values underlined by the most surface knowledge of religious jurisprudence on these questions. An MA thesis by Martin St-Jean (2015, 29) similarly found socially conservative attitudes among Palestinian nurse and midwifery students in the West Bank regarding provision of abortion and contraception to unmarried women even in situations allowed by law to save a woman's life.

About 15 percent of pregnancies among Palestinian women in the West Bank are estimated to be aborted, and "approximately one-third of these are unsafe, either because they are self-induced ... or because they are performed by an untrained provider" (Daoud and Foster 2016, 58–60; also Shahawy and Diamond 2018, 297–298). Abortion in Palestinian hospitals today is putatively limited to married women whose husbands consent if the woman or fetus is deemed to suffer from certain medical conditions. A hospital committee decides whether a married woman may receive a termination in cases of hypertension, malignant illness, fetal "mongolism" (Downs syndrome), congenital heart disease, or to save her life. In practice, abortions are undertaken outside legally allowed categories and if they reach the threshold of a private physician's office or a hospital they are usually recorded as "something else," including "vaginal bleeding" or a "fetus incompatible with life," which is likely true for the many women who self-induce abortions and go to a physician's office or hospital for completion and care. A physician explained, "doctors always have available to them this kind of [vague] documentation," although they develop a "bad reputation" if they regularly conduct abortions. Another explained that some male (Palestinian) physicians in private practice have earned their bad reputation by overcharging women in need of an abortion or "exploiting them sexually." It may be that most abortions in the Palestinian Territories are hybrid, using a combination of informal and over-the-counter methods that also require medical care in a hospital or clinic for completion and health maintenance.

Married and unmarried Palestinian women's access to healthcare and contraceptive and abortion services in the Occupied West Bank

dramatically decreased after the Palestinian uprising of 2000, which
was followed by the Israeli government building walls that separate
Palestinians in the West Bank from Jerusalem, an area dense with
Palestinian and Israeli medical institutions that provide contraception,
abortion, and aftercare. West Bank pharmacists report that "contraceptive failure" occurs at a high rate among married women, especially
"in areas like Bethlehem and Qaqiliyah," where Israeli-built barriers
"impeded women's access to health services and consistent access to
contraception, thereby affecting women's ability to continue the cor-
rect use of methods like oral contraceptive pills." A number of pharmacists mentioned in addition that "restrictions on freedom of
movement affected unmarried women's ability to obtain contraception, as they were less able to travel outside of their home community to
get more confidential services" (Daoud and Foster 2016, 65). New
Israeli policies include a humiliating "abortion travel permit" for
Palestinian women seeking care in Jerusalem (58–60). The walls,
checkpoints, closed zones, and highly militarized Jewish settlements
built on stolen land expand the time/distance it takes Palestinians to get
to any part of historic Palestine. Apartheid barriers have even more
dramatically contained Palestinians in the Gaza Strip from all directions, a carceral reality that combined with poverty reduces access to
effective "family planning" and maternal and infant health services
(Bosmans et al. 2008; Giacaman et al. 2005), let alone sexual and
reproductive freedom.

This chapter substantiates continuities rather than radical historical shifts
on birth control in historic Palestine, although religion- and morality-
based arguments against abortion amplified in the 1990s for Palestinians,
shaped largely by the conservative masculinist priorities of secular and
religious political elites. It is incontrovertible that abortion was a regular
and largely undocumented practice during the Mandate period despite
being illegal and condemned for Jews by Zionist elites for demographic
reasons. It was and remains not unusual for Palestinian women across
religiosity, class, education, and type of residency (rural, urban, refugee
camp) to use abortion as a birth control method in modern Palestine. As
Reem al-Botmeh explained to me in a January 2016 conversation,
Palestinian women's abortion explanations are always "about birth and

life, not death." They ask perfectly reasonable questions like "What kind of life will this child have? How will it affect my life?" In the next chapter, I make the case that scholarship on fertility problematically projects political demographic motivations onto Palestinians, ideologically shaped by what are in fact *Zionist and Western* geopolitical frames of analysis, anxieties, and priorities. The chapter then takes an analytical detour into Afrofuturist, Afropessimist, and queer scholarship to consider the implications of futurities grounded in biological reproduction, termination, and life itself under conditions that abjected groups cannot choose. It concludes by analyzing a selection of Palestinian literature and film to show that death rather than reproduction is the dominant theme in Palestinian futurities after 1948.

6 | "The Art of Death in Life"
Palestinian Futurism and Reproduction after 1948

"That's the way our family is and why we bear the name Pessoptimist. For this word combines two qualities, pessimism and optimism, that have been blended perfectly in the character of all members of our family since our first divorced mother, the Cypriot."

(Habiby 2003, 12)

In *The Secret Life of Saeed the Pessoptimist* (2003), the absurdist irreverent novel published in 1974 under the more evocative Arabic title *Al-waqa'i` al-ghariba fi ikhtifa' sa`id abi al-nahis al-mutasha'il* (*Strange Events in the Disappearance of Sa`id the Unlucky Pessoptimist*), Palestinian author Emile Habiby consolidates the Arabic words "optimist" (*mutafa'il*) and "pessimist" (*mutasha'im*) to coin the term *mutasha'il* (pessoptimist).[1] The novel brilliantly tells the leitmotif of disappearance – social and political death – prominently found in Palestinian literature published after 1948. Habiby's neologism offers a discursive aperture to speculate on reproduction, death, and futurity in Palestinian imaginations with the occupation of 1948 Palestine and the expulsion and containment of Palestinian bodies in settings that include 1948 Israel, where *The Secret Life of Saeed* was set and where Emile Habiby lived.

This chapter is concerned with whether demographic competition with Jews has been relevant to Palestinian reproductive desires and practices since 1948, when they viscerally and universally recognized the importance to Zionism of the double action of "Judaizing" and "de-Arabizing" the land. This realization, I argue, did not translate into a Palestinian futurity oriented to reproductively competing with Israel. Demographic concerns have been largely inconsequential to

---

[1] I am grateful to Sherene Seikaly for suggesting I consider this novel when I presented initial thoughts on reproduction and futurity at the March 2018 New Directions in Palestinian Studies workshop at Brown University, "The Shadow Years: Material Histories of Everyday Life."

Palestinian reproductive practices despite their continuing centrality to Zionist settler-colonialism in historic Palestine. The operations of Zionist demographic biopower and Palestinian resistance shift, exist as pluralities in the same time and place, and are never totalizing, as Michel Foucault would have guessed.

Representing Palestinians as hyperbolically reproductive has had at least three consequences. First, it projects and magnifies onto Palestinians what are in fact Zionist and Western pathologies and anxieties reflected in the policies and priorities of their governments, knowledge industries, and foundations, motivated by geopolitical, ideological, and material interests. Second, it misses the range of socio-economic, psychic, and contextual factors that have shaped Palestinian reproductive and anti-reproductive desires and practices. Third, it distorts our ability to see the emphasis on creative, political, and social struggle and regeneration in the face of social and political death in the Palestinian futurities articulated after 1948. Indeed, I found death more relevant than reproduction in my analysis of Palestinian poetry, fiction, and film.

The first section of the chapter questions demographic competition as an explanation for Palestinian reproductive desires and practices even as the establishment of Israel amplified and empowered Zionist demographic anxieties based on religion. The section that follows explores anti-normative African-American, African, transatlantic Black feminist, and Western queer scholarship to put them in conversation with Palestinian reproduction and futurity after 1948. The final section explores futurity in Palestinian literature, film, and decolonial queer activism, showing the primacy after 1948 of political and creative struggle rather than biological reproduction in contexts of ongoing physical and social death.

Palestinian Fertility and the Reproductive Family after 1948

Zionist forces expelled about 90 percent of Palestinians from the war borders claimed by Israel in 1948, making them refugees, not including those internally displaced in the new state. Many Palestinians became refugees twice over when the 1967 war expanded Israel's military borders. Depending on their location in Palestine, resources, and familial networks, 1948 refugees were largely dislocated to the Gaza District, which came under Egyptian jurisdiction until 1967; to the

newly coined "West Bank" region, which included the remainder of
Jerusalem and eventually came under Jordanian jurisdiction until
1967; and to Lebanon, Syria, and Jordan. Palestinians after 1948
continued to differ socioeconomically and by region of origin. New
categories and identities joined the old ones, including for well-off
families from pre-1948 Palestine who lost homes, businesses, and
other properties but continued to carry their social and cultural capital.
Those registered as refugees with the UN Relief and Works Agency for
Palestine Refugees (UNRWA) in the West Bank, Gaza, Jordan, Syria,
and Lebanon became eligible for medical care and schooling.
Palestinians who remained in Israel were eligible for universal healthcare. Residency type, proximity to healthcare institutions, and class
and wealth influenced healthcare access and health outcomes in every
location, although this is not a matter the chapter explores.

    The coordinated massacre of Palestinians by Zionist militias in the
Jerusalem village of Deir Yassin on April 8, 1948, is a foundational
terror event that worked on embodied, symbolic, and discursive levels
to communicate the Zionist commitment to cleanse as much land and
property as possible of non-Jewish inhabitants. Many elder Palestinian
women interviewed for the PalestineRemembered.com oral history
project recalled that their family members left in 1948 upon hearing
accounts of the Deir Yassin massacre. Signaling the salience and horror
of this dimension in Palestinian collective memory of 1948, some
mentioned that Zionist fighters had split open the belly of a pregnant
Palestinian woman.[2] An elder woman I interviewed, married to a man

---

[2] The Deir Yassin massacre was one of tens of massacres committed by Zionist
militias in 1948 Palestine. On June 22, 2017, I interviewed in the Jalazon refugee
camp in Ramallah a survivor of Zionist massacres in 1948 Lyd that killed her
husband and largely emptied the town of Palestinians. Fatima ʿAbdelwafi ʿAnati
(born circa 1924 in Lyd) was mourning the death of her youngest sister twelve
days previously when interviewed. She and her daughter-in-law insisted I ask for
her account of the 1948 trauma, which I ultimately did. She explained that
Zionist militias ("the Jews") had come to their home and taken her husband with
six other Palestinian men "in their trucks." "They had shot on the mosque the
previous night and killed everyone in the mosque." They ordered the seven men
to carry the dead out of the mosque and "burn them." "My husband, God have
mercy on him, said by God I will not burn them. They moved the dead men from
the mosque and all refused to burn them. They shot and killed all seven men …
We walked from Lyd to Niʿlin with my [three] children [the youngest an eight-
month-old daughter] and their grandfather [and her other in-laws]. My father-in-
law put the children in the pockets of the wool saddlebag of our mule … He

killed during the massacre, fled Deir Yassin while pregnant with her third child, a girl born afterward in her natal Jerusalem village. She explained that her eight-month-old son became ill "from fear [*khawfa*]" during the massacre and died soon after.[3]

The violence of Deir Yassin sent a number of sexual and gendered messages to Palestinians. Elsewhere I examine the massacre, its aftermath, and its deployments in Palestinian nationalist discourse after 1948 with attention to the "honor" rather than reproductive dimensions (Hasso 2000). Based on her oral history research with Palestinian refugees in 1970s Lebanon, Rosemary Sayigh writes that Zionist forces, who had studied Palestinian village life, carefully amplified the massacre, using the name of the village in a "psychological warfare" campaign of terror to assure "that the news spread through the Palestinian population ... In the following months Zionist radio stations and loudspeaker vans were to make good use of the emotive words 'Deir Yasseen' to panic villages about to be attacked" and reduce the number of resistance fighters they would face in battles that continued through late summer 1948 as men chose between staying and leaving to protect children and womenfolk (Sayigh 1979, 75–77). Refugees in Lebanon also circulated an account of "the cutting open of the womb of a nine months' pregnant woman" (76).

Palestinian infant and child deaths were lower in the 1950s, although we have no fine-grained data that systematically track such deaths by socioeconomic status, relevant healthcare institutions, and juridical setting in which a community lived (e.g., Israel, West Bank, Gaza, Jordan, Lebanon, Syria). Data on Palestinian reproduction rates and birth control practices are similarly fragmentary and often gathered based on the priorities of the sponsoring research organization. The nonsystemic data I gleaned from oral histories and my interviews with elder women of reproductive age during the 1940s and 1950s indicate that infant and

---

would go everywhere looking for water for the thirsty children." Her sister-in-law's baby died during the *hijra*, during which "there was no food."

[3] Fatima Khamis Zaydan was born in 1929 in Rammoun and moved to Deir Yassin when she married. She had her first two children in the British Jerusalem government hospital and the last child at home before the midwife arrived. She never remarried. Interviewed on June 17, 2017 in El-Bireh, Palestine.

child death remained common, but so did a high total fertility rate, particularly among women born in villages.

The massive uprooting and dispersal transformed family life, which always differed by class, wealth, urban/rural, educational, and regional backgrounds, and a family's sensibilities and culture. It would be surprising if the Palestinian reproductive family did not become more central to survival in an existential conflict that left Palestinians without a country or political representation. Socially speaking, the "uprooting" "tore apart the natural groupings of clan and village," some of which refugees "reassembled in the camps" (127). New borders divided scattered populations and poverty made communication and travel difficult for many (127). Uprooted Palestinians did everything they could to reestablish "family solidarity" and "family reproduction" after 1948, including through early marriage (128).

Commitment to sustaining kin ties differs from having babies for the purpose of demographically competing with Jews, a sensibility often sloppily projected onto "Palestinians" writ large as if it explains actual reproductive practices and fertility rates. My nonsystematic detour into fertility studies indicates rare efforts to break down Palestinian data by socioeconomic class, refugee/non-refugee status, or urban/rural residency, even in Israel, limiting their value as studies of "Palestinian fertility," which is essentialized, and masking our ability to understand the causal factors at play in different settings and times. Total fertility rates are sensitive to many factors, most of which are not studied with the exception of access to contraception and desire for sons. Systematic fertility data that account for Palestinians' multiple statuses within and across different geographic sites and sovereignties over time are nonexistent.

Some of the problems in the literature on Palestinian fertility are illustrated in an otherwise thoughtful lengthy article by demographic historian Philippe Fargues, "Protracted National Conflict and Fertility Change: Palestinians and Israelis in the Twentieth Century" (Fargues 2000). While the article shows the axiomatic importance of Palestinian fertility to Western powers given the "exceptional political history of these populations [Jewish and Palestinian], in which demography played a major role for both sides in nation-building" (441, 444), the second clause presents demographic fertility as a strategy for "both sides." The discursive framing of the fertility question occasionally traffics in other empirical sleights of hand: "Two extremes of fertility transition [are] found side by side ranging from barely above replacement level among Jews born in Europe and among Christian Arab Israelis (2.13 and 2.10 respectively in 1992–96), to the highest level recorded in today's world among Palestinians of the Gaza Strip (7.73 in 1991–95)" (441). Instead of comparing Palestinian Christian, Palestinian Muslim, and Jewish Israeli fertility rates in Israel, which would be closer to "side by side" despite Israel's apartheid-like geography and legal scaffolding within 1948 borders, Fargues compares Israeli Palestinian Christian, Israeli Jewish, and Gaza Palestinian fertility rates. The fertility of the largely refugee women living in the militarized open-air prison of Gaza frequently becomes synecdoche for Palestinian fertility.

Fargues acknowledges that the "plurality of residential destination is not easily dealt with for Palestinians … because their national identity has long been denied or because statistical reconstruction of a population dispersed over the globe, with no internationally recognized nationality, would be a hopeless endeavor" (442, 474n2). While recognizing the unreliable nature of Israeli data on Palestinians, he uses them to explore "the relationship between belligerence and fertility" (443, 442). Fargues posits that demographic transition theory, whose hypothesis is that fertility rates decrease after infant mortality rates decrease in an industrialized society, occurred for Israeli Jews but not for Palestinians, although he also shows the theory does not ahistorically apply to Jews in Israel.[4] The higher fertility rates of Jews who immigrated to Israel from African and Asian societies did decrease over time to match the rates of Jews from Western societies given "equalization of social conditions," access to birth control, social integration through Israeli institutions, intermarriage, and a common language (448–450). However, level of religiosity challenges the logic of Israeli Jewish fertility conformity to demographic transition theory. For example, a 1987 fertility study showed Ultra-Orthodox Jewish women to have higher fertility in comparison to other Jewish and Palestinian women in Israel. By 1996 the total fertility rate for Ultra-Orthodox Jewish women in Israel was 7.61 children. Ultra-Orthodox political leaders had long explicitly

---

[4] For an overview of demographic transition theory, see "What Is the Demographic Transition Model?" by Drew Grover (October 13, 2014), PopEd Blog (accessed May 13, 2020): https://populationeducation.org/what-demographic-transition-model/.

promoted large families to "increase their weight" in elections and "seize political power within Israel by democratic means" (451). Moreover, the average fertility among Jews in Israel at the time the article was published was higher than in "Tunisia, Turkey, or Lebanon," Muslim-majority countries ranked "far behind Israel in standard of living and political participation" (451). Fargues shows the importance of Jewish demographic dominance to the shape of Israeli law and policy, Zionist anxiety about high rates of Jewish intermarriage outside Israel and low rates of Jewish immigration to Israel, and Zionist concern with "low Jewish fertility" relative to "excessive Arab fertility" in Israel (453–458).

For Palestinians, Fargues argues, migrant work in oil-rich countries fostered "a high Palestinian fertility," as did support for Palestinian refugees from the UN and Arab governments, both of which "alleviated the costs of childrearing" and "may have inhibited fertility decline" (459). He makes compelling and not-so-compelling socioeconomic and political arguments to explain fertility differentials between Jews and Palestinians in Israel (460–461), and between Palestinians in the West Bank and Gaza (462–467). None of the claims, however, indicate that demographic competition with Jews explains Palestinian fertility rates, irrespective of Palestinian pronatalist nationalist discourse that developed in the 1980s and 1990s (468–469).

Demographic reports abound that compare Palestinian to Jewish fertility and life expectancy rates in pre-1967 Israel, with Palestinians usually described as "Moslems" (Schellekens and Eisenbach 2002, 546). The ever-present dilemma for Israeli policy makers is "encouraging the Jewish birth rate without encouraging the Arabs to multiply too," writes Rhoda Kanaaneh in her book *Birthing the Nation: Strategies of Palestinian Women in Israel* (Kanaaneh 2002, 38; also Yuval-Davis 1989, 92, 94, 95).[5] Israeli policies designed to "curb" the Palestinian fertility rate and encourage Jewish fertility and immigration are continuous, as is the related concern "to counteract negative Jewish demographic trends" exacerbated by the 1967 occupation of the remainder of historic Palestine, populated by Palestinians (Rousso-Schindler 2009, 287, 289–290; Yuval-Davis 1989, 95, 96). Encouragement of Jewish

---

[5] Kanaaneh's "Babies and Boundaries" chapter is an excellent analysis of the racialized workings of Israeli pronatalism (Kanaaneh 2002, 23–80).

fertility, especially by religious and right-wing parties, has at various points, certainly by the 1980s, competed with "quality not quantity" bourgeois Zionist positions concerned with poverty and lower rates of education in families with more children, which also affected legal debates related to abortion policy (Yuval-Davis 1989, 97–100). On the plane of ideological continuities between liberal and right-wing Zionists, "it was widely known among [Israeli] ministry [of health] employees that approval for a general clinic in an Arab area [of Israel] was difficult to get, but approval was all but guaranteed if the proposed clinic included a family planning unit" (Kanaaneh 2002, 37). Israel made contraceptives available gratis to Palestinian women in Israel but not to Jewish women (Yuval-Davis 1989, 100).

Research findings on post-1948 Palestinian fertility are mixed and variable over time, but show declining rates. Palestinian fertility is difficult to address systematically given that Palestinian communities are dispersed, live in multiple types of settings (villages, cities, refugee camps, etc.), and are forcibly separated from each other in historic Palestine.[6] Nevertheless, scholarship sometimes rehearses the idea of

---

[6] I provide a few snapshots of Palestinian fertility. In 1975 the average number of children among married Palestinian women in the West Bank, including Jerusalem, was 5.8, with lower fertility rates for city and town residents and higher rates for villagers (Husseini 1981, 13, table 11). An early 1980s ethnographic study of childbirth and childhood in multiple West Bank villages found that for many women from the Nakba generation it was more important to have babies after 1948, especially boys, because husbands often worked farther from home and in other countries and "girls needed brothers" (Kanaana et al. 1984, 40). In her doctoral dissertation study between 1981 and 1984 of 272 married women in three Palestinian villages, Rita Giacaman found them to continue to marry relatively young, increasing a woman's years of fecundity. Proletarianization meant more family reliance on grown children for subsistence agricultural work, factory work in Israel, and remittances from abroad. Kinship remained crucial for grown children whose low-wage labor did not provide enough to allow them freedom and distance from their parents (Giacaman 1988, 95–96). In a 1993 study of 301 married women in the West Bank village of Sinjil, Aida J. Hudson found them to marry at a mean age of eighteen and to have a mean number of 3.8 births, spaced by approximately 1.6 years. Fifty-five percent considered four children the ideal number, while 23 percent preferred to have more than four (Hudson 1998, 98, 99). Rhoda Kanaaneh's ethnography includes a table that lists the following total fertility rates for 1995 in 1948 Israel: 2.63 for European or American-born Jews; 5.86 for Asian or African-born Jews; 3.64 for Jews overall; 7.96 for Palestinians categorized as Muslims; 4.85 for

a Palestinian demographic sensibility, in the process unintentionally skirting over the range of personal and social motivations of actual Palestinian fertility decisions. For example, "The higher the birth rate, the larger the number of Palestinians, and the better future ability to conquer the aggressor, the logic goes" (Giacaman 1988, 96). Or, in Israel, where population policy locates "the site of political contest in women's wombs," "Palestinians [living in the Galilee in the mid-1990s] have advocated either having larger families (to outbreed Jews, just as the Israelis fear) or smaller families (in order to afford to modernize them and thus to challenge Israeli domination with the quality of their children

Palestinians and Russian immigrants categorized as Christians; and 6.58 for Palestinians categorized as Druze. Notably, the 1995 total fertility rate significantly increased for each group in comparison to the rate in 1990. Marwan Khawaja compares the mid-1990s fertility rates of Palestinian refugees with non-refugee or host populations in the West Bank, Gaza Strip, Jordan, and Lebanon. Age of marriage seemed to be the main factor differentiating women's fertility rates, given that most Palestinian women have their children in their twenties (Khawaja 2003, 282–284, 287–288, 292). He found that Palestinian refugee women's fertility was similar to the non-refugee or host population fertility rate except for the West Bank, where refugee women had lower fertility in comparison to villagers. A study of Palestinian fertility between 1991 and 1994 found 4.9 births per woman in Jordan and 5.8 births per woman in the West Bank, whereas in Gaza the fertility rate was 7.7 children per woman (282–283). In a mid-1990s study of 841 Gaza women of reproductive age, Serena Donati and her colleagues found the majority desired four to six children. The study found a gap between "fertility preference and achievement" – women preferred fewer children but had "constraints on free reproductive choice" that included lack of access to healthcare infrastructure and contraceptive services and information (Donati et al. 2000, 843, 845, 848). The total fertility rate for Palestinian women by 2003 fell to 4 children per woman in the West Bank and 5.7 per woman in Gaza. Notably, Palestinians in Gaza are more urbanized than Palestinians in the West Bank and Gaza women are more likely to complete high school, although Gaza has higher poverty and unemployment rates (Khawaja et al. 2009, 158, 155, 159). Marwan Khawaja and his colleagues theorize that lowered fertility rates are mostly due to an increased proportion of "never married" women, especially in the West Bank (165–166). About 25 percent of women in Gaza and 23 percent of women in the West Bank reported "unmet need" for birth control (167–170). Analyzing large-scale surveys, Weeam Hammoudeh and Dennis P. Hogan found that by 2006 "contraceptive use accounted for the greatest fall in fertility" among Palestinians in the West Bank, where there was a 16.8 percent decrease, and in the Gaza Strip, where there was a 14.7 percent decrease. Additional factors explaining decreased fertility by order of importance included "fewer marriages in the younger age groups" of fifteen to twenty-four-year-olds in Gaza and "increased duration of breastfeeding" in both the West Bank and Gaza (Hammoudeh and Hogan 2012).

rather than the quantity)" (Kanaaneh 2002, 17–18, 82).[7] In the Coda, I revisit the ideological work of popular rhetoric that frames Palestinian reproduction as motivated by demographic competition.

Idiographic studies of Palestinian women's reproductive and anti-reproductive motivations and decision-making are notably limited. A short report from a 2011 study that relied on interviews with a sample of eight mothers with between one and six children in the Qalandia refugee camp in the West Bank found that "political reasons" were relevant to fertility decisions for seven of them in the sense that they "feared death or imprisonment of their adolescent sons by the Israeli military." While most of these women were motivated to "have more children to counter such losses," mothers with imprisoned or killed sons "had fewer children because of the loss of an income provider and because they were scared of losing another child." Moreover, mothers who did not articulate a connection between fertility and "national struggle were having many children" (Hansson et al. 2013). Consciously or unconsciously, some Palestinians may worry about needing "a replacement child because this one might be killed," as an experienced nurse-midwife mused during an interview I conducted with her in Palestine in 2018, which should not be reduced to a *nationalist demographic* motivation. Indeed, none of the "political" reasons given in the Qalandia refugee camp study were based on demographic grounds.

A valuable qualitative study by Gaza public health researcher Khitam Abu Hamad in 2020 based on six focus groups with married women (nine in each focus group) aged between fifteen and forty-nine years who had at least one child younger than five years old offers some insights on the relevance of demographic competition to fertility in present-day Gaza. Abu Hamad divided the women evenly between contraceptive users (three focus groups) and non-contraceptive users (three focus groups) (Abu Hamad 2020). Problematically, the article frames Gazans as living in conditions of "economic transition" of improved "socio-economic conditions" and lower infant mortality rates that should lower fertility rates (1). Abu Hamad describes as high the 4.5 total fertility rate for Gaza women according to 2018 data from the Palestinian Central Bureau of Statistics (1), although it is significantly lower than the 5.7 total fertility rate in 2003 (Khawaja et al. 2009).

---

[7] Kanaaneh develops the consumption dimension of Palestinian reproductive modernity in the Galilee in the "Luxurious Necessities" chapter (2002, 81–103).

Abu Hamad's findings from the focus group research are the following: Gaza women and their families viewed having four to five children as ideal and preferred childbearing to be completed in a woman's twenties. They understood children as "an asset and source of social security" in old age (Abu Hamad 2020, 2). They expressed the familiar understanding that their "ability to reproduce, particularly sons," shapes their "social standing, recognition, and marital stability," and discussed the common practice of not using a contraceptive until a son is born. All the women "stated that son preference is one of the main motivating factors for having many children within a short interval" (2). Women were familiar with contraceptive methods, with the IUD the most preferred and used, followed by the pill. Women who did not use contraception noted a variety of reasons, including high unemployment, which led to "spare time" and boredom, encouraging them to get pregnant (3). Religiosity was largely irrelevant to their decisions, although they debated among each other the nature of Islamic teachings on contraceptive use (3).

The majority of women in the study reported that the political conflict affected family size decisions in ways that led to *more* or *fewer* children (4). For those who wanted more children, the thousands of Palestinians killed in Israel's wars on Gaza required "a reservoir" within a family to "compensate" for martyred children. A quarter of the women, in contrast, reported that the wars increased their desire to use contraceptives because of the devastation of having children killed. They explained that "many families do not want to bring children into the world to suffer and perhaps die ['like chickens'] without being able to offer them a good life." It was noticeably more difficult, they shared, to evacuate and protect children during Israeli air attacks when a family had more of them. A mother of six said that she and other women relatives requested insertion of an IUD immediately following the 2014 war on Gaza for these reasons (4). None of the women expressed demographic competition with Israel as a motivation for large family size, although the author nevertheless projected it onto them (3, 6).

Rather than resolving the structural repression of Palestinians, governments and national, international, and bilateral development, population, and public health organizations consistently rely on limited technocratic solutions and hyperbolize fertility, paradoxically magnifying it. Palestinians in Gaza, for example, live in overwhelming conditions of Israeli enclosure and apartheid that penetrate all dimensions of life, a system largely funded and supported by Western governments, especially the United States. Ending Israel's racist carceral policies and laws and justly resolving the status of refugees and internally displaced Palestinians would have far more impact on their sexual and reproductive agency than another study of fertility. Demographic competition is an unwarranted projection onto Palestinians but is persistent and overwhelmingly documented for Zionism as a settler-colonial project in Palestine.

Black, Feminist, and Queer Futurities

This section considers African-American, African, Black feminist, and Western queer scholarship on death, futurity, reproduction, and liberation to further illuminate my investigation of Palestinian life and death without analogizing the transatlantic slave trade, slavery, the historical statuses of Black people in the United States or anywhere, or Western queerness and queer debates, to Palestinian conditions. Rather, Afrofuturist and Afropessimist debates and creative production offer insights on Palestinian creativity and biological and social struggle and survival as imperial, capitalist, and settler-colonial powers continue to deliver erasure and death to groups they deem disposable. Queer-inflected deliberations on optimism and pessimism, moreover, invited me to push harder against the seam of Palestinian anti-reproductive desire by considering forms of flourishing and belonging that do not require heteronormative reproductivity.

In 1998 Alondra Nelson used the "umbrella term" *Afrofuturism* to name a listserv designed to discuss "science fiction metaphors and technocultural production in the African diaspora" (Nelson 2002, 14n23, 15n24, 9).[8] The online community's purpose was to explore "theoretical territory" and "incubate ideas" related to "sci-fi imagery, futurist themes, and technological innovation" (9). Late-1990s Afrofuturism challenged reigning fantasies of a "placeless, raceless, bodiless near future enabled by technological progress" that excluded Black communities hegemonically framed as on the wrong side of the "digital divide." To Afrofuturist theorists, this reading ignored

---

[8] Nelson explains that Mark Dery coined the term in a 1993 introductory essay to an interview he conducted with three US Black cultural critics and producers. The listserv and a September 1999 forum held at New York University by the same title focused on "the future of black cultural production" (Nelson 2002, 9).

African-American cultural (music, art, and literature), scientific, and intellectual history and reinforced "preconceived ideas of black technical handicaps and 'Western' technological superiority" (1, 5, 6). Afrofuturists analyze a long history of Black diasporic literary, artistic, scientific, and entrepreneurial creation oriented toward the future but informed by past and present life, including transatlantic enslavement and the institutions of slavery (7). Afrofuturism "relies on not just the injection of futurity, fantasy, and technology, but also an ever-present orientation toward black liberation that draws its strength from liberation movements in the past" (Hamilton 2017, 19).

Afropessimism, on the other hand, describes a range of theoretical orientations and positions expressed in artistic production, cultural studies, and economic, legal, and philosophical analysis that are arguably negative regarding the potential for decolonization and freedom for Black people in African and African diasporic settings. The main reason for this negativity is the assumed universality and permanence of anti-Black racism after slavery given its necessity to the consolidation and survival of white supremacy. Some Afropessimist scholarship is articulated in the vein of "what went wrong" in postcolonial African settings (Rieff 1998/1999). Philosopher Achille Mbembe, for example, maintains that postcolonial African politics and philosophy made renaissance difficult because they too often lacked "self-reflexivity," instrumentalized "knowledge and science" in the "service of partisan struggle," reproduced colonial fictions of racial purity, and "reenchant[ed] tradition" (2002, 253–254, 243, 255–256, 265). He contends that while the transatlantic slave trade was a "co-invention" of Western actors and "African auxiliaries seeking profit," too many contemporary African politicians deliberately forget the shame of this collaboration (262). The "value of things," he argues, has come to surpass "that of people," leading to "massacres of civilians, genocides, various kinds of maiming" (268).[9]

Mbembe shares the anti-humanist critique at the heart of Afrofuturist and Afropessimist theories and practices. Liberal humanism always required an excluded, subordinated, expellable Other (Mbembe 2019, 157–166). His inter-articulated analysis depends on an equivalent critique of capitalism (177). Capitalism was from the

---

[9] Writing about the continent, Boulou Ebanda B'béri and P. Eric Louw offer a useful critique and analytical overview of Afropessimist social science scholarship, dividing its approaches and arguments into strands (B'béri and Louw 2011).

beginning "effectively impelled" by "three sorts of drives": "the constant manufacturing of races, or species (as it happens, *Negroes*)," "seeking to calculate and convert everything into exchangeable commodities (law of *generalized exchange relations*)," and "the attempt to maintain a monopoly over the manufacture of the living as such." The "civilizational process" "tempered" these drives at various historical moments in modernity, but "all the dikes collapse" in "the age of neoliberalism," which abolished "taboos" and released "all sorts of drives" to serve "an endless process of accumulation and abstraction" (177–178).

The transatlantic slave trade and slavery in the Western hemisphere forcibly separated African-origin peoples from their families and communities of birth (Wilderson 2010, 10–11, 17, 18–19, 27), the definition of social death. Black feminist scholars in Afrofuturist and Afropessimist traditions theorize the embodied, reproductive, and family dimensions of such displacement and violence, exploring its continuing ideological (embedded, for example, in law and policy) and material (reflected, for example, in less access to resources and disproportionate subjection to chronic illness and early death) effects (Sharpe 2016). In her classic article, "Mama's Baby, Papa's Maybe: An American Grammar Book," Hortense J. Spillers (1987) draws on Lacanian psychoanalytic concepts to argue that African-American women are overdetermined split subjects because of an "American grammar," or symbolic system encoded into the legal system, produced by the transatlantic slave trade and slavery. This grammar is oriented to disrupting "Black African culture" and Black family life by disconnecting mothers and fathers from their progeny (66, 68, 72, 80). "Living in/the wake of slavery," writes Christina Sharpe, "is living 'the afterlife of property' and living the afterlife of *partus sequitur ventrem* (that which is brought forth follows the womb), in which the Black child inherits the non/status, the non/being of the mother. That inheritance of a non/status is everywhere apparent now in the ongoing criminalization of Black women and children" (Sharpe 2016, 15).

Jared Sexton and other humanist critics wrangle with the implications of some Afropessimist ideas. A lively debate refuses the inscription of Black (ontological) pathology and "a certain conflation of the fact of blackness with the lived experience of the black" person historically and in the present. Sexton argues, for example, that "the concept of social death cannot be generalized [to all Black people across time, place and situation]. It is indexed to slavery and it does not travel"

(Sexton 2011, 21, 22, 24). The more important matter may be to "speak of a type of living on that survives after a type of death" (23). For Sexton, Afropessimism does not claim there is "no black (social) life." Rather, it posits that "Black life is not lived in the world that the world lives in, but it is lived underground, in outer space" (28), creating imaginative and practical spaces of escape. In African and African diasporic literature, art, and music, for example, the figure of the "Afronaut," or Black space traveler, imagines and creates possibilities for "finding safe spaces for black life" in sites "out of reach of racial stereotypes" (Hamilton and Bristow in Hamilton 2017, 18).

Lee Edelman takes on the reproductive dimensions of futurity in his polemical *No Future: Queer Theory and the Death Drive* (2004). Like Spillers, Edelman relies on a Lacanian approach (8, 114), but challenges the value of the innocent child as a figure to whom the future is transmitted, as well as ideological deployments of the reproductive family as extra-political (2–3). Queerness, in this analysis, names the position of those who do not fight for the children (3, 13). Queerness should accept its negative figural status as representing the death of child-centered futurism and the social and political order's death drive (4, 9, 11, 14, 115). Allow the queer to represent "reality's abortion," Edelman insists, the undoing of a heteronormative reproductive futurity, and encourage its disturbance of identity (7, 17, 116, 132).

Edelman's anti-normative *No Future* has drawn a range of its own anti-normative critical scholarship for its unidimensional framing of "the child" in class and racial terms, its unacknowledged male embodied positionality, and its equation of queerness with anti-relational and anti-political ontologies. Jennifer Doyle, for example, notes that Edelman is "hailed" by an antiabortion billboard framed around the belly of a pregnant woman in Cambridge, Massachusetts. Edelman, Doyle points out, makes a correspondence between "abortion and queerness" as "against" reproduction, futurity, and thus life (Doyle 2009, 27, 29). Edelman is not interested in abortion as a normal part of women's lives, the termination of a pregnancy. Doyle contends this signals that the figurations and embodiments in Edelman's queer anti-futurity are male (26–28). Doyle highlights Edelman's rejection of "reparative" and "overly political commitments" in queer scholarship, which Edelman argues are normatizing (28). Doyle draws on feminist scholarship and practice that detach sexual and reproductive agency from liberal theory's autonomous subject and imagines an "alternative politics" that is "deeply relational," including in how it imagines the fetus or embryo in relation to the pregnant woman's body (30–46).

Drawing on the works of a long genealogy of playwrights, scholars, artists, performers, and poets, the late José Esteban Muñoz (2007) argues for "a counter-narrative to political nihilism, a form of inquiry that promotes what I am calling queer futurity," even a "queer utopia" and "queer temporality" that "sidesteps straight time's heteronormative bent" (353, 360). Queer futurity "is not an end but an opening or horizon" (360). While sympathetic to Edelman's negative reading of reproductive futurity centered on the child, Muñoz refuses "to give up hope on concepts like politics, hope, and a future that is not 'kid's stuff'" (361). Anti-relationality "is imaginable only if one can frame queerness as a singular abstraction that can be subtracted and isolated from the larger social matrix." Just as "all queers are not the stealth-universal-white-gay-man invoked in queer anti-relational formations, all children are not privileged white babies to whom contemporary society caters" (363).

James Bliss also challenges the unraced child figure at the center of Edelman's analysis and calls for reckoning "with antiblackness as a structuring force in the contemporary world" (Bliss 2015, 85, 86, 89). Bliss proposes "reproduction without futurity," taking exception to "interventions called queer negativity" and their politics of "hope-lessness." Black feminist theory, he contends, contains the "prefigur-ations" of a politics of hope even as it "anticipates or, rather, haunts the political imaginary articulated in queer negativity" (83). Edelman, Bliss argues, "does not account for those modes of reproduction that are not future-oriented, the children who do not register as such, and the 'families' that are not granted the security of nuclear bonds" (86). Bliss recommends theorizing "from the vantage of Black female sub-jectivity" in order to "think the utopian without being beholden to the dictates of hope" or "mired in futurity" (89–90). He argues for the "beautiful or generative" in pessimism and the possibility that embra-cing it "might also create space for thinking beyond the nuclear family, for thinking a Black feminism that follows neither the father nor the mother, but that embraces the sorts of queer kinship networks that have always shaped Black life in the New World" (94).

Analyzing Octavia Butler's 1987 science fiction novel *Dawn*, which articulates a post–nuclear war reproductive futurity of human/non-human hybridity whose unwilling mother is the Black woman sur-vivor Lilith Ayapo, Justin Louis Mann advances the ambivalent concept of "pessimistic futurism," which "couches the prospects of tomorrow in the uncertainties conditioned by the past and present" (Mann 2018, 62). Referring to a scene in the novel, he writes, "trapped though she is in a limiting situation, Lilith consistently chooses survival over self-abnegation, retreat or forfeit" (63).[10] Mann reads Afropessimism and Afrofuturism as "complementary" projects, the "critical mode" he understands Butler uses in the novel. The pessimistic futurism at whose core is reproduction under conditions not of ones choosing "looks to the potential that lives in the future, acknowledges the unknowability of that future and then speculates about the possible position of black subjects when the future arrives" (65).

Palestinian literature and film after 1948, I show in the following section, rarely set a stake in biological reproductive futurities, reduced Palestinian women to their reproductive lives, capacities, and potential, or offered reproductive competition as a path to victory over Zionism. These works of poetry, prose, and film, which sometimes rely on speculative form, are most likely to express conditions of social and biological death even as life and struggle go on in insecure and often devastating conditions not of Palestinian choosing.

Death and Futurity in Palestinian Literature and Film

> Waste no regrets on S
> Fixed on the star's deception
> She brought the art of death in life
> To perfection.
>   "The Woman" – excerpt of poem by Salma Khadra Jayyusi (Jayyusi
>   1992b, 183, trans. Jayyusi and John Heath-Stubbs)

Palestinian nationalist movement discourse after 1948 reproduced masculinist modernist motifs, including a self-critique that blamed the defeat on "backward" investments in family honor (Hasso 2000), but it rarely expressed a futurity that fetishized women as reproducers

---

[10] I taught the trilogy by Octavia E. Butler, which begins with *Dawn*, in the Gender, Sexuality and Feminist Studies senior seminar at Duke University in spring 2019 and spring 2020. I am grateful to the students who enthusiastically participated in the endeavor, even in pandemic conditions. *Adulthood Rites* and *Imago* are the second and third novels in the trilogy (Butler 2000).

in a demographic battle with Zionism. Mary Layoun foregrounds familiar nationalist tropes in the Palestinian Declaration of Independence released on November 15, 1988: "We render special tribute to the brave Palestinian woman, guardian of sustenance and life, keeper of our people's perennial flame" (Layoun 1992, 407). This gendered and heteronormative statement expresses political and social rather than biological reproductive futurity. In comparison to nationalist rhetoric, which rarely reflects ambivalence or opacity, this section makes the case that a prominent theme in Palestinian literary and cinematic work after 1948 is the coexistence of social and political death with social and political resistance and regeneration. While such cultural production is similar to nationalist motifs in not linking emancipation with demographic competition and in foregrounding political and social survival, it is much more likely to express nuanced and contrapuntal sensibilities and negative futurities. My readings of the selected texts do not address matters of form and style, which I leave to creators and scholars of Palestinian literature and film.[11]

Repeated destruction of Palestinian social worlds and separation and dispersal of communities inevitably informed Palestinian literature in the second half of the twentieth century (Jayyusi 1992a, 3, 4–5, 16). Poetry is the privileged Arabic artistic form (Jayyusi 1992a, 2; Rahman 2015, 6). After 1948 the most widely read Palestinian poets in Israel lived in villages under Israeli military rule until it was lifted in 1966. Given they were "highly influenced by communist notions of a backward/ progressive dichotomy, as well as Marx's contention that religion is the masses' opiate, Palestinian poets criticized cultural and religious values that they believed subjected their society to reactionary conditions and brought defeat upon them" (Ghanim 2009, 30). The poems often made sense of the past and articulated Palestinian futurities that amplified the value of land, family, and notions of honor invested in chastity and masculine valor (33). These are gendered tropes, certainly, but not concerned with Palestinian reproduction in a demographic battle.

The following thematics and concerns emerged from my analysis of post-1948 writing in Salma Khadra Jayyusi's *Anthology of Modern Palestinian Literature* (1992b): unstable temporalities (flashbacks, fluidity of time, mutability of time, disrupted time, stretched time,

---

[11] I am grateful to Nadia Yaqub and Dima Ayoub for their generous comments and source suggestions for this chapter.

waiting), alienation, suffering, exile, grief, longing to return, resistance, redemption, and survival. Writers occasionally refer to reproduction and fertility, but not in the service of a demographic futurity. For example, the final verse of "A Song," a poem by Yusuf `Abdel `Aziz, links heteronormative reproduction to creating future strugglers, a not uncommon theme in Palestinian visual and literary culture:

> She stretched her hands out to me
> and we embraced at the gateway of defeat,
> breeding fighters in all directions.
> > "The Song" – excerpt of poem by `Abel `Aziz (Jayyusi 1992b, 85,
> > trans. May Jayyusi and Naomi Shihab Nye).[12]

Writing about three decades before `Abdel `Aziz, poet and novelist Tawfiq Sayigh "was among the few early authors to . . . incorporate the fertility myths that became very fashionable in Arabic poetry in the late fifties" (Jayyusi 1992b, 21). In such myths, "the god arises from death and the world is again filled with fertility and life," which Jayyusi reads as reflecting "a profound hope in the resurgence of the Arab spirit after the catastrophe of 1948, a renewed faith in the possibility of resurrection after symbolic death" (22).

Mahmoud Darwish (1941–2008) is the most celebrated Palestinian poet and authored significant works of prose. He understood, writes Najat Rahman, that "all poetry is preoccupied with a future and is in this sense political" (Rahman 2015, 10).[13] Two of the "most significant themes" in his work, writes Ibrahim Muhawi, are "memory and presence" (2009, 5). Collective death, moments he randomly survived, and his own impending death are also important concerns in Darwish's

---

[12] Born in 1956, `Abdel `Aziz became a refugee from his West Bank village during the 1967 war, after which he and his family were dislocated to Amman. He likely wrote this poem in the 1980s given his birth year and the 1992 publication of the anthology.

[13] Darwish, "a lyric poet with a capacity for ceaseless innovation," drew thousands of fans to his poetry readings until the end of his life, although he was ambivalent about his designation as a "national poet" or "resistance poet" (Rahman 2015, 3, 16, 18; Muhawi 2009, 6–7). In a 2007 interview with a journalist Darwish complained of "the Palestinian who wishes to imprison me in my old poems, and the Arab who wants modernism for himself, and bad poetry for me" (Muhawi 2009, 6–7). The discourse around the museum dedicated to his life and work in Ramallah, which includes a mausoleum for his body, arguably participates in this confinement, for example, referring to "safeguard[ing]" his "cultural, literary and intellectual legacy": http://mah mouddarwish.ps/en/article/6/About-the-museum.

work, I found. I explore reproduction and death in two iconic Darwish poems, "Identity Card" and "The Dice Player," the first from early and the second from late in his career.

Darwish was born to a middling peasant family in the village of Birweh in northern Palestine, which Zionists emptied of its Palestinian inhabitants in 1948, appropriated, and settled with Jews. The family "infiltrated" Palestine from Lebanon after a year. They relocated to Galilee to become "present-absentees," an Israeli legal category for dislocated Palestinians and their descendants present in historic Palestine but deemed "absent" from their appropriated properties (Rahman 2015, 17). Darwish became fluent in literary Hebrew and left Israel for multiple exilic destinations in 1970 until he "returned" to Ramallah in 1996, after it came under the limited jurisdiction of the Palestinian National Authority, "but exile remained at the heart of his poetry" (18; also Muhawi 2009, 3).

Darwish authored the renowned poem "Identity Card" (*Bitaqat Hawiyya*) in 1964 at age twenty-three (Darwish 1964), which led to Israel imprisoning him. The early verses, addressed to an Israeli state that refuses to hail Palestinians as such, are typically interpreted to promote Palestinian demographic competition with Israeli Jews. The poem relies on repetition and expresses Darwish's recognized musical style, influenced by classical Arabic meters (Rahman 2015, 18):

> Write down
> I am an Arab
> and my identity card number is fifty thousand
> I have eight children
> and the ninth will arrive after a summer
> Will you be angry
> Write down
> I am an Arab
> I work with my toiling comrades in a quarry
> and I have eight children
> I produce for them bread,
> clothing and notebooks out of the stone
> I do not beg for charity nor demean myself
> at your doorstep's tiles.
> Does that anger you?
> > "Identity Card" – excerpt of poem by Darwish (Darwish 1964,
> > consolidated translation sources, including my own)

The remainder of the poem expresses the steadfast determination of a Palestinian people rooted for generations but victims of displacement and theft, as well as the danger to Israel of their anger and hunger. Overdetermined by the racialized demographic logic of Zionism, the poem's reference to eight children and a ninth on the way is often read as a Palestinian reproductive threat. That is only one reading, I suggest, given the multiple messages in the poem and the dynamic and nuanced understanding of belonging in Darwish's work (Rahman 2015, 20–21). It is reductive, I insist, to understand the verse as a manifesto that encourages Palestinians to have more children to threaten Israel demographically, let alone that Palestinians used the poem as a manual for a fertility-based liberation struggle. Notably, Darwish was twice married but did not himself have children, truncating his own biological line. His poetry and prose till the fields of suffering and death more than they do reproductive futurities.

Darwish struggled with heart disease and other ailments from childhood (Jayyusi 1992a, 73n16). He died in a Houston hospital on August 9, 2008, three days after a nonemergency open-heart surgery (his third) that he had scheduled for August 6 (Muhawi 2009, 9). Muhawi, who translated one of Darwish's major works of prose, *Memory for Forgetfulness: August, Beirut, 1982* (Darwish 2013, trans. Muhawi; original Arabic 1986), which reflects on the 1982 Israeli invasion of Lebanon and 88-day siege of Beirut, speculates that the chosen surgery date was significant to Darwish because it remembers other deathly events. During the war on Beirut, "the Israeli air force dropped a vacuum, or concussion, bomb on a twelve-story building, leveling it to the ground . . . The book . . . condenses the whole siege into a single day, August 6." For Darwish, August 6 remembers this act of war on civilians and "Hiroshima . . . Vanquished remnants of the Nazi army in Berlin . . . Headlines that jumble past with present, urging the present to hurry on. A future sold in a lottery. A Greek fate lying in wait for young heroes . . . on this day, on the anniversary of the Hiroshima bomb, they are trying out a vacuum bomb on our flesh, and the experiment is successful" (Darwish in Muhawi 2009, 9).

La'ib al-nard ("The Dice Player") is one of Darwish's last poems, which he read during his final public performance at the Ramallah Summer Cultural Festival in June 2008 (aired on Al Jazeera television) (Joudah in Darwish 2008a). Fady Joudah, who translated the poem, writes that Darwish knew "he was walking towards death, in full dignity, not without a hope for life through a surgery against the odds" (Joudah quoted in Darwish 2008b).[14] The poem, which begins with Darwish reflecting on his birth in 1941 in Birweh, expresses the randomness of life and death and the impossibility of living as if a secure future is possible:

> Who am I to say to you
> what I say to you?
> when I'm not a stone burnished by water
> to become a face
> or a reed punctured by wind
> to become a flute ...
> I'm a dice player
> I win some and lose some
> just like you or a little less ...
> born by the water well
> and three lonely trees like nuns,
> without parade or midwife,
> I was given my name by chance
> belonged to a family by chance
> and inherited its traits, features and illnesses:
> First, arterial disease and high blood pressure
> Second, shyness when addressing my parents
> and the tree – my grandmother
> Third, a hope in being cured of influenza
> with a cup of hot chamomile
>
> > "The Dice Player" – excerpt of poem by Darwish (Darwish 2008b,
> > trans. Fady Joudah)

In the remainder of the poem, the narrator makes clear he had little hand in his birth, was by coincidence born a male, "did not try hard to find a mole" in "his most private body parts," could have been like "my sister who screamed then died" an hour after birth, coincidentally did not take the school bus in which other children died in an accident, and by chance survived "the sea" he played in as a child. He could have become "an olive tree, a geography teacher." "Who am I to say to you/I could have not been who I am/I could have not been here/The plane

---

[14] The poem "employs a quieter lyric and more conversational tone that he has been developing since 2002 with [the poetry collections] *State of Siege* and *Don't Apologize for What You've Done*: a rebirth that exhibits ... how he always coaxed his readers beyond a fixed reading of his work" (Joudah quoted in Darwish 2008b).

could have crashed/with me on board that morning/but it is my good fortune that I sleep in/I could not have seen Damascus or Cairo the Louvre or the magical towns/ . . . And had I been a fast walker/I might have become shrapnel" (Darwish 2008b, trans. by Joudah). If anything, Darwish's creative oeuvre is pessimistic, ruminating on social and biological death, a ubiquitous theme in Palestinian cultural production since 1948, not reproductive futurity in its biological or demographic registers.

I opened this chapter with an epigraph from Emile Habiby's 1974 satirical novel, whose protagonist is Saeed, "the Pessoptimist" (Habiby 2003), which I maintain is concerned with social rather than biological reproduction and transformation and, similar to work by Darwish and other Palestinian artists, is not oriented to an optimistic futurity. Habiby, a member of the Communist Party throughout his life, was born in Haifa, Palestine, in 1922 and died in Nazareth, Israel, in 1996 (Jayyusi 1992a, 33).[15] The novel meditates on the political and ontological condition of being present and absent at the same time.

In the first of the novel's three "books," the narrator reports the account of Saeed ("happy" in Arabic) from Haifa, who had written a letter asking that his "strange" story be told since he has "disappeared," as he had wanted and "expected all his life," but was "not dead." Rather, Saeed the "office boy" is in "outer space" in the "company" of "creatures" with whom he is "soaring" (Habiby 2003, 3–5). His father, a collaborator with Zionist forces, was shot and killed (presumably by Palestinians) in 1948. Saeed escaped death "because a stray donkey came into the line of fire." The ass "died in place of me. My subsequent life in Israel, then, was really a gift from that unfortunate beast. What value, then, honored sir, should we assign to this life of mine?" (6, 9). Under no circumstances is Saeed a fighter or a resistor; he is "remarkable" because he is like "the rest" (7). The "nobility" of his "Pessoptimist" family, he explains, is traced to a fourteenth-century "Cypriot girl from Aleppo" who "ran off with a Bedouin" who divorced her because of an affair she had with another man who also divorced her in Beersheba (8). He continues:

[15] *Saeed the Pessoptimist* "was published serially in *Al-Ittihad*, the Arabic newspaper of the Israeli Communist Party, as a response to the 1967 June War" (Mir 2015, 143), before it was published as a novel in Jerusalem in 1974.

"Our forefathers went on divorcing our grandmothers until our journey brought us to a flat and fragrant land on the shore of the sea called Acre, then on to Haifa at the other side of the bay. We continued this practice of divorcing our wives right up until the state [of Israel] was founded" (8). At that point, the family scattered to live "in all of the Arab countries not yet occupied" (9).

When 24-year-old Saeed and his remaining family ran out of money in Lebanon by the end of 1948, he returned to work as a collaborator for the same "Mr. Adon Safsarsheck" who had employed his father (9, 11, 27). Saeed, a self-serving dim-witted coward, is never sure whether he is a pessimist or an optimist since if "harm befalls me during the day, I thank Him that it was no worse" (12, 15, 43). His Israeli espionage assignment is to pretend to be a member of a Palestinian workers' union and to target Communist activists (43). He reconnects with his adolescent love object, Yu`ad ("shall return"), until the state deports her for being "an infiltrator" (61–62). In return for an obviously mendacious Israeli government promise to allow this first beloved to return, Saeed continues to spy on Palestinians until he comes to reside in a `Acca mental institution in the early 1970s (65).

The second book centers on Baqiyya ("the remainer"), "the girl who stayed," and is again narrated by a person who received a letter from Saeed. Saeed writes he is living with his "brothers from outer space . . . in the catacombs of Acre, safe but not secure" (69). Saeed has a secret he needs to tell the world; it is Baqiyya's secret, who he married by arrangement of his Israeli employers, who wanted to control her family (78, 87). Baqiyya wants Saeed to help her return to her village of Tantura and find a hidden family treasure (88–89). He now has two secrets to keep, that he is a collaborator and Baqiyya's family treasure. His Israeli boss forces them to name their only child Walaa ("loyalty") (97). Saeed and Baqiyya continue looking for the treasure as their son grows up (98–99). In 1966 Saeed's boss informs him with rage that the sixteen-year-old Walaa, who had learned to speak little out loud during his life, had become a Palestinian guerrilla fighter. Baqiyya had told him and his friends where to find the treasure, which included "weapons and gold" (106). When his parents find him in a hiding place "in the ruins" of Tantura, Walaa "resolved to die a martyr rather than surrender" (107, 108). Saeed's Israeli employers, "out of compassion" for Saeed and his mother, want them to "persuade him to abandon this

adolescent death wish" and threaten to kill all of them if he does not
(108). After a long conversation between Walaa and Baqiyya, she
decides to join him in the cave, taking one of the machine guns (112).
Mother and son escape by "diving into the sea" until "they had disappeared into the water" and were likely one of the units that fought in
the 1967 Israeli war (113, 114).

Book three, titled "The Second Returner [Yu`ad]," once again
begins with a narrator reading a letter from Saeed, who has awakened
"on top of a stake," although he isn't sure if he is in a nightmare (117–
118). Saeed decides it is best not to risk finding out by waking up
"until I met Yu`ad once again and felt warm for the first time in
a thousand years" (118–119). During the 1967 war, he explains, he
was imprisoned and expected to spy on Palestinians in the Shatta
prison; prison guards beat him badly to prove he was not
a collaborator (122, 129, 130). In prison, he briefly cared for and
was impressed by a badly wounded younger Saeed who had crossed
into Palestine from Lebanon to fight and had a twenty-year-old sister
named Yu`ad, with whom the older Saeed quickly becomes infatuated
(132–133). Saeed has little choice but to continue working for the
Israelis as a spy in and outside of his fake prison stints (134–135). At
various points Saeed repeats his pessoptimist family's intergenerational rationalization, or "philosophy," of "how there is a kind of
death which is better than another, and one, indeed, better than life
itself" (145).

The novel's form relies on repeated cross-generational reproduc-
tions of the status quo and interruptions by younger doubles. The
young Yu`ad ultimately reveals to the protagonist Saeed that her dead
mother was Yu`ad, his love from long ago. In addition to naming her
daughter Yu`ad, she had named her son Saeed, the beaten young
guerrilla fighter Saeed cared for initially in prison (150–151, 153–
154). In a scene that almost exactly repeats events from decades
earlier, Yu`ad fiercely fights the soldiers as her mother had, but they
deport her for illegally entering Israel; she promises, "I will return!"
(155). In life or a dream, Saeed continues "holding on tight to his
stake" despite various figures from his life encouraging him to leave
Israel or join the Palestinian fight (158–159). He ultimately turns to
another being from the sky, apparently God, who says: "When you
can bear the misery of your reality no longer but will not pay the price
necessary to change it, only then you come to me" (159). In the

epilogue, we learn that all the letters were postmarked from an Israeli mental hospital in `Acca (161).

The threads of expulsion, disappearance, intergenerational conflict, struggles to return, and the paradoxes of living under settler-colonialism bind *The Secret Life of Saeed* (Habiby 2003). It is difficult to argue, however, that the novel grounds pessimism or optimism in biological proliferation of the family. For one thing, the novel at various points forecloses Palestinian biological reproduction. After her husband was killed in a crane accident while he was working at the port of Haifa, Saeed's brother's widow ran "off with another man two years later and he turned out to be sterile. When my mother [also a pessoptimist] heard that he was so, she repeated her favorite saying, 'And why should we not praise God?'" Saeed follows by rhetorically asking the reader, "So what are we then? Optimists or pessimists?" (13). Male sterility comes up again when the wife of Saeed's missing great uncle, who during the Mandate period had gone in search of a treasure lost for centuries but never returned, "found another husband, one who was not sterile" (29). Saeed and Baqiyya limit their own progeny to one child after their son, Walaa, is born in Israel: "Since I realized birth control was a proof of loyalty, we had no more children" (97).

The Secret Life of Saeed invests in younger Palestinian generations the hope of return and political and social regeneration: "Walaa, my only son, that shy, skinny young man, whose dinner any cat could steal, had become a *fedaiy*, a guerrilla, and had taken up arms in rebellion against the state!" (106). Walaa, who turns out to be more his mother's son, with "two of his schoolmates, had founded a secret cell. Then he had retrieved, from a cave in a deep hollow in the rocks off the deserted beach of Tanturah, a well-made strongbox, shut tight so that no moisture could penetrate it. It was filled with weapons and gold." When Saeed reprimands his wife for telling their son, Walaa, the secret of the treasure, she replies: "But Saeed, Saeed, our children are our only hope!" (106). Similarly, the younger Saeed, son of the expelled lover Yu`ad, is the fighter who crosses the border into Palestine.

With the exception of his beaten down and resigned mother, women characters such as Saeed's lover Yu`ad, his wife Baqiyya, and Yu`ad's daughter Yu`ad are distinctly bold and courageous refusers. Some of them marry and have children, but they also join the resistance, search for resources, and socialize children to remember and fight for exist-ence. The majority, however, termed "the rest" by Saeed, do the best they can in their conditions. The novel challenges authenticist and biologist definitions of belonging and does not traffic in honor discourse, puritanical sexual norms, or heteronormative family values. It does, however, harshly judge Saeed and others like him who will do anything to survive, even as it shows the impossible absurdities Palestinians must negotiate and the choices they make to do so.

The ontological state of being dead yet alive connects Habiby's novel to another published forty years later by Palestinian author Ibtisam Azem titled *Sifr al-Ikhtifa'* (*The Book of Disappearance*) (Azem 2019, trans. Antoon). The novel opens with the voice of Alaa, a single forty-year-old Palestinian with an apartment in Tel Aviv who describes his fearful mother running through the streets of the 'Ajami neighborhood in Jaffa searching for his grandmother "from house to house" (1–3). Alaa ultimately finds her dead "on an old wooden bench gazing at the sea" (5). Azem describes contemporary Jaffa as a scene of haunting, the aftermath of an ethnic expulsion and continuing politics of death: "All the Jaffans who stayed here see a shadow walking next to them when they walk through the old city. Even the Jews say they hear voices at night, but when they go out to see who it is, they don't find anyone" (4). Alaa's grandmother had refused to leave Jaffa in 1948, although her natal family and husband left and were unable to return. Speaking in the present tense about 1948, she explains to her grandson: "I'm six months pregnant. What would we do if something happened on the way there? How could one leave Jaffa anyway? What would I do in Beirut?" (10–13).

Like Saeed, Alaa wrote a story of the self and Palestinian past and present. He purchased a "red notebook" from a stationary store and began "writing his memoirs" (13), "addressing you directly" (14), speaking to his grandmother, whose stories about the past, he realized too late, had many "holes" (15). His grandmother was expelled from her home in al-Manshiyye neighborhood in 1948 and "forced to live in 'Ajami," which the new state barbed in with its remaining Palestinians; Jaffa was emptied of all except four thousand of its one hundred thousand Palestinian residents (16–18).

In the fourth chapter *The Book of Disappearance* introduces "Ariel," a liberal Jewish newspaper journalist whose father had insisted he learn Arabic to "know thy enemy" (79–81). Ariel was friends with Alaa and lived in the same apartment building in Tel Aviv, on a lower floor (23). Alaa was not seen again after a party the previous evening.[16] Chapter nine, titled "A Building," makes clear that *all* Palestinians in Israel and the West Bank and Gaza have completely disappeared, disrupting an Israeli normalcy that relies on their existence as marginals (49–53). For Israelis, "the Arabs are gone" (56). By chapter fifteen, Ariel had used Alaa's "spare key," which they had exchanged in case they were locked out, to enter his apartment and closely explore it. He begins thumbing through Alaa's memoir (75–81), followed by sleeping in his bed and taking over his apartment.

From Alaa's memoir, read by Ariel, we learn that his mother decided to have a hysterectomy early in her marriage (121, 122). Deliberate self-extinguishing of biological futurity is an overriding message in the novel, as is the ontological status of living death for Palestinians in an Israeli settler-colonial context. For Jewish Israelis, in contrast, the novel ends with a massive celebration to mark the disappearance of all Palestinians from historic Palestine, "the biggest festival in the young country's history." "In modern states people chase the future. The victors never look back. They only look forward." Part of this Zionist forward motion is to finalize the erasure of traces of Palestinian existence, including replacing Arabic names of streets and places with Hebrew or English names (219). At this point, Ariel has moved into Alaa's apartment permanently because he much preferred it to his own.

Wedding in Galilee, `Urs al-jalil* in Arabic (Khleifi 1987), is the first feature-length Palestinian film made in historic Palestine by a Palestinian. The film is iconic and relevant to my focus on Palestinian reproduction and futurity. As with Habiby's novel, it is ambivalent in its treatment of marriage and thus reproductive futurity. Set in a contemporary "extremist" Palestinian village in the Nazareth area that was under military curfew for "blood shed" four months previously, the story centers on a father (Abu `Adel), the *mukhtar* of the village, committed to holding a wedding to marry off his son despite bans on large gatherings. The Israelis agree to allow the wedding on condition that Abu `Adel invites the military governor as a guest. Abu `Adel agrees but makes the entourage commit to stay through the very end of an elaborate wedding with its food, clothing, music, and ritual

---

[16] Four chapters follow that offer snippets of Palestinian-Israeli labor and social interactions in Israel, including on a "flower farm," at a "bus stop," in "Prison 48," and in a "hospital."

dimensions, which lasts a day and a night, during which the curfew is suspended. The conditions for the wedding divide the family and villagers. Abu `Adel's adult nephew is a collaborator with the Israelis who is in charge of maintaining peace and security during the wedding. Many dramas and narrative threads unfold during the film, including homoerotic scenes and an ultimately foiled plot to kill the military governor by young village men who had suffered Israeli torture.

The son, `Adel, who badly wanted to get married, is ashamed about the conditions for the wedding. His mother replies, "We have no choice." Most interesting for my purposes is that the consummation between bride and groom is unsuccessful because `Adel is unable to have an erection despite repeated attempts initiated by himself or Samya during a long evening, although the couple make love. They cannot provide evidence of blood from a broken hymen, which devastates both sets of parents, who seek each other's counsel outside the bedroom and turn to prayer while events continue to unfold. `Adel's father is especially frantic since he views his honor as dependent on signaling successful penetrative consummation and recognizes that the plotting against the military authorities while the festivities continued outside was increasingly dangerous.

In the bedroom, `Adel tells Samya in frustration that the only solution is for him to kill his father, who he understands to be the source of his suffering and failure, to which she replies, "violence does not solve anything." *Wedding in Galilee* expresses the bitterness of Palestinian children against ineffectual fathers understood to have conceded their dignity to survive under Israeli authority. Samya ultimately decides to "protect everyone's honor" by undressing and penetrating herself with her hand, producing blood evidence on her white nightgown. Before doing so, she asks `Adel, "If a woman's honor is her virginity, where does one find evidence of the honor of men?" The marriage is publicly completed when Samya forecloses biological reproduction by queerly penetrating herself. Anticlimax and failure are the messages in *Wedding in Galilee*. An uncle who disapproves of the wedding held under the imposed conditions nevertheless foils the plan by younger men to kill the military entourage. The internal foiling of the attack on the entourage is the definition of a defeated people. The Palestinian wedding in Galilee ultimately occurs under the conditions set by the Israeli military authorities.

Two more recent Palestinian short films address reproductive and anti-reproductive futurities. *Bonbone*, a crowd-funded production by Rakan Mayasi released in 2017, opens with a few young Palestinian men in an Israeli prison showering. After returning to his cell, the male protagonist deeply inhales the fragrance of a piece of candy wrapped in two layers of plastic, one green and one clear, unwraps it, and tries to masturbate in bed but is unsuccessful. Arriving on a bus with multiple women the same day, his wife visits with him after an Israeli woman soldier wearing latex gloves slowly searches her naked back, loosens her long hair, rubs her scalp, and has her crouch to search her anally. The husband and wife communicate by phone separated by a glass partition whose seam was broken by other prisoners and visitors to create a small opening. The plan had been for him to hand semen to her through the opening. She asks, "if it turns out to be a boy, what would you name him?" Revisiting the motif of male sexual and reproductive failure, he explains with shame that he could not ejaculate. "I am damaged" (*kharban*). She responds by seducing him through the glass until they both have orgasms. He wraps the semen into the two layers of the small candy wrapper, twists the ends, and slips it to her through the seam. Before the long bus ride home from the prison begins, she sets a six-hour timer. When twenty-two minutes are left, she decides to inseminate herself on the bus, which is half full of mostly dozing women, some with children. She takes off her heeled shoes, crouches on the seat, and inserts the semen into her vagina. The film ends with a panel of text informing viewers that West Bank Palestinian women have conceived more than fifty babies with imprisoned husbands thus far using such methods.

Mohammed Hamdan (2019) analyzes the Palestinian smuggled semen phenomenon among men sentenced to life in prison,[17] arguing they are "biopolitical acts of resistance" to a carceral system designed to cut the men off from the outside world physically and communicatively (528–530). Using a Derridean analysis of masturbation and semen transmission, Hamdan argues that Palestinian women's use of IVF to conceive in such cases has the unintended consequence of

---

[17] Five thousand Palestinian men are serving life sentences "for offences that range from stone throwing and burning tires to killing Israeli soldiers. They are normally classified by Israeli authorities as security prisoners, a designation that subjects them to extra restrictions by Israeli prison laws, especially the denial of conjugal visits" (Hamdan 2019, 526).

empowering them by alienating the biological father from reproduction (529–530, 538–539). This strategy, he contends, reclaims a futurity invested in nationalist reproduction despite Israel's imprisonment of activists (527–528). The resulting "child/trace not only comes as present affirmation of the absent Palestinian other/father who is denied by the Israelis; the child/trace also manifests the prisoners' nonorigin in their society only to affirm their powerful return to presence and symbolize their resistance to the Israeli policing of subversive correspondence" (527). The born child "symbolizes a state of aspiration – the aspiration for the impossible, or the reworking of the impossible" and "proof" of the prisoner's existence (531). Sperm smuggling and successful insemination cross the barriers made when Israeli settler-colonialism "cuts" Palestinians from the land and each other (531, 532).

I find persuasive Hamdan's reading of sperm smuggled out of prison as a missive or correspondence that communicates presence – not unlike the letters Saeed sends from a mental institution and the memoir written by Alaa and read by Ariel after he disappears. Hamdan's provocative reading of sperm smuggling is more optimistic than mine, however, regarding the potential for women's empowerment when reproduction occurs outside coitus. Reproduction within marriage, ideally of a son who will be counted toward the patrilineal line, is an authorized Palestinian cultural aspiration and accomplishment and source of great social pressure. I am unconvinced that nationalist reproductive futurities motivate impregnation in such circumstances, although I concede it is impossible to pull apart stated from unstated motivations, let alone the unconscious workings of desire. The desire to fulfill the requirements of a gendered heteronormative status quo can easily explain Palestinian efforts to reproduce despite settler-colonial carcerality.

Celebratory sperm smuggling and nationalist reproductive accounts leave little space for Palestinian *anti-reproductive desire* and the difficulties of fulfilling it in settler-colonial conditions. *Condom Lead* (2013), a short film by Gaza brothers Tarzan Abu Nasser and Arab Abu Nasser, illustrates this very dilemma, among others. Set in an upper-floor middle-class Gaza apartment, the film features a married couple in their thirties who repeatedly try to have nonreproductive sex but are foiled by the overwhelming, nonstop sounds and lights of war in a screenplay with no dialogue except for the occasional gurgles and terrified cries of a toddler child. The film opens with the baby crawling among multicolored pastel balloons we later learn are unused condoms the father has blown up. In the evening, the constant sounds of drones and warplanes in the sky and sirens on the ground take up all sonic space and often move the mother to comfort the terrified toddler awakened or unable to fall asleep as a result. Weariness is the overwhelming affect produced by living in Gaza, a prison whose land, air, and water borders Israel guards. After he washes his bearded face, the male protagonist watches staccato news clips while his wife takes her turn looking in the bathroom mirror, washing and stretching her face, releasing her hair. Lying in bed side by side, facing upward, she touches his feet and then his arm; he reaches for her and as they caress, he opens a condom wrapper.

As the baby listens to a drone become louder and louder, clashing into a crescendo that includes shooting and sirens, she starts to cry and the woman once again leaves the bed to rock her cradle. The husband blows up and ties another condom balloon, illustrating the incessance of Israeli violence and the repetition necessary for Palestinians to continue. A few days later, another attempt to have sex, another explosion, flashing lights of war illuminate the apartment through its windows, another terrified cry by the child, and another balloon is on the floor. Twenty-two days later, tens of blown up transparent condoms gently float on the apartment floor. In the last scene, the male protagonist is on the balcony in the morning. We look at his back and watch with him dozens of blown up empty condoms floating over the skies released by other Gazans.

Palestinian geographer Walaa Alqaisiya (2018) takes Palestinian anti-reproductive desire a step further in her "decolonial queer" analysis of the activist and intellectual work of alQaws for Sexual and Gender Diversity in Palestinian Society. AlQaws challenges "the racialized worldview that informs Israeli social life, which divides the world into binaries of civilized versus uncivilized, pride versus homophobia, democracy versus terror" (32). Working within the geographic frame of historic Palestine, and thus persistently crossing the physical walls, borders, and barriers separating and compartmentalizing Palestinians, alQaws "has a presence in Haifa and Jaffa … East Jerusalem, Ramallah, and Bayt Jala" (34, 36). Decolonial queering "rejects singling out sexuality as a discrete site of oppression disconnected from the power structure of settler colonialism" (36). AlQaws, Alqaisiya argues, "dares to image Palestine otherwise."

Decolonial queering aims for a politically and sexually transformed Palestinian futurity. While not taking "an anti-national stance," it challenges the "heteronormative reproduction of [a] Palestine" that foregrounds heroic masculinity and disavows homosexuality, nonmarital sexuality, and sex work, which are condemned as sources of collaboration with Israel and dishonor (36, 37). It "provides room for gender and sexual performances that *disidentify* with the dominant gendered paradigms enshrined in Palestinian nationalist thought" and the queer assimilation requirements of Zionist LGBTQ frames (38, 35). It challenges the nationalist silencing of "queer and native feminists" and insists on recognizing that the edifices of Israeli settler-colonialism are "heteronormative structures" reproduced in "Palestinian imaginings of liberation." A Palestinian decolonial queer futurity refuses liberation on the terms set by these systems of "subjugation" (39).

~~~~~~~~~~

This chapter challenges the assumption that Palestinians after 1948 absorbed the demographic competitive logic of Zionism and followed it in their reproductive decision-making. It shows how demographic research on Palestinian fertility, however, often reproduces Zionist ideological assumptions and projections. These methods leave little space for Palestinian motivations and desires – which span the range of possibilities – let alone Palestinian thriving. The second section draws on African diasporic, Black feminist, and queer scholarship on reproduction, futurity, and death to illuminate my analysis of death and reproduction for Palestinians after 1948. Drawing on a selection of iconic and newer post-1948 Palestinian poetry, prose, and film, the final section shows that Palestinian creative work has been more likely to express pessimistic futurities, dwelling on the grounds of social and biological death rather than reproduction. It extends the book's argument further by making an affirmative case for Palestinian anti-reproductive desire as another dimension of the Palestinian past and decolonized present and future. As a whole, the chapter offers additional substantiation for my argument that a racialized demographic logic has been the central compulsion *of Zionism* as a settler-colonial movement that always required ethnically cleansing the land of its indigenous inhabitants by all available means and appropriating their lands, natural resources, and built environments. The coda concludes *Buried in the Red Dirt* by tracking and analyzing the rise of an explicitly reproductive Palestinian nationalist theme in 1980s and 1990s discourse and iconography and briefly dwells on the multifaceted ways Palestinians have addressed death, struggle, and regeneration in life and art.

CODA: *Life, Death, Regeneration*

Buried in the Red Dirt excavates quotidian dimensions of reproduction, illness, death, and birth control, topics peripheralized in the historiography and history of Palestinians who lived under British colonial rule. It also tells a larger systemic story about how colonialism produced suffering and premature death. The book "resists the event," to use Megha Anwer's terms, reorienting us to less "colossal" and catastrophic scales of history and experience (Anwer 2014, 2, 7). It emphasizes nonevents such as the structural maldistribution of illness, disease, injury, hunger, and early death because of colonial, racial, and class status, as well as the sexual inequalities that allocate power, resources, pain, and pleasure unevenly. It reminds us that extraction of labor and life are the very grounds of imperialism and colonialism and are always legitimated by racializing the abjected group. It shows the prevalence of Zionist demographic competition in modern Palestine for well over a hundred years, an agenda too frequently paradoxically projected onto Palestinians. In challenging the ideological hyperbolization of Palestinian reproduction, the book also takes seriously Palestinian anti-reproductive desires and practices. It conveys that political and social regeneration and survival dominated in Palestinian literature and film after 1948, articulated on scattered ground colored by the prevalence of loss, forced dispersal and premature death.

The book does not claim that Palestinians are unaware of Israel's less than subtle racial demographic project in historic Palestine, supported by Western powers, or that every Palestinian is immune to its competitive dimensions in their reproductive lives. In the late 1980s during the first Intifada, Palestinian nationalist iconography occasionally expressed such competitive reproductive desire. For example, I saw popular porcelain artwork that fetishized the Palestinian woman's pregnant womb, with a gender-indistinguishable embryo armed and prepared to battle, when I interned in 1989 with the

Palestinian Federation of Women's Action Committees. Even during this period, however, the Palestinian mother was most likely to be symbolically represented as a source of steadfastness. A famous 1988 poster by the renowned Sliman Mansour of the Palestinian Liberation Art Movement, "Portrait of the Intifada ... the Mother" (*"lawhat al-intifada ... al-umm"*), shows a fully clothed woman in Palestinian village dress with a multitude of resistant adult men and women emerging from between her large magnified hands and crouched legs.[1] I read the Mansour poster image as valorizing the ubiquitous participation of women as fighters, defenders and protectors and reinforcing the quintessential place of mothers in Palestinian life and nationalism.

In reviewing almost ninety years of Palestinian posters indexed by the Palestine Poster Project Archive, I found that the Palestinian woman as breeder was not a discernable dimension of resistance representational discourse and symbolism. Even sentimental maternalist representations were rare. Most of the posters were created beginning in the 1960s by committed artists affiliated with the Palestine Liberation Organization's Plastic Arts Section and Arts and Heritage Section. The artists created work in the inexpensive poster format to make it widely available to everyday Palestinians even as they also produced painting, sculptor, glasswork, and reliefs (Farhat and Halaby 2012). When depicting a Palestinian woman, the images are much more likely to present her as a fighter, usually carrying a weapon, such as in the 1976 poster titled "Palestinian Motherhood," also by Mansour (see Figure 7.1).

Mansour uses brutal realist lines in shades of brown and orange broken only by a white hair cover and the yellow line of a rising or setting sun. In the poster, he figures the Palestinian woman as a gargantuan exhausted mother, hair strands damp with sweat escaping downward around her bent profile as she sits on a cloth covering tumultuous terra. Her large strong left hand props a weapon and equally large right hand supports an infant's head as it nurses from an exposed breast that emerges from her rippled brown chest.

When I probed friends and acquaintances for Palestinian rhetoric regarding demographic competition, some mentioned statements

---

[1] The Palestine Poster Project Archives, "Mother Intifada" by Sliman Mansour 1988: www.palestineposterproject.org/poster/mother-intifada.

Figure 7.1 "Palestinian Motherhood" poster, Sliman Mansour, 1976. Used with the kind permission of the artist.

attributed to the late PLO leader Yasir Arafat. Research into the provenance of the first statement shared with me, "*Rahm al-mar'a al-'arabiyya huwa silahi al-aqwa*" ("The Arab woman's womb is my strongest weapon"), invariably led me to Zionist sources. For example, the statement takes center stage in an August 2019 article by Yehuda Shalim published in the religious right Zionist newspaper *Israel Today*.[2] The article was translated and published in English- and Arabic-language venues, amplifying its message. I read it in Arabic translation in the London-based online newspaper *Al-Quds al-'Arabi*. Shalim repeats the "womb" statement putatively made by Arafat to editorialize about Palestinian Authority Prime Minister Muhammad Ashtiyya insisting that Palestinians are a majority "between the river and the sea" and thus Israel cannot continue to colonize Palestinian land. This claim,

---

[2] Shalim is listed as a researcher and resident of the Ariel (Jewish) settlement in the West Bank.

Shalim asserts, is a postmortem release of Arafat's "demographic demon," a "scarecrow" that frightened Israeli leaders into giving up land to the Palestinians in the 1990s Oslo Accords. There is no reason for Jews not to keep what they've taken and to go further by confiscating the remaining lands of "Greater Israel," he concludes, since as of 2009, Palestinian and Jewish fertility rates in historic Palestine are essentially equal.[3]

If Arafat had indeed made the statement attributed to him, he would have more likely said *the Palestinian woman's womb* and not *the Arab woman's womb*, the latter a Zionist rhetoric of erasure. When I circulated the statement in Arabic to a WhatsApp group of researchers discussing COVID-19 in Jordan in May 2020, some were aware of it, but not of its provenance. One participant offered a different statement he attributed to Arafat: "`Indahum al-qunbila al-nawawiyya wa ihna `indana al-qunbila al-namawiyya*" ("They have the nuclear bomb but we have the sperm bomb"). While I was unable to find a credible source substantiating that Arafat had made either statement, each reproduces a commonsense understanding of Palestinian reproduction as motivated by demographic competition.

Arafat's nom de guerre from the 1960s, Abu `Ammar, ironically connotes his lack of biological reproductivity, at least of sons. A father in Arabic carries the honorific title "father of" (Abu ...) the firstborn son's name if he has one, or his oldest daughter's name if he does not. Arafat had no biological sons and one biological daughter was born late in his life from his only marriage in 1990; he had adopted Palestinian war orphans (two girls and three boys) in the 1980s.[4] The name "Abu `Ammar," however, does not refer to one of Arafat's children. Instead, it denotes his status as a "builder" of the national

---

[3] "*Al-I`lam al-Israili: 'Al-Shaytan al-dimughrafi' ... fiza`at `Arafat `ala lisan Ashtiyya*" ["The Israeli Press: 'The Demographic Demon': Arafat's Scarecrow in the Words of Ashtiyya"], by Yehuda Shalim, *Al-Quds al-`Arabi* newspaper (August 14, 2019), accessed June 23, 2020. www.alquds.co.uk/%d8%a7%d9%84%d8%a5%d8%b9%d9%84%d8%a7%d9%85-%d8%a7%d9%84%d8%a5%d8%b3%d8%b1%d8%a7%d8%a6%d9%8a%d9%84%d9%8a-%d8%a7%d9%84%d8%b4%d9%8a%d8%b7%d8%a7%d9%86-%d8%a7%d9%84%d8%af%d9%8a%d9%85%d8%ba%d8%b1%d8%a7/.

[4] "Arafat's Orphans Due in Gaza by Weekend with Palestinian-Arafat, Bjt," July 12, 1994 (accessed June 24, 2020): https://apnews.com/817b88e545021e1a69e0cdfa1f732451.

resistance movement (he was trained as an engineer) even as the appellation reminds its users, listeners, and readers that he did not biologically sire any sons as far as we know.

Palestinian life, death, and regeneration have been folded together since 1948. Moataz Dajani's installation "Besieged Shrines: Soul Houses to Epic Lives," first exhibited in 2002, refashioned Palestinian stories and memories using terracotta, testimonial audio, personal photographs, found objects, stones, lit candles, artificial light, and natural life such as living vine planted in dirt, to create miniature houses and "womb-like" caves. "Besieged Shrines," in his words during an interview, "memorializes the epic in people's lives and struggles" as they "created life and hope amidst insurmountable adversity." The shrines, which force viewers to bear witness, were inspired by "diverse ancient and folk arts and rituals from the Arab fertile crescent region, including story boxes and Canaanite ossuaries in Palestine." The soul houses, he explained, "highlight magical fertility rituals and the life cycle of birth, growth, death, and regeneration."[5]

The following images are of three miniature Besieged Shrines I had the privilege of viewing in their multidimensionality in Amman in May 2018 (see Figures 7.2, 7.3, 7.4). The image of a fourth shrine from the exhibit, "Shrine of Witness," is printed on the book's cover. The shrines illustrate how Palestinian responses to loss and death since 1948 have been to regenerate through retelling, remembering, and rebuilding families and communities. The shrines and their captions evidence the pervasiveness of Israeli attempts to biologically, politically, and socially extinguish Palestinians. More importantly, they beautifully express stubborn endurance through kinship, politics, and creativity. The refusal to forget or be disappeared is cultivated in each Palestinian generation that follows.

---

[5] Author interview with Moataz Dajani on May 17, 2018, in Amman, Jordan. Email correspondence with Dajani between late June and early July 2020.

Figure 7.2 Besieged Shrine to Hands of Thyme and Stone (1). Title from the Mahmoud Darwish poem. The shrine is dedicated to Nabil, Munir, and their children. Their father and half of the father's extended family were massacred by Lebanese fascist militias in the Tel El Za`atar camp in east Beirut in 1976. The remaining family moved to the Shatila camp, where the mother and some of her children were killed by Lebanese militias during a 1982 siege by Israeli forces. Munir, the youngest child, was badly injured, while his oldest brother, Nabil, survived. Shrine of wood with thyme tree growing out of a rock. Scroll written on layers of silk and papyrus. Moataz Dajani. Used with kind permission of the artist.

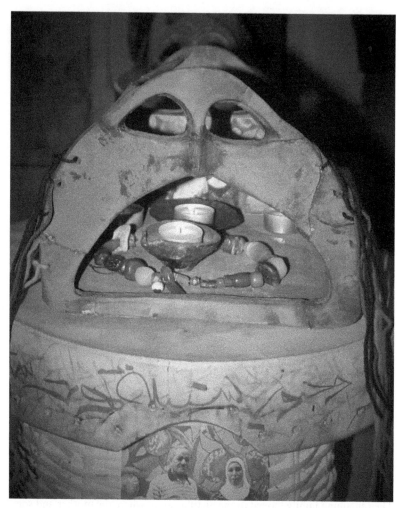

Figure 7.3 Soul house to Kamal, Mariam, and their new children. Kamal and Mariam lost all five of their children in a shelter that Israel attacked with phosphorus bombs in the Borj Shmali camp, Tyre, south Lebanon, during the invasion of June 1982. Mariam was badly burned. They lived in Beirut while Mariam was being treated and returned to Borj Shmali to rebuild their lives and bring to life six new children. Terracotta, yarn, photographs, and found objects. Moataz Dajani. Used with kind permission of the artist.

Figure 7.4 Shrine to Bassam and his children. The seated figurine is modeled after a Canaanite goddess found near Ashdud in Palestine. An audiotape inside the basket plays the family story narrated by Bassam: "In 2007, I was carrying my mom to safety out of [the] Nahr el Bared camp under shelling from the Lebanese army. When we were out and safe she started crying. I said, "Mom, we are safe. Why are you crying?" She said, "I remembered 1948, when my mother carried me under shelling as we fled our village. Then I remembered when I carried you out of [the] Shatila camp during the massacre of 1982, when your father, sister, and brother were killed. Don't let your children carry you out ... leave Lebanon." Silver seated figurine of a mother suckling a shell in a terracotta womb-like cave. Moataz Dajani. Used with kind permission of the artist.

Bibliography

Abdul Hadi, and Aouni Bey. 1932. "The Balfour Declaration." *Annals of the American Academy of Political and Social Science. Special Issue: Palestine. A Decade of Development* 164 (November): 12–21.

Abdulhadi, Faiha. 2006a. *Adwar al-mar'a al-falastiniyya fi al-intidab: al-musahama al-siyasiyya lil-mar'a al-falastiniyya, 1930s* [*Palestinian Women's Roles in the Mandate: Palestinian Women's Political Participation, 1930s*]. El-Bireh: Palestinian Women's Research and Documentation Center.

Abdulhadi, Faiha. 2006b. *The Political Role of Palestinian Women in the 1930s: The Political Participation of Palestinian Women, Women's Oral History Narratives.* El-Bireh: Palestinian Women's Research and Documentation Center.

Abu El-Haj, Nadia. 2012. *The Genealogical Science: The Search for Jewish Origins and the Politics of Epistemology.* Chicago: University of Chicago Press.

Abu Hamad, Khitam. 2020. "Determinants of Fertility and Contraceptive Use among Palestinian Women in the Gaza Strip: A Qualitative Study." *Journal of Women's Health Care* 9(485): 1–7. www.longdom.org/open-access/determinants-of-fertility-and-contraceptive-use-among-palestinian-women-in-the-gaza-strip-qualitative-study.pdf

Abu-Lughod, Lila, and Ahmad H. Sa`di. 2007. "Introduction: The Claims of Memory." In *Nakba: Palestine, 1948, and the Claims of Memory.* Edited by Ahmad H. Sa`di and Lila Abu-Lughod, 1–24. New York: Columbia University Press.

Abu Nasser, (Ahmed) Tarzan, and (Mohamed) Arab Abu Nasser (screenwriters). 2013. *Condom Lead.* Amman. Produced by Rashid Abdelhamid.

Abu-Rabia, Aref. 2005. "Bedouin Health Services in Mandated Palestine." *Middle Eastern Studies* 41(3): 421–429.

Alqaisiya, Walaa. 2018. "Decolonial Queering: The Politics of Being Queer in Palestine." *Journal of Palestine Studies* 47(3): 29–44.

Alrifai, Ayesha. 2018. "Abortion As a Contested Right in Occupied Palestine." *Journal of Middle East Women's Studies* 14(3) (November): 384–389.

Anderson, Matthew R., Lanny Smith, and Victor W. Sidel. 2005. "What Is Social Medicine?" *Monthly Review: An Independent Socialist Magazine* 56(8) (January 1). https://monthlyreview.org/2005/01/01/what-is-social-medicine

Anderson, Warwick. 2006. *Colonial Pathologies: American Tropical Medicine, Race, and Hygiene in the Philippines.* Durham, NC: Duke University Press.

Anglo-American Committee of Inquiry. 1946. *A Survey of Palestine, Vols. I and II.* Prepared in December 1945 and January 1946 for the information of the Anglo-American Committee of Inquiry. Palestine Government Printer.

Anwer, Megha. 2014. "Resisting the Event: Aesthetics of the Non-event in the Contemporary South Asian Novel." *Ariel: A Review of International English Literature* 45(4) (October): 1–30.

Arab Office. 1946. *The Problem of Palestine: Evidence Submitted by the Arab Office, Jerusalem, to the Anglo-American Committee of Inquiry, March 1946.* Washington, DC: Arab Office. Pamphlet Collection, Duke University Library.

Arnold, David. 1993. *Colonizing the Body: State Medicine and Epidemic Disease in Nineteenth-Century India.* Berkeley: University of California Press.

Asad, Talal. 1976. "Class Transformation under the Mandate." *MERIP Reports*, No. 53 (December): 3–8, 23.

Azem, Ibtisam. 2019. *The Book of Disappearance.* Translated from the Arabic by Sinan Antoon. Syracuse, NY: Syracuse University Press.

Bachi, Roberto. 1970. "Abortion in Israel." In *Abortion in a Changing World, Volume 1.* Edited by Robert E. Hall, 274–283. New York: Columbia University Press.

Bachi, Roberto, and Judah Matras. 1962. "Contraception and Induced Abortions among Jewish Maternity Cases in Israel." *Milbank Memorial Fund Quarterly* 40(2) (April): 207–229.

Balsoy, Gülhan. 2009. "Gender and the Politics of the Female Body: Midwifery, Abortion, and Pregnancy in Ottoman Society (1838–1890s)." PhD Dissertation, Binghamton University, State University of New York, Department of History.

Banko, Lauren. 2012. "Occupational Hazards, Revisited: Palestinian Historiography." *Middle East Journal* 66(3) (Summer): 440–452.

al-Barghuthi, Omar Bey Salih. 1932. "Local Self-Government: Past and Present." *Annals of the American Academy of Political and Social Science* 164(1) (November): 34–38.

Baron, Beth. 2020. "Perilous Beginnings: Infant Mortality, Public Health and the State in Egypt." In *Gendering Global Humanitarianism in the*

Twentieth Century: Practice, Politics and the Power of Representation. Edited by Esther Möller, Johannes Paulmann, and Katharina Stornig, 195–219. New York: Palgrave MacMillan.

Basker, Eileen. 1980. "Belief Systems, Cultural Milieu and Reproductive Behavior: Women Seeking Abortions in a Hospital in Israel." PhD Dissertation, Hebrew University. National Library of Israel.

Baumberg, Christine. 1998. "Ripples from Europe: The Dunedin Jewish Community in the 1930s and 1940s." A dissertation submitted in partial fulfillment of the requirements for the degree of BA (Hons) in history and German at the University of Otago, Dunedin, New Zealand.

de B'béri, Boulou Ebanda, and P. Eric Louw. 2011. "Afropessimism: A Genealogy of Discourse." *Critical Arts* 25(3): 335–346.

Beattie, James. 2011. "Natural History, Conservation and Health: Scottish-Trained Doctors in New Zealand, 1790–1920s." *Immigrants & Minorities* 29(3): 281–307.

Becquemont, Daniel. 2011. "Social Darwinism: From Reality to Myth and from Myth to Reality. *Studies in History and Philosophy of Biological and Biomedical Sciences* 42: 12–19.

Bentwich, Norman (Compiled by the Attorney-General of Palestine). 1926. *Legislation of Palestine, 1918–1925, Including the Orders-in-Council, Ordinances, Public Notices, Proclamations, Regulations, Etc. Volume 1: Orders-in-Council and Ordinances.* Alexandria: Printed for the Government of Palestine by Whitehead Morris Limited.

Bentwich, Norman. 1928. *The Criminal Law of Palestine 1928.* Jerusalem: Government Printing Office.

Bentwich, Norman. 1938. "The New Criminal Code for Palestine." *Journal of Comparative Legislation and International Law* 20(1): 71–79.

Blacklock, Mary G. 1936. "Certain Aspects of the Welfare of Women and Children in the Colonies." *Annals of Tropical Medicine & Parasitology* 30 (2) (June 19): 221–264.

Bliss, James. 2015. "Hope against Hope: Queer Negativity, Black Feminist Theorizing, and Reproduction without Futurity." *Mosaic* 48(1) (March): 83–98.

Bosmans, Marleen, Dina Nasser, Umaiyeh Khammash, Patricia Claeys, and Marleen Temmerman. 2008. "Palestinian Women's Sexual and Reproductive Health Rights in a Longstanding Humanitarian Crisis." *Reproductive Health Matters: An International Journal on Sexual and Reproductive Health and Rights* 16(31): 103–111.

Bourmaud, Philippe. 2005. "Public Space and Private Spheres: The Foundation of St. Luke's Hospital of Nablus by the CMS (1891–1901)." In *New Faith in Ancient Lands: Western Missions in the Middle East in the*

Nineteenth and Early Twentieth Centuries. Edited by Heleen L. Murre-Van den Berg, 133–150. Leiden: Brill Academic.

Bourmaud, Philippe. 2009. "Pride and Prejudice: Hospitals, Medical Authority and Public Voice in Late Ottoman Southern Bilad al-Sham." In *From Western Medicine to Global Medicine: The Hospital beyond the West.* Edited by Mark Harrison, Margaret Jones, and Helen Sweet, 274–302. New Delhi: Orient BlackSwan.

Bourmaud, Philippe. 2012. "Experts at Large: Physicians, Public Debate and the Press in Late Ottoman Palestine." *Oriental Archive* 80 (Prague): 295–337.

Bourmaud, Philippe. 2013. "Guest Editor's Introduction: Internationalizing Perspectives: Re-reading Mandate History through a Health Policy Lens." *CBMH/BCHM [Canadian Bulletin of Medical History]* 30(2): 9–21.

Breslow, Lori. 1991. "Sins against Nature: The Condemnation of Birth Control in Early Christianity." *Atlantis* 17(1) (Fall–Winter): 52–60.

Brockopp, Jonathan E., ed. 2003. *Islamic Ethics of Life: Abortion, War, and Euthanasia. Studies in Comparative Religion.* Columbia: University of South Carolina Press.

Brownson, Elizabeth. 2000. "Gender, Muslim Family Law, and Contesting Patriarchy in Mandate Palestine, 1925–1939." PhD Dissertation, University of California, Santa Barbara, Department of History.

Brownson, Elizabeth. 2017. "Enacting Imperial Control: Midwifery Regulation in Mandate Palestine." *Journal of Palestine Studies* 46(3) (Spring): 27–42.

Bucknill, John A. S., and Haig Apisoghom S. Utidjian. 1913. *The Imperial Ottoman Penal Code: A Translation from the Turkish Text, with Latest Additions and Amendments Together with Annotations and Explanatory Commentaries upon the Text and Containing an Appendix Dealing with the Special Amendments in Force in Cyprus and the Judicial Decisions of the Cyprus Courts.* London: H. Milford, Oxford University Press.

Bunton, Martin. 2007. *Colonial Land Policies in Palestine, 1917–1936.* Oxford: Oxford University Press.

Burdon, R. M. 1945. *New Zealand Notables, Series Two.* Christchurch: Caxton Press.

Burkman, Thomas W. 2007. *Japan and the League of Nations: Empire and World Order 1914–1938.* Honolulu: University of Hawaii Press.

Butler, Octavia E. 2000. *Lilith's Brood.* New York: Grand Central.

Campbell, Chloe. 2007. *Race and Empire: Eugenics in Colonial Kenya.* Manchester: Manchester University Press.

Campbell, Oona, and Gillian Lewando-Hundt, with members of the Maximizing Arab Maternal Health Network. 1998. "Profiling Maternal Health in Egypt, Jordan, Lebanon, Palestine, and Syria." In *Reproductive Health and Infectious Disease in the Middle East.* Edited by Robin Barlow and Joseph W. Brown, 22–44. Aldershot: Ashgate.

Canaan, Tawfik. 1927. "The Child in Palestinian Arab Superstitions." *Journal of the Palestine Oriental Society* 7: 159–186.

Canaan, Tawfik. 1946. "The Hygienic and Sanitary Conditions of the Arabs of Palestine. The Palestine Arab Medical Association." Pamphlet Vol. 5747 (March). Jerusalem: Economic Press, Mamilla Road. National Library of Medicine, Bethesda, MD.

Climie, Hugh. 1942. "Immunization against Typhoid and Paratyphoid with Alcohol-Killed, Alcohol-Preserved and Heat-Killed, Phenol-Preserved, Vaccine." *Journal of Hygiene* 42(4) (July): 411–415.

Coale, Ansley J. 1983. "Frank W. Notestein, 1902–1983." *Population Index* 49(1) (Spring): 3–12.

Cohen, Rivka. 1987. "The Israeli Health System: Power, Politics and Policies." PhD Dissertation, University of Toronto, Faculty of Medicine.

Constantine, Stephen. 1984. *The Making of British Colonial Development Policy 1914–1940*. London: Frank Cass.

Cullather, Nick. 2007. "The Foreign Policy of the Calorie." *American Historical Review* 112(2) (April): 337–364.

Daoud, Francoise, and Angel M. Foster. 2016. "Navigating Barriers to Abortion Access: Misoprostol in the West Bank." In *Abortion Pills, Test Tube Babies, and Sex Toys: Emerging Sexual and Reproductive Technologies in the Middle East and North Africa*. Edited by L. L. Wynn and Angel M. Foster, 58–68. Nashville, TN: Vanderbilt University Press.

Darwin, Charles. 1859. *The Origin of Species by Means of Natural Selection: Or the Preservation of Favored Races in the Struggle for Life*. London: John Murray.

Darwish, Mahmud. 1964. *"Bitaqatu Hawiyya"* (poem), in Awraq al-Zaytun. Haifa: Matba`at al-ittihad al-ta`awuniyya. Also (accessed May 20, 2020): https://tinyurl.com/ybksa8jw

Darwish, Mahmud. 2008a. *"La`ib al-nard"* (poem). Al-kalima: Majalla adabiyya fikriyya shahriyya. No. 20 (August). Also (accessed July 27, 2021): www.alkalimah.net/Articles/Read/1481

Darwish, Mahmoud. 2008b. "The Dice Player" (poem). Translated by Fady Joudah. *Poetry Nation Review* 35(2) (November/December): 16–19.

Darwish, Mahmoud. 2013. *Memory for Forgetfulness: August, Beirut, 1982*. 2nd edition. Translation and Introduction by Ibrahim Muhawi. New foreword by Sinan Antoon. Original Arabic 1986. Berkeley: University of California Press.

Davidovitch, Nadav, and Zalman Greenberg. 2007. "Public Health, Culture, and Colonial Medicine: Smallpox and Variolation in Palestine during the British Mandate." *Public Health Reports* 122(3) (May–June): 398–406.

Davidovitch, Nadav, and Rakefet Zalashik. 2010. "Pasteur in Palestine: The Politics of the Laboratory." *Science in Context* 23(4): 401–425.

DCAF (Geneva Centre for the Democratic Control of Armed Forces). 2012. *Palestinian Women and Security: A Legal Collection.* Geneva: Geneva Centre for Security Sector Governance. www.dcaf.ch/sites/default/files/p ublications/documents/Legal_Collection_Women_EN.pdf

Demirci, Tuba, and Selçuk Akşin Somel. 2008. "Women's Bodies, Demography, and Public Health: Abortion Policy and Perspectives in the Ottoman Empire of the Nineteenth Century." *Journal of the History of Sexuality* 17(3) (September): 377–420.

Dickens, Bernard M., and Rebecca J. Cook. 1979. "Development of Commonwealth Abortion Laws." *International and Comparative Law Quarterly* 28 (July): 424–457.

Donati, Serena, Rawia Hamam, and Emanuela Medda. 2000. "Family Planning KAP Survey in Gaza." *Social Science & Medicine* 50: 841–849.

Doumani, Beshara. 2009. "Archiving Palestine and the Palestinians: The Patrimony of Ihsan Nimr." *Jerusalem Quarterly* No. 36 (Winter): 3–12. www.palestine-studies.org/en/node/165402

Doyle, Jennifer. 2009. "Blind Spots and Failed Performance: Abortion, Feminism, and Queer Theory." *Qui Parle: Critical Humanities and Social Sciences* 18(1) (Fall/Winter): 25–52.

Du Bois, W. E. B. 1900a. "To the Nations of the World." In *The Oxford W. E. B. Du Bois Reader.* Edited by Eric J. Sundquist (1996), 625–627. Oxford: Oxford University Press.

Du Bois, W. E. B. 1900b. "The Present Outlook for the Dark Races of Mankind." In *The Oxford W .E. B. Du Bois Reader*, 47–54.

Du Bois, W. E. B. 1919. "Africa, Colonialism, and Zionism." *In The Oxford W. E. B. Du Bois Reader*, 637–640.

Du Bois, W. E. B. 1920. "The Souls of White Folk." *In The Oxford W. E. B. Du Bois Reader*, 497–509.

Du Bois, W. E. B. 1921. *Darkwater: Voices from within the Veil.* New York: Harcourt, Brace.

Du Bois, W. E. B. 1948. "The Case for the Jews." In *The Oxford W. E. B. Du Bois Reader*, 461–464.

Edelman, Lee. 2004. *No Future: Queer Theory and the Death Drive.* Durham, NC: Duke University Press.

El-Eini, Roza I. 1997. "Government Fiscal Policy in Mandatory Palestine in the 1930s." *Middle Eastern Studies* 33(3) (July): 570–596.

Ertem, Ece Cihan. 2011. "Anti-abortion Policies in Late Ottoman Empire and Early Republican Turkey: Intervention of State on Women's Body and

Reproductivity." *Fe Dergi: Feminist Eleştiri* 3(1): 47–55. http://cins
.ankara.edu.tr/20111.html

Falk, Raphael. 2017. *Zionism and the Biology of the Jews*. Cham: Springer
International.

Farge, Arlette. 2013. *The Allure of the Archives*. Translated by Thomas
Scott-Railton. Forward by Natalie Zemon Davis. New Haven, CT: Yale
University Press.

Fargues, Philippe. 2000. "Protracted National Conflict and Fertility Change:
Palestinians and Israelis in the Twentieth Century." *Population and
Development Review* 26(3) (September): 441–482.

Farhat, Maymanah, and Samia Halaby. 2012. "On 'Liberation Art' and
Revolutionary Aesthetics: An Interview with Samia Halaby." Jadaliyya
.com (June 22) (accessed June 27, 2021). www.jadaliyya.com/Details/26
316/On-Liberation-Art-and-Revolutionary-Aesthetics-An-Interview-with
-Samia-Halaby

Feldman, David M. 1968. *Birth Control in Jewish Law: Marital Relations,
Contraception, and Abortion As Set Forth in the Classic Texts of Jewish
Law*. New York: New York University Press.

Felix, Arthur. 1935. "Clinical Trials with a New Antityphoid Serum." *The
Lancet* (April 6): 799–802.

Felix, Arthur. 1951. "The Preparation, Testing and Standardization of
Typhoid Vaccine." *Journal of Hygiene* 49(2/3) (September): 268–287.

Felix, Arthur, K. S. Krikorian, and Rudolph Reitler. 1935. "The Occurrence
of Typhoid Bacilli Containing Vi Antigen in Cases of Typhoid Fever and of
Vi Antibody in Their Sera." *Journal of Epidemiology and Infection* 35(3):
421–427.

Felix, Arthur, and R. Margaret Pitt. 1934. "A New Antigen of B. *Typhosus*:
Its Relation to Virulence and to Active and Passive Immunisation." *The
Lancet* (July 28): 186–191.

Fleischmann, Ellen L. 1996. "Crossing the Boundaries of History: Exploring
Oral History in Researching Palestinian Women in the Mandate Period."
Women's History Review 5(3): 351–371.

Fleischmann, Ellen L. 2003. *The Nation and Its "New" Women: The
Palestinian Women's Movement, 1920–1948*. Berkeley: University of
California Press.

Foucault, Michel. 1978. *The History of Sexuality, Volume I: An
Introduction*. Translated from the French by Robert Hurley. New York:
Vintage Books.

Ghani, Miriam. 2012. "A Brief History of Collapses." Two-channel color
video project, with sound. 22 minutes. Solomon R. Guggenheim Museum,
New York. Produced for Documenta 13, Kassel, Germany. https://vimeo

.com/100683295. Interview with Ghani on the project in 2016: www
.guggenheim.org/video/mariam-ghani-on-a-brief-history-of-collapses

Ghani, Miriam. 2015. "'What We Left Unfinished': The Artist and the
Archive." In *Dissonant Archives: Contemporary Visual Culture and
Contested Narratives in the Middle East*. Edited by Anthony Downey,
43–63. London: I. B. Tauris.

Ghanim, Honaida. 2009. "Poetics of Disaster: Nationalism, Gender, and
Social Change among Palestinian Poets in Israel after Nakba."
International Journal of Politics, Culture, and Society 22: 22–39.

Giacaman, Rita. 1988. *Life & Health in Three Palestinian Villages*. London
and Atlantic Highlands: Ithaca Press.

Giacaman, Rita, Laura Wick, Hanan Abdul-Rahim, and Livia Wick. 2005.
"The Politics of Childbirth in the Context of Conflict: Policies or De Facto
Practices?" *Health Policy*. 72(2): 129–139.

Giladi, Avner. 2015. *Muslim Midwives: The Craft of Birthing in the
Premodern Middle East*. Cambridge Studies in Islamic Civilization.
New York: Cambridge University Press.

Government of Cyprus. 1928. *The Cyprus Criminal Code, Order in Council,
1928, with an Appendix Containing a Summary of References to the
Principal Offences*. Published by Authority. Nicosia: Government
Printing Office.

Government of Palestine. 1921a. Local Councils Ordinance, Order for
Jericho.

Government of Palestine. 1921b. Local Councils Ordinance, Order for
Rameh.

Government of Palestine. 1922. Local Councils Ordinance, Order for Bir Zeit.

Government of Palestine. 1929. "An Ordinance to Regulate the Practice of
Midwifery." ("Midwives Ordinance") *Official Gazette of the
Government of Palestine*, No. 226, Jerusalem (April 1): 260–264.

Government of Palestine (W. J. Johnson, R. E. H. Crosbie, et al.). 1930.
*Report of a Committee on the Economic Condition of Agriculturalists in
Palestine and the Fiscal Measures of Government in Relation Thereto*.
Jerusalem: Government Printing Office.

Government of Palestine. 1938. *Report by the Treasurer on the Financial
Transactions of the Palestine Government for the Year 1937–38*.
Jerusalem: Government Printing Office.

Government of Palestine. 1939. *Report by the Treasurer on the Financial
Transactions of the Palestine Government for the Year 1938–39*.
Jerusalem: Government Printing Office.

Government of Palestine, Department of Health. 1923. *Annual Report of the
Department of Health for the Year 1923*. Institute of Community and
Public Health, Birzeit University.

Government of Palestine, Department of Health. 1927. *Annual Report of the Department of Health for the Year 1927.* Institute of Community and Public Health, Birzeit University.

Government of Palestine, Department of Health. 1929. *Annual Report of the Department of Health for the Year 1929.* Institute of Community and Public Health, Birzeit University.

Government of Palestine, Department of Health. 1930. *List of Doctors, Pharmacists, Dentists and Midwives Who Have Been Licensed in Accordance with the Various Ordinances Regulating Their Professions.* Jerusalem: Government Printing Press. National Library of Israel, Ein Kerem.

Government of Palestine, Department of Health. 1931. *Annual Report of the Department of Health for the Year 1931.* Institute of Community and Public Health, Birzeit University.

Government of Palestine, Department of Health. 1934. *Annual Report of the Department of Health for the Year 1934.* United States National Library of Medicine.

Government of Palestine, Department of Health. 1935a. *Annual Report of the Department of Health for the Year 1935.* United States National Library of Medicine.

Government of Palestine, Department of Health. 1935b. *List of Doctors, Dentists, Dental Practitioners, Pharmacists, Assistant Pharmacists and Midwives Who Have Been Licensed to Practise Their Professions in Palestine Including a Supplement of Licensed Veterinary Surgeons.* Jerusalem: Government Printing Press. National Library of Israel, Ein Kerem.

Government of Palestine, Department of Health. (July) 1936. *List of Medical Practitioners, Dentists, Dental Practitioners, Pharmacists, Assistant Pharmacists and Midwives Licensed by the Director of Medical Services to Practise Their Professions in Palestine Including a Supplement of Licensed Veterinary Surgeons.* Jerusalem: Government Printing Press. National Library of Israel, Ein Kerem.

Government of Palestine, Department of Health. 1938. *List of Medical Practitioners, Dentists, Dental Practitioners, Pharmacists, Assistant Pharmacists and Midwives Licensed by the Director of Medical Services to Practise Their Professions in Palestine Including a Supplement of Licensed Veterinary Surgeons.* Jerusalem: Government Printing Press. National Library of Israel, Ein Kerem.

Government of Palestine, Department of Health. 1940. *List of Medical Practitioners, Dentists, Dental Practitioners, Pharmacists, Assistant Pharmacists and Midwives Licensed by the Director of Medical Services to Practise Their Professions in Palestine Including a Supplement of Licensed Veterinary Surgeons.* Jerusalem: Government Printing Press. National Library of Israel, Ein Kerem.

Government of Palestine, Department of Health. 1946. *List of Medical Practitioners, Dentists, Dental Practitioners, Pharmacists, Assistant Pharmacists and Midwives Licensed by the Director of Medical Services to Practise Their Professions in Palestine Including a Supplement of Licensed Veterinary Surgeons.* Jerusalem: Government Printing Press. National Library of Israel, Ein Kerem.

Granqvist, Hilma. 1947. *Birth and Childhood among the Arabs: Studies in a Muhammadan Village in Palestine.* Helsingfors: Soderstrom and Company Forlagsaktiebolag.

Granqvist, Hilma. 1950. *Child Problems among the Arabs: Studies in a Muhammadan Village in Palestine.* Helsingfors and Copenhagen: Soderstrom and Company and Ejnar Munksgaard.

Granqvist, Hilma. 1965. *Muslim Death and Burial: Arab Customs and Traditions Studied in a Village in Jordan.* Soceitas Scientiarum Fenneca, Commentationes Humanarum Litterarum. XXXIV.1. Helsinki: Centraltryckeriet Helsingfors.

Greenberg, Ela. 2010. *Preparing the Mothers of Tomorrow: Education and Islam in Mandate Palestine.* Austin: University of Texas Press.

Gudorf, Christine E. 2003. "Contraception and Abortion in Roman Catholicism." In *Sacred Rights: The Case for Contraception and Abortion in World Religions.* Edited by Daniel C. Maguire, 56–76. Oxford: Oxford Scholarship Online.

Habiby, Emile. 1974. *al-Waqai` al-Ghariba fi Ikhtifa' Sa`id abi al-Nahs al-Mutasha'il.* Jerusalem: Manshurat Salah al Din.

Habiby, Emile. 2003. *The Secret Life of Saeed the Pessoptimist.* Translated by Salma K. Jayyusi and Trevor LeGassick. Northampton, MA: Interlink.

Hamdan, Mohammed. 2019. "'Every Sperm Is Sacred': Palestinian Prisoners, Smuggled Semen, and Derrida's Prophecy." *International Journal of Middle East Studies* 51: 525–545.

Hamilton, Elizabeth C. 2017. "Afrofuturism and the Technologies of Survival." *African Arts* 50(4) (Winter): 18–23.

Hammoudeh, Weeam, and Dennis P. Hogan. 2012. "Proximate Determinants of Palestinian Fertility: A Decomposition Analysis." *The Lancet* 380, Special Issue S20 (October 1).

Hanssen, Jens. 2005. *Fin de Siècle Beirut: The Making of an Ottoman Capital.* Oxford: Clarendon Press.

Hansson, Liv Nanna, Siri Tellier, Lotte Buch Segal, Maysoon Bseiso. 2013. "Political Fertility in the Occupied Palestinian Territory: An Ethnographic Study." *The Lancet.* 382, Special Issue S17 (December 5).

Hart, Mitchell B. 2007. *The Healthy Jew: The Symbiosis of Judaism and Modern Medicine.* Cambridge: Cambridge University Press.

Hasso, Frances S. 2000. "Modernity and Gender in Arab Accounts of the 1948 and 1967 Defeats." *International Journal of Middle East Studies* 32 (4): 491–510.

Hatem, Mervat F. 1997. "The Professionalization of Health and the Control of Women's Bodies as Modern Governmentalities in Nineteenth-Century Egypt." In *Women in the Ottoman Empire: Middle Eastern Women in the Early Modern Era*. Edited by Madeline C. Zilfi, 66–104. Leiden: Brill.

Hirsch, Dafna. 2008. "'Interpreters of Occident to the Awakening Orient': The Jewish Public Health Nurse in Mandate Palestine." *Comparative Studies in Society and History* 50(1): 227–255.

Hirsch, Dafna. 2009. "'We Are Here to Bring the West, Not only to Ourselves': Zionist Occidentalism and the Discourse of Hygiene in Mandate Palestine." *International Journal of Middle East Studies* 41: 577–594.

Hong, Grace Kyungwon. 2015. *Death beyond Disavowal: The Impossible Politics of Difference*. Minneapolis: University of Minnesota Press.

Horton, Richard. 2013. "Comment: Public Health or Social Medicine? It Matters." *The Lancet* 382, Special Issue (November 29): 1.

Hourani, Albert. 2005. "The Case against a Jewish State in Palestine: Albert Hourani's Statement to the Anglo-American Committee of Enquiry of 1946." *Journal of Palestine Studies* 37, no. 1 (Autumn), 80–90.

Hudson, Aida J. 1998. "Fertility and Family Planning in a West Bank Village." In *Reproductive Health and Infectious Disease in the Middle East*. Edited by Robin Barlow and Joseph W. Brown, 92–113. Aldershot: Ashgate.

Hughes, Matthew. 2013. "A British 'Foreign Legion'? The British Police in Mandate Palestine." *Middle Eastern Studies* 49(5): 696–711.

Husseini, Salim F. 1981. *Women & Abortion in the West Bank of Jordan: A Pilot Study*. Jerusalem: Jordan Family Planning and Protection Association.

Israel: Reproduction and Abortion: Law and Policy. 2012. Washington, DC: Law Library of Congress, Global Legal Research Center. HeinOnline through J. Michael Goodson Law Library.

Ittmann, Karl. 2013. *A Problem of Great Importance: Population, Race, and Power in the British Empire, 1918–1973*. Berkeley Series in British Studies 7. Berkeley: University of California Press.

Jad, Islah. 2005. "Re-reading the Mandate: Palestinian Women and the Double Jeopardy of Colonialism." *Review of Women's Studies* 3: 8–29. Institute of Women's Studies, Birzeit University.

Jarman, Robert L., ed. 2001. *Political Diaries of the Arab World: Palestine & Jordan, Vol. 1: 1920–1923*. London: Archive International Group. Bilad ash-Sham Library, University of Jordan.

Jayyusi, Lena. 2007. "Iterability, Cumulativity, and Presence: The Relational Figures of Palestinian Memory." In *Nakba: Palestine, 1948, and the*

Claims of Memory. Edited by Ahmad H. Saʿdi and Lila Abu-Lughod, 107–133. New York: Columbia University Press.

Jayyusi, Salma Khadra. 1992a. "Introduction: Palestinian Literature in Modern Times." In *Anthology of Modern Palestinian Literature*. Edited by Salma Khadra Jayyusi, 1–80. New York: Columbia University Press.

Jayyusi, Salma Khadra, ed. 1992b. *Anthology of Modern Palestinian Literature*. New York: Columbia University Press.

Jellett, Henry, and J. Bernard Dawson. 1948. *A Short Practice of Midwifery for Nurses*. 14th edition. London: J. & A. Churchill.

Jewish Agency for Palestine. 1946 (March). "Memorandum Submitted to the Anglo-American Committee of Inquiry on Palestine by the Jewish Agency for Palestine." Jerusalem: Jewish Agency for Palestine.

Jung, Moon-Kie. 2015. "The Problem of the Color Lines: Studies of Racism and Resistance." *Critical Sociology* 41(2): 193–199.

Kahn, Susan Martha. 2013. "Commentary: Who are the Jews? New Formulations of an Age-Old Question." *Human Biology* 85(6): 919–924.

Kanaana, Sharif, ʿAbd al-ʿAziz Abu Hadba, ʿUmar Hamdan, Nabil ʿAlqam, and Walid Rabiʿ. 1984. *Al-Injab wal-Tufuleh: Dirasa fi al-Thaqafa wal-Mujtamaʿ al-Falastini* [*Birth and Childhood: A Study of Palestinian Society and Culture*]. El-Bireh, Palestine: Inʿash al-Usra Association, Palestinian Social and Popular Heritage Research Committee. Printer: Awfasat Hasan Abu Dalu, Beit Safafa, Jerusalem.

Kanaaneh, Rhoda Ann. 2002. *Birthing the Nation: Strategies of Palestinian Women in Israel*. Berkeley: University of California Press.

Katvan, Eyal, and Nira Bartal. 2010. "The Midwives Ordinance of Palestine, 1929: Historical Perspectives and Current Lessons." *Nursing Inquiry* 17 (2):165–172.

Katz, Marion Holmes. 2002. "The Problem of Abortion in Classical Sunni *Fiqh*." In *Islamic Ethics of Life: Abortion, War, and Euthanasia*. Edited by Jonathan E. Brockopp, 25–50. Columbia: University of South Carolina Press.

Kelm, Mary Ellen. 2005. "Diagnosing the Discursive Indian: Medicine, Gender, and the 'Dying Race.'" *Ethnohistory* 52(2) (Spring): 371–406.

Keown, John. 1988. *Abortion, Doctors and the Law: Some Aspects of the Legal Regulation of Abortion in England from 1803 to 1982*. Cambridge: Cambridge University Press.

Khalaf, Issa. 1997. "The Effects of Socioeconomic Change on Arab Societal Collapse in Mandate Palestine." *International Journal of Middle East Studies* 29(1) (February): 93–112.

Khalidi, Aziza. 1996. "Indicators of Social Transformation and Infant Survival: A Conceptual Framework and an Application to the Populations of Palestine from 1927 to 1944." DSc Dissertation, Johns Hopkins University, Health Policy and Management.

Khalidi, Tarif. 1981. "Palestinian Historiography: 1900–1948." *Journal of Palestine Studies* 10(3) (Spring): 59–76.

Khawaja, Marwan. 2003. "The Fertility of Palestinian Women in Gaza, the West Bank, Jordan and Lebanon." *Population* 58(3): 273–302.

Khawaja, Marwan, Shireen Assaf, and Yara Jarallah. 2009. "The Transition to Lower Fertility in the West Bank and Gaza Strip: Evidence from Recent Surveys." *Journal of Population Research* 26(2) (June): 153–174.

Khleifi, Michel (Director, Producer, Screenwriter). 1987 (2004 video). `Urs al-jalil (*Wedding in Galilee*). Produced by Jacqueline Louis and Bernard Lorain. Marisa Films (Brussels); Les Productions Audiovisuelles (Paris). Distributed by Kino on Video, New York (116 minutes).

King, Frederick Truby. 1913. *Feeding and Care of Baby*. London and Calcutta: Macmillan. Accessed June 27, 2021. https://dlcs.io/pdf/well come/pdf-item/b21512115/0

King, Frederick Truby. 1918. *Natural Feeding of Infants*. Introduction by J. S. Fairbairn, M.D. B.Ch. Oxon, F.R.C.S. London. London: Whitcombe & Tombs.

Kligler, Israel Jacob. 1931. "An Inquiry into the Diets of the Population of Palestine." *Palestine & Near East Economic Magazine: A Fortnightly for Trade, Industry & Agriculture* 6 (December 15): 389–418. Tel Aviv, Palestine: Publication and Exhibition Company.

Kligler, Israel Jacob. 1932. "Public Health in Palestine." *Annals of the American Academy of Political and Social Science* 164. Palestine. A Decade of Development (November): 167–177.

Kozma, Liat. 2010. "Sexology in the Yishuv: The Rise and Decline of Sexual Consultation in Tel Aviv, 1930–1939." *International Journal of Middle East Studies* 42(2) (May): 231–249.

Lake, Marilyn, and Henry Reynolds. 2008. *Drawing the Global Colour Line: White Men's Countries and the International Challenge of Racial Equality*. Cambridge: Cambridge University Press.

Laukötter, Anja. 2016. "How Films Entered the Classroom: The Sciences and the Emotional Education of Youth through Health Education Films in the United States and Germany, 1910–30." *OSIRIS: History of Science Society* 31: 181–200.

Layoun, Mary. 1992. "Telling Spaces: Palestinian Women and the Engendering of National Narratives." In *Nationalisms & Sexualities*. Edited by Andrew Parker, Mary Russo, Doris Sommer, and Patricia Yaeger, 407–423. New York: Routledge.

Ledbetter, Rosanna. 1976. *A History of the Malthusian League, 1877–1927*. Columbus: Ohio State University Press.

Leon, Jacob V. 1947. *Criminal Code Ordinance No. 74 of 1936 (As in Force on 1st December 1947). Consolidated Edition with References to Cases*

Decided by the Supreme Court and District Courts of Palestine. Jerusalem: Hamadpis Lipshitz Press.

Levine, Philippa, and Alison Bashford. 2010. "Introduction: Eugenics and the Modern World." In *The Oxford Handbook of the History of Eugenics.* Edited by Alison Bashford and Philippa Levine, 3–24. Oxford: Oxford University Press.

Liddiard, Mabel. 1925. *The Mothercraft Manual or The Expectant and Nursing Mother and Baby's First Two Years.* Introduction by J. S. Fairbairn. 3rd edition. London: J.& A. Churchill.

Lindner, Ulrike. 2014. "The Transfer of European Social Policy Concepts to Tropical Africa, 1900–50: The Example of Maternal and Child Welfare." *Journal of Global History* 9: 208–231.

MacLennan, Norman M. 1935. Tuberculosis in Palestine (A Preliminary Survey). MD, DPH, DTM &H, Senior Medical Officer, Department of Health, Palestine, July 20. Access to a personal copy of the report provided courtesy of Walid Khalidi (Amman).

MacQueen, John (M.B., C.M. Edin., Department of Health, Jerusalem). 1926. "Small-pox and Variolation in a Village in Palestine in December, 1921." *The Lancet* (January 23): 212–214.

Manderson, Lenore. 1998. "Shaping Reproduction: Maternity in Early Twentieth-Century Malaya." In *Maternities and Modernities: Colonial and Postcolonial Experiences in Asia and the Pacific.* Edited by Kalpana Ram and Margaret Jolly, 26–49. Cambridge: Cambridge University Press.

Mann, Justin Louis. 2018. "Pessimistic Futurism: Survival and Reproduction in Octavia Butler's *Dawn.*" *Feminist Theory* 19(1): 61–76.

March, Norah. 1917. "The Eugenic Aspects of National Baby Week." *Eugenics Review* 9(2) (July): 95–108. www.ncbi.nlm.nih.gov/pmc/art icles/PMC2942200

Masalha, Nur. 2008. "Remembering the Palestinian Nakba: Commemoration, Oral History and Narratives of Memory." *Holy Land Studies: A Multidisciplinary Journal* 7(2) (November): 123–156.

Mayasi, Rakan (Screenwriter, Director, Producer). 2017. *Bonbone.* Distribution by MAD and Salaud Morisset. Palestine, Lebanon, 15 minutes. Co-screenwriter, Parine Jaddo. Produced by Groundglass 235 with Postoffice and Mod4Films. www.youtube.com/watch?v=LNkn552kEYA

Mbembe, Achille. 2002. Translated by Steven Rendell. "African Modes of Self-Writing." *Public Culture* 14(1) (Winter): 239–273.

Mbembe, Achille. 2019. Translated by Steven Corcoran. *Necropolitics.* Durham, NC: Duke University Press.

Mbembe, Joseph-Achille. 2003. Translated by Libby Meintjes. "Necropolitics." *Public Culture* 15(1) (Winter): 11–40.

McCarthy, Justin. 1990. *The Population of Palestine: Population History and Statistics of the Late Ottoman Period and the Mandate*. Institute for Palestine Studies Series. New York: Columbia University Press.

McSweeney, C. J. 1935. "Clinical Trials with a New Antityphoid Serum." *The Lancet* (May 11): 1095–1098.

McSweeney, C. J. 1937. "Serum Treatment of Typhoid Fever." *British Medical Journal* 2(4013) (December 4): 1118–1119.

Meiton, Fredrik. 2019. *Electrical Palestine: Capital and Technology from Empire to Nation*. Oakland: University of California Press.

Miller, David Hunter. 1928 (January). *The Drafting of the Covenant*. Vol. 2. London: G. P. Putnam's Sons.

Miller, Ylana N. 1985. *Government and Society in Rural Palestine, 1920–1948*. Modern Middle East Series 9. Austin: University of Texas Press.

Milns, Susan, and Brian Thompson. 1994. "Constructing British Abortion Law: The Role of the Legislature, the Judiciary and the European Institutions." *Parliamentary Affairs* 47(2) (April): n.p.

Mir, Salam. 2015. "The Art and Politics of Emile Habiby II." *Arab Studies Quarterly* 37(2) (Spring): 142–160.

Mogannam, E. Theodore. 1952. "Developments in the Legal System in Jordan." *Middle East Journal* 6(2) (Spring): 194–206.

Morris, Anne E., and Michael A. Jones. 2007. *Blackstone's Statues: Medical Law*. 5th edition. Oxford: Oxford University Press.

Mortensen, Berit. 2011. "To be Veiled – or Not to Be? What Unites Is the Question: Experiences from Continuous Midwifery Care in Occupied Palestine and in Norway." Master in Practical Knowledge Thesis. University of Nordland. Kindly provided by author.

Muhawi, Ibrahim. 2009. "Contexts of Language in Mahmoud Darwish." Occasional Papers. Center for Contemporary Arab Studies, Edmund A. Walsh School of Foreign Service. Washington, DC: Georgetown University.

Mukherjee, Siddhartha. 2016. *The Gene: An Intimate History*. New York: Scribner.

Muñoz, José Esteban. 2007. "Cruising the Toilet: LeRoi Jones/Amiri Baraka, Radical Black Traditions, and Queer Futurity." *GLQ: A Journal of Lesbian and Gay Studies* 13(2–3): 353–367.

Musallam, Basim F. 1981. "Why Islam Permitted Birth Control." *Arab Studies Quarterly*. 3(2) (Spring): 181–197.

Musallam, Basim F. 1983. *Sex and Society in Islam: Birth Control before the Nineteenth Century*. Cambridge Studies in Islamic Civilization. Cambridge: Cambridge University Press.

Nashef, Khaled. 2002. Tawfik Canaan: His Life and Works. *Jerusalem Quarterly*. No. 16. www.palestine-studies.org/jq/fulltext/78010

Nazzal, Nafez. 1978. *The Palestinian Exodus from Galilee, 1948.* Monograph Series No. 59. Beirut: Institute for Palestine Studies.

Nelson, Alondra. 2002. "Introduction: Future Texts." *Social Text* 20(2) (Summer): 1–15.

El-Nimr, Sonia. 1990. "The Arab Revolt of 1936–1939 in Palestine: A Study Based on Oral Sources." PhD Dissertation, University of Exeter, Arabic and Islamic Studies. Kindly provided by author.

Noonan, John T., Jr. 1967. "Abortion and the Catholic Church: A Summary History." *Natural Law Forum* 12: 85–131.

Noonan, John T., Jr. 1986. *Contraception: A History of Its Treatment by the Catholic Theologians and Canonists.* Cambridge, MA: Harvard University Press.

Norris, Jacob. 2013. *Land of Progress: Palestine in the Age of Colonial Development, 1905–1948.* Oxford: Oxford University Press.

Norris, Jacob. 2017. "Transforming the Holy Land: The Ideology of Development and the British Mandate in Palestine." *Humanity: An International Journal of Human Rights, Humanitarianism, and Development* 8(2) (Summer): 269–286.

Notestein, Frank W., and Ernest Jurkat. 1945. "Population Problems in Palestine." *Milbank Memorial Fund Quarterly* 23(4) (October): 307–352.

Olssen, Erik. 1981. "Truby King and the Plunket Society: An Analysis of a Prescriptive Ideology." *New Zealand Journal of History* 15: 3–23.

Oppenheimer, W. 1958. "Prevention of Pregnancy by the Graefenberg Ring Method: A Re-evaluation after 28 Years' Experience." *American Journal of Obstetrics and Gynecology* 78(2) (August): 446–454.

Pad.ma. 2010. "10 Theses on the Archive." April. Beirut, Lebanon. https:// pad.ma/documents/OH

Palestine and Transjordan Administration Reports 1918–1948, Vol. 1, 1918–1924. 1995. London: Archive International Group. Bilad ash-Sham Library, University of Jordan.

Palestine and Transjordan Administration Reports 1918–1948, Vol. 2, 1925–1928. 1995. London: Archive International Group. Bilad ash-Sham Library, University of Jordan.

Palestine and Transjordan Administration Reports 1918–1948, Vol. 3, 1929–1931. 1995. London: Archive International Group. Bilad ash-Sham Library, University of Jordan.

Palestine and Transjordan Administration Reports 1918–1948, Vol. 4, 1932–1933. 1995. London: Archive International Group. Bilad ash-Sham Library, University of Jordan.

Palestine and Transjordan Administration Reports 1918–1948, Vol. 5, 1934–1935. 1995. London: Archive International Group. Bilad ash-Sham Library, University of Jordan.

Palestine Women's Council. 1922. *Report 1921–1922.* Kindly provided by Ellen Fleischmann.

Pappé, Ilan. 2006. *The Ethnic Cleansing of Palestine.* London: Oneworld.

Porath, Yehoshua. 1974. *The Emergence of the Palestinian-Arab National Movement, 1918–1929.* London: Frank Cass.

Pursley, Sara. 2019. *Familiar Futures: Time, Selfhood, and Sovereignty in Iraq.* Stanford, CA: Stanford University Press.

Qafisheh, Mutaz M. 2012. "Human Rights Gaps in the Palestinian Criminal System: A United Nations Role?" *International Journal of Human Rights* 16(2): 358–377.

Qasimiyya, Khayriyya, ed. 2002. *Mudhakarat ʿAwni ʿAbdulhadi.* Introduction by Khayriyya Qasimiyya. Beirut: Markaz Dirasat al-Wihda al-ʿArabiyya.

Rabinow, Paul, ed. 1984. *The Foucault Reader.* New York: Pantheon Books.

Raghavan, V. V., and P. M. Bakshi. 2000. *Law of Crimes: Exhaustive Commentary on Indian Penal Code, 1860 [Act No. 45 of 1860].* Vol. 2 (Secs. 301 to End). 5th edition. New Delhi: India Law House.

Rahman, Najat. 2015. *In the Wake of the Poetic: Palestinian Artists after Darwish.* Syracuse, NY: Syracuse University Press.

Ramsden, Edmund. 2009. "Confronting the Stigma of Eugenics: Genetics, Demography and the Problems of Population." *Social Studies of Science* 39(6) (December): 853–884.

Reilly, Philip R. 2015. "Eugenics and Involuntary Sterilization: 1907–2015." *Annual Review Genomics and Human Genetics* 16: 351–368.

Report by His Majesty's Government in the United Kingdom and Northern Ireland to the Council of the League of Nations on the administration of Palestine and Transjordan for the year 1938: 1930 to 1938. 1938. London: His Majesty's Stationery Office, 1931–1939. LLMC Digital Law Library.

Reşit Paşa, Mustafa, Mehmed Fuad Paşa, and Âli Paşa. 1872. *Muharrerat-ı Nadire.* Desaadet: Dar-i Şura-yı Bab-ı Alinik Matbaasi.

Rieff, David. 1998/1999. "In Defense of Afro-Pessimism." *World Policy Journal* 15(4) (Winter): 10–22.

Robbins, Joan D., and John B. Robbins. 1984. "Reexamination of the Protective Role of the Capsular Polysaccharide (Vi antigen) of *Salmonella Typhi.*" *Journal of Infectious Diseases* 150(3) (September): 436–449.

Rogers, Therisa. 1999. "The Islamic Ethics of Abortion in the Traditional Islamic Sources." *Muslim World* 89(2) (April): 122–129.

Rogers, Vena (Winifred Ellen). 1934. "Midwifery Work in Palestine." *International Nursing Review* 9: 102–109.

Rosenau, M. J., and Charles F. Wilinsky. 1928. "Part III. A Sanitary Survey of Palestine." In *Reports of the Experts Submitted to the Joint Palestine Survey Commission. October 1.* Edited by P. C. Melchett, et al., 537–741. Boston, MA: Press of Daniels.

Rosenberg-Friedman, Lilach. 2015. "Abortion in the Yishuv during the British Mandate Period: A Case Study of the Place of the Individual in a Nationalistic Society." *Jewish History* 29: 331–359.

Rothenberg, Celia E. 2004. *Spirits of Palestine: Gender, Society, and Stories of the Jinn.* Lanham, MD: Lexington Books.

Rousso-Schindler, Steven. 2009. "Discourses of Modernization and Child Allowances: Israeli Population Politics and Their Impact on Palestinian Citizens of Israel." In *Between Life and Death: Governing Populations in the Era of Human Rights.* Edited by Sabine Berking and Magdalena Zolkos, 287–302. Frankfurt: Peter Lang.

Safwat, Najda Fathi, ed. 1988. *Mudhakarat Rustum Haydar.* Introduction by Najda Fathi Safwat. Beirut: Al-Dar al-`Arabiyya lil-Mawsu`at.

Saha, Ranjana. 2017. "Milk, 'Race' and Nation: Medical Advice on Breastfeeding in Colonial Bengal." *South Asia Research* 37(2): 147–165.

Sasson, Isaac, and Ronen Shamir. 2020. "The 1931 Census of Palestine and the Statistical (Un)making of an Arab Landless Class." *Middle Eastern Studies* 56(2): 239–256.

Sayigh, Rosemary. 1979. *Palestinians: From Peasants to Revolutionaries. A People's History Recorded by Rosemary Sayigh from Interviews with Camp Palestinians in Lebanon.* With an Introduction by Noam Chomsky. London: Zed Press.

Sayigh, Rosemary. 2007. "Women's Nakba Stories: Between Being and Knowing." In *Nakba: Palestine, 1948, and the Claims of Memory.* Edited by Ahmad H. Sa`di and Lila Abu-Lughod, 135–158. New York: Columbia University Press.

Schellekens, Jona, and Zvi Eisenbach. 2002. "The Predecline Rise in Israeli Moslem Fertility." *Economic Development and Cultural Change* 50(3) (April): 541–555.

Schenk, Faith, and A. S. Parkes. 1968. "The Activities of the Eugenics Society." *Eugenics Review* 60(3): 142–161.

Schull, Kent Fielding. 2007. "Penal Institutions, Nation-State Construction, and Modernity in the Late Ottoman Empire, 1908–1919." PhD Dissertation, University of California, Los Angeles, Department of History.

Schwartz, Yardena. 2015. "Dispatch: Palestine's Abortion Problem." *Foreign Policy* (December 4).

Seikaly, Sherene. 2014. "Bodies and Needs: Lessons from Palestine." *International Journal of Middle East Studies* 46(4) (November): 784–786.

Seikaly, Sherene. 2016. *Men of Capital: Scarcity and Economy in Mandate Palestine*. Stanford, CA: Stanford University Press.

Sekaleshfar, Farrokh B. 2008. "Abortion Perspectives of Shiah Islam." *Studies in Ethics, Law, and Technology* 2, no. 3: 1–15.

Sexton, Jared. 2011. "The Social Life of Social Death: On Afro-Pessimism and Black Optimism." *Tensions*, No. 5 (Fall/Winter): 1–47.

Shahawy, Sarrah, and Megan B. Diamond. 2018. "Perspectives on Induced Abortion among Palestinian Women: Religion, Culture and Access in the Occupied Palestinian Territories." *Culture, Health & Sexuality* 20(3): 289–305.

Sharafi, Mitra. 2020. "Abortion in South Asia, 1860–1947: A Medico-legal History." *Modern Asian Studies*: 1–58.

Sharpe, Christina. 2016. *In the Wake: On Blackness and Being*. Durham, NC: Duke University Press.

Shimazu, Naoko. 1998. *Japan, Race and Equality: The Racial Equality Proposal of 1919*. New York: Taylor & Francis Group.

Simoni, Marcella. 2000. "At the Roots of Division: A New Perspective on Arabs and Jews, 1930–39." *Middle Eastern Studies* 36(3) (July): 52–92.

Sleiman, Hana, and Kaoukab Chebaro. 2018. "Narrating Palestine: The Palestinian Oral History Archive." *Journal of Palestine Studies* 47(2) (Winter): 63–76.

Smuts, Jans Christiaan. 1919. *The League of Nations: A Practical Suggestion*. New York: Nation Press. Courtesy of HathiTrust.org (accessed June 27, 2021). https://hdl.handle.net/2027/hvd.hny6cg

Soloway, Richard A. 1988. "Eugenics and Pronatalism in Wartime Britain." In *The Upheaval of War: Family, Work, and Welfare in Europe, 1914–1918*. Edited by Richard Wall and Jay Winter, 369–388. Cambridge: Cambridge University Press.

Soloway, Richard A. 1990. *Demography and Degeneration: Eugenics and the Declining Birthrate in Twentieth-Century Britain*. Chapel Hill: University of North Carolina Press.

Somel, Selçuk Akşin. 2002. "The Issue of Abortion in 19th Century Ottoman Empire." Unpublished paper presented at the IXth International Congress of Economic and Social History of Turkey. Dubrovnik, Croatia. August 20–23 (accessed June 27, 2021). http://research.sabanciuniv.edu/1277/1/3011800000289.pdf

Spillers, Hortense J. 1987. "Mama's Baby, Papa's Maybe: An American Grammar Book." *Diacritics. Culture and Countermemory: The "American" Connection* 17(2) (Summer): 64–81.

Steinfeld, Rebecca. 2015. "War of the Wombs: Struggles over Abortion Policies in Israel." *Israel Studies* 20(2): 1–26.

Stern, Alexandra Minna. 2002. "Making Better Babies: Public Health and Race Betterment in Indiana, 1920–1935." *American Journal of Public Health* 92(5) (May): 742–753.

Stoler, Ann Laura. 2009. *Against the Archival Grain: Epistemic Anxieties and Colonial Common Sense.* Princeton, NJ: Princeton University Press.

Summers, Carol. 1991. "Intimate Colonialism: The Imperial Production of Reproduction in Uganda, 1907–1925." *Signs: Journal of Women in Culture and Society* 16(4): 787–807.

St-Jean, Martin. 2015. "Assessing Nursing and Midwifery Students' Attitudes toward Abortion and Contraception: Results of a National Survey in the Occupied Palestinian Territories." Master of Science in Interdisciplinary Health Sciences Thesis, University of Ottawa, August.

Stockdale, Nancy L. 2007. *Colonial Encounters among English and Palestinian Women, 1800–1948.* Gainesville: University Press of Florida.

Sufian, Sandra M. 2007. *Healing the Land and the Nation: Malaria and the Zionist Project in Palestine, 1920–1947.* Chicago: University of Chicago Press.

Sufian, Sandra M. 2015. "Healing Jerusalem: Colonial Medicine and Arab Health from World War I to 1948." In *Jerusalem Interrupted: Modernity and Colonial Transformation, 1917–Present.* Edited and introduced by Lena Jayyusi, 114–138. Northampton, MA: Olive Branch Press.

Symeonides, Symeon C. 2003. "The Mixed Legal System of the Republic of Cyprus." *Tulane Law Review* 78(1–2) (December): 441–456.

Takeshita, Chikako. 2011. *The Global Politics of the IUD: How Science Constructs Contraceptive Users and Women's Bodies.* Cambridge, MA: MIT Press.

Tamari, Salim. 2009. *Mountains against the Sea: Essays on Palestinian Society and Culture.* Berkeley: University of California Press.

Tilley, Helen. 2011. *Africa As a Living Laboratory: Empire, Development, and the Problem of Scientific Knowledge, 1870–1950.* Chicago: University of Chicago Press.

Tilley, Helen. 2014. "Racial Science, Geopolitics, and Empires." *Isis: History of Science and Society* 105: 773–781.

Totah, Faedah M. 2018. "The Palestinian Cause in Syrian Nationalism." *Dialectical Anthropology* 42(4) (December): 429–441.

Vickers, W. J. 1944. *A Nutritional Economic Survey of Wartime Palestine, 1942–1943.* Foreword by Colonel Sir George Heron, Director of Medical Services. No. 8. Jerusalem, Palestine: Department of Health.

Von Tol, Deanne. 2007. "Mothers, Babies, and the Colonial State: The Introduction of Maternal and Infant Welfare Services in Nigeria, 1925–1945." *Spontaneous Generations: A Journal for the History & Philosophy of Science* 1(1): 110–131.

Waddams, Herbert. 1945. "Survey of Social and Economic Conditions in Arab Villages, 1944." *General Monthly Bulletin of Current Statistics* 10 (7–9) (July–September): 426–447, 509–517, 559–567.

Wandieen, Abdennaim M. A. 1987. "The Role of the Constitution and Domestic Law in the Implementation of the Modern International Standards of Human Rights: A Case Study of Jordan." PhD Dissertation in the Faculty of Law, University of London.

Weindling, Paul, ed. 1995. *International Health Organisations and Movements, 1918–1939.* Cambridge History of Medicine. Cambridge: Cambridge University Press.

Wick, Alexis. 2004. "Of Missing Actors: Palestine and Arab Diplomacy in Europe, 1919–1920." Master of Arts in History Thesis. Columbia University. Kindly provided by author.

Wilderson III, Frank B. 2010. *Red, White & Black: Cinema and the Structure of US Antagonisms.* Durham, NC: Duke University Press.

Williams, H.C. Maurice. 1941. "Inoculation with T.A.B.C. Vaccine in Southhampton: Analysis of Reactions." The British Medical Journal (January 18). Vol. 1(4176): 84.

Wilson, G. S. 1957. "Obituary Notices of Deceased Members: Arthur Felix, 3rd April 1887–14th January 1956." *Journal of Pathology and Bacteriology* 73: 281–294.

Yahya, Abbad. 2017. "Oral History and Dual Marginalization." *Jerusalem Quarterly.* No. 70: 96–110. www.palestine-studies.org/en/node/214132

Young, Elise G. 2011. *Gender and Nation Building in the Middle East: The Political Economy of Health from Mandate Palestine to Refugee Camps in Jordan.* London: I. B. Tauris.

Yuval-Davis, Nira. 1989. "National Reproduction and 'the Demographic Race' in Israel." In *Woman-Nation-State.* Edited by Nira Yuval-Davis and Floya Anthias, 92–109. New York: Palgrave MacMillan.

Zangwill, Israel. 1911. "The Jewish Race." In *Papers on Inter-racial Progress: Communicated to the First Universal Races Congress Held at the University of London, July 26–29, 1911.* Edited by Gustav Spiller, 268–279. London: P.S. King & Son.

Zu'bi, Nahla. 1984. "The Development of Capitalism in Palestine: The Expropriation of the Palestinian Direct Producers." *Journal of Palestine Studies* 13(4) (Summer): 88–109.

Zurayk, Constantin. 1948. *Ma`na al-nakba (The Meaning of the Disaster).* Beirut: Kashaf Press.

Index

Page numbers in **bold** refer to notes. Pages numbers in *italic* refer to figures or tables.

Ottoman Penal Code, 165–167, 171, 172, 176, **188**
Ottoman period
  abortion laws, 161–167
  birth control laws and traditions, 161
  hospitals, 18, 82–83, **118**
  land registration, 55
  local authority, **52**
  religious categorization, 125
  resistance to Jewish settlement, 36
  transportation links, 53

Pad.ma, 6
Palestine. *see also* racism, Palestine Mandate, Palestinian women, eugenics, British Palestine colonial governance, demographics and colonial policies, towns, villages, and camps, Palestinian futurities in literature and film, Palestinian futurities, Zionism and demographics
  demographic discourse, 132–134
  ethnic cleansing, 8, 212
Palestine Arab Medical Association, 72, 74
Palestine Broadcasting Service, 17
Palestine Criminal Code (1928), 171–172
Palestine Liberation Organization's Plastic Arts Section and Arts and Heritage Section, 245
Palestine Mandate, 40, 51, *see also* League of Nations, Versailles Peace Conference (1919), British Palestine colonial governance, British Palestine Department of Health, Palestine
Palestine Police constables, 87–89
Palestine Poster Project Archive, 245
Palestine Women's Council, 100
PalestineRemembered.com oral history project, 8, 13–16, 212
Palestinian Authority (PA). *see* Palestinian National Authority (PNA)
Palestinian Diaspora and Refugee Center, 10

Palestinian futurities, 210–211, 242, *see also* fertility, futurities, Black, feminist, and queer, Palestinian futurities in literature and film
  post-1948 fertility and reproductive family, 211–221
  queer-inflected, 241
Palestinian futurities in literature and film, 226–228, *see also* futurities, Black, feminist, and queer, Palestinian futurities
  Bonbone (Mayasi), 239–240
  Condom Lead (Abu Nasser and Abu Nasser), 240–241
  Emile Habiby, 232–236
  Ibtisam Azem, 236–237
  Mahmoud Darwish, 228–232
  The Secret Life of Saeed the Pessoptimist (Habiby), 232–236
  Tawfiq Sayigh, 228
  Wedding in Galilee (Khleifi), 237–238
  Yusuf `Abdel `Aziz, 228
Palestinian Motherhood poster, 245, 246
Palestinian National Authority (PNA), 246
  abortion laws, 180–181, 206
Palestinian national identity
  challenges to dominant narrative of Nakba, 17
  historiography, 3
  oral histories, 8
  reproductive decision-making, 219, 239
  reproductive desires, 210–211, 245–247
  reproductive desires in iconography, 244–248
Palestinian physicians
  advocacy by, 74–76
  extraction from, 20
Palestinian prisoners, **239**
Palestinian women. *see also* Palestinians
  effects of 1948, 10
  interactions with Jews pre-1948
  hijra, 10, 13

Milton Keynes UK
Ingram Content Group UK Ltd.
UKHW030805300124
436963UK00019B/517